MARYLAND POLITICS AND GOVERNMENT

Politics and Governments
of the American States

Founding Editor

Daniel J. Elazar

Published by the University of
Nebraska Press in association
with the Center for the Study
of Federalism at the Robert B.
and Helen S. Meyner Center
for the Study of State and Local
Government, Lafayette College

HERBERT C. SMITH AND JOHN T. WILLIS

Maryland Politics and Government

DEMOCRATIC DOMINANCE

UNIVERSITY OF NEBRASKA PRESS

LINCOLN AND LONDON

Library of Congress Cataloging-in-Publication Data

Smith, Herbert C. (Herbert Charles), 1946–

Maryland politics and government: democratic

dominance / Herbert C. Smith and John T. Willis.

p. cm.— (Politics and governments of the

American states)

Includes bibliographical references and index.

ISBN 978-0-8032-3790-2 (pbk.: alk. paper)

1. Maryland—Politics and government.

I. Willis, John T., 1946– II. Title.

JK3816.S65 2012

320.9752—dc23   2011024769

CONTENTS

TABLES

MAPS

FIGURES

Preface

As a state, Maryland has rarely received wide national recognition. Tucked between the larger and historically more illustrious commonwealths of Pennsylvania and Virginia, Marylanders in general have remained content to enjoy the diversities of environment, economics, and people in the self-proclaimed "land of pleasant living."

Despite the state's less than imposing physical stature, it is the contention of this book that Maryland, its government, its politics, and its policies are eminently worthy of both sustained scrutiny and a measure of acclaim. First, in a state of ample and growing affluence, Maryland's elected officials, predominantly Democrats, have long steered a stable and persistent course of fiscal prudence. The state's and many of its counties' bond ratings consistently score at the triple-A level, a very public rebuke to those who automatically denigrate governmental financial stewardship.

Second, in many respects Maryland does deserve the slogan "America in Miniature" that sometimes adorns its promotional literature. Its terrains are diverse and varied, from the Chesapeake Tidewater to Baltimore City's upscale gentrified communities and desperate drug-infested neighborhoods depicted on *Homicide* and *The Wire*, suburban and rural Piedmont, and Appalachian highlands. Maryland's population, multiracial from its inception, has grown even more diverse as immigrants from other states and countries have made the state one of the most demographically distinct in the nation. Balancing the disparate needs of region, culture, and people in a pluralistic tapestry has long been a requirement of successful Maryland politicians.

The result has been a mix of progressive and pragmatic policies that have proven responsive, fair, and effective. These range from "Smart Growth" programs, designed to channel residential growth to already developed areas, to extensive civil rights protections, educational funding mechanisms to pay for school construction and equalize educational opportunities, strong support for public and private higher education, environmental protection for "critical areas," marshland and buffers surrounding the Chesapeake Bay, expansive health care benefits, strict air emissions automobile standards, and a mandated "living wage" provision for state contracts.

Finally, Maryland's long-established Democratic Party has achieved consistent dominance in state politics unparalleled south of the Mason-Dixon Line or, for that matter, in most states north of that demarcation. Only Democratic bastions such as Hawaii, Massachusetts, and Rhode Island rival Maryland's propensity to elect and reelect Democrats to govern at the state level.

Although Maryland once was similar to other southern states in its reliance on segregationist appeals based on states' rights, its Democrats reformed and transformed in the civil rights era to forge a persistent and durable biracial majority. In the modern, post–World War II era only three Republicans governors have been elected, serving a total of fourteen years, while the state legislature, the general assembly, has maintained overwhelming Democratic majorities. How Maryland Democrats have continued their electoral supremacy in an age of polarized politics is a testament to their organization, flexible policies, and political pragmatism.

For us it was a labor of love to describe, detail, and explain the dynamics of contemporary Maryland politics and government. We have long served as active participants and observers of the process at both the local and state levels. Herbert C. Smith is a transplanted Philadelphian who arrived in Baltimore for his doctoral work in political science at the Johns Hopkins University and stayed, teaching at McDaniel College since 1973. He managed his first political campaign while still in graduate school in 1971. John T. Willis was born in Baltimore City, grew up in Carroll County, graduated from Harvard Law School, returned to Maryland to practice law after seven years in the U.S. Army Judge Advocate Generals Corp, taught at Western Maryland College (now McDaniel College), and is currently teaching at the University of Baltimore. He served as vice chair of the Maryland Democratic Party and on the Democratic National Committee before his appointment as the Maryland secretary of state for eight years in Governor Parris N. Glendening's administration. In 1982, when John ran for the Maryland House of Delegates, a number of Herb's students served as campaign volunteers. Over the years Herb and John often appeared together on radio and television shows, and their commentaries have peppered newspaper accounts of Maryland campaigns and elections. Their collaboration emerged from an earlier working group at the William Donald Schaefer Center for Public Policy, housed at the University of Baltimore.

The "Maryland Book," as it came to be called, has occupied our research commitment for the past five years. In contemporary times no other text on Maryland politics and government encompasses the scope and focus of this work. Our motivation has been to detail the democratic processes, the governmental structures, and a broad array of public policies through a political lens that explains the partisan dynamics that have determined electoral outcomes and influenced policy decisions in the Maryland context.

The first chapter explores the Maryland identity; the second examines the historic development of the state and its consequences for modern Maryland. Subsequent chapters deal with contemporary political behavior, Maryland public opinion, political parties, interest groups, and political corruption, the state constitution, the Maryland General Assembly, the governor and the executive branch, the state judiciary, and such policy areas as taxation and spending, environmental protection, land use, and transportation. The nature of intergovernmental relations is examined and future thoughts on government and politics in Maryland are presented.

We sincerely appreciate the substantial support of academic sabbaticals and the helpful resources of McDaniel College and the University of Baltimore. Former students played a major role as well. Our appreciation is extended to M. James Kaufman for lending his research on Maryland lobbyists, Natalie Brown Olson for her work on the full-time commitment of Maryland legislators to the General Assembly, and Karyn Strickler for her insights on the Question 6 pro-choice referendum.

We also wish to thank the many Maryland public officials we have known and worked with during the past four decades. Marylanders should be proud of their hard work and dedication to public service. Among those who spoke with us about this project and have our special appreciation for their thoughts and insight are former governors Parris N. Glendening and Harry R. Hughes, former Maryland attorney general J. Joseph Curran Jr., former Baltimore County executive Theodore G. Venetoulis, former Maryland state senators Julian L. Lapides and George W. Della Jr., former delegates Paul Weisengoff and Donald Lamb, and current delegates A. Wade Kach, and Samuel I. (Sandy) Rosenberg. Public officials who have shared their perspectives in our classrooms include Chief Judge Robert Bell, former secretary of corrections and public safety Stuart Simms, former secretary of the environment Jane Nashida, and delegates Talmadge Branch, Brian McHale, and Nancy Stocksdale.

We also recognize our enduring debt to several distinguished political mentors: former comptroller Louis L. Goldstein, former congressman Goodloe Byron (Dem: 6th), Johns Hopkins University professor Milton Cummings, and the esteemed pioneer education advocate C. Milson Raver. They taught us how to judge political events, keep a long-range perspective, and respect the citizen-voter.

We dedicate this book to the two women who kept our spirits elevated and egos checked throughout the long hard slog to the completion of this project: our wives, Beth A. Smith and Kathy S. Mangan.

MARYLAND POLITICS AND GOVERNMENT

CHAPTER ONE

The Maryland Identity

We Marylanders may look at our State realistically, and still find it lovely. It has variety, it has color, and it has a certain touch of mystery.
H. L. Mencken

In Annapolis they stand like bronze bookends with the Maryland Capitol Building between them. Both native Marylanders, both U.S. Supreme Court Justices, and the similarities end there. From a marble chair a robed statue of Chief Justice Roger Brooke Taney gazes down the historic capitol lawn. It is usually quiet there, with old shade trees and lush green grass. A short distance down the hill lies the harbor, where boats under full sail or motor's hum ply the Chesapeake waters. Taney's counterpart stands young and vital amid a group sculpture of African American students on the opposite side of the capitol. Sculpted when he served as the chief counsel for the NAACP on the eve of the historic *Brown v. Board of Education* decision, Thurgood Marshall greets the hordes of tourists before they climb the steps to enter America's oldest continuously used state legislative chambers. The Marshall sculptures occupy the middle of "Lawyers Mall," with Government House, the governor's official residence, on the south side, the Legislative Services Building on the north, and the state capitol to the east. The sculptures mark the focal point of Maryland state government.

Taney's career spanned half a century of political activism as he rose from the Maryland House of Delegates to the nation's highest court. Though he personally abhorred slavery, he signed the infamous *Dred Scott v. Sandford* (1857) decision that held American blacks had "no rights which any white man was bound to respect."[1] Marshall, born in Baltimore, was the first African American appointed to the U.S. Supreme Court, serving from 1967 to 1991. Justice Marshall championed liberal judicial activism on the nation's highest court, arguing for First Amendment freedoms, the rights of individuals, and affirmative action. Together these iconic figures represent the diversity and paradoxes of Maryland past, present, and future.

Maryland's development has long reflected its considerable geographic and demographic diversity as well as the crosscurrents between North and South. Described accurately as a "cartographer's nightmare," Maryland is also something of a political scientist's dilemma.[2] Sometimes depicted as the southernmost northern state and sometimes as the northernmost southern state, in many regards Maryland acts like neither and defies most conventional categorizations. A small state in land area, ranking forty-second in the country, Maryland contained 5,773,552 people in the 2010 census, placing it nineteenth among the fifty states. With the second highest median household income in the nation from 2005 to 2007 and ranking fifth in population density in the nation, it is far more affluent and urbanized than other border states.[3] Established Maryland public policies on affirmative action, environmental protection, gun control, health care, and abortion rights are considerably more progressive than those in the states included in the "South Atlantic" grouping devised by the U.S. Census Bureau. Maryland is also decidedly more dominated by Democrats than most states in the Northeast or Mid-Atlantic regional blocs. Contemporary political pundits complain of the "ambiguous identity" of Maryland.[4] Indeed as early as 1776 the essence of Maryland befuddled such an astute political analyst as John Adams, who confessed, "It is so eccentric a colony—sometimes so hot, sometimes so cold, now so high, then so low—that I know not what to say about or expect from it."[5]

The Maryland way seems to confound patterns of consistent political predictability. Maryland was the first colony to establish religious tolerance as government policy, and then repeal it. It was the first border state to abolish slavery, yet rejected ratification of the Fourteenth and Fifteenth Amendments in 1867 and 1870, only symbolically ratifying these civil rights amendments in 1959 and 1973. The Progressive Era brought a host of election reforms; however, the national women's suffrage movement was perceived as a major threat to the male political establishment. The Maryland General Assembly, fixated on states' rights, overwhelmingly rejected ratification of the Nineteenth Amendment in 1920. While Maryland is a national leader in boards and commissions enforcing stringent governmental ethics regulations, the state has periodically seen unsavory political corruption at both high and low levels, making one twentieth-century period a veritable "postmark for corruption."[6]

The gubernatorial election of 2002 was another case manifesting the state's perplexing nature. After eight consecutive Democratic gubernatorial victories, the longest winning streak in Maryland history, Republican Congressman Robert Ehrlich defeated Democratic Lieutenant Governor Kathleen Kennedy Townsend. He was the first of his party the state had seen since Spiro Agnew was elected in 1966. The same election witnessed a significant change in the Maryland congressional delegation. For ten years deadlocked with four Democrats balanced by four Republican members serving in the U.S. House of Representatives, the Democrats picked up two seats, giving them a 6–2 advantage. In 2002 Maryland was the only state where Democrats gained more than one congressional seat from their opponents in a decidedly Republican year. Four years later Ehrlich was decisively defeated for reelection by Baltimore City Mayor Martin J. O'Malley and was the only incumbent governor of either party in the nation rejected by voters during the 2006 general election. In the 2008 presidential election Maryland Democrats added a seventh congressional seat (the first district, comprising the nine Eastern Shore counties and parts of Anne Arundel, Baltimore, and Harford counties), and Barack Obama received the fourth highest margin of victory for a presidential candidate in Maryland since the two-party election era began in the nineteenth century. In the 2010 gubernatorial election, incumbent Governor O'Malley easily defeated Ehrlich, again counter to national trends.

Even the state nickname remains somewhat unsettled. Displayed on the U.S. Mint's state series quarter is the oldest, "The Old Line State," dating to the American Revolution, when the Maryland Line, the four hundred–strong state militia, covered the retreat of Washington's army during the Battle of Long Island in 1776.[7] Another nickname, "The Free State," stems from the Prohibition era, when many of Maryland's elected officials and much of its public openly ignored the "noble experiment." The federal Bureau of Prohibition complained, "We have no cooperation in the State of Maryland."[8] The Free State nickname was popularized by the *Baltimore Sun*, especially its most iconoclastic reporter, H. L. Mencken, and it remains in use today mainly in media sources.

Undoubtedly the appellation most popular with the Maryland tourist industry is "America in Miniature," reflecting the state's distinct geographic regions. These range from the coastal plains of Southern Maryland and the Eastern Shore to the Appalachian hinterlands of Western Maryland and the sprawling metropolitan areas of Baltimore and Washington DC, with a mul-

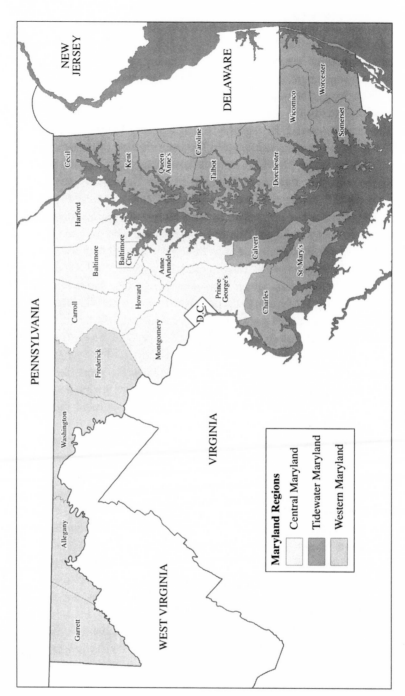

Map 1-1. Maryland regions

titude of suburbs and edge cities along the Interstate 95 corridor that connects them. Founded on simple geography, the state has a regional diversity whose demographic, economic, and political differences reflect to some extent national patterns.

TIDEWATER: THE EASTERN SHORE AND SOUTHERN MARYLAND

The 195-mile-long, 3,237-square-mile Chesapeake Bay, the largest estuary on the North American continent, cuts deeply into and divides the Maryland landmass into the eastern and western shores. Formed from the prehistoric drowned valley of the lower Susquehanna River, the Chesapeake ranges from three to twenty-five miles wide and is punctuated by a multitude of rivers and tidal creeks. The Bay is Maryland's single most distinctive geographic feature. The Eastern Shore, part of the larger Delmarva Peninsula shared with Delaware and Virginia, contains nine Maryland counties (Caroline, Cecil, Dorchester, Kent, Queen Anne's, Somerset, Talbot, Wicomico, and Worcester). Together with the three southernmost counties of the Western Shore (Calvert, Charles, and St. Mary's), they display a similar flat topography, the eroded heritage of an ancient Miocene-epoch sea. The Tidewater is predominately rural; though it contains half of the state's counties, it accounts for less than 14 percent of the total state population. Twenty percent of Tidewater residents are African American.

It was in the Tidewater region that the initial colonization of Maryland took place. Throughout the seventeenth and eighteenth centuries the region attracted settlers drawn by the abundant and fertile land, the seafood bounty of the Bay, and the meandering rivers that provided easy water transit for goods and supplies. In effect the Chesapeake was "one expansive port," and concentrated settlements were the exception rather than the rule.[9] For much of Maryland's early history these counties were bolstered by a robust plantation tobacco economy that produced much of the state's wealth and growth. This tobacco monoculture and plantation society came at considerable human costs. Slavery flourished in the Tidewater region; by 1790 close to 60 percent of all slaves living in Maryland worked there, comprising over 40 percent of the region's population.[10] Most Marylanders lived in this region during the first few generations of colonial settlement; a plurality, 44 percent, still resided in the Tidewater at the time of the 1800 Census. But population growth slowed considerably in the second half of the nineteenth century and the first half of the twentieth in comparison to other regions (see Table 1-1).

Along the Chesapeake's edge, in the myriad creeks and tidal estuaries, crabs, fish, oysters, and waterfowl provided a living for generations of wa-

Table 1-1: Maryland regional populations

Region	1800	1850	1900	1950	2000
Tidewater Maryland	149,550	168,010	241,071	275,249	677,223
	44%	29%	20%	12%	13%
Western Maryland	56,476	94,604	168,448	251,988	431,976
	17%	16%	14%	12%	8%
Central Maryland	135,522	320,420	778,525	1,815,764	4,187,287
	40%	55%	66%	77%	79%
Total Maryland Population	341,548	583,034	1,188,044	2,343,001	5,296,486

Source: U.S. Census Bureau.

termen and their families. This once largely subsistence economy boomed shortly after the Civil War, when the Chesapeake Bay oyster was transformed into the primary cash crop of the region. The growing national railroad network and innovations in the canning industry fueled the bonanza, especially in the town of Crisfield, just north of the Virginia border on the lower Eastern Shore. There oyster shucking and canning facilities abounded. At the zenith of the oyster age, in 1884, fifteen million bushels of oysters were harvested, and Crisfield was home port to more than six hundred oyster boats that dredged or tonged the Bay bottoms and bars.[11] The inevitable overharvesting, as well as water pollution and increased sedimentation, reduced the once prolific oyster bars to largely barren outcroppings on the Bay's bottom. For much of the twentieth century Chesapeake Bay watermen turned to the blue crab, though here too environmental degradation of the Bay has considerably reduced crustacean stocks and shortened seasons. Tightening size and catch limits has often set the state government and the watermen communities at political loggerheads.

Separated from the rest of Maryland by the Bay, the Eastern Shore has been described as "the most self-conscious" area in the state.[12] To defuse the periodic outbursts of separatist sentiment (which once in the 1830s prompted the Delaware legislature to propose a merger) the governorship was rotated regionally from 1838 until 1864, and the two Maryland seats in the U.S. Senate were divided between the Western and Eastern Shores by the state legislature from 1789 until 1896. Eastern Shore secession remains an issue, but not a serious one. Occasionally a delegate or state senator will file a separation bill, but does so more for the inevitable publicity and as reinforcement of regional pride and identity than with serious intent.

The three southern counties were equally detached by customs, if not geography, from the rest of the Western Shore for most of the state's history. A southern-style conservatism, complete with courthouse political machines that ran the counties with a certain degree of moral laxity, dominated for generations. By local ordinance slot machines were legal in Calvert, Charles, and St. Mary's counties, and also Anne Arundel County, from the 1940s well into the 1960s. They were scattered throughout the area, in restaurants, package stores, motels, and virtually every bar. Small-time graft and corruption flourished in this poorly regulated enterprise and pervaded some aspects of local governance in the mid-twentieth century.

The Eastern Shore and Southern Maryland produced a disproportionate share of the state's early master politicians from 1776 until the First World War. Throughout most of the twentieth century modernization bypassed the area, and the politics of the Tidewater grew more distant and aloof from and more reactionary toward the state norm; residents often voted Democratic for local and state offices but Republican in national elections. While the central core of Maryland grew and prospered, growth was perceived not as an opportunity but as a threat to the established order. When the first Chesapeake Bay Bridge was debated in 1947, much of the Eastern Shore delegation in the general assembly was fiercely opposed. In the small towns and tidewater hamlets people sang, "We don't give a damn for the whole state of Maryland / We're from the Eastern Shore!"[13] Their opposition was brushed aside and the bridge was constructed, opening Maryland's short Atlantic coast to tourist hordes. With the completion of the second span in 1973, the Eastern Shore became even more accessible. Recreational activities joined agribusiness and seafood as the region's primary economic pursuits. In a substantial reversal of long-term trends, the 1980s and 1990s brought dynamic population growth to the Coastal Plain counties near the eastern terminus of the twin Bay Bridges. Suburban sprawl, long-distance commuting, and new retirement communities produced a 23 percent increase in population from 1980 to 1990 and 20 percent in the 1990s, almost double the state average for the two decades.

This sometimes explosive growth sprang from different sources. Southern Maryland was and remains under the influence of Washington metropolitan development. For example, the population of Charles County expanded from 23,415 in 1950 to 120,546 in 2000, more than a fivefold increase, with another 21.6 percent jump to 146,551 in 2010. In neighboring St. Mary's County the sprawling Patuxent Naval Air Station and research facilities helped push the population from 14,626 in 1950 to 86,211 in 2000, and to 105,151 in 2010. On the Eastern Shore, Annapolis, and even metropolitan Baltimore and Washington commuters have been attracted by open spaces, good roads, low crime rates, and some of the lowest property tax rates in the state. Suburbanization was accompanied by a growth in Republican registration and electoral victories at all levels in the region. Today most parts of the Eastern Shore and Southern Maryland, with the exception of Charles County, are something of an equal conservative political partner to Western Maryland, on the other geographic end of the state, in their support for statewide Republican candidates.

THE HIGHLANDS: WESTERN MARYLAND

Westward across the length of the state, in the time-worn Catoctin and Appalachian Mountains, are the four counties, Allegany, Frederick, Garrett, and Washington, conventionally considered Western Maryland, the last settled region of the state. The highest point in Maryland is found in its westernmost subdivision, Garrett County. There Hoye Crest on Backbone Mountain tops off at 3,360 feet, which by most national and international standards is hardly mountainous. Yet for settlers coming from the Maryland Coastal Plain or Piedmont areas, the geographic ridges of Western Maryland appeared very high indeed.

The Western Maryland region has never accounted for even 20 percent of the state's population, and today holds only slightly more than 8 percent (see Table 1-1). Western Maryland shares with the Eastern Shore and Southern Maryland a sense of protracted distance from state power and concern. Although it is the most racially homogeneous area in the state, with an African American population of over 8 percent, the politics of Western Maryland are based on a diverse combination of ethnic, class, and occupational cleavages.

The region was settled initially in the 1700s by English and Scots farmers from Maryland's Eastern Shore and Virginia as well as German immigrants who farmed the fertile rolling hills and sheltered valleys. The mixed farming economy in the valleys was quickly augmented by the exploitation of other natural resources. George Washington was one of the first to observe that the region was blessed with abundant and easily mined surface beds of bituminous coal, which he called "the fuel of the future."[14]

The development of the region was a consequence of American westward expansion and Marylanders' desire to promote trade and commerce with the Ohio Valley. The transportation infrastructure of Western Maryland received a substantial boost in 1807, when Congress appropriated funds for the National Road, or Cumberland Road. Originally a wagon trail, it ran from Cumberland in Allegany County to Wheeling, West Virginia, and was the first "internal improvement" funded by the federal government. The

Maryland General Assembly provided substantial financial support for the construction of the Chesapeake and Ohio Canal along the Potomac River as well as the Baltimore and Ohio Railroad. In addition the state legislature incorporated a dozen mining companies in the region from 1828 to 1838.[15] Industrial development followed these ventures as factories, mills, and mines attracted waves of Irish, Welsh, German, and Scots Irish, both immigrants and native-born. Miners were much more likely to be foreign-born as mine owners recruited experienced workers from Europe.[16]

With an established transportation grid, Western Maryland became a nationally significant initial economic gateway to the Ohio Valley and helped fuel Baltimore's industrial expansion. The B&O Railroad shipped 193,000 tons of coal to Baltimore in 1850, which escalated to 493,000 tons in 1860.[17] The C&O Canal, with five hundred canal boats in operation, carried a record-setting 973,805 tons of freight in 1875.[18] Hagerstown in Washington County has long served as a transportation center and crossroads. Nicknamed "Hub City" for the six railroad lines that met there, Hagerstown links the Shenandoah Valley of Virginia with Maryland and central Pennsylvania through the Great Valley of Appalachia. Significant family businesses developed in the larger towns of Cumberland, Frederick, and Hagerstown and smaller neighboring towns, including glass works, tanneries, cement plants, canneries, and knitting mills.

This region was by far the most pro-Union during the Civil War. Republican sentiments were eventually balanced by Western Maryland industrial workers, who formed the core constituency of a powerful and enduring labor union movement in the late nineteenth century and twentieth century. The region suffered during the Great Depression and recovered somewhat during the production boom of the World War II, but was continually plagued by plant closings in the second half of the twentieth century. This is especially true of Allegany County, which has steadily lost population since 1950. In that year's census the county had a population of 89,556; by 2000 the number had declined to 74,930, with a slight increase to 75,087 in 2010.

Efforts to improve economic vitality in the two westernmost counties (Allegany and Garrett) have focused on the development and promotion of recreational opportunities and even the construction of state correctional facilities, public works projects that often produce a NIMBY ("Not in my backyard") reaction in more prosperous sections of the state.

In contrast to the economic malaise in Garrett, Allegany, and Washington counties is the thriving easternmost member of this region, Frederick County. Containing 233,385 people, according to the 2010 census, Frederick is the most heavily populated county in the region. Its growth rate from 1990 to 2000 was 23 percent, the third highest in the state. Southern Frederick became an increasingly popular residence for Washington metro commuters and for workers employed in the technology corridor along Interstate 270 in Montgomery County. Suburban issues such as land use and schools began to supplant traditional rural concerns. In addition Frederick County hosts the U.S. Army's sprawling biomedical research center, Fort Detrick, and the world-renowned presidential retreat, Camp David.

Politically Western Maryland produced the only stable, long-term, two-party competitive system at the state legislative and local levels for much of the twentieth century. Political contests in the region, where even the fluoridation of the water supply remains a contentious issue, almost always pit conservative Democrats against even more conservative Republicans. Although Democrats certainly remain competitive in the towns and more densely populated legislative districts, Republicans now win most races in this region. Similar to the Tidewater area, family allegiances and long-term ties to the Western Maryland region have been of considerable importance. Two generations of the Byron family, both husbands and wives, served as Democratic members of the House of Representatives from Maryland's Sixth Congressional District. Conservative Republican Roscoe Bartlett, who succeeded the last Byron in 1992 and was reelected to a tenth term in 2010, is Western Maryland's congressman. In federal and statewide elections at the beginning of the twenty-first century Western Maryland voters have reliably produced large Republican majority margins.

THE MIDSTATE MAJORITY: CENTRAL MARYLAND

The economic, social, and political drive wheel of Maryland is the Piedmont region of the Western Shore, its original topography of rolling forested hills and fields now mostly obscured by urban and suburban developments. In 1800 this area accounted for 40 percent of the state's population; in 2000 almost 80 percent of Marylanders called this region home (see Table 1-1). Central Maryland contains 88 percent of the state's African American population and is over 40 percent nonwhite according to the 2010 census.

Statewide electoral outcomes reflect the growth and population dominance of this region. The six Maryland governors since 1967 and all U.S. senators since 1976 have resided in this region. The central core consists of two major metropolitan areas, Baltimore and Washington, connected by the Interstate 95 corridor. The Baltimore area, consisting of a central city and surrounding suburbs, provided a classic case in the second half of the twentieth century of a declining urban base and prosperous suburban ring. The Washington metropolitan area contains the first and second most populous counties in the state. Montgomery is one of the nation's most wealthy, large urban subdivisions, and Prince George's is home to the most highly educated and affluent majority African American population in the country. Together with Baltimore City, Montgomery and Prince George's counties form the core urban base of Democratic voters in the state. Two Central Maryland subdivisions, fast-growing Carroll and Harford counties, are almost exclusively suburban and predominantly white and provide a conservative Republican block of votes in the region. The three remaining subdivisions—Anne Arundel, Baltimore, and Howard counties—were the focus of shifting party fortunes in the last third of the twentieth century. Baltimore County and Howard County have recently trended more Democratic, while Anne Arundel remains a two-party competitive jurisdiction.

The economy of Central Maryland is exceptionally diverse, ranging from federal installations in the Washington metropolitan area such as the National Institutes of Health and National Aeronautics and Space Administration and biotechnology ventures at the Johns Hopkins Hospital in Baltimore City to corporate manufacturing facilities such as Black and Decker and Severstal Steel in Baltimore County and Northrop Grumman in Anne Arundel County. An educated and skilled labor force has helped make the I-95 corridor one of the most attractive in the country for startup businesses, and the region's intellectual capital is an increasingly vital asset. In the 2000 census Maryland ranked first among the states in percentage (26.4) of professional and management workers and placed third among the states in percentage (31.4) of the population age twenty-five and over with at least a bachelor's degree.[19]

Even with the proliferation of biotech, software, and other twenty-first-century ventures and venues, one element has remained the same since the early 1800s: the geographic transportation advantage of Baltimore. Situated farther west than any other East Coast seaport, the Port of Baltimore remains a vital component of the state economy. Container ships have replaced the Baltimore clippers, allowing international commerce valued at $41.9 billion (in 2007) to pass through port terminals. Ranking ninth in the country, the Port of Baltimore directly employs 18,400 and indirectly supports an additional 107,900 in the labor force.[20] In addition the Baltimore-Washington International Thurgood Marshall Airport, located eighteen miles from downtown Baltimore in the heart of the I-95 corridor, is the second fastest growing airport in the country and serves as a hub for Southwest Airlines.

Explosive growth in the I-95 corridor and the resulting education, transportation, housing, and environmental issues have occupied center stage in Maryland politics since the Second World War. Maryland was a veritable staging area for the arsenal of democracy during the war years, and migration into the state was massive for nearly thirty years afterward. From 1940 to 1970 the state jumped from twenty-eighth in population to eighteenth, a surge that mirrored that of distant Sunbelt states. The state's 27 percent population increase during the 1960s was twice the national average. In 1961 Governor Millard Tawes noted the urgency to "reckon . . . with sheer numbers," and most governors since have felt the same pressure.[21] The bulk of the growth was focused in the Baltimore and Washington metropolitan suburbs, where populations doubled from 1946 to 1951, doubled again from 1951 to 1961, and doubled yet a third time from 1961 to 1981.[22] Growth slowed somewhat in the 1990s, when the population increased 11 percent, to 5,296,486, compared to a national increase of 13 percent. The resulting congested highways, neighborhoods, and schools will remain problems for decades.

Central Maryland political styles vary considerably. Montgomery and Howard counties form the base of an idealistic, reform-driven approach. Both have experienced explosive growth since 1950, with Montgomery becoming the most populous subdivision in Maryland; it had 971,777 residents according to 2010 census. Howard had only 23,119 people in 1950 and was seventeenth in population out of twenty-four subdivisions; after the 2010 census Howard contained 287,085 residents and ranked sixth. In both counties the new arrivals have been predominantly affluent and well educated, influencing local public policy. Howard, for example, was the first Maryland subdivision to mandate bike helmets for youngsters and in 2007 launched the Healthy Howard Plan, a national model program to extend health coverage to its uninsured adult citizens.[23] Columbia, the enlightened famed developer Jim Rouse's acclaimed "new town," consists of clustered villages bound by deeded restrictive covenants and exemplifies community-based planning and regulation. There are no billboards in Columbia, and mailboxes are often grouped together so neighbors will have an opportunity to interact.[24] Montgomery County liberalism is a given in Maryland politics. Montgomery prizes an exacting rectitude in political morality above all else in its elected officials and consistently supports "civil rights, welfare, consumer and environmentalist legislation."[25]

Professional politicians may still be found in portions of Baltimore City, Baltimore County, and Prince George's County, where a dwindling number of old-style Democratic organizations make politics pay. Former Baltimore mayor Thomas D'Alesandro once summarized the prevalent 1950s attitude this way: "Let the Republicans have the two-party system, give the Democrats the political jobs."[26] That mind-set often came with a price: political corruption. Maryland was plagued with investigations, indictments, and convictions of prominent Democratic and Republican politicians during the 1960s and 1970s. Reform Democrats sometimes capitalized on such misfortunes, as did an occasional Republican at the local level.

The dynamics of Maryland policymaking are often based on the interplay between a reformist imperative to improve society and the more guarded, practical-minded political temperament. The outputs of the resultant conflict and compromise between diverse interests and principles are often progressive yet pragmatic policies. Politicians who understand this, and can manage the process, succeed. For example, in 1968, when Maryland voters rejected a boldly progressive state constitution, it was the machine-bred governor Marvin Mandel who helped orchestrate a piecemeal acceptance of many of the modernized reorganization proposals through the general assembly and subsequent ratification by the voters.

The result of this political dynamic is a policy system that proceeds with well-crafted and thought-out policies, often innovative yet realistic in scope. These policies range across the spectrum, from Maryland's much acclaimed Smart Growth land use and environmental initiatives to progressive health care programs. Even with often activist policy stances Maryland has long held the coveted triple-A bond rating from Wall Street, reflective of an underlying and consistent fiscal prudence.[27]

UNDERSTANDING MARYLAND POLITICS

Three major factors characterize Maryland politics: growing diversity, long-term Democratic Party dominance of the state government, and the sheer pragmatism of that party, its leaders, and its policies through nearly a century and a half of political and governmental control.

At first glance Maryland may seem paradoxical, inconsistent, and ambiguous. But what is at work is not simple contrariness, but diversity. By virtue of participation differentials—who votes and which groups dominate in decision making—diversity itself can produce multiple and conflicting outcomes that a more homogeneous state would find bewildering. Maryland's diversity operates on three levels. First is demographic diversity. As a refuge for assorted groups since its origin, Maryland has had a heterogeneous collection of people and continues to attract more. Fully one-third of the state's population growth in the 1990s came from foreign-born immigrants. The 1,700,298 African American residents enumerated by the 2010 census ranked fifth in the nation for percentage of population (29.4).[28] The rapid growth of Hispanic (8.2 percent) and Asian (5.5 percent) populations in the 1990s has continued into the twenty-first century. The now 58 percent white majority contains multiple ethnic identities, reflecting the panoply of European immigration over four centuries. Religious diversity is present as well. While Protestant affiliations claim the majority of Maryland's citizens, the state was founded by the Catholic Lord Calvert, and a significant Roman Catholic minority has been present since colonial times. The state also has more than 235,000 Jewish residents, earning the ranking of eighth in the nation.[29]

The second level of diversity is displayed by Maryland's economy, which spans traditional folk craft artisans of the Appalachian valleys, farmers on the Eastern Shore, civil servants at the Social Security Administration Headquarters in Baltimore County, and research scientists at Johns Hopkins University and the University of Maryland. The state's labor force distribution reflects the diversity of jobs and occupations.[30] Approximately 19 percent of the labor force is within the public sector. Of these 479,115 workers during the second quarter of 2008, 53 percent were employed by local governments and 21 percent by the state. Over 26 percent of government-sector workers were employed by the federal government. The private sector accounts for over 81 percent of total employment. Maryland has a fully developed service economy; nearly 85 percent of private-sector employment is classified as "service providing." Only 12.3 percent of the workforce was producing tangible goods in 2008. In the private sector professional and business services are the largest grouping of jobs in the state, at 19.3 percent. Next, at over 18 percent, are trade, transportation, and utilities, followed by education and health services (14 percent), leisure and hospitality services (9.5 percent), construction (7 percent), financial activities (6 percent), manufacturing (only 5 percent), and information services (2 percent).

The third significant category of diversity derives from the geography of Maryland, which produces a wide array of environmental pressures. State policymakers must respond not only to declining fish and shellfish stocks in the Chesapeake Bay, but also chronic and complex urban pollution in Baltimore, acidic runoff from abandoned mines in Western Maryland, and poultry waste on the Eastern Shore. This physical diversity is amplified by social and economic diversity. Differences in class, race, religion, and ethnicity were once accented by a well-defined regionalism, although sustained population growth in the central core of the state and significant partisan changes have redefined the relative importance of traditional regional divisions. Yet although the three regions—the Eastern Shore and Southern Maryland Tidewater, the Highlands of Western Maryland, and the populous Central Maryland core of the state—help explain the state geographically, they fall short as a basis for political analysis. Nor is the conflict between the urban, suburban, and rural subdivisions sufficient to explain the shift in the state's party affiliation. A new paradigm for Maryland politics, a "two Marylands" approach, is necessary. A description of the growing and intensifying polarization between Maryland Democrats and Republicans is detailed and discussed throughout this text.

The second major factor characterizing Maryland politics is the persistent dominance of the Democratic Party in public affairs. In the thirty-seven gubernatorial elections conducted since 1867 Maryland Democratic candidates have won thirty times, a success rate of 81.1 percent. In the twentieth century eight Democratic governors were elected for two or more terms, compared to only one Republican governor. Democratic dominance has been even greater in the state legislature, the Maryland General Assembly. Beginning with the legislative session of 1868 Democrats have controlled the state senate in every year but two (1898–99) and been the majority in the house of delegates for every year but six (1896–99 and 1918–19). Republicans held majorities in both chambers only once, for a single legislative session following the elections of 1897. Maryland Republicans generated a surge in electoral competitiveness at virtually every level of state and local government in the late 1980s, culminating in the election of Robert Ehrlich in 2002. However, the gain of Government House, the chief executive's Annapolis mansion, was reversed in 2006 by the Democratic mayor of Baltimore City, Martin O'Malley, who handily defeated Ehrlich's reelection bid. Statewide Democratic dominance had returned and was strongly reinforced in 2010, when O'Malley doubled his 2006 victory margin in a rematch with Ehrlich. The Republican goal of establishing a two-party competitive system at the state level was deferred yet again.

The final major factor explaining Maryland politics has been an underlying political pragmatism exercised by state Democratic elected leaders in keeping with a very utilitarian approach to politics and policies. This pragmatism, a consequences-based approach to governing rather than an ideological one, also resonates with what historians identify as a central trait of the Maryland character: a "middle temperament" of "compromise and accommodation" quite in keeping with the diverse backgrounds and interests of the state population.[31] In tune with the times, Maryland Democrats were generally conservative, fiscally prudent, and minimalist in state services for almost a century following the Civil War. With the advent of the New Deal and the Roosevelt realignment, those themes became less relevant and politically productive, and state Democrats moved to a more activist state model, advancing programs and regulations that reflected the changes in Maryland after World War II. Many of these policies are progressive and in keeping with the expressed interests of Democratic support groups. Pragmatism has made the Maryland Democratic Party positively adaptive to changing socioeconomic conditions in the past, the present, and, presumably, the future.

TWO MARYLANDS

Politically there are two Marylands today. Democratic Maryland is multiracial and multiethnic and spans all socioeconomic classes. This Maryland straddles the I-95 corridor that transects the most heavily populated and racially integrated sections and connects the Baltimore and Washington metropolitan areas. These communities are either urban or suburban, with population densities exceeding 1,500 people per square mile or greater. The majority of Maryland's African American citizens live in this corridor and vote overwhelmingly Democratic. White voters in this area support Democrats as well, although at reduced levels. The core subdivisions of the Democratic base are vote-rich Baltimore City, Montgomery County, and Prince George's County, where statewide Democratic candidates routinely win with 60 to 80 percent of the vote, providing a substantial foundation for electoral dominance. Additional urban and suburban Democratic bases of support are scattered across the remainder of the state in such cities and places as Cumberland, Frederick, and Hagerstown in Western Maryland; Cambridge, Chestertown, Salisbury, and Princess Anne on the Eastern Shore; Leonardtown and Waldorf in Southern Maryland; and Annapolis, Columbia, Owings Mills, and Randallstown in Central Maryland.

Republican Maryland is predominantly rural or suburban, predominantly white, and increasingly conservative. Much of the Maryland Tidewater and Western Maryland counties now fall within this category in statewide elections. In Central Maryland, Carroll County and Harford County are virtual citadels of Republican strength in county, state, and federal elections.

The early twenty-first-century Maryland Republican Party is different from decades past, when the party was often progressive in comparison to the more fiscally and socially conservative Democrats who usually defeated their candidates. Contemporary Republican candidates, especially statewide and legislative, are more likely to reflect the policy positions of their national party: pro-business, antigovernment, antitax, anti-abortion, and strongly protective of gun and property rights. Their opposition to Democratic dominance is deep-seated, and the level of political polarization produced by this challenge is notably more intense and spirited than in modern Maryland history.

Maryland politics has never been sedate, but the clash of partisan politics in the twenty-first century has increased in every election cycle as negative campaign tactics have proliferated and percolated down from national elections to statewide, legislative, and even local contests. Governing, never an easy task, has become more demanding as elective, administrative, and judicial leaders confront the pressures of a diverse polity in the context of this partisan polarization. It is in the multiple decisions of the three governmental branches of its state and local units that the continual redefining of the Maryland identity takes place. The succeeding chapters detail that process and its results.

CHAPTER TWO

A Maryland Political History

Heaven and earth never agreed better to frame a place for man's habitation.

Capt. John Smith on the Chesapeake Bay shores

Maryland began on March 25, 1634, when the *Ark* and the *Dove*, two ships of Cecil Calvert, the second Lord Baltimore, anchored off St. Clement's Island in the mouth of the Potomac River. His father, George Calvert, a knight of the realm and secretary of state under James I, had lobbied tenaciously for a royal land grant in the New World. Ultimately Calvert succeeded, but it was only after his death that King Charles I extended a charter for a proprietary colony named for his wife, Queen Henrietta Maria. Cecil inherited the "Terra Maria," or Mary's Land, and organized an expedition sending his brother Leonard to serve as the first governor of the colony.

Maryland was the first colony to establish religious freedom, in part in a pragmatic reaction to the Calverts' Catholicism in predominantly Protestant England. Cecil Calvert's instructions to his brother stressed the preservation of "unity and peace" among the Protestant and Catholic settlers and cautioned his fellow and distinctly minority Catholics to maintain a subdued profile in religious matters.[1] The free exercise of the Christian religion was broadened in 1649, when the Maryland Assembly passed the Toleration Act. In the context of the seventeenth century, "when conformity under compulsion was the universal practice" and religious prejudice was almost everywhere rampant, this was a considerable achievement.[2] Proprietary tolerance served to establish the colony as a safe haven for persecuted minorities and set the early pattern for subsequent pluralistic development.[3]

Although the royal grant provided Lord Baltimore the authoritative powers of a feudal lord, the colonists who actually took the very real risks of life in early Maryland quickly asserted themselves. The first legislative body of freemen assembled in St. Mary's City in February 1635. Their deliberations produced a body of "wholesome laws" that was wholly rejected by Cecil Calvert. After a second confrontation Calvert relented, and the assembly established a semblance of independent legislative initiative.[4] Political, religious, and economic tensions between the proprietor and the freemen were institutionally separated in 1650, when the assembly began meeting as a bicameral body, with an upper house appointed by Lord Baltimore or his governor. Direct election of the lower house came in 1658.

Despite the prerogatives of a proprietary charter that far exceeded the powers of any royal governor in adjacent colonies, the Lords Baltimore had to maneuver a fine political line.[5] From the inception of Calvert's ambition of a New World legacy, the prime directive was to make money. In fact the historian George Callcott estimates that "the Calverts collected as profit about 6% of the total product of the settlers for 150 years."[6] In this context, political pragmatism again was imperative, first, to entice the largely Protestant English immigrants to brave the North Atlantic to come to the new colony, and second, to persuade them to stay. Indeed life in the 1600s was a constant struggle for the Maryland colonists, for, as the historian Robert Brugger observed, "the Chesapeake region both enticed newcomers with its richness and killed them with its illness."[7] Despite high mortality rates, the colony grew. Tobacco flourished in the settled Tidewater regions. With this labor-intensive crop came the slave trade, attended by brutality and disregard for human rights. By the end of the seventeenth century Maryland ranked second to Virginia in the importation of African slaves.

The tides of English politics engulfed Maryland as the English Civil War brought Puritan ascendancy to the colony and an end to the Toleration Act. Catholics were barred from voting and Lord Baltimore's proprietary rights effectively suspended. Cecil Calvert, possessing the persuasive skills of his father, convinced Lord Protector Oliver Cromwell to restore his franchise to Maryland. However, conflicts between the Protestants, usually the owners of small freeholds, and Catholic insiders, who continued to enjoy patronage appointments and prime real estate, remained the major source of political tension. The elected delegates of the lower house of the Maryland Assembly clashed with proprietary governance over concerns of personal rights and liberties they felt due them as citizens. Matters culminated in the aftermath of the English "Glorious Revolution" of 1688. Opponents of Calvert rule formed a Protestant Association, armed themselves, and marched on St. Mary's City. The capital fell without significant resistance, and shortly thereafter Maryland became a royal colony, remaining so for twenty-five years. The change was political, not economic, as the Calverts retained their claim to proprietary lands and the Crown collected the rents due Lord Baltimore.

By the end of the seventeenth century Maryland was a well-established enterprise with a total population of about 30,000. The colony had eleven counties completely encircling the Chesapeake Bay, six on the Western Shore and five on the Eastern Shore. These were administered by justices of the peace who were appointed by the governor and served in both judicial and administrative capacities. A long-term increase in tobacco prices brought growing economic prosperity. With population growth came expansion northward, up the Chesapeake Bay, and westward, toward the Allegheny Mountains. These areas were not well suited to tobacco cultivation, and wheat, corn, and other cereal grains became the agricultural base. German farmers from Pennsylvania began to migrate south to the fertile Maryland Piedmont in substantial numbers, adding a significant new ethnic base to the Maryland mix.

Monarchial change in England again reverberated in the Chesapeake in 1715. A year after the death of Queen Anne, King George I, the first king of the Hanover line, restored the full proprietary rights of the Calvert charter to Benedict Leonard Calvert. Calvert Catholicism was no longer at issue; Benedict had converted to the High Church of England and was safely Protestant. However, the colonial Maryland Assembly remained troublesome. The colony was no longer populated by mainly English-bred immigrants accustomed to aristocratic hierarchy. Most were native-born Marylanders, and by the early eighteenth century they had developed a distinctive identity that deeply resented external authority and control. In addition they were skilled and experienced by birth and training, as public office was passed from one generation to the next.[8] The political debates raised in Annapolis pitted "proprietary prerogatives versus popular aspirations" and a republican and independent ethos steadily grew.[9]

Maryland was growing as well. In 1729 the Maryland Assembly chartered Baltimore Town on the northern side of the Patapsco River. Soon to follow was the Baltimore Company, founded to mine iron ore deposits throughout the Patapsco drainage basin. By midcentury Baltimore and nearby smelters were producing iron at an annual rate equal to almost one-seventh of the far more industrialized England.[10] Baltimore itself grew slowly immediately following its inception. In 1752 it contained a mere twenty-five houses; by 1788 the young city held approximately 14,000 people in more than 2,000 residences.[11]

Land speculation was another potentially lucrative venue. Charles Calvert, the fifth Lord Baltimore, wanted western expansion to secure his proprietary claims against intrusions by Pennsylvania and Virginia settlers. After the Maryland Assembly peacefully bought off the indigenous Indian tribes, Western Maryland was open for full-scale settlement. Wealthy and well-positioned planters purchased huge tracts, laid out Frederick Town, named for Calvert's son, and enticed European farmers with bargain-basement prices. With roads connecting Frederick to Baltimore and Annapolis, the western region was soon developing. This growth produced conflict with William Penn's colony to the north, as colonists settled disputes with frontier justice. Ultimately the boundary disputes, resolved by a British court and accepted by the Calvert and Penn families, led to one of the most significant demarcation lines in the country: the Mason-Dixon Line.

ROAD TO REVOLUTION: "FULL OF SIN AND POLITICS"

The prosperity of the colonies in the second half of the eighteenth century did not go unnoticed by the British government. Faced with the enormous expenses of the French and Indian War and the continuing costs of defending the frontier, the Grenville administration in Great Britain enacted the Stamp Act, a tax measure that provided the colonists with a common cause of defiance. Negative reactions ran the gamut. There was the principled intellectual critique of Maryland's attorney general Daniel Dulaney Jr., whose lengthy and influential essay "Considerations on the Propriety of Imposing Taxes in the British Colonies" questioned the validity of taxation without representation. He decried the mercantile mentality of Parliament and cautioned, "The Mother Country might be devouring the hen that laid golden eggs."[12] While Dulaney's brief provided a basis for conservative and even elite opposition, resistance to the Stamp Act was also violent. Annapolis mobs destroyed the warehouse where the despised stamps were allegedly stored and hung the stamp collector in effigy. In 1766 chapters of the Sons of Liberty, led by later signatories of the Declaration of Independence William Paca and Samuel Chase, were formed in Baltimore and Annapolis. The Tea Act of 1774 served as the catalytic event as the British "March of Folly" continued.[13] In Boston crates of tea were dumped into the harbor. In Annapolis matters were carried to a greater extreme. Not only was the tea destroyed, but the ship that carried the cargo, the *Peggy Stewart*, was put to the torch by its owner, who faced the choice of tar and feathers or self-inflicted arson by a crowd of radicalized patriots.[14]

Revolutionary fervor was not universal in Maryland. Loyalists were in

evidence, especially on the lower Eastern Shore, and even the most experienced and respected "first citizens" were somewhat reluctant revolution-
aries. Francis Asbury, the founder of the Maryland Methodist movement,
castigated revolutionary leaders as "full of sin and politics."[15] Maryland's
delegates to the Continental Congress often steered a moderate and pragmatic course, reflecting the economic concerns of the merchant planters
who depended on English trade and credit, at times frustrating John Adams
and Thomas Jefferson.[16]

From revolutionary county associations came a call for a provincial convention. Once elected the delegates convened as a council of safety and
served as the de facto government, with uneasy coexistence with Governor
Robert Eden, Lord Baltimore's final proprietary executive, who left Maryland under relatively cordial terms a scant two weeks before July 4, 1776.
Independence for Marylanders meant an end to both British and the more
immediate proprietary rule. Self-governance produced the first Maryland
Constitution and the Declaration of Rights, fundamental documents that
balanced democratic egalitarianism with a prudent and pragmatic republican conservatism.

The hostilities of the Revolutionary War scarcely touched Maryland.
There were naval skirmishes in the lower Chesapeake Bay, and Baltimore
privateers ravaged British merchant ships up and down the Atlantic sea-
board. The soldiers of the Maryland Line performed superbly throughout
the war, covering Washington's retreat at the Battle of Long Island and
earning the high praise of Gen. Nathaniel Greene in the culminating battles of the southern campaign that led to ultimately to Yorktown. "Nothing
could exceed the gallantry of the Maryland Line," Greene observed of the
troops that constituted a third of his army.[17]

Maryland emerged from the Revolution literally and figuratively in the
midst of the great American experiment. Maryland was a middle state between the northern and southern boundaries of the thirteen former colonies.
In 1790 the geographic population center of the United States was twenty-
three miles east of Baltimore, in Kent County, and eighteen miles west in
1800. By the 1800 census Maryland had grown to 341,548 people. During
the 1700s eight new county governments were organized. The three new
jurisdictions in Western Maryland (Frederick, Washington, and Allegany)
demonstrated expansion pressures on Maryland's distinctly limited frontier. The other counties were subdivided out of existing counties in central
Maryland and the Eastern Shore.

A considerable portion of the population growth centered in Baltimore,
then the fledgling republic's third largest city, surpassed only by the con-

siderably older Philadelphia and New York. Baltimore's assets included an accessible harbor, a growing network of roads, and abundant water power from area streams with steep gradients. The consequences of having a transportation and trade economy significantly and consistently enlarged Maryland's perspectives. Although insular concerns and parochial priorities certainly did exist, they usually failed to flourish. Linkages and connections based on that ultimate of American realities, trade and economic interests, grew between Maryland, the Northeast, the Midwest, and trade partners in Europe, the Caribbean, and later Asia.

The peculiar institution of slavery was also impacted by Maryland's location. Although the Maryland version of slavery did not approach the massive plantation system of the slave states farther south, it was present in the tobacco estates and farms in the Tidewater counties of Southern Maryland and the Eastern Shore. These farms were generally smaller scale operations that promoted a different working relationship between masters and slaves.[18] The slave system also existed at reduced numbers throughout the state and encompassed other labor-intensive occupations and domestic work. In the first federal census of 1790 nearly one-third of Maryland's residents (103,036) were counted as slaves.

Maryland slavery was pressured by both the doctrine of revolutionary-era human rights promulgated in the Declaration of Independence and progressive Christian theology. Maryland Quakers opposed slavery before the Revolutionary War; those who refused to free their slaves were disowned by the church.[19] John Wesley was also scornful of slavery, and Maryland's multiplying Methodist congregations often reflected their founder's position. The revolution itself produced egalitarian impulses. The initial draft of the 1776 Maryland Declaration of Rights called for the cessation of the slave trade. The issue was also debated in the Maryland General Assembly in 1789, when Charles Carroll, a signatory of the Declaration of Independence, introduced a plan to end slavery incrementally. The measure failed, but Carroll's advocacy was indicative of a growing disconnect between some of the Maryland elite and the slavery system.

Both religious beliefs and political ideals provided rationales against bondage, and there were compelling economic rationales as well. The tobacco culture declined in the nineteenth century for a number of reasons. First, as a crop, tobacco wore out its welcome by exhausting the soil. Second, wars in Europe disrupted the principal market for Maryland "sot weed."[20] As the focus of Maryland's agrarian economy shifted decisively to grains and corn, agricultural commodities less suited to slave labor, the number of freed slaves in the state soared. No less an observer than Alexis de Tocqueville in *Democracy in America* predicted the imminent demise of slavery in Maryland.[21] In contrast to more southern states, where manumission was limited to the selective few, in Maryland it was practiced more broadly and inclusively, with the slaves of entire estates frequently freed.[22] The results were dramatic. In 1810 the ratio of slaves to free blacks was three to one. Twenty years before, in 1790, it was nearly thirteen to one.[23] By the eve of the Civil War free African Americans in Maryland virtually equaled the number of slaves, making the state the home of the largest free black community in the country. Again, unlike the more southern states, Maryland's free African Americans had more practical, if not legal, civil and property rights.

THE NEW REPUBLIC: "DEFENSE OF FORT MCHENRY"

The egalitarian idealism of the American Revolution coupled with competition between the Federalists and the Democratic-Republicans finally swept away the Maryland property qualification for voting in state elections in 1802 and federal elections in 1810. The workers in Baltimore's growing and diversified economy provided Maryland's support base for Thomas Jefferson's Democratic-Republicans, while Federalist Party strength rested predominantly in the rural counties of Western and Southern Maryland as well as the Eastern Shore.

Partisan conflict was intense; on the eve of the War of 1812 violence erupted when a Baltimore mob attacked and destroyed the office of the pro-Federalist newspaper, *The Federal Republican*. After its editor, Alexander Hanson, fortified a new facility and manned it with armed friends and supporters, his citadel was again attacked in what Brugger called one of the worst civil disorders in the country to that time.[24] The Democratic-Republicans paid an electoral price, losing Maryland state elections that fall, but the second conflict with the British politically destroyed the Federalists, who had criticized and, in some instances, impeded the American cause.

Maryland provided the arena for the absolute low and high points of the War of 1812. The former was the Battle of Bladensburg, where the state militia collapsed against the British regulars. The subsequent burning of Washington compelled Baltimore to rely on its own resources to repulse the British forces, which it did with willful determination. Gen. Samuel Smith, veteran of the Revolutionary War and a U.S. senator, commanded and co-ordinated the citizen volunteers and Maryland militia units. Smith cut corners, persuaded Baltimore merchants and banks to bankroll supplies, and provided enthusiastic, positive, and above all practical leadership. Once the British landed, Smith attacked, sending a small force down the North Point peninsula on September 12, 1814, to the east of the city while holding most of his forces in reserve behind massive earthworks. The Americans were repulsed, but not before two young sharpshooters killed the commander of the British ground forces, Gen. Robert Ross. While the Battle of North Point raged, the British fleet moved into position to bombard Fort McHenry, the key to the defense of Baltimore's inner harbor. Throughout September 13 and well into the night the warships pounded the American fortifications. With the dawn of September 14 a Maryland attorney, Francis Scott Key, saw the huge American flag still waving above the star-shaped battlements and quickly penned a poem, "Defence of Fort M'Henry." First published in Baltimore, what eventually became "The Star Spangled Banner" forever links our nation with the common folk of the Chesapeake Bay who beat back the British tide. Defenders' Day, September 12, is celebrated each year in Maryland as a state holiday to commemorate their triumph.[25]

Following the war the concerns of Maryland state government focused on the development of a transportation infrastructure, or, in the parlance of the time, "internal improvements." Although the Federalists as an organization were fractured, the Hamiltonian concept of government actively encouraging private business ventures remained relevant. The locale and focus of these projects also revealed a regional shift in priorities. The counties of original settlement in Southern Maryland and the lower Eastern Shore increasingly became backwaters to "North America's first boom town," Baltimore, its immediate environs, and Western Maryland.[26] The first federally funded infrastructure project was the National Road, originating in Cumberland, which was authorized in 1806, during the second term of President Jefferson; construction began in 1811 under President Madison, and in 1818 the road reached Wheeling, Virginia (now West Virginia), under President Monroe.[27]

The construction of the Erie Canal in New York spurred a multitude of similar projects in other states, and Maryland was no exception. The most ambitious was the Chesapeake and Ohio Canal, which was to follow the Potomac River from Georgetown to a projected terminus in Wheeling along the Ohio River. The Maryland legislature incorporated the c&o Company in 1824 and, with a pledge of continued financial support, committed the state to an eventual fiscal nightmare. By 1840 Maryland had sunk $7.2 million, almost half of the total state debt, into the project. During much of that decade the state was technically in default, making no interest payments from 1842 until 1848.[28] Facing far greater engineering challenges than the Erie Canal, the c&o made slow progress; after twenty-two years of construction it reached Cumberland in Western Maryland, 185 miles from its Washington DC origin. But there it stopped, never fulfilling its name, as the Ohio River basin remained an unobtainable goal because of the steep elevations of the Allegheny Mountains. Within Maryland the C&O was an important transportation asset for much of the nineteenth century, as barges hauled farm produce and coal from the western counties. The year 1875 marked the heaviest volume for the canal, when 973,805 tons of cargo moved along the waterway.[29] The canal fell into disuse and disrepair and was purchased by the federal government in 1938. The Chesapeake and Ohio Canal National Historical Park was opened in 1971. Today the towpaths once used by mules to haul the canal barges are popular with joggers, hikers, and bikers along the scenic Potomac River Valley.

Competing with the C&O Canal for access to the west in the nineteenth century was a new transportation technology: the railroad. A group of Maryland businessmen, including the now venerable and venerated Charles Carroll and Thomas Ellicott, whose mills clustered along the Patapsco Valley west of Baltimore City, created the Baltimore and Ohio Railroad. The railroad was incorporated by the Maryland General Assembly in 1827 with a state tax exemption that lasted until 1878. In one of the ironies of Maryland history both of these massive transportation projects were publicly begun on the same day, July 4, 1828. President John Quincy Adams turned the first shovel of dirt on the C&O Canal just north of Georgetown, while the ninety-one-year-old Carroll played a modest role in laying the cornerstone of the B&O. Within two years the B&O connected Baltimore with Ellicott Mills in nearby Howard County. The railroad tracks reached Cumberland in 1842, eight years before the C&O Canal finally arrived there and stopped. But the B&O rolled on, and by 1852 residents of Wheeling heard its train whistles. Five years later, in 1857, B&O rails stretched as far west as St. Louis.

Together with other lines, such as the Western Maryland Railroad, the B&O spurred economic and industrial growth across much of the state. Iron and coal from the western counties were shipped to Baltimore, and a coal depot was constructed at Locust Point. Chesapeake Bay striped bass, or "rockfish," as they are known in the Bay region, and oysters were shipped west to the Ohio Valley and points beyond. The railroads served to incorporate Maryland with the "industrializing northern culture."[30] Technological innovations were also encouraged by the extensive and diverse transportation grid. For example, Samuel Morse first demonstrated the telegraph along the B&O line that connected Baltimore with Washington in 1844.

Competition between the B&O and the C&O often transcended the marketplace and involved the state government. Issues such as rights of way and the suppression of labor unions occupied the policy agenda through much of the nineteenth century. Executive positions in the companies provided the financial springboard to elective office. Thomas Swann, the Unionist-Democrat governor of Maryland immediately following the Civil War, was president of the B&O. The importance of the B&O in Maryland politics during the Gilded Age is reflected in the naming of the final and westernmost Maryland subdivision, Garrett County, in honor of John W. Garrett, another president of the B&O, in 1872.

PARTISAN UPWARD MOBILITY: "POLITICS IS A COMPLETE TRADE"

Mass-based political parties emerged in Maryland with the rise of Andrew Jackson as a national political figure in the 1820s and 1830s. First and foremost Jackson's Democratic Party established deep and enduring organizational roots in the state, a necessary precondition for the electoral dominance that was to follow. The resumption of party competition after the Era of Good Feelings siesta created a new type of party, popular-based, with campaigns and elections that were not for the fainthearted. The polarization that defined the John Quincy Adams and Jackson contests of 1824 and 1828 rearranged the old Federalist and Democratic Republican alignments in Maryland, and prominent political personalities with them. The Baltimore attorney Roger Brooke Taney, the husband of Francis Scott Key's sister, and U.S. senator Samuel Smith, the hero of the Battle of Baltimore, led the Jackson forces. They were instrumental in organizing the first statewide political party in Baltimore on May 21, 1827, with the formation of a state central committee chaired by Taney and a permanent party organization to monitor, solicit, and promote party matters. Adams's supporters soon followed that organizational template, and the electoral battle was joined.

As the new parties emerged, a new type of Maryland politician also evolved. Before the Jackson era the vast majority of state leaders reflected a privileged culture. The governmental system they ruled was elitist and exclusive, and so were they. About two-thirds emerged from the planter class of rural Southern Maryland and the Eastern Shore. They enjoyed the comfortable lifestyle of large and extensive estates complete with slaves. Socially well-connected and often well-educated, they were first and foremost gentry politicians of the old school. By the early 1840s the planter politicians were eclipsed by younger, ambitious men on the make. Largely lawyers, they came from Baltimore or established towns and county seats from areas that had gone underrepresented in the past.[31] To them politics was both a means of social ascent and a course of economic betterment. Politics was their business; elections were about jobs, contracts, and governmental preferments. The parties often established a flexible take-back allotment for such favors, and patronage employees were "maced" a percentage of their salaries. As Brugger observed of the quid pro quo, "Organizational loyalty became an end in itself."[32] Taney's career well illustrates the pattern. Born in Calvert County, Southern Maryland, Taney moved to Frederick, where he developed a successful law practice. Ambitious for a larger stage and frustrated by county politics, he moved again, to Baltimore City, where his work for the presidential campaigns of Andrew Jackson propelled him to national prominence. First named attorney general in Jackson's cabinet, he parlayed that post into secretary of the treasury and ultimately chief justice of the U.S. Supreme Court.

For old-school politicians who saw social position and political position as synonymous, the change was frustrating and bitter. A former conservative congressman from the Eastern Shore, John Leeds Kerr, complained, "Politics is now become a complete trade and what is worse every fellow follows it, fool or knave & aspires to the best jobs."[33] Repugnant or not to the rural gentry, this opportunistic political approach emphasized utilitarian and pragmatic concerns and came to dominate Maryland politics and government while providing a legitimate channel for social and economic mobility.[34]

The patronage-based parties, Jacksonian Democrats, Adams's National Republicans, and later the Whigs were organized more around prominent political personalities than philosophies of governance and more on personal advancement than principled disagreement on issues. Without much in the way of competing distractions, Marylanders and Americans in general were consumed by the political process. Tocqueville was amazed at the centrality of politics in the young republic: "The political activity prevailing in the United States is something one could never understand unless one has seen it. . . . To take a hand in the government of society, and to talk about it, is his most important business and, so to say, the only pleasure an American knows."[35]

Newspapers of the era were almost invariably partisan and reinforced political competition. *The Baltimore Sun*, founded in 1837, was Democratic in inclination, while *Niles' Weekly Register* was reliably on the side of the Whigs. The parties organized with almost military precision massive rallies, parades, and speeches. The party-centered process continued through election day, when voters selected from ballots prepared, printed, and distributed by party loyalists. As almost every analyst and historian has noted, such a system "almost invited election fraud," in Maryland as elsewhere.[36]

Baltimore City was to earn an unsavory and somewhat enduring reputation as "Mobtown" for its corrupt and often coercive election practices by the time of its full bloom in the 1850s. The newspaper publisher Hezekiah Niles despairingly wrote to the Whig leader Henry Clay before elections in 1830, "Whiskey flows like water & money abounds very much."[37] The votes of "loafers, rounders, and rowdies," the homeless and unemployed by chance or choice were cast repeatedly by the simple expedient of taking such men from polling place to polling place.[38] Recent immigrants were quickly schooled in the lessons of such democracy; as Brugger notes, "Election day made a native out of many a newcomer."[39] Because voting was a public act, intimidation at the polling places was a standard tactic in some Baltimore wards dominated by Democrats. Despite this, voter turnout in the period soared to new heights. The 1828 Jackson-Adams rematch attracted over 70 percent of the eligible Maryland voters, which was substantially above the national average of 58 percent. In 1840, the "Tippecanoe and Tyler too" contest, turnout approached 85 percent of the eligible voting population and again exceeded the national average of 80 percent.[40]

Campaigns of the period vilified the opposition, and the personal political attacks were far more savage than any contemporary negative television commercial. Excessive and semidemagogic rhetoric was very much a staple of the day. For example, in 1836 Governor Thomas W. Veazey, a Whig, charged that Democrats were promoting "unspeakable calamities of anarchy, intestine commotion, and civil war."[41] Despite such polarizing rhetoric, the Whigs and Democrats were generally similar in their composition and constituents. The most striking disparity between the parties was in Baltimore City, where recent immigrants were more likely to support Democrats.[42]

Although the Democrats were the first to organize, winning Maryland for their presidential candidates proved elusive. Because of district contests for electors until 1840, the state did not deliver all its electoral votes to a Democrat until the 1852 presidential election. At the state level Democrats were quite competitive with the anti-Jackson forces, the Whigs. Elections for governor were hard fought and tightly won. In the five gubernatorial contests from 1838 to 1850 the victory margin averaged only 745 votes, with the Democrats controlling the governor's mansion for twelve of fifteen years. The Whigs held majorities in the Maryland General Assembly for eleven of those same years.

The competitive parity between Democrats and Whigs helped produce governmental reforms that modernized and democratized Maryland government and politics. In accordance with the Jacksonian imperative to broaden self-governance and the more pragmatic goal of winning additional legislative seats, Maryland Democrats campaigned for direct popular elections of the governor and state senators during the early 1830s.[43] The Whig-controlled general assembly bowed to the pressure and passed constitutional amendments that gave Maryland citizens the right to vote directly for the governor and state senators.

During the 1830s Baltimore became the national convention center for American political parties. With sectional antagonisms increasing, simple geography played to the city's advantage. Neither wholly northern nor wholly southern, its centrality provided some semblance of neutral ground and its forty-mile distance from the national capital was convenient for travel. The newly organized Democrats held their first six conventions in Baltimore, from 1832 through 1852, a tribute both to the logic of the city as a convenient meeting place and the energy of the Maryland Democratic Party. The National Republicans nominated Henry Clay in Baltimore in 1832, and the Whigs returned in 1844 and 1852. In the confused and critical year of 1860 Baltimore hosted three of four national party conventions: the Constitutional Union Party, the regular Democrats, and the secessionist Democrats. During the Civil War the Unionist Party renominated Abraham Lincoln for a second term in 1864 in Baltimore, and the Democrats returned in 1872 to nominate Horace Greeley to run against President Ulysses S. Grant. After that Baltimore fell almost completely out of political convention vogue, supplanted by midwestern cities such as Chicago and St. Louis. Baltimore hosted its final convention when the Democrats nominated Woodrow Wilson in 1912.

Within Maryland Baltimore City was both prized and feared. For some it was the "soul of the state," yet others saw its rapid growth and economic dominance as a very real threat to traditional Maryland customs and life.[44] By midcentury the city had twice as many residents as it did in 1820. Its 1850 population of 169,054 was almost 30 percent of the statewide total. Much of the demographic growth came from European immigration, especially from the Germanic states and Ireland. After New York, Philadelphia, and Boston, Baltimore was a popular destination, with almost 11,000 arriving in 1847 alone.[45] Of the Germans and Irish that came, almost 70 percent stayed in the city. With more than 50,000 foreign-born residents by 1850, the number of immigrants in Maryland far exceeded that of other states below the Mason-Dixon Line. By 1850 southern states averaged thirty-two foreign-born per 1,000 people. In Maryland the rate was 114, only one per-

son below the national average of 115 per 1,000.[46] Coupled with the growing number of free blacks, the population of Maryland was far more diverse
and pluralistic than most states, either north or south. This growing demographic diversity divided the state more than ever before.

ERA OF THE KNOW NOTHINGS:
"AMERICANS SHALL RULE AMERICA"

The final decade before the Civil War was scarcely Maryland's finest. A
"primal political evil" flourished in the 1850s, dominating elective offices
from the local level to the governor's mansion in Annapolis.[47] Called the
"Know Nothings" by their detractors for their secretive manners, the American Party began as small, covert societies organized around the premise
that only "Americans shall rule America."[48] In Maryland sporadic economic growth and a fierce competition for jobs by immigrants and free blacks,
especially in Baltimore, gave political resonance to the Know Nothing
message. Nativist rhetoric translated into a political agenda that "mingled
hate, clannishness, and fear."[49]

The Know Nothings feared the influence of the Maryland Catholic community. They feared the growing influence of the Baltimore Jewish community. Above all they feared "foreign ungrateful refugees."[50] They promised
a return to purer republican ways, a simpler politics devoid of maneuvers
and manipulations. The party attracted to their cause young, successful
businessmen from the urban and small-town middle class. They were often
newcomers to the political process and stood in stark contrast to the professional and established politicians of the Maryland Democratic Party.[51]

With the rapid political collapse of the Whigs after the election of 1852,
the Know Nothings began a meteoric rise to power in Maryland. The party's first electoral successes came in 1854 in the Western Maryland cities
of Hagerstown and Cumberland, where the Know Nothings exploited the
frequent strikes by immigrant miners. Later that year the Know Nothings
won a majority of municipal offices in Baltimore City with the assistance
of a ballot that duplicated the design of the Democratic version and confused immigrants, who constituted much of the city's Democratic base. In
1855 the Know Nothing tide continued to roll. The nativists won fifty-four
of seventy-four seats in the Maryland House of Delegates and enticed several Whig remnants in the state senate to join their cause, giving them control of the upper body. In 1856 the Know Nothings mounted a national
presidential campaign, nominating former Whig president Millard Fillmore
as their standard-bearer. In Baltimore local elections preceded the presi-

dential election, and a close mayoral contest took election day violence to a whole other level. The nineteenth-century Maryland historian Thomas Scharf described the voting experience: "In various parts of the city pitched battles raged all day; muskets and pistols were freely used, and even cannon brought out into the streets. Nightfall alone put a close to a scene more like the storming of a town than a peaceful election."[52]

At a cost of four lives and scores wounded, the Know Nothing candidate for mayor, Thomas Swann, former president of the B&O Railroad, was elected. The presidential election riot was worse, with a death toll of ten and more than two hundred injured in widespread fighting at city polling places. In Maryland the nativists triumphed, with Fillmore besting Democrat James Buchanan. Maryland was the only state Fillmore carried and was the only slave state that did not support Buchanan. The newly formed Republican Party barely registered in the Maryland electorate, with its candidate, former Gen. John Fremont, receiving a pittance of 285 votes out of 86,862 votes cast.

Nationally the Know Nothings quickly fragmented; however, the party held on for a few more years in Maryland. In certain Baltimore wards street gangs with such names as the "Plug Uglies" and the "Blood Tubs" reigned on election days and permitted only Know Nothing ballots to be cast and counted. Their favorite weapons for intimidating would-be Democratic voters were the shoemaker's awl, similar to an ice pick, and tubs filled with slaughterhouse blood to pour over the heads of uncooperative voters. To further pad the Know Nothing vote counts, their operatives also practiced "cooping." This referred to the kidnapping of drunkards and other unfortunates a few days before an election, drugging them to keep them manageable, and locking them up in convenient basements or even abandoned chicken coops. Once the voting started they were dragooned to vote repeatedly the length and breadth of the city.[53]

As mob rule influenced Baltimore election outcomes, Know Nothing rule continued statewide. In 1857 the American Know Nothing Party elected its first governor, Thomas Hicks, and four of the state's six congressional representatives and maintained its control of the general assembly, although with reduced majorities. Holding power, the Know Nothings were quiescent, making "little effort to translate rhetoric into law."[54] As the historian Jean Baker observes, the attraction of the party for "young, self-made Marylanders" was essentially "position, power, and prestige."[55] Beyond that, there was little to the Know Nothing agenda. With increased Democratic competition, full-blown nativism took a backseat to pragmatic expediency. Soon the American Know Nothing Party extolled first and fore-most the virtues of conservative unionism, a precursor of the Constitutional Union Party and then the Civil War–era Union Party in Maryland.

In Baltimore City a mounting political reaction against Know Nothing control was mobilizing. As the national reputation of Baltimore slipped fur-ther into disrepute, independents and Democrats organized a City Reform Association and won seats on the city council. By 1859 the nativists were in full retreat. In the statewide elections they lost everywhere except Bal-timore, and there the returns were contested. Maryland Democrats retali-ated in the general assembly. They stripped police power from Baltimore's mayor, impeached a Know Nothing city judge, and unseated the entire Bal-timore City delegation.

The Maryland Democratic Party had benefited substantially from the new state constitution of 1851. Representing the last wave of Jacksonian-era "long ballot" reform, the constitution significantly expanded voter par-ticipation in state and local government.[56] Under the new constitution the state comptroller, four commissioners of public works, the commissioner of land office, all circuit court and appeals judges, clerks of the various county courts, registers of wills, state's attorneys, county commissioners, county surveyors, justices of the peace, constables, and road supervisors all became elective posts. With the extension of the ballot patronage patterns shifted. The governor's appointive powers sharply declined, and that of lo-cal elected officials greatly increased. Over time county political organiza-tions, especially the Democrats, grew more powerful and entrenched.

As the Know Nothings scapegoated immigrants, Maryland's African Americans, free and slave alike, were scapegoated by the Democrats. John Brown's raid on Harper's Ferry in 1859 "heightened negrophobia," which was exploited by the Democrats.[57] The party supported southern states' rights and sought to diminish the size and rights of a growing Maryland free black population. Legislative measures to prohibit future manumission and require the registration of free African Americans won the support of many of the state's 14,000 slave owners. A bill creating a board of commis-sioners in selected counties with the power to summon free Negroes and auction them for a term of one year if they could not provide evidence of being employed was passed during the 1860 regular session of the general assembly.[58] This statute never took effect as it required an affirmative vote of the citizens of affected counties but was instead soundly rejected at the polls. In part this was due to the political efforts of free Maryland blacks who lobbied and organized against the legislation. The movement was

based in the black Baltimore churches such as the African Methodist Epis-
copal Church (AME), long "the spiritual and psychological bedrock" of the
black community.[59] Enlisting the support of sympathetic whites, including
two hundred women who petitioned against the proposed laws, Baltimore's
free blacks helped beat back the oppressive proposals. They displayed a
considerable sense of "racial identity and solidarity" within a "cohesive urban community," attributes and virtues they would have to call on again
and again in the years to come.[60]

There was no question that free blacks faced a more precarious economic and political environment. With African Americans constituting one
fifth of the population and the number of free blacks increasing and slaves
declining, state politicians moved to preserve white supremacy. Maryland was the first state to provide an annual appropriation to its Colonization Society, designed to send free African Americans to Haiti or Liberia.
Although its efforts were largely ineffectual, the state government maintained annual appropriations until the Civil War.[61] Economic competition
from German and Irish immigrants often provoked violence. Shortly before
Frederick Douglass escaped to the North, he was brutally assaulted while
working as a contracted-out slave in a Baltimore shipyard. As the numbers
of foreign-born whites increased, economic opportunity for Maryland African Americans declined. In Baltimore black employment dropped by almost 21 percent during the 1850s.[62] The city, once regarded by blacks as a
place of refuge, "lost its status as a safe haven."[63]

Although Maryland slaves were as legally disadvantaged as their Deep
South counterparts, some historians have concluded that "Maryland's black
code was far less severe in practice than in theory."[64] Politically Maryland
was quite different from most slave states. The planter class and the plantation system did not dominate but coexisted with a rapidly diversifying
economy within an increasingly pluralistic social context. This meant that
Maryland slave masters often "lived in the midst of outspoken antislavery
sentiment," where they constituted a distinct minority interest.[65] The numbers were simply against them. In 1800 slaves constituted almost 31 percent of the Maryland population. By 1830 the percentage had dropped to
23, and by 1860 it shrank to less than 13. In Baltimore City slavery was
even more uncommon. African Americans held in bondage accounted for
11 percent of the city's population in 1800, but by 1860 slaves numbered
only 2,218, or 1 percent of the city's 212,418 residents. In contrast Baltimore free blacks were 12 percent of populace.[66]

In general Maryland slaveholders may have acted less harshly given their geographic vulnerability.[67] Though the proximity to Pennsylvania made a dash to freedom alluring, relatively few made the journey. An exception was Harriet Tubman; born a slave in Dorchester County, on the lower Eastern Shore, she escaped bondage through the Underground Railroad in 1849. Tubman returned to her home state fifteen times to lead an estimated three hundred slaves to northern safety, earning her the title "the Moses of her people."

MARYLAND'S CIVIL WAR: "PATRIOTIC GORE"

Over Antietam's killing fields the Maryland Monument rises thirty-five feet high. Unlike many Civil War battlefield monuments it does not eulogize solely the Union or the Confederate dead; it recognizes both sides of the terrible and costly conflict. Financed by the Maryland General Assembly and dedicated on Memorial Day 1900, its plaque reads, "Erected by the State of Maryland to her sons, who on this field offered their lives in maintenance of their principles."[68] As it divided the nation the Civil War polarized Maryland; while 46,638 Marylanders wore Union blue, some 12,000 to 16,000 went south to fight for the Confederacy. Troop numbers reflected Marylanders being pulled in multiple directions, as did the 1860 presidential election, in which the national mainstream candidates, Democrat Stephen A. Douglas and Republican Abraham Lincoln, ran a distant third and fourth, with Douglas receiving only 6,080 votes and Lincoln a meager 2,296. Marylanders seemed to be searching for a middle course when such compromise solutions were no longer possible in the nation.

The first shots of the Civil War were fired in Charlestown Harbor, and the first deaths of the conflict were recorded on the streets of Baltimore. A week after the attack on Fort Sumter, on April 19, 1861, a Baltimore mob assaulted troops of the Sixth Massachusetts Regiment marching along Pratt Street between train stations en route to defend the nation's capital. After enduring rocks and sporadic gunfire that killed four of their company, the soldiers shot back. At the melee's end twelve Baltimoreans lay dead. Despite the courageous efforts of the reform mayor George Brown and Chief of Police George Kane, who personally put themselves at physical risk to protect the troops, the city was "engulfed by hysteria."[69] In Washington alarmed federal authorities made plans for military intervention. Hundreds of miles to the south, in Louisiana, a young English teacher and transplanted Baltimorean, James Ryder Randall, after learning of the riot, penned an emotional, poetic plea to his native state to leave the Union. The first and final stanzas are as follows:

The despot's heel is on thy shore, Maryland!

His torch is at thy temple door, Maryland!

Avenge the patriotic gore that flecked the streets of Baltimore,

And be the battle queen of yore, Maryland, my Maryland!

I hear the distant thunder-hum, Maryland!

The Old Line bugle, fife and drum, Maryland!

She is not dead, nor deaf, nor dumb.

Huzza! She spurns the Northern scum!

She breathes! She burns! She'll Come! She'll Come!

Maryland! My Maryland![70]

Maryland, of course, did not secede, though commentators disagree over whether this was a function of the rapid federal military occupation that smothered the secessionist impulse or a prevailing public sentiment for the Union.[71] With a diverse and commerce-based economy, an extensive transportation infrastructure, two-party politics, and a pluralistic population, Maryland was hardly a typical southern state.[72] Certainly there were areas, chiefly Southern Maryland and the Eastern Shore, where a substantial number, if not absolute majorities of white citizens sympathized and actively supported the Confederate cause. This posed an almost constant wartime concern in Washington. In fact President Lincoln's first secretary of war, Simon Cameron, seriously proposed dismembering and abolishing the state.[73] As Robert Brugger observed, in the months before open hostilities "most Marylanders probably wanted to be left alone."[74] Events, Maryland's strategic location, and the vulnerability of the District of Columbia dictated otherwise.

During the mounting crisis Governor Hicks's policy of "masterly inactivity" was pragmatic to a fault.[75] While he criticized "union by coercion," he defused contention by ignoring calls for a secessionist convention and helped Maryland stay in the Union by something close to political default.[76] When he finally yielded to pressure and called a special session of the general assembly in late April 1861, Hicks directed the legislature to meet in Frederick, away from any center of slavery sentiment. In this session the majority of legislators declared that they possessed no authority to secede and rejected a call for a statewide secession convention. The Lincoln administration would take no chances as many state political leaders remained critical of federal actions. Habeas corpus was suspended, and in mid-May Baltimore was occupied. On the heights of the inner harbor's Federal Hill Union cannon pointed directly at the city center. In command was Gen. Benjamin Butler, who regarded most Marylanders as "malignant and traitorous."[77]

Federal authorities applied their unlimited powers of arrest and uncharged detention with considerable energy. Twenty-seven state legislators were detained, along with Mayor Brown of Baltimore and all four of the city's police commissioners, former governor Thomas Pratt, a pro-peace congressman, newspaper editors suspected of secessionist sentiments, and scores of private citizens. An Eastern Shore circuit court judge, Richard Carmichael, protested what he considered illegal arrests and for his troubles was forcibly removed from his courtroom and beaten by federal troops. Even U.S. Supreme Court Chief Justice Taney felt endangered. Ruling against the administration in *Ex parte Merryman* over the arrest of a Baltimore County Democrat, the eighty-four-year-old judge confessed to the mayor of Baltimore after his ruling, "I am an old man, a very old man, but perhaps I was preserved for this occasion."[78]

Under the circumstances the most salient political issue was the Lincoln administration and its war policy. The prewar political organizations "virtually disappeared."[79] Weakened by defections to the Confederate Army and federal detentions, some Maryland Democrats joined forces with a new States' Rights Party. The Constitutional Union Party morphed into the Unionists, along with some former Democrats, with a platform that "wrapped itself in the patriotic garb of defending the Constitution and Union against treason."[80] Maryland elections were subject to control in certain areas, with federal troops and loyalty oaths that discouraged turnout and promoted Union Party success. State Democrats claimed the outcomes were "elections by sword" at the cost of the "trampled ballot." They would recycle and exploit those charges for years in Maryland politics.[81] The Unionists pushed through a new state constitution in 1864 that emancipated Maryland's slaves, the first border state to do so. The new constitution also mandated a strict and all-inclusive loyalty oath as a requirement for voting, which served to disenfranchise a portion of the Maryland electorate and to ensure the control of the Union Party.

While the Civil War produced sweeping political changes in Maryland, these proved "curiously transitory and superficial."[82] The hiatus of a unified state Democratic Party soon ended. At war's end Maryland was not covered by the executive orders and congressional acts that imposed conditions and restrictions on the states of the defeated Confederacy. Instead Maryland began reconstruction on its own terms. The Union Party, fragmented by personality clashes and policy divisions, became the Republican Party, associated, like it or not, with the federal occupation and suffrage for blacks. Opportunistic political actors quickly perceived the shifting electoral power. Montgomery Blair, who helped defend Dred Scott, organized the

Maryland Republican Party before the Civil War, and served as Lincoln's postmaster general, moved over to the Democrats. So did Thomas Swann, past president of the B&O, Know Nothing mayor of Baltimore, and Unionist governor. He aided the reemerging Democrats by appointing voter registrars for the 1866 legislative elections who loosely applied or conveniently ignored the loyalty requirements of the 1864 state constitution. Democratic voters returned en masse to the polls, and the results were a predictable change of substantial Democratic control of the general assembly.

Shortly after the newly elected legislature convened in 1867 another constitutional convention was called, approved, and held. It was presided over by Judge Carmichael, the same jurist pulled off the bench and imprisoned by Union troops in 1862. The 1867 constitution discarded the loyalty oath for elective office and increased legislative representation in strong Democratic areas. Constitutional changes were, in the main, "political in nature."[83] By 1868 the Democrats held every statewide office. Swann, justly labeled a "political acrobat," was elected as a Democratic congressman in 1868.[84]

DEMOCRATIC GILDED AGE DOMINANCE:
"THAT FELLOW GORMAN IS NO FOOL"

Once restored to power the Maryland Democratic Party seemed "entrenched and impregnable."[85] Organized at the local level in Democratic clubs that served social, economic, and political functions, Democrats could depend on high voter turnouts to consistently turn back Republican statewide challenges. From 1868 through 1895 all nine Maryland governors were Democrats, with ample Democratic majorities in both houses of the general assembly throughout the period.

There was little in the way of a programmatic approach to state politics. Democrats championed states' rights and fiscal conservatism and reminded voters of the Civil War occupation. Playing the race card was their strongest suit. Carl Bode asserts that the only issue that really mattered was voting rights for blacks, which "the Democrats were fiercely against and the Republicans uneasily for."[86] In 1870 the Democratic state legislature unanimously rejected ratification of the Fifteenth Amendment, forbidding race discrimination in voting. As soon as it was ratified nationally, however, the Democratic State Central Committee and the Democratic-dominated legislature did support revised voter registration and authorized voting by black male citizens. If the Gilded Age Maryland Democrats were anything, they were pragmatic.[87]

Republicans did enjoy substantial support in the counties of Western

Maryland, counties in the Tidewater region, and Montgomery County, which had large African American populations, but in the seven gubernatorial elections from 1867 through 1891 they averaged only 42 percent of the statewide vote, winning none. The absence of statewide elected opposition coupled with the mechanics of party politics created fertile conditions for the development of party bosses. There was no open primary election process, and candidates for office were "endorsed" on the county and state levels by party conventions. These were gatherings of party activists whose fortunes and life stations depended on personal relationships and their ability to create and collect on political debts. With businesses booming, industries expanding, and unions developing there was certainly a place for political power brokers who could provide the legal exemptions and sweetheart deals that made the Gilded Age glitter.

In Maryland their names were Arthur Pue Gorman, of rural Howard County and I. Freeman Rasin, the boss of Baltimore City. As a team they sparked a political synergy that influenced the course of Maryland politics for three decades and established a reliance on corruption that persisted for generations.[88] Their marriage of political convenience was based on mutual admiration. Rasin, the hard-edged insider, observed of his partner, "That fellow Gorman is no fool."[89] Rasin marshaled his ward organizations from his position as clerk of the court of common pleas in Baltimore City but delivered only one public speech in his forty years in politics.[90] The Baltimore boss "knew everything and everybody," and when votes were needed he delivered.[91] Prior to election day Rasin's lieutenants would distribute "walking-around money" to precinct captains to buy drinks and votes from the city electorate. Intimidation at the polls and voting repeaters were stock and trade. If reform pressure grew too intense, Rasin was not above "perfuming" the Democratic ticket with machine-connected but trusted citizens of good repute.[92]

While Rasin attended to urban matters, Gorman played on a larger stage. His political education began at age eleven, as page to the U.S. Senate. There he stayed during the Civil War, serving as assistant postmaster in the U.S. Senate post office. He was elected to the house of delegates in 1869, the speakership in 1873, and in 1880 returned to the U.S. Senate as a member from Maryland elected by the state legislature. Gorman's power base included the presidency of the Chesapeake and Ohio Canal Company, a post he acquired as a reward for political favors. Armed with public- and private-sector patronage, Gorman constructed his statewide machine and a loyal following within the general assembly. The Gorman-Rasin ring employed such tactics as "bell-ringer" legislation, proposals such as new taxes on then unregulated utilities such as the Baltimore Gas and Electric Company. To kill the bill business lobbyists would distribute "cash by the bagful."[93] It was no wonder that the *Baltimore Sun* described the Gorman-Rasin system as "corrupt to the core."[94] Yet despite their abundant resources in patronage and contributions, machine control of Maryland was never absolute.

PROGRESSIVES AND IMPERFECT REFORMS

In the states as well as the federal system ambition tends to counteract ambition, just as James Madison envisioned in Federalist Number 51. Over time the Gorman-Rasin machine accumulated a critical mass of political enemies who fueled the development of reform movements, comprised of independent-minded Democrats and Republicans. As almost always in politics, motivations were mixed. Some reformers were idealistic citizens who sincerely believed a public office is a public trust. Others, such as John K. Cowen, the general counsel of the B&O Railroad, were simply out for a modicum of vengeance in response to biased policy decisions. First the Citizens Reform Association and then the Baltimore Reform League took aim at "Gormanism" and all that it represented. By the mid-1890s progressive reformism was a national trend as muckraking, crusading newspapers exposed official malfeasance. In Baltimore the standard operating procedures of the machine were exposed for all to see. In 1895 the Reform League investigated voter registration and found grossly inflated rolls in Rasin's strongholds. In the Ninth Ward three houses were listed as containing 186 voters, where only a year before there were only eleven registered.[95] With 1,500 League poll watchers in place, the machine went down to defeat as Lloyd Lowndes, a banker from Western Maryland, became the first Republican governor in Maryland history. Democrats lost control of the general assembly two years later, and the GOP majority replaced Gorman in the U.S. Senate with the Republican Louis McComas.

Although reform measures such as the Australian secret ballot, primary elections, and a professional and bipartisan administration of the local boards of supervisors of elections were all instituted, the demise of the Gorman-Rasin machine was decidedly exaggerated. Maryland Republicans provided unwitting life support. They were as fond of patronage and lucrative conflicts of interests as their political nemesis. Governor Lowndes, an investor in an Allegany County coal company, vetoed mine safety bills, and House of Delegates Speaker Sydney Mudd described an honest politician as one "who will stay bought."[96] The Republican politics-as-usual approach helped the Democrats regain control of the governorship and the state legislature in the next election. The general assembly promptly again elected Gorman to the U.S. Senate in 1901. The Democratic restoration spawned a series of attempts to cripple the Maryland Republican Party by taking aim at the more than 57,000 African American registered voters who constituted its strongest and most reliable electoral bloc.

Through the assorted devices of literacy tests, poll taxes, white primaries, and the grandfather clause, the wholesale disenfranchisement of black voters in states to the south had not gone unnoticed by the machine leadership. Cloaking his proposal in the reform guise of "good government," Gorman devised, with the aid of John Prentiss Poe, dean of the University of Maryland Law School, a constitutional amendment that coupled the grandfather clause to the literacy test. The "Poe Amendment" would have restricted voting to adult males who were entitled to vote on January 1, 1869, or to their descendants. Only native-born white males, of course, could qualify. Otherwise, prospective voters, white or black, would have to give a "reasonable explanation" of any part of the Maryland Constitution selected at the discretion of an election judge. Republicans, reform Democrats, and African Americans were hardly fooled. One independent Democratic leader observed, "I fear much more the old Democratic ring than I do the bugaboo of Negro domination."[97] A variety of Jim Crow statutes involving public transportation, accommodations, parks, and education were enacted, making segregation the rule across the state. But the African American community was not defenseless. They had helped elect black city councilmen in Baltimore City and aldermen in Annapolis and Cambridge and were "better organized" than in other southern states.[98] Joining a newly formed Negro Suffrage League in opposition were immigrant groups, the Republicans, and reform Democrats, a coalition almost identical to the one that first defeated the Gorman-Rasin machine in 1895. The results were even more decisive. The proposed constitutional amendment was overwhelmingly defeated, 104,286 (60 percent) to 70,227 (40 percent), in the 1905 general election.[99]

Following the deaths of Senator Gorman in 1906 and Rasin in 1907, the machine faltered and progressive causes gained adherents in the Democratic Party. But as the historian Margaret Callcott observed, "Racism . . . remained constant."[100] Maryland Democrats tried two other measures to disqualify black voters but were again soundly rejected by voters in 1909 and 1911. The final attempt was blatantly racist and of dubious constitutionality; it provided the vote to all white males subject to age and residence restrictions, but African American men had to have paid real estate or personal property taxes for two consecutive years. This proposal generated national criticism and was crushed at the polls, 83,070 (64 percent) to 45,988 (36 percent), in the 1911 general election. Ironically the same election sounded the death knell of the machine as Arthur Pue Gorman Jr., the power broker's son, lost his bid to become governor of Maryland by 2,997 votes to Phillips Lee Goldsborough, who previously served from 1898 to 1900 as the only Republican elected as comptroller of Maryland under the 1867 constitution.

During the Progressive era Maryland Republicans enjoyed unprecedented electoral success at the federal level. From 1896 through 1928 Maryland voters supported the Republican presidential candidate in seven out of nine elections. They won three of the seven direct elections for U.S. senator and nearly broke even in the U.S. House of Representatives, capturing forty-eight of the 102 congressional races. However, at the state level Republicans remained a distinct minority. Two Republican governors were elected in 1895 and 1911, but only the 1898 session of the Maryland General Assembly had Republican majorities in the house of delegates and state senate. The Republicans were generally the party most associated with reform and progressive measures; for example, they supported women's suffrage in contrast to Maryland's Democratic leadership, which considered female political participation as mostly a "nuisance."[101]

The Progressive movement also championed an activist governmental role in the social welfare public policy sphere. In efforts to reform child labor and the excesses of sweatshop labor, Maryland women became involved as never before. Leaders came from newly chartered women's colleges, such as Goucher and Notre Dame, America's first Catholic college for women. Maryland was scarcely a national leader in progressive causes, yet substantial reforms in public health, utility regulation, and public education were enacted. State reform Democrats and Republicans, often outnumbered by conservative rural Democrats in the malapportioned general assembly, were by circumstance political pragmatists, settling for halfway measures rather than the hoped-for ideal. As James Crooks concludes in his study of the Maryland Progressive movement, "The striking phenomenon is not that they failed to do more, but that they accomplished as much as they did."[102]

Maryland fell far short of either ideal or compromised reform in responding to the women's suffrage movement. The state went unrepresented at national suffrage conventions until 1889, and the Maryland Woman's Suffrage Association had fewer than two hundred members in 1904.[103] Efforts to influence the state legislature were tactically divided, and the Maryland General Assembly unceremoniously tabled the various proposals.[104] In

1920 thirty-six states quickly ratified the Nineteenth Amendment, but the Maryland legislature voted against ratification.

By the end of the nineteenth century the Maryland subdivision count was complete at twenty-three counties and the City of Baltimore. During the 1800s three counties, Carroll, Howard, and westernmost Garrett, were created on the Western Shore, and Wicomico, a product of the 1867 constitution, was formed on the Eastern Shore. The Maryland economy was changing as the percentage of agricultural workers fell below that in manufacturing by 1900. Although the state was never a national leader in industry, ranking fourteenth in the value of products per capita in 1900, Maryland was first in the South Atlantic region. Baltimore, with well-established clothing, canning, and iron and steel facilities, produced almost two-thirds of the state's industrial output.[105] Demographic shifts gave Maryland a clear distinction between the rural counties and Baltimore. Almost 43 percent of the state population lived in Baltimore City by 1900, and this increased to an all-time high of 51 percent in 1920. But state legislative malapportionment remained the rule.[106]

THE REIGN OF RITCHIE: GUBERNATORIAL GODFATHER

Despite Progressive-era reforms Maryland state government and the governor's office itself were mired in nineteenth-century inefficiencies. No governor had ever been reelected by the people, and though many were distinguished and able, no single governor had left an enduring mark on the office. But then Albert Ritchie was elected. Labeled by some contemporaries and state historians Maryland's "greatest" and "most remarkable" governor, Ritchie barely eked out a 165-vote victory over Harry Nice, the Republican candidate in 1919. Educated at Johns Hopkins University and the University of Maryland Law School, Ritchie ascended the political ladder quickly. He served as Baltimore's assistant city solicitor from 1903 to 1910 and as assistant general counsel to the Public Service Commission from 1910 to 1913 before being elected Maryland's attorney general in 1915. During the First World War he was appointed general counsel to the War Industries Board by President Wilson, where he gained national government experience.

With the Maryland Democratic Party splintered by factionalism between Baltimore City and rural leaders, Ritchie became the focus of party fortunes for the next fifteen years after his election as the state's chief executive in 1919. Ritchie was not a progressive reformer, although he used selected progressive rhetoric and reforms as pragmatic tools to further his

political interests. His first reform was to strengthen the institutional resources of the gubernatorial office and overhaul the cumbersome machin-
ery of executive agencies to produce greater efficiencies. As H. L. Mencken
wrote, Ritchie was a "genuine Jeffersonian" Democrat, but he had distinct
"energy in the executive," Hamiltonian impulses.[107]

During Ritchie's four terms he personalized the executive budget by
presenting it before joint sessions of the state legislature. He established
central purchasing for state supplies and supported a state constitutional
amendment that shifted all state and most county elections to a presidential
midterm system that persists to this day. He provided general fund revenue
sharing for county school systems and greatly extended the merit system
for state employees. When Ritchie embarked on executive reorganization
he "Marylandized" an out-of-state study by appointing a state reorganization committee to redraft the bureaucratic consolidation. All 108 members
of the committee were Democrats, illustrative of Ritchie's additional political interests. He "overlooked no chance for party growth" and likewise
never seemed to neglect a chance to promote himself.[108]

At Ritchie's ideological core was an unwavering commitment to dual
federalism. For him the line of responsibilities and powers between the federal and state governments was a clear and inviolate boundary. His defense
of states' rights during Prohibition made him "a national rallying point in
the struggle against dry tyranny."[109] His hostility to the Volstead Act cli-
maxed at a 1922 Washington luncheon hosted by President Warren Hard-
ing. After the president had implored the fifteen governors in attendance to
vigorously enforce Prohibition, Ritchie stood and launched a counterpoint
diatribe against "an unnecessary and drastic federal infringement on their
state and personal rights." Ritchie's defense of states' rights did not extend
to overtly racist sentiments typical of contemporary southern governors.
He took steps to frustrate the activities of the Ku Klux Klan in the 1920s.
When the lower Eastern Shore became the scene of the state's last two racist lynchings, in 1931 and 1933, Ritchie made efforts, albeit unsuccessful,
to bring to justice those responsible.[110]

Articulate and handsome, energetic and intelligent, Ritchie harbored
presidential ambitions. Following the scholastic Wilson model, he authored
scores of articles on the art of governance and the principles of states'
rights. He delivered countless speeches, and through his "Ritchie Leagues"
(groups of likeminded Democratic activists) presidential boomlets began in
1924, 1928, and 1932. However, each ended in frustration for Maryland's
governor. Frank Kent, a columnist and advisor for Sunpapers, concluded
that in each Democratic convention Ritchie "had more friends and few-

er votes than any other candidate."[111] Although his presidential bids didn't amount to much, his legacy in rejuvenating and organizing the Maryland Democratic Party has endured far beyond his death in 1936.[112]

For much of his career Ritchie could count on the constant support of the *Baltimore Sun*, which had become Maryland's dominant newspaper. With writers such as Kent, Mencken, and Gerald Johnson, the newspaper "usually located common sense and sound judgment in Albert C. Ritchie."[113] Mencken, whose national reputation as an iconoclast with a keen wit and barbed pen soared during the 1920s, shared with Ritchie an antipathy to Prohibition. The *Sun* editor called the Noble Experiment "the Thirteen Dreadful Years."[114]

The Great Depression presented Ritchie with a dilemma, a choice between his principles and his pragmatism. Unlike in more industrialized states, Maryland's economy went into a slow freeze rather than a free fall, but by 1932 the state was in deep trouble. Unemployment in Baltimore City was over 20 percent, coal companies went bankrupt in Western Maryland, and canneries were closed on the Eastern Shore. Ritchie, committed to voluntarism, refused to request federal loans from the Hoover administration, but once the New Deal grants were in place he agreed "to get all we can."[115] Despite the governor's philosophical aversion to the emerging doctrine of cooperative federalism, he attempted to run for a fifth term, this time as a New Dealer, in the 1934 general election after being sharply and closely challenged by a progressive Democrat in the primary. His primary opponent charged that the incumbent had succumbed to "governitis contageosus," and Maryland Republicans asked whether his slogan was "Ritchie Forever."[116] In an almost mythical turn of political irony Ritchie's 1919 Republican opponent, Harry Nice, resurfaced as the Republican gubernatorial nominee. Nice, the Baltimore City state's attorney, campaigned as the better New Dealer, even appropriating the FDR theme song "Happy Days Are Here Again." Nice squeezed out a 6,149-vote victory, consistent with the twentieth-century political template for Maryland Republican gubernatorial candidates: Republicans could win if they were more liberal than their Democratic opponents, who also suffered from intraparty conflict. Nice's bid for reelection in 1938 was dashed by Democrat Herbert O'Conor, Ritchie's attorney general and ticket mate in 1934 and a self-described protégé of both Ritchie and Roosevelt. A pragmatist's pragmatist, O'Conor "sensed the public mood and played to it."[117] Ritchie's four-term run will never be equaled, as Maryland voters ratified a constitutional amendment in 1948 that mandates a limit of two consecutive terms for governor.

THE MAKING OF MODERN MARYLAND

The New Deal left its mark on Maryland beyond the programs that lifted public spirits and incomes. Although the state initially gathered less New Deal funds per capita than most because of Ritchie's reluctance to participate in dollar-matching grants, 21,000 Civil Conservation corpsmen cleared forest trails, restored historic forts and monuments, and improved drainage on Eastern Shore farmland.[118] Public works included bridges over the Potomac and the Susquehanna Rivers, dredging of the Chesapeake and Delaware Bay Canal, and the acquisition and conversion of the Chesapeake and Ohio Canal into a national park. The Works Progress Administration alone expended nearly $38 million on public facility construction.[119] Maryland unions, now protected by the Wagner Act, organized throughout the state as the Congress of Industrial Organizations (CIO) and the American Federation of Labor (AFL), gaining thousands of members. The growth of the FDR's federal government was noticeably felt, especially in Prince George's County and Montgomery County, where the population soared 37 percent from 1930 to 1940.[120]

The New Deal established the importance, range, and scope of the federal government in social welfare and economic policies. As Washington grew in importance, so did Maryland, in the main as a function of simple proximity. But what transformed and modernized Maryland even more completely than the New Deal was the second critical test of the "Greatest Generation": the Second World War. Before that global conflict the state was southern in some social aspects, with Jim Crow–style segregation in public accommodations and a relatively high illiteracy rate, twenty-eighth in the nation, but northern in urbanization, where it ranked ninth, and in per student public school expenditures, where it ranked twelfth.[121] Before the war Maryland, tucked below the Mason-Dixon Line, had no national prominence. World War II and its aftermath changed that forever.

The global conflict produced unprecedented national demands in military preparations and industrial production; Maryland would become a center for both. Armed service bases were expanded or constructed anew. First established in 1917 in Harford County, Aberdeen Proving Grounds, with a compliment of 30,000 military personnel, occupied 36,000 acres; it developed, tested, and shipped ordnance from small arms to tanks. Andrews Air Force Base in Prince George's County served as a training facility, along with the sprawling 14,000-acre Fort George G. Meade in Anne Arundel County. The Bethesda Naval Medical Center in Montgomery County and Walter Reed Army Hospital in Washington DC both researched and treated the inevitable consequences of war. The Patuxent Naval Air Station, the primary naval aircraft testing facility in the country, doubled the prewar population of then rural St. Mary's County. Maryland continues to rank high in the number of military and defense installations, an important legacy of the World War II mobilization.

With $5.5 billion in war contracts, state factories boomed. Aircraft and ship building were the dominant endeavors. Baltimore shipyards launched more than six hundred vessels from 1942 to 1945. The Glenn L. Martin Company, which made aviation history in the 1930s with Pan Am Clippers, built the Army Air Force B-26 Marauders and the Navy's Mariner, a flying boat patrol bomber. The Martin facilities at Middle River in Baltimore County employed more than 53,000 workers at its peak. Along forty miles of the Chesapeake Bay, from Cecil County at its headwaters to the Baltimore Harbor, industrial plants attracted tens of thousands of workers recruited from adjacent states. They came to work at the Bethlehem Steel complex at Sparrows Point, the second largest steel producer in the nation, whose output ranged from "nails to Liberty ships."[122] Or they found work at Continental Can, where white and black women accounted for 60 percent of all employees.[123] Long-established gender and racial stereotypes began to unravel during the war years as women and blacks filled occupational roles once the exclusive province of white males. Maryland African American employment surged as the black percentage of the Maryland labor force increased from 7 to 17.[124] Just as important, whites and African Americans worked together, often for the first time, for a common goal that superseded the racial conventions of the day.

The vast majority of growth was focused in the Baltimore and Washington metropolitan areas. Many towns and communities on the Eastern Shore and Western Maryland actually lost population during the war years because of military service and the allure of high-paying jobs in the central core of the state. Prosperity changed lives and expectations. By war's end Marylanders, like their counterparts throughout the nation, were eager for the fruits of victory.

Presiding over Maryland during the war years was Governor O'Conor, who, in keeping with his pragmatic instinct, took national and state security measures very seriously. He organized an ad hoc state Minuteman, 12,000 strong, to take the place of departed National Guard units and patrol Maryland's shores and watch the skies. A fiscal conservative like his mentor Ritchie, O'Conor maintained budgetary austerity during his administration, reducing state spending and boasting of a surplus. By 1946 the fiscally conservative Democratic approach was wearing thin among Maryland voters. The state's per capita expenditures stood at $36.68, a full 14 percent below the national average. Reflecting voter sentiment, outgoing Governor O'Conor barely won a seat in the U.S. Senate by 1,624 votes.[125]

The end of sustained sacrifice, pent-up demand, and a baby boom of staggering demographic proportions produced an economic surge that confounded predictions of a postwar slump. In Maryland suburbanization accelerated with a vengeance. As the historian George Callcott reports, over the five-year period from 1947 to 1952 in Anne Arundel, Baltimore, Montgomery, and Prince George's counties "more new houses sprang up . . . than had been built there in all the preceding centuries."[126]

Faced with unprecedented challenges across almost the entire public policy spectrum, newly elected governor William Preston Lane Jr. turned state government to a far more activist role than it had played in the past. Favorably compared to Harry Truman in his practical-minded assertiveness, Lane pushed through a revenue package that initiated the first Maryland sales tax, set at 2 percent, and increased gasoline, corporate, and investment income taxes. Coupled with a robust economy, Maryland state expenditures soared during Lane's administration, growing by almost 25 percent a year. By 1950 they stood slightly above the national average.[127]

Aid to counties, largely for public education, increased 821 percent beginning in 1945, appropriations for highway construction jumped 409 percent, and capital improvement bonds went up by 451 percent. With elementary school enrollments skyrocketing and veterans filling the state's classrooms of higher education well past the point of capacity, Lane focused most on improving Maryland education from top to bottom. More than two hundred new schools were built, teachers' salaries were raised substantially, and the budgets for Maryland public colleges and universities almost tripled.[128] In addition construction began on a long-deferred dream, a bridge across the Chesapeake, between Sandy Point on the Western Shore and Kent Island on the Eastern. Although Lane's achievements transformed Maryland into a "liberal state," according to George Callcott, it was one gubernatorial patronage decision that helped end the governor's political career and disrupted Democratic dominance of Maryland's statewide elections.[129]

George P. Mahoney was a hard-edged Baltimore paving contractor, grown wealthy on city contracts. He was also a friend of Governor O'Conor, who had appointed Mahoney to the Maryland Racing Commission. There, in the citadel of Maryland landed gentry and luxurious horse farms, Mahoney's "sandpaper personality" found little acceptance but plenty of targets for his ire.[130] He became the self-proclaimed and well-publicized champion of the average citizen, the two-dollar bettor, who Mahoney charged was victimized by fixed races and corrupt practices. While the racing industry fumed, Mahoney developed a substantial following that credited him with reforming Maryland's racetracks. Lane responded by replacing Mahoney with a pillar of the Maryland racing establishment, Stuart Symington Janney Jr., who owned and rode a Maryland steeplechase champion.[131] Mahoney did not go quietly. He challenged Lane's 1950 reelection bid in the Democratic primary, condemning the sales tax and echoing the derisive catcall "Pennies for Lane" that had emanated from disgruntled businesses and taxpayers.[132] Although Mahoney garnered more total votes, Lane won sixteen of the twenty-four subdivisions and captured the nomination under a county unit rule system utilized by the Democratic Party. The incumbent governor survived the Mahoney challenge, but faced another in November.

In the 1950 general election Theodore R. McKeldin, the wartime mayor of Baltimore City, compiled the greatest Republican gubernatorial majority in history, defeating Lane by a 57 percent to 43 percent margin. McKeldin, a pro–civil rights, liberal Republican, echoed Mahoney's disdain for the sales tax throughout the campaign and pledged to repeal it, but once in office he quickly recognized the benefit of the sales tax to Maryland's coffers. McKeldin became Maryland's sole two-term Republican governor. Mahoney moved on as well. He ran statewide eight more times, capturing the Democratic nominations for U.S. Senate in 1952 and 1956 and for governor in 1966. He fatally weakened the bruised Democratic primary winner all but once, when he did not win the primary and lost in the general election, whenever he captured a nomination. Despite Mahoney's divisive primaries and resulting Republican victories, Democrats continued to dominate Maryland elections at the state legislative and local levels.

On July 30, 1952, the William P. Lane Jr. Bridge, better known as the Chesapeake Bay Bridge, was dedicated and opened to the public. The steel and concrete span, four and a half miles long, linked the western and eastern shores of Maryland. That same year the legendary Baltimore Colts began play in the National Football League, followed two years later by the return of Major League Baseball in the faces and uniforms of the Baltimore Orioles. Professional sports recognized the growing Maryland market and stamped the "major league" seal of approval on the Free State. By the early 1950s the patterns of subsequent Maryland political history were well established. In the context of a rapidly growing and diverse population with a dynamically complex and mixed economy, modern Maryland had begun.

CHAPTER THREE

Contemporary Political Patterns

Q: Would you vote for the Democrat even if the Democrat was the devil?
A: Well, maybe not in the primary.
Louis Goldstein, Maryland comptroller, 1959–98

Few states can match the success of Maryland's Democratic Party from the post–Civil War era into the twenty-first century. Although the core constituencies and policy positions of both the Democratic and Republican parties have radically changed, the net result remains virtually identical in Maryland: one-party domination of state governmental structures extending across time, with decades stretching into centuries.

This is extremely unusual for two reasons. First, Maryland ranks high in the socioeconomic measures of income and educational attainment most commonly associated with competitive state two-party systems. Second, at a time when party affiliation means less and election outcomes are more determined by money, personalities, and campaign dynamics than party label, Democrats have retained a substantial competitive advantage in Maryland.

Contemporary Democratic strength is increasingly concentrated within an urban and older suburban corridor that stretches along Interstate 95 from Harford County through Baltimore City and southward to the Washington metropolitan counties of Prince George's and Montgomery. This area contains almost 70 percent of the total Maryland population. With the exception of a handful of adjacent counties that are two-party competitive, the rest of the state votes solidly Republican in federal elections and most statewide elections. Politically there are two Marylands, and the state today is more politically polarized than at any time since the Civil War.

Back in 1911 Frank Kent of the *Baltimore Sun* observed, "From the close of the Civil War to 1895, the political history of Maryland is the history of the Democratic Party. In that period, the Republicans had practically no voice in either city or state government."[1] Kent's generalization remains largely accurate today. Before Robert Ehrlich's 2002 gubernatorial victory, the last Republican election triumph for a statewide office was in 1980, when U.S. Senator Charles McC. Mathias, a liberal Republican, won his third and final term. Few if any other states can claim such an enduring dominance by one party.

The basis of the state's nineteenth-century Democratic control began with a county-based organization created in 1827 to support Andrew Jackson's bid for the presidency. It was substantially enhanced by the Maryland Constitution of 1851, itself inspired by Jacksonian reform, which provided for the popular election of local officials and county commissioners. Democrats emerged with a solid base of electoral triumphs and began party building from a broad base of patronage dispersed throughout much of the state. This early party structure and dominance was consolidated in the immediate aftermath of the Civil War. The federal occupation of Baltimore and other areas of the state coupled with the Democrats' exploitation of racial issues helped fuel a persistent anti-Republican bias. Unconditional Unionists controlled state offices during the war, but Democrats quickly surged back into power and firm control of the state once the war ended.

From 1866 until 1895 Democrats such as State Senator Arthur Gorman and Baltimore City boss Freeman Rasin constructed a statewide machine of Tammany Hall–like proportion and controlled most federal and state elections. The expansive growth of Baltimore City was the political key. By 1890 it accounted for 42 percent of the state population, permitting Rasin and his lieutenants to turn out the needed votes on demand. While Lincoln Republicans in Western Maryland and counties with substantial African American voters in Southern Maryland and the Eastern Shore kept those jurisdictions two-party competitive at the local level, their votes were regularly overcome by the Baltimore area's Democratic majorities in statewide races.

Accompanying the adoption of Progressive-era reforms such as the secret ballot, direct primary elections, and voter registration rules, Maryland Republicans, joined by anti-machine Democrats, did establish a modicum of two-party statewide competitiveness for nearly twenty years, winning their first gubernatorial election in 1895 and their second in 1911. However, Democratic governors Emerson Harrington (1915–19) and four-term governor Albert Ritchie (1919–34) undercut much of the Republican appeal by adhering to a fiscally conservative and states' rights approach while modernizing the structures and functions of state government. By effectively employing the state executive budget and administrative powers, Ritchie reconsolidated Democratic dominance in state government. Without party-building patronage controlled by the state house, the Maryland Republican Party declined to something of a token force, contesting, but never conquering, Democratic dominance in state politics for most of the twentieth century.

The boom of burgeoning paychecks, enormous population growth, and burgeoning suburbs after the Second World War led to a brief period of Republican competitiveness in the 1950s for governor and federal offices. A series of divisive Democratic primaries and the personal appeal of the pro–civil rights Republican mayor of Baltimore, Theodore McKeldin, provided the GOP with its only two-term Maryland governor and a template for statewide electoral victory. Maryland Republicans could win statewide if two conditions were met. First, Maryland Democrats must engage in a fratricidal, divisive primary. McKeldin himself acknowledged that reality, remarking, "Republicans only get into office in Maryland when the Democrats split."[2]

Beginning in 1950 George P. Mahoney, a demagogic conservative Democratic, independently wealthy, and with a following of at least 100,000 voters, obliged.[3] Mahoney ran first in 1950 and every second year thereafter through 1958 and again in 1962, 1966, and 1968. He was the master of the divisive Democratic primary, either crippling the winner or winning the primary himself. He never won a general election. Mahoney's heated primary challenge to incumbent governor Lane helped elect McKeldin to the statehouse. Sixteen years later, in 1966, Mahoney propelled Spiro Agnew to the Maryland governorship by narrowly capturing the Democratic primary. Two years after Agnew's victory Mahoney assisted Mathias's initial U.S. Senate triumph by running as an independent candidate and attracting 13 percent of the vote.

The second ingredient for Republican success in a statewide contest rested on positioning, especially on civil rights, in a state that has historically prided itself on tolerance. Both McKeldin and Agnew were considered progressive Republicans when they ran for the statehouse. A former mayor of overwhelmingly Democratic Baltimore, McKeldin turned his eloquent rhetorical wrath on his more conservative Democratic opponents. In his 1954 reelection campaign he chastised H. C. "Curley" Byrd's opposition to the *Brown v. Board* decision with "Come, come Dr. Byrd. Come out of the bog of bigotry, out of the puddle of prejudice."[4] Agnew's meteoric rise from local politics to governor in 1966 followed the McKeldin model.

Agnew was elected Baltimore County executive in 1962, following an all-out divisive primary between factional leaders of the entrenched county machine. His credentials as a racial moderate were established when he publicly supported a limited state open accommodations law that was not favored by Baltimore County voters in a 1964 statewide referendum vote. In the 1966 gubernatorial campaign Agnew faced George Mahoney, whose 30 percent plurality in the crowded Democratic primary field was achieved by championing defiance of civil rights with the slogan "Your Home Is Your Castle—Protect It." Agnew appeared liberal in comparison and was backed by enthusiastic front-page *Baltimore Sun* editorial endorsements. As the historian George Callcott wryly observed, in the general election Agnew won the support "of everyone in Maryland who was on this side of the Dark Ages."[5] These successes proved transient for Maryland Republicans. Neither McKeldin nor Agnew was a party builder; besides, Agnew served as governor for only two years before his midlife conversion into the partisan pit bull of the Nixon administration as vice president.

By the late 1960s many older Maryland Democratic leaders, who had traditionally reflected southern conservative Democratic concerns such as states' rights, fiscal conservatism, and minimal services, were replaced by younger, more liberal and reform-minded activists in the state legislature and Congress. The U.S. Supreme Court "one person, one vote" decisions mandated reapportionments of the Maryland House of Delegates and the state senate in 1966 and helped usher in this new breed of Maryland Democrats. More formally educated and more sensitive to the needs of urban and suburban constituencies, politicians such as Ben Cardin, Steny Hoyer, and Paul Sarbanes began their lengthy careers during this era. At the national level U.S. Senator Joseph Tydings and at-large Congressman Carleton Sickles reflected national trends and events in the 1960s and advanced civil rights. Especially after the reapportionment decisions of the 1960s, African American candidates running as Democrats won elections for the state legislature and local offices in increasing numbers. In 1970 Parren J. Mitchell, a political science professor at Morgan State University, integrated the Maryland congressional delegation by winning the West Baltimore Seventh Congressional District by thirty-eight votes in a primary challenge to the incumbent. That same year Milton B. Allen won the state's attorney contest and Paul Chester was elected clerk of the court of common pleas as African American Democratic candidates.

Meanwhile Republican gubernatorial candidates in Maryland, and most federal and statewide candidates, echoed the Nixon southern strategy by moving toward public positions that were socially conservative, pro-business, and decidedly mute on racial issues. For the rest of the twentieth century that posture yielded continual defeat for Republican statewide candidates in the Maryland political environment. Despite contested and often divisive Democratic gubernatorial primaries, every eight years after 1970, when the incumbent governor was term-limited, Maryland Republicans were unable, and perhaps unwilling, to follow the McKeldin template. Maryland Republican futility ended in 2002, when Congressman Ehrlich won the governorship, but the aspirations of lasting two-party competition withered just four years later. Defeated by Baltimore City mayor Martin O'Malley, Ehrlich was the only gubernatorial incumbent in the entire nation to lose in the 2006 election cycle. His defeat and that of his lieutenant governor, Michael Steele, in the U.S. Senate contest to Congressman Benjamin Cardin were very visible signs that Democratic dominance in Maryland had been restored.

VOTER REGISTRATION

Democratic dominance in Maryland can be explained in very simple terms. Since voters first registered statewide by party in 1914, Democrats have substantially outnumbered Republicans. Because Maryland has long been a closed primary state, where voters must be registered in a party to be able to vote in that party's primary, voter registration preferences are relatively more meaningful than in other states. Democrats bested Republicans by a margin of better than 2.5 to 1 for much of the post–World War II era, with Democratic registration peaking at 72 percent compared to Republicans' 23 percent in 1966. This margin gradually diminished over decades and, for the 2010 general election, was 56 percent to 27 percent (see Table 3-1). Unaffiliated voters are the fastest growing cohort of Maryland registered voters, and along with various third-party registrants have increased from a mere 2 percent in 1966 to over 17 percent in 2010. In the measure that counts the most, the highest numerical difference between Democratic and Republican registered voters, 1,031,665, was reached during the 2010 gubernatorial election cycle.

For the gubernatorial general election in November 2010 Maryland registered voters numbered 1,957,279 Democrats compared to 925,614 Republicans and 585,392 designated as unaffiliated or registered with a minor party. Democrats held registration pluralities in fifteen of Maryland's twenty-four subdivisions, including substantial majorities in Baltimore Country (290,998 Democrats to 128,638 Republicans, a 59 to 26 percent advantage) and Montgomery County (324,195 to 123,253; 57 to 21 percent), as well as better than 8 to 1 Democratic to Republican margins in Prince George's County (403,582 to 46,641; 78 to 9 percent) and Baltimore City (289,776

Table 3-1: Voter registration percentages by party, 1962–2010

	Democrats	Republicans	Others or Independent	Democratic Registration Advantage
1962	70	27	2	560,201
1966	72	26	2	654,894
1970	71	27	3	701,800
1974	70	26	5	768,440
1978	70	23	7	891,573
1982	69	24	7	896,472
1986	67	25	7	907,045
1990	63	29	8	730,907
1994	61	29	10	747,945
1998	58	30	12	701,285
2002	56	30	14	723,312
2006	55	29	16	823,866
2008	57	27	16	1,019,025
2010	56	26	17	1,031,665

Source: Compiled by authors from official records.

to 32,027; 79 to 9 percent). These are by far the four most populous jurisdictions in the state. Republican registrants outnumber Democrats in the four westernmost counties (Frederick, Washington, Allegany, and Garrett) as well as in Caroline, Queen Anne's, and Talbot counties on the Eastern Shore and in Carroll and Harford counties, outer suburban Baltimore metropolitan subdivisions.

VOTER TURNOUT PATTERNS

Like voters in all states, the Maryland electorate regularly votes at higher frequencies in presidential election years. Among registered voters turnout has averaged 76 percent for the past eight presidential elections (1980–2008), with a high of 81 percent in 1992 for the Bush-Clinton-Perot contest; four years later it dropped to 70 percent, the lowest turnout for the period. Four of these six presidential election turnouts tallied 75 percent, a very consistent level of participation. Belying the state's strong educational and economic rankings, voter turnout as a percentage of voting-age population generally lagged below the national average in presidential elections over the past several decades but rose to slightly above the average in 2000, 2004 and 2008.[6] Republican and Democratic presidential candidates and their campaigns have bypassed Maryland in recent decades, assuming a foregone Democratic victory. In the 2000 presidential campaign the state's television stations ran the fewest number of political presidential commercials and received the least political ad revenue of any state in the country.[7] In 2008 Obama supporters in Maryland were routinely outsourced and carpooled to nearby Virginia and Pennsylvania precincts for canvassing and phone bank duties.

Maryland elections for the statewide offices of governor, lieutenant governor, attorney general, and comptroller, the Maryland General Assembly, and the vast majority of local offices are scheduled in the even-year non–presidential election cycle. Total voter turnouts of registered voters are substantially lower in these years, averaging 58 percent for the eight gubernatorial elections from 1982 to 2010. The highest turnout occurred in 1994, when 61 percent of the registered voters recorded their choices. The lowest was 1990 with 54 percent.

VOTING PATTERNS IN PRESIDENTIAL ELECTIONS

In terms of presidential elections, contemporary Maryland voters actually are more likely to support Democratic candidates than they were in the past. Between 1884 and 1988 Maryland was close to a bellwether state, supporting the presidential winner 78 percent of the time in twenty-one out of twenty-seven elections. In eleven of these elections Maryland cast its electoral votes for Republican presidential candidates, most recently in 1988, when George H. W. Bush edged Michael Dukakis, 51 to 48 percent. However, from 1992 through 2008 the state recorded a popular vote for Democratic presidential candidates averaging a full 7 percent above the national average. Maryland was Bill Clinton's third strongest state in 1992 and fifth best in 1996. In 2000 57 percent of Maryland voters chose Al Gore, his fourth best state; in 2004 John Kerry tallied 56 percent of the Maryland popular vote, ranking just behind the senator's home state of Massachusetts and its neighboring states of New York, Rhode Island, and Vermont. In 2008 Maryland ranked sixth among the fifty states in supporting the Democratic ticket, behind only Obama's birth state of Hawaii and the northeastern states of New York, Rhode Island, and Vermont and .02 percent behind neighboring Delaware, the home state of Vice President Joe Biden.

VOTING PATTERNS IN CONGRESSIONAL ELECTIONS

With a success rate of over 71 percent Democrats have won twenty-five out of thirty-five U.S. Senate elections in Maryland since 1913 and the past eleven consecutive state elections since 1982. Two liberal Democrats from the Baltimore metro area, Barbara A. Mikulski, first elected in 1986, and Benjamin L. Cardin, elected in 2006, represent Maryland in the U.S. Senate. Both have deep family roots in the state and had lengthy prior legislative service, a typical feature of election to this elevated post in Maryland. Mikulski is a product of southeast Baltimore's white ethnic neighborhoods, where her parents owned and operated a popular bakery. A social worker who taught at Loyola College, Mikulski served on the Baltimore City Council and as a member of the U.S. House of Representatives before her U.S. Senate career. Cardin succeeded U.S. Senator Paul S. Sarbanes, who retired after five terms, the longest U.S. Senate service in the history of the state. Cardin's family has extensive ties throughout the Baltimore Jewish community. His father, Meyer Cardin, was a member of the House of Delegates and completed a ten-year term as a circuit court judge. Cardin's uncle Maurice was a member of the House of Delegates from 1951 through 1966, representing northwest Baltimore City. When Maurice retired, he cleared the way for his twenty-two-year-old nephew, Ben, still in Maryland Law School, to assume the seat. In Annapolis Ben was a consummate, well-respected legislator and was elected speaker of the house in 1979. In 1986 he was elected to the U.S. House of Representatives from the Third Congressional District when Mikulski first ran for the U.S. Senate. In 2006, after a forty-year legislative career, Cardin won the Democratic senatorial primary, defeating former U.S. congressman Kweisi Mfume 44 to 40 percent, and faced Republican Lieutenant Governor Michael Steele in the general election. Although Steele won media acclaim and attention for his polished style and clever media advertising, his conservative positions on embryonic stem cell research and abortion rights along with steadfast support for the war in Iraq (Cardin had voted against the 2003 congressional authorization) doomed him on Election Day. Cardin won handily, 54 to 44 percent.

In senatorial elections many Republican candidates have either been individuals with scant Maryland connection other than an official residence or distinctly second-tier candidates without meaningful national party support. Democratic candidates since 1982 have typically rolled up huge majorities in the Baltimore-Washington corridor subdivisions and lost most of the outlaying suburban and rural but far less vote-heavy counties. In her reelection campaigns in 2004 and 2010 Mikulski easily cruised to victory with over 65 percent of the vote. In 2000 Sarbanes waited until five days before the election to run any TV spots but still won by 63 to 37 percent.

From 1980 through 2010 Maryland's U.S. House of Representatives delegation went from six Democrats and two Republicans to a four-four split before returning to a 6 to 2 Democratic margin in 2006, rising to 7 to 1 in 2008 and returning to 6 to 2 after the 2010 general election. During this period eight incumbent members of the House of Representatives were defeated for reelection. Four were unseated as a result of conventional partisan competition. Congressman Clarence Long (Dem: 2nd), an eleven-term incumbent, was turned out by Republican Helen Delich Bentley in 1984; Congressman Roy Dyson (Dem: 1st) was upset in the wake of a scandal by Republican Wayne Gilchrest in 1990; and Congresswoman Constance Morella (Rep: 8th), the only incumbent Republican representative in the country to lose a general election in 2002, was defeated by Democrat Christopher Van Hollen after a favorable Democratic redistricting. In 2010 one-term Democratic incumbent Frank Kratovil was defeated in a rematch with his 2008 Republican opponent, state senator Andrew Harris. One congressman, Democrat Tom McMillen, was unseated in 1992 when redistricting moved him from his Fourth District to compete with Congressman Gilchrest in a newly drawn First Congressional District. Three representatives were defeated in hotly contested intraparty races, with the more ideological candidate prevailing in each. Congresswoman Beverly Byron was defeated in the 1992 Democratic primary by a state legislator, Delegate Thomas Hattery, who then lost the Sixth District seat to the current Republican congressman, Roscoe Bartlett. In the 2008 presidential primary moderate Eastern Shore Republican Wayne Gilchrest was defeated in a multicandidate race for the First Congressional District by staunch conservative state senator Andrew Harris of Baltimore County, who then lost in the general election to Democrat Frank Kratovil, the Queen's County state's attorney. Also in the 2008 primary Fourth District congressman Al Wynn was defeated by Democratic challenger Donna Edwards, who garnered the backing of numerous union and progressive interest groups dissatisfied with the eight-term incumbent. In 2006 John P. Sarbanes, the son of retiring U.S. Senator Paul Sarbanes, easily won the open Third Congressional District seat vacated by Ben Cardin with over 64 percent of the vote.

VOTING PATTERNS FOR GUBERNATORIAL AND OTHER STATEWIDE ELECTED OFFICES

Since the departure of Spiro Agnew in 1968, five Maryland Democrats—Marvin Mandel (elected in 1970 and 1974), Harry Hughes (1978 and 1982), William Donald Schaefer (1986 and 1990), Parris Glendening (1994 and 1998), and Martin O'Malley (2006 and 2010)—were elected to two terms each (see Table 3-2). Glendening's 1998 reelection marked the eighth con-

Table 3-2: Maryland gubernatorial elections, 1966–2010

	Democratic candidate	Vote for Democrat (%)	Republican candidate	Vote for Republican (%)
1966[1]	Mahoney	373,543 (40.6)	**Agnew**	455,318 (49.5)
1970	**Mandel**	639,579 (66)	Blair	314,336 (32)
1974	**Mandel**	602,648 (64)	Gore	346,449 (37)
1978	**Hughes**	718,328 (71)	Beall	293,635 (29)
1982	**Hughes**	705,910 (62)	Pascal	432,826 (38)
1986	**Schaefer**	907,301 (82)	Mooney	194,187 (18)
1990	**Schaefer**	664,015 (60)	Shepard	446,980 (40)
1994	**Glendening**	708,094 (50.2)	Sauerbrey	702,101 (49.8)
1998	**Glendening**	846,972 (55)	Sauerbrey	688,357 (45)
2002	Townsend	813,422 (48)	**Ehrlich**	879,592 (52)
2006	**O'Malley**	942,279 (53)	Ehrlich	825,464 (46)
2010	**O'Malley**	1,044,961 (56)	Ehrlich	776,319 (42)

Source: Official election returns, compiled by authors.
Note: The winning candidate is designated in bold.

[1] In 1996 Baltimore City comptroller Democrat Hyman Pressman ran as an independent candidate for governor in protest of Mahoney's nomination and received almost 10 percent of the popular vote. In no subsequent Maryland gubernatorial election has an independent or third-party candidate received more than 2 percent.

secutive Democratic gubernatorial win, a record unprecedented in Maryland political history. Republican Robert Ehrlich broke the streak in 2002, only to be turned out of the gubernatorial office four years later by Baltimore City mayor Martin O'Malley and defeated again in their 2010 rematch.

In addition the only two other separately elected statewide offices, attorney general and comptroller, have been won by Democrats since every election since 1923 and 1899, respectively. Only occasionally have Maryland Republicans mounted serious efforts for these offices in modern times. The last significant challenge came in 1994, when a former U.S. district attorney for Maryland, Richard D. Bennett, waged an aggressive "law and order" campaign despite the absence of a state constitutional mandate for the attorney general to fight street crime. Although achieving virtual fundraising parity, Bennett lost to Attorney General J. Joseph Curran Jr. by eight points, 54 to 46 percent.

Former attorney general Joe Curran reflected the pattern of seeming electoral life tenure in these offices. Once a Democrat wins, he holds the office for an appreciable time. Curran was first elected statewide in 1982 as Harry Hughes's second-term lieutenant governor. Curran won the attorney general position in 1986 and in four subsequent reelection bids. The father-in-law of Governor O'Malley, Curran retired in 2006. Montgomery County state's attorney Douglas F. Gansler won the competitive Democratic primary and defeated Frederick County state's attorney Republican Scott Rolle by a margin of over 360,000 votes (61 to 39 percent) in the general election. In 2010 Gansler was unopposed in the primary and general elections.

The archetype of Maryland political longevity is Louis L. Goldstein, the state comptroller from 1958 until his death in 1998. A natural politician in the best sense of the word, Goldstein was first elected to the Maryland House of Delegates from his native Calvert County when he was twenty-six, in 1938, and was elected to the state senate in 1946 after serving as a marine in World War II. After a twelve-year stint in the state senate he was elected comptroller in 1958 and was then reelected nine consecutive times. No one has ever served longer in Maryland statewide elective office. The present comptroller, Peter Franchot, a member of the house of delegates from Montgomery County, defeated two-term incumbent (and former governor) William Donald Schaefer in a closely contested three-way September 2006 Democratic primary. Franchot then cruised to a 59 to 41 percent victory over Republican Anne McCarthy, the former dean of the University of Baltimore Business School and a state resident for only four years. In 2010 Franchot was reelected comptroller with nominal opposition.

VOTING PATTERNS FOR STATE LEGISLATURE

Historically Maryland voters have elected Democratic legislators to the general assembly in overwhelming numbers. Since the Civil War Republicans have held majorities in the lower house of delegates only three times, after the general elections of 1895, 1897, and 1917. A Republican majority was elected to the Maryland State Senate only once, in 1897. In the twentieth century Democrats averaged winning 79 percent of all the state legislative seats. Over the past five state elections, from 1994 through 2010,

Republicans have increased their legislative presence to nearly 30 percent, reflecting statewide voter registration patterns. Partisan representation also displays the growing political polarization of Maryland regional areas. Most of the state senators and the vast majority of state delegates from Western Maryland and the Eastern Shore districts are Republicans, while Baltimore City, Montgomery County, and Prince George's County are Democratic monopolies. The remaining Baltimore and Washington metro suburban jurisdictions elect divided delegations and serve as the current political battlegrounds between the two parties.

VOTING PATTERNS FOR ELECTED COUNTY OFFICES

Democrats hold half of Maryland's local elective partisan offices, this number represents a considerable reduction from the 72 percent held in 1990 (see Table 3-3). Such positions run the gamut from powerful county executives who represent and serve more people than the governors of several small states to the overworked and underpaid rural county commissioners who rotate administrative responsibilities in such areas as zoning, public education, and county roadways.

The seven most populous Maryland subdivisions have charter home rule, and Democrats hold four of the six county executive positions in addition to the mayor of Baltimore City. Democrats also hold council majorities in the same five subdivisions. There are no Republican elected officials in Baltimore City, Montgomery County, or Prince George's County. In 2006 and 2010 only Anne Arundel and Harford counties elected Republican executives and have Republican majorities on their county councils. Four Eastern Shore counties—Cecil, Dorchester, Talbot, and Wicomico—also have charter home rule and have replaced the traditional county commissioner governance form with a council. In 2006 Wicomico elected its first county executive, Democrat Richard M. Pollitt, who was reelected in 2010. After the 2010 general election only Dorchester County had a majority Democratic county council. The remaining thirteen counties are administered by county commissioners; the Republicans hold all or a majority of the seats in ten counties and Democrats in three after the 2010 election cycle.

EXPLAINING DEMOCRATIC DOMINANCE

In almost all forms of electoral behavior, from voter registration to presidential and gubernatorial choices and voting for the register of wills, Marylanders have favored Democrats. Indeed the state has proven to be one of

Table 3-3: Party affiliation of local officials (percentages)

	1986	1990	1994	1998	2002	2006	2010
Democrat	75	72	56	62	58	60	50
Republican	25	28	44	38	42	40	50

Source: Official election returns from city and county boards of elections, compiled by authors.

the most reliably Democratic in the nation. Although Republican strength has increased in recent years, the persistence of Democratic dominance at all electoral levels has been remarkable. Maryland voters elect and reelect Democratic candidates for a wide variety of reasons; four of the most significant are the following.

1. Large and Activist African American Voting Bloc: Ranking behind only the Deep South states of Mississippi, Louisiana, South Carolina, and Georgia, Maryland's African Americans make up 29 percent of the state population. Blacks form a substantial majority in two of the four most populous Maryland subdivisions, Prince George's County (65 percent) and Baltimore City (64 percent), and constitute a significant percentage of the population in the remaining half of the "Big Four," with Baltimore and Montgomery counties at 21 and 16 percent, respectively. African Americans have a long tradition of civic and political activism in Maryland. Black candidates were first elected to the Baltimore City Council in 1891 and to the Maryland General Assembly in 1954. Once civil rights issues broke firmly against the Republicans in the 1960s, the African American votes in the Democratic column escalated to well above the 80 percent range and stayed that way. Two of Maryland's eight-member U.S. House of Representatives delegation are black: Donna Edwards (Dem: 4th) and Elijah Cummings (Dem: 7th). African Americans, all Democrats, comprise 22 percent of the Maryland General Assembly. The county executives in the state's two most populous counties, Montgomery (Isiah "Ike" Leggett) and Prince George's (Rushern Baker), are African American Democrats, as is the mayor of Baltimore City (Stephanie Rawlings-Blake).

2. The Bureaucracy Factor: Since the New Deal the Democratic Party has been rightly termed the "party of government." With a multitude of federal installations and Maryland's proximity to Washington, the state has a high percentage of government employees in its labor force. Almost a fifth of Maryland's labor force is directly employed by federal, state, or local government. In addition a significant portion of the private Maryland economy is heavily dependent on governmental contracts. The state ranked fourth in total, and third per capita, in federal procurement expenditures during the 2009 federal fiscal year.[8]

3. Organized Interest Groups: Traditional Democratic support groups such as unions, teachers' associations, and gun control, abortion rights, and environmental organizations have a long history of energetic and committed involvement in Maryland politics. For example, the major labor unions have more than 400,000 members in the Baltimore-Washington area, and union officials and interests are well represented in Maryland Democratic politics and policies. The Maryland State Teachers Association, some 65,000 strong with forty-one local chapters and affiliates, has rewarded endorsed candidates, usually Democrats, with extensive campaign support. Advocacy groups such as Progressive Maryland, CeaseFire Maryland (which lobbied for stricter controls on firearms), the abortion rights supporters of NARAL Pro-Choice Maryland, and Harriet's List (which aids mostly liberal female candidates) have also promoted many Democratic officeholders. Protection of the Chesapeake Bay and Maryland environs has produced scores of environmental organizations, such as the Maryland League of Conservation Voters, 1000 Friends of Maryland, the Assateague Coastal Trust, and the Maryland Public Interest Research Group. Their policy agendas and concerns almost always coincide with those of Democratic elected officials.

4. The Policy Connection: Democratic governors, legislative leaders, and federal representatives have initiated issues and policies favorable to Democratic support groups. These include civil rights, environmental protection, a "smart growth" approach to residential and commercial development in both suburban and revitalized urban communities, gun control, health care, abortion rights, supportive labor policies, and enhanced public education funding at both the local and college levels. From a comparative perspective these may seem to be liberal causes, but most reflect the diversity of interests represented in Maryland and as such are best considered pragmatic and progressive. Maryland Democrats are rarely crusaders; the policies that emerge reflect both grassroots and organized group support subject to normal political compromise and negotiation.

The persistence of Democratic domination in Maryland is a function of multiple causes that range from powerful demographic and occupational bases in the electorate that are favorably predisposed to support Democrats to skillful and pragmatic leadership that has adapted to changing circumstances. Before World War II Maryland Democrats stood for states' rights and other conservative causes. Today they are aligned with far more liberal positions on a wide variety of social welfare and quality-of-life issues. Yet Maryland politics is changing, and state Republicans may fashion a more competitive future. To understand this, consider how far Maryland Republicans have come from their absolute political nadir.

The year was 1986, and in the gubernatorial election four-term Baltimore City mayor William Donald Schaefer defeated the Republican candidate Thomas Mooney by 713,114 votes, an 82 to 18 percent margin. Schaefer's margin was the largest for a first-time governor in modern U.S. history. Mooney, a formerly obscure Democratic member of the House of Delegates, had switched parties to make the race. Without significant campaign funding he offered only token opposition and received fewer total votes than any Republican candidate for governor since 1942. In contrast Schaefer brushed aside the primary challenge of the well-regarded two-term Maryland attorney general Stephen Sachs and cruised to an even easier general election victory. The proclaimed political architect of a "Baltimore Renaissance" that transformed the inner harbor of the port with such tourist attractions as the Harborplace Pavilions and the National Aquarium, Schaefer in 1986 was more a force of nature than a mere politician. His campaign emphasized his intense work ethic and a "do it now" approach to activist governance. He carried every Maryland subdivision by extraordinary margins; his Baltimore City base gave him 92 percent of their votes. Even westernmost Garrett County, then the only jurisdiction with a registered Republican majority, fell to the Schaefer juggernaut by a 61 percent margin.

No Republicans even filed for either attorney general or comptroller, leaving the only remaining statewide posts to the Democrats J. Joseph Curran Jr. and Louis L. Goldstein. In the Maryland General Assembly Republican ranks were thinned to a mere 12 percent of the legislature; voter registration stood at 67 percent Democrat to 23 percent Republican.

An initial weakening of Maryland Democratic dominance appeared first in 1988, when George H. W. Bush defeated Michael Dukakis by 51 to 48 percent. Although Bush lost both Baltimore City and Prince George's County by wide margins, he ran almost even with Dukakis in vote-rich Montgomery County and captured over 60 percent of the votes in sixteen other subdivisions. The trend continued two years later, in the 1990 state and local elections. As the incumbent governor, Schaefer cruised to reelection by a 60 to 40 percent margin, but local vote totals revealed sharply growing Republican strength in the rural and suburban counties of the state. Outside of the heavily Democratic subdivisions of Baltimore City and Montgomery and Prince George's counties, Republican challenger William S. Shepard held Schaefer to a virtual dead heat. In the remaining twenty-one counties the governor barely edged his challenger, 325,883 votes to 325,756. This was surprising because Shepard was not a major figure in Maryland Republican politics prior to the 1990 election. A retired U.S. State Department official who had never held elective office, his cause appeared so hopeless that no Republican of substance was willing to run with him as lieutenant governor. Against the deadline to select a running mate, Shepard picked his wife, Lois. While the Shepard and Shepard ticket caused some humorous reappraisals of the old nostrum "Politics makes strange bedfellows," it did carry twelve Maryland counties.

Doubtless some of the Shepard votes were attributable to anti-Schaefer sentiment. What had been dismissed as offbeat eccentricities when he served as mayor became character liabilities at the more elevated gubernatorial position. Schaefer had berated reporters, state legislators, and even private citizens who disagreed with his policies. He was accustomed to dominating a compliant and all-Democratic Baltimore City Council, and the independence of the Maryland General Assembly often provoked sarcastic tirades that were duly communicated by a state capitol press corps unawed by the Schaefer mystique. The national economic downturn of 1990 and resultant state budget crunch compounded his problems. Less than half a year after his reelection Schaefer's performance ratings had plummeted from 58 percent (excellent or good) to 35 percent.[9]

A pattern of increased Republican strength in predominantly white rural and suburban Maryland subdivisions was unmistakable. Shepard won three of the four Western Maryland counties, seven of the nine Eastern Shore counties, and Anne Arundel and Carroll counties in the Baltimore metropolitan area. In the presidential election of 1992 the pattern continued. While Clinton piled up insurmountable majorities in Baltimore City, Montgomery County, and Prince George's County on his way to capturing 50 percent of the statewide Maryland vote, President Bush compiled a 50,000-vote majority in the rest of the state and Ross Perot attracted 14 percent statewide. The relatively easy Clinton victory masked significant changes in the partisan balance that were revealed two years later.

1994: A REPUBLICAN NEAR MISS

Maryland Republicans had some cause for uncustomary optimism in 1994. With Schaefer term-limited out, an open, competitive, and potentially divisive Democratic gubernatorial primary loomed. Aiding the Republican cause was continued suburban growth, the decline of Baltimore City as a percentage of the state vote, and a reduction in the Democratic voter registration majority. As recently as 1978 registered Maryland Republicans were outnumbered 3 to 1. By 1994 the margin had narrowed to a still formidable 2 to 1. These factors helped produce a rarity in Maryland: hotly contested Republican primaries for governor and the U.S. Senate. The gubernatorial field hosted three candidates: conventional wisdom's front-runner, Congresswoman Helen Delich Bentley, a five-term legislator from Baltimore County's Second Congressional District with proven crossover Democratic appeal; Delegate Ellen R. Sauerbrey, the minority leader of the House of Delegates who revitalized the Republican caucus through her energized and confrontational conservative style; and Shepard, who believed his 1990 showing against Schaefer demonstrated statewide appeal.

The campaign quickly developed into a two-woman race. Sauerbrey waged a relentless negative campaign against the favored Bentley for her failure to attend candidate forums, her past close associations with Governor Schaefer, and a purportedly liberal voting record. It was Sauerbrey's play of a major tax cut, the so-called Whitman card adopted by Republican gubernatorial candidates across the nation in 1994, that defined and focused her message. Similar to strategy utilized by New Jersey governor Christine Whitman a year earlier, Sauerbrey pledged a 24 percent reduction in the Maryland personal income tax phased in over four years. While Bentley outspent Sauerbrey almost 2 to 1 and ran well ahead in early polls, Sauerbrey routed the congresswoman on primary day as legions of Sauerbrey's volunteers carried posters that proclaimed "Vote Yourself a Tax Cut" and manned the polling places.

On the Democratic side the open gubernatorial seat produced several serious aspirants, but a close contest never developed. The initial front-runner, two-term lieutenant governor Melvin Steinberg, suffered from the open hostility of Governor Schaefer, an extravagant and ever-changing campaign staff, and a subsequent lack of campaign focus or direction. A full six months before the primary Steinberg's early advantage had evaporated and his lead was lost to three-term Prince George's County executive Parris Glendening. A professor of political science at the University of Maryland with a doctorate in urban policy and intergovernmental relations, Glendening had established a reputation for meticulous planning and cautious but always progressively pragmatic policy positions. His run for the Democratic nomination exemplified those political traits. He had traversed the state for years working with his colleagues in the Maryland Municipal

League and the Maryland Association of Counties. By the time primary season began, Glendening had assembled an extensive coalition of supporters among local government officials, unions, educators, environmentalists, and former students, some 9,000 in number. In addition he proved to be a prodigious fund-raiser, with over $3.2 million in his coffers for the Democratic primary. Outmaneuvered and outspent, Glendening's rivals, Steinberg and State Senators American Joe Miedusiewski and Mary Boergers, provided limited competition. Glendening won 53 percent of the primary vote and every county, finishing thirty-six points ahead of his closest competitor. In all previous elections such a decisive Democratic primary triumph would presage a comfortable November victory over the Republican. What Glendening faced was something very different.

In gubernatorial election years Maryland primaries are conducted on the second Tuesday in September, just seven weeks before the general election, a time when many voters first begin to focus on their statewide choices. Sauerbrey's surprising primary victory produced a media bounce of considerable proportion. Polls had accurately predicted Glendening's victory, but Sauerbrey's upset of Bentley was unanticipated, hence its intrinsic value to the Maryland news media. As a result Sauerbrey established herself as a major statewide political competitor with essentially free media. This was imperative for her because her campaign coffers were empty, exhausted by Republican primary expenses. For both the primary and general elections Sauerbrey had opted to take public financing from Maryland's limited plan for gubernatorial elections. For the general election she received approximately $1 million that had slowly accumulated from a voluntary tax check-off on state income tax returns since the Watergate-era plan was approved and was spared the necessity of personal fund-raising during the short eight-week general election campaign.

The Glendening campaign quickly recognized the Republican threat and began an incessant attack, assailing Sauerbrey as a right-wing extremist with an anti-abortion, anti-environment, and pro-gun record far out of touch with the mainstream of Maryland values. Sauerbrey's campaign centerpiece, the 24 percent tax cut, was critically dissected as unrealistic and misleading. Bolstered by a campaign treasury that had raised an all-time state record of nearly $6 million for an individual candidate, Glendening flooded the Maryland airwaves with negative media ads. For a time it seemed the strategy was working; October surveys gave Glendening an 11 percent lead. Sauerbrey persistently stayed on her antitax, anti–big government message, which resonated with the national Republican "Contract with America" motif, and her campaign began to attain the ever elusive "traction." Nationally it was very much a Republican year, and Sauerbrey's theme was consistent with that dynamic. As Election Day drew closer polls showed a tightening race; the final surveys were within the margin of error and "too close to call."[10]

Close it was indeed. By election's end Glendening held a razor-thin lead of 5,993 votes. With an overall turnout of 61 percent of registered voters, twenty-one counties set individual records for the total votes cast for governor. The statewide total, 1,437,450, broke the previous record by 271,023. Again it was the three heavily Democratic subdivisions that provided the electoral foundation for maintaining the Democratic gubernatorial winning streak. Glendening won only these, but he carried Baltimore City (75 percent), his home base Prince George's County (68 percent), and Montgomery County (59 percent) by strong majorities. These three subdivisions accounted for 41 percent of the total statewide vote and made up 53 percent of Glendening's total vote. Elsewhere in Maryland Sauerbrey piled up substantial majorities, winning twenty-one counties and holding Glendening to under 40 percent of the vote in fifteen. While many pundits focused on the three Democratic jurisdictions rather than the twenty-one Republican counties, more was at work than that. Glendening won areas with high population density and urban precincts located throughout Maryland, including Salisbury, Cambridge, and Chestertown on the Eastern Shore, Havre de Grace in otherwise Republican Harford County, Annapolis in Anne Arundel County, Columbia in Howard County, and Leonardtown in Southern Maryland. In rock-ribbed Republican Western Maryland he won precincts in the cities of Frederick, Hagerstown, and Cumberland. In terms of voting patterns, the first Glendening-Sauerbrey contest revealed a classic urban versus rural and suburban contest.

For some the 1994 Maryland gubernatorial election will live forever as the election with an asterisk. The controversy began on election night, when early suburban county returns put Sauerbrey substantially ahead. Once Prince George's County and Baltimore City urban precincts came in, the contest tightened; well past midnight, when the final returns came in from predominantly African American West Baltimore, Sauerbrey trailed by about 7,000 votes. For some Maryland Republicans the lateness and lopsided nature of the returns raised suspicions and evoked comparisons of Mayor Richard Daley holding back votes in Chicago to ensure Democratic victories.

Sauerbrey refused to concede and remained in a combative mode. At press conferences she aired charges of fraud, corruption, ballot tampering, and the dead walking the earth on Election Day and casting votes for

Glendening. An investigation and legal challenge were organized against the votes of the three Maryland subdivisions carried by the Democrat. In the subsequent trial, conducted days before the gubernatorial inaugural, sweeping accusations of massive corruption were scaled down by Sauerbrey's legal team. Originally some 51,000 votes were challenged. Her attorneys reduced that to 3,600 and abandoned charges of fraud. Once the Anne Arundel County Circuit Court convened, rules of evidence applied and it became clear that much of the Sauerbrey case was longer on rhetoric then on actual fact. Absent was testimony from any of the thousands of Republican election judges who helped administer the election in Montgomery County, Prince George's County, and Baltimore City. The one point that Sauerbrey's legal team scored was that some 1,800 Baltimore City residents who voted should have been purged from the registration list because of inactivity (a disqualification no longer permitted under federal and state law). The voters were predominantly Democrats, as is Baltimore City as a whole. Republican attorneys proved bureaucratic failures but little more. After the judge dismissed the case Sauerbrey remained defiant, charging, "This election was stolen and the ballots were stuffed."[11] Two subsequent investigations by the Maryland state prosecutor and the Federal Bureau of Investigation confirmed "error, poor judgment, and outright incompetence" by election officials but no outright vote fraud.[12]

1998: THE REMATCH

The expected Glendening-Sauerbrey rematch came four years later. Sauerbrey had maintained a high profile as a part-time talk radio host, a Maryland GOP national committeewoman, and the purported victim of a "stolen" election, so called in at least some Republican circles.[13] There would be no hotly contested Republican primary this time or the meager public campaign financing that Sauerbrey resorted to in 1994. Republican fund-raisers pointed to her razor-thin defeat and the contributions flowed in. Political demographics appeared equally positive as continued suburban growth increased the potential Republican vote. In addition surveys taken at the midpoint of Glendening's first term provided encouragement to the Republican cause. One Mason-Dixon survey reported that only 24 percent believed the governor's performance merited reelection.[14]

Glendening initially faced challenges within the Democratic Party arising from his antigambling stance and spending priorities, but his strongest assets were the products of his governing. Admitting to missteps, Glendening acknowledged his responsibility and focused his campaign on policy and budgetary achievements, with a "Promises Made, Promises Kept" theme. These included a sustained focus on improving education. State education funding increased 33 percent during his first four years, and his administration committed $633 million to new school construction or renovation. When pfiesteria, a toxic microorganism, threatened Chesapeake Bay recreation and seafood, the governor promptly closed infected estuaries and convinced the general assembly to enact tougher regulations on agricultural runoff. Together with his Smart Growth policy that provided state incentives to funnel new growth into already developed areas, stricter gun control laws, and increased aid for the developmentally disabled, Glendening's résumé of accomplishments was lengthy and substantial, and he easily turned back party insurgency, winning 70 percent of the primary vote.

In the fall campaign Sauerbrey's centerpiece 1994 issue, a 24 percent income tax cut, was partially preempted by a phased-in 10 percent reduction that Glendening had ushered through the Maryland General Assembly in 1997. Sauerbrey persisted with her position, advocating an additional 14 percent cut, and proposed more than doubling the state income tax exemption on retirement income. However, much of the antitax, antigovernment drumbeat that so marked the 1994 Republican campaign was decidedly muted. Instead Sauerbrey accentuated kinder and gentler personality attributes and more moderate policies. Upbeat and positive biographical polyspots stressed the narrative of her childhood in Baltimore and her union steelworker father, despite her reputation as one of the most anti-union, "right to work" legislators in the Maryland General Assembly. Absent from Sauerbrey's agenda were her 1994 proposals for school vouchers and the fingerprinting of welfare recipients. She echoed Glendening on the environment and, despite a strong and strident pro-life legislative record of sixteen years, promised not to threaten Maryland law that protected abortion rights. On education Sauerbrey almost matched a Glendening pledge to hire 1,100 new teachers with a proposal to hire 1,001.

The challenger did attack the incumbent governor on issues of honesty, integrity, and misplaced priorities. Negative TV ads featured the newly constructed Ravens stadium and charged that the governor "built stadiums instead of schools"; other ads condemned Glendening for running "a campaign of fear." On the Democratic side Sauerbrey's move to the center was critically challenged. The Glendening campaign broadcast attack ads that condemned her legislative record on environmental protection, gun control, and civil rights. Scott Wilson, a *Washington Post* reporter, judged the debate via television commercials as "the most sustained assault of negative political advertising in state history."[15] Maryland voters didn't seem to mind, however; the 61 percent turnout matched the level recorded four years before. But Sauerbrey was unable to build on her near miss of 1994. Governor Glendening won handily, tallying 846,972 votes to Sauerbrey's 688,357. With a ten-point victory margin (55 to 45 percent), Glendening received more votes in 1998 than he had four years earlier in every Maryland subdivision. The pattern of Baltimore City, Prince George's County, and Montgomery County providing the basis for a Democratic victory continued. Glendening took 81 percent of the vote in Baltimore City, 74 percent in Prince George's County, and 62 percent in Montgomery County. He carried two other subdivisions, Allegany and Howard counties, and nearly upset Sauerbrey in her home, Baltimore County, losing narrowly 51 to 49 percent. Glendening's reelection was the eighth consecutive Democratic victory for governor, the longest gubernatorial winning streak in Maryland history. For a time it seemed that the Sauerbrey challenge represented a Republican tide that had crested and receded, a function of the Republican Revolution of 1994, orchestrated by Newt Gingrich, that had brought congressional control to the GOP. In Maryland the flood came close to overcoming the Democratic bastion, but four years later the political tide was ebbing.

The freak tidal fluctuation metaphor was still apt two years later, when Vice President Al Gore handily won Maryland by some 330,000 votes, with a seventeen-point advantage (57 to 40 percent) over George W. Bush. Gore carried Baltimore City and Montgomery and Prince George's counties by huge majorities, captured suburban Baltimore and Howard counties, and even edged Bush in Southern Maryland's Charles County and Somerset County on the Eastern Shore. The scene was set for the gubernatorial election of 2002 when Glendening, term-limited, would leave an open seat. His lieutenant governor, Kathleen Kennedy Townsend, was reasonably popular at the beginning of the campaign and had cultivated a mainstream Democratic posture. Active in the Democratic Leadership Council, Townsend had focused on juvenile justice administration and economic development during her eight years in state government. Most analysts and observers believed the Democratic winning streak would be extended.[16]

2002: EHRLICH'S BREAKTHROUGH

According to the McKeldin template, Townsend stood a very good chance for election. She successfully preempted potential Democratic rivals such as Baltimore City mayor Martin O'Malley and Montgomery County executive Douglas M. Duncan through a strategy of vigorous fund-raising and a host of endorsements. No divisive primary loomed. In January 2002 Townsend held a comfortable but not commanding 51 to 36 percent lead over her Republican challenger, four-term congressman Robert L. Ehrlich Jr. of Baltimore County. Keith Haller of Potomac Survey Research did caution, "There are a few dark clouds on the horizon."[17] Both the Glendening and Townsend favorability ratings had eroded considerably from earlier polls, and voters expressed almost equal confidence in state Republicans and Democrats handling Maryland problems.

But Townsend faced the dilemma of all second-in-commands seeking election in their own right: Do you run on the record of the administration or strike an independent course? Considering that only 29 percent of all lieutenant governors who run for the top post succeed, it is a dilemma not often resolved to the voters' satisfaction.[18] Townsend ultimately chose distance from Glendening. She stopped meeting privately with him, and some of his critics within the Democratic Party assumed increasing roles of prominence on her campaign advisory councils. The lieutenant governor had her reasons. Governor Glendening was mired in personal and political problems on a number of fronts. His longtime marriage had unraveled in the summer of 2000, and it was widely known that he had an intimate relationship with a member of his staff. The governor's presumed desire once leaving office to become chancellor of the University of Maryland system was also subject to both rumors and criticism of pro-Glendening appointments to the board of regents, the governing body that would ultimately select the chancellor. Although the Glendening administration had crafted a record of productive leadership in aid to education, environmental protection, and economic development, such policy accomplishments seemed off the Townsend campaign table. When Townsend was interviewed by the *Daily Record*, Baltimore's legal newspaper, and asked the standard opening question, "Why do you want to be governor?" she replied, "I think Maryland has great potential. And I think I'm best situated to lead the state to reach that potential."[19] With that comment the lieutenant governor erased the previous eight years of her service; she employed the rhetoric of a challenger and not an incumbent. An ever shifting campaign focus and obvious unease in the role of administration defender plagued the Townsend effort. By midsummer the contest had considerably tightened, and the Townsend lead dwindled to a mere three points. It was apparent that Ehrlich represented a very real threat to continued Democratic dominance.

The reasons were multiple. First, Ehrlich, a native Marylander, had an appealing life story of rising from western Baltimore County working-class origins to graduate from Gilman, a prestigious Baltimore preparatory school, Princeton, where he captained the football team, and law school at Wake Forest University. Over the course of the campaign Ehrlich perfected autobiographical narrative politics that contrasted his humble beginnings with the more privileged start of his opponent. An early Ehrlich fundraising letter began, "I grew up in a row house, not a castle in Camelot."[20] When Townsend held her annual $2,000 per person fund-raiser in the Kennedy compound at Hyannis Port, Ehrlich countered the same day with a $20 per person crab feast at his native Arbutus community center. There he remarked, "The lieutenant governor is home and I am home."[21]

Second, over his two-term, eight-year career in the Maryland House of Delegates Ehrlich had compiled a voting record of moderation as a Republican, but just as important, he had established a friendly rapport with many Democrats in the general assembly. However, when Ehrlich made the jump to a congressional seat in the ultra-Republican year of 1994 he was very much a part of the "Gingrich Revolution," voting loyally with the conservative Republican House leadership. Since Sauerbrey's 1998 defeat Ehrlich had established himself as the Republican "best hope" for statewide office. His U.S. House record solidified his legitimacy with state party regular Republicans, and his personal appeal and residual Annapolis ties held very real crossover potential among Maryland Democrats, especially in the Baltimore metropolitan area. While some cynics wondered "which Bobby would show up" on the campaign trail, the Gingrich clone or the popular Annapolis insider, the answer was never in doubt. Ehrlich consistently displayed a responsive pragmatism throughout his career. He did what it took to win. Before he announced for governor, he demanded Maryland Republican unity at the party's annual convention, arguing, "To the extent that there is intramural fighting among you, stop it now, please. I am really tired of it."[22] For Ehrlich winning took precedence over ideological purity. He had defeated Maryland Democrats before and understood that a united Republican Party was imperative.

In response to Ehrlich, the Townsend campaign copied a battle-tested Democratic campaign strategy: label the Republican nominee a dangerous reactionary, too conservative for Maryland, and deliver the message with a barrage of negative political thirty-second spots. But the strategy did not work in 2002, perhaps because Ehrlich's and Townsend's stances were, in many respects, almost indistinguishable.

Ehrlich did not campaign as a conservative. "Moderate" was the favorite word in his campaign lexicon and a popular graphic in many of his political commercials. "Practical" was the most apt description of his policy approach. In some policy areas his position was identical to, if not more liberal than Townsend's. For example, both favored construction in Montgomery County of the Intercounty Connector, a long-proposed superhighway link between I-95 and I-270 that had been shelved by the Glendening administration for environmental and fiscal reasons. Ehrlich also voiced his support for the Smart Growth policies of the Glendening administration, and he favored marijuana use for medical purposes, unlike his Democratic opponent. Finally, Ehrlich's pro-gambling stance and call for legalized slot machines at Maryland racetracks clearly represented a considerable departure from his party's prior position. In 1995 the Republican caucus in the Maryland House of Delegates had pledged to vote as a bloc in opposition to legalized casino-style gambling. Both Governor Glendening and Townsend strongly opposed expansion of legalized gambling. Ehrlich argued that legalizing slots represented a substantial remedy to the projected $1.7 billion budgetary shortfall.[23]

Perhaps the most striking difference in the Townsend and Ehrlich campaigns was their choice for running mate. Both candidates counterprogrammed their choices. Townsend selected former admiral Charles Larson, who had served as the commandant of the Naval Academy in Annapolis and was a registered Republican until just a few weeks before his selection. Larson brought impressive military and administrative credentials but little else to the Democratic ticket. His selection infuriated some establishment Democrats, and Townsend found herself spending valuable time mending political breaches and ruffled egos long after the Larson announcement. In contrast Ehrlich tapped Michael Steele, chairman of the Maryland Republican Party and an African American from Prince George's County. This choice of inclusion reinforced Ehrlich's moderate claims and helped redefine what contemporary Maryland Republicans stood for over the course of the campaign.

Also aiding Ehrlich were widening defections in the Maryland Democratic Party. Glendening, the first governor from the metropolitan Washington suburbs in modern times, was far from beloved in metro Baltimore Democratic circles. Although Townsend made her home in Baltimore County, she was scarcely regarded as a party mainstay in that area. Prior to her two terms as Glendening's running mate, her only venture into electoral politics was a 1986 run for Congress against Republican incumbent Helen Bentley, who won reelection easily (59 to 41 percent). Townsend's problems were reflected by the behavior of state comptroller Schaefer's inner circle. Schaefer, the former Baltimore mayor and governor, had a legendary personal animosity toward Glendening, his gubernatorial successor. Although he formally supported Townsend and was featured in endorsement commercials, easily half of his immediate political entourage and longtime major contributors opted for Ehrlich.[24] The Republican candidate's Democrats for Ehrlich Committee was not for mere show, as Louis Grasmick and John Paterakis, businessmen of significant influence in Maryland politics, lent their support and opened their checkbooks, as did others. Ehrlich's campaign funds topped $10.4 million, shattering the previous state record. Townsend collected $8.7 million, but in the final stage of the campaign she trailed her Republican challenger. Ehrlich received $3.7 million in the two months before the election, with 88 percent of his contributors from Maryland. Townsend gathered only $1 million, and 42 percent of her contributions were from out of state.[25] Ehrlich also ran a leaner, more cost-effective campaign, paying almost less than half of what Townsend paid in staff salaries.[26]

As the campaign moved into its final stage, tragedies stunned the state and partially froze the campaigns. From October 3 to 24, 2002, a wave of mysterious and savage sniper attacks plagued the Washington metropolitan area. Beginning with the slaying of five Montgomery County residents murdered at random while performing the tasks of everyday life, the sniper threat paralyzed the state. Afterschool activities and outdoor athletic events were postponed or cancelled, shopping malls saw attendance plummet, and citizens pumped their gas at service stations in defensive postures. Then, on October 16, a fire-bombing arson in an East Baltimore City row house killed an entire family of seven people, including five children. The Dawson family was burned to death by a twenty-one-year-old on probation for drug offenses. The mother, Angela Dawson, had confronted neighborhood drug dealers and called city police repeatedly for assistance. Together with the sniper attacks, the horrific deaths of the Dawson family presented both the image and the reality of crime out of control. Within days Ehrlich's campaign aired "law and order" ads that spotlighted Maryland's violent crime rate, third highest in the nation, and attacked the "negligent management" of the Glendening-Townsend administration.[27] Ehrlich poured resources into the Baltimore metropolitan area during the final week, with direct mail and telephone appeals reaching a level of saturation unusual for Maryland Republican statewide efforts.

By Election Day it was obvious that Ehrlich had momentum. The final pre-election Sunpapers survey had the challenger four points ahead, within the error margin of the poll. But the trend line was clear: Townsend was in deep trouble.[28] The GOTV (Get Out the Vote) and Election Day efforts of the Ehrlich campaign represented a level of organizational competence not normally associated with Maryland Republican campaigns. The result was a narrow but impressive Ehrlich victory (51.6 to 47.7 percent). His support set all-time state records for the most votes statewide by a Republican candidate (879,592), the most votes in twenty out of twenty-three counties for a Republican candidate, and the highest percentage vote ever for a Republican gubernatorial candidate in seventeen out of the twenty-three counties.

Winning elections involves turnouts and ratios, and Ehrlich had both in his favor. Republican voter mobilization was crucial to his success. The 67.4 percent turnout of Republican registered voters was a modern record and almost 5 percent higher than in 1998. It was especially strong in the northern suburban section of the Baltimore metropolitan area in or near Ehrlich's former Second Congressional District, with Baltimore County (up by 10 percent), Carroll County (up by 9 percent), and Harford County (up by 6 percent) delivering a 142,253-vote (67 percent) majority for Ehrlich, well in excess of the 66,170 statewide vote differential out of the record 1,706,179 votes cast for governor. In contrast turnout among the state's majority Democrats was relatively flat; at 63 percent it was slightly under the 1998 rate. Subdivision support repeated the 1994 election pattern. Townsend carried only three to Ehrlich's twenty-one. While Baltimore City (75 percent), Montgomery County (61 percent), and Prince George's County (77 percent) returned strong votes for Townsend, Democratic turnout in these critical Democratic core jurisdictions was significantly lower, down 1.65 percent in Montgomery County and down 6.1 percent in Prince George's County. The Townsend majorities from these three subdivisions were outweighed by lopsided Republican margins that exceeded 70 percent in five counties. Townsend lost ten counties by better than 2 to 1 margins, and the aggregate deficit was more than the three-subdivision Democratic base could overcome. A disturbing portent for Democrats was the increasing proportion of the statewide Democratic vote concentrated in their base. In 1986 Baltimore City and Montgomery and Prince George's counties accounted for 44 percent of the statewide Democratic gubernatorial vote; by 2002 that percentage had risen to almost 56 (see Table 3-4).

Ehrlich's upset victory was a decidedly personal and campaign-driven triumph. Although issues played a role, the differences in the personalities and leadership qualities of the two candidates proved critical. Townsend seemed an unenthusiastic, even unhappy campaign warrior. As the political science professor Thomas F. Schaller of the University of Maryland, Baltimore County, observed, she was far too often "awkward on the stump, visibly uncomfortable."[29] Glendening judged the Townsend effort "one of the worst run campaigns in the country," and few fellow Maryland Democrats questioned that critique.

Table 3-4: Big Three vote for Democratic gubernatorial candidates

Subdivisions	1986	1990	1994	1998	2002	2006	2010
Baltimore City	152,553	81,542	114,022	125,686	120,070	115,136	133,068
Montgomery County	147,946	143,948	149,015	171,800	180,576	190,873	198,950
Prince George's County	102,611	102,642	114,256	146,746	150,927	162,899	203,957
Total Big Three Dem. vote	403,110	328,132	377,293	444,232	451,573	468,908	535,975
Total vote for Democrat	907,301	664,015	708,094	846,972	813,422	942,279	1,044,961
Big Three percentage of Total Democratic vote	44.4	49.4	53.3	52.5	55.5	49.8	51.3

Source: Compiled by authors from official election returns maintained by the Maryland State Board of Elections.

Results below the top of the ticket showed little evidence of a party re-alignment in Maryland. Despite massive Ehrlich majorities outside of the Democratic base of Baltimore City and Montgomery and Prince George's counties, his coattails were considerably shortened. Republicans picked up nine seats in the Maryland General Assembly, compared to the four-teen gained in Sauerbrey's 1994 defeat. Democrats won or were reelected to county executive posts, and former Baltimore County executive Dutch Ruppersberger, a Democrat, succeeded Ehrlich in the redrawn Second Con-gressional District.

The McKeldin formula for Republican success in Maryland was fol-lowed in spirit, if not in fact. Townsend went into the campaign season with a reasonably united Democratic Party, but her inept campaign and selection of Larson as her running mate, coupled with Ehrlich's success in attracting elite Democratic defectors in the Baltimore metro area, helped fragment party cohesion and reduce its organizational effectiveness. Ehrlich's posi-tioning as a pragmatic moderate defused Townsend's attempts to portray him as a far-right extremist of the Sauerbrey variety. This represented the second half of the McKeldin template: Republicans must run to the left of their Democratic opponent. Though Ehrlich certainly did not campaign as a progressive, he was the candidate of change. His positions on the budget crisis, on crime, and on what he characterized as the Annapolis "culture of corruption," a function of one-party rule, all represented moving away from the status quo.

2006: DEMOCRATIC DOMINANCE RESTORED

While the election of 2002 demonstrated that Robert Ehrlich knew how to campaign, his four years as Maryland chief executive raised the troubling question of whether he knew how to govern. As a candidate he was energetic and telegenic, a gifted political tactician and a superb opportunist in the best sense of the word. As governor he clashed repeatedly with the Democratic leadership of the general assembly, constantly railed against his coverage in the "dishonest" *Baltimore Sun*, and appeared frequently as a guest on right-wing talk radio shows, where his gubernatorial "facts" were never checked.[30] His legislative achievements paled in comparison to those of his Democratic predecessors. Ehrlich called two special sessions of the general assembly, one on medical malpractice insurance in 2004 and the second on energy rate hikes in 2006. Both concluded with legislative overrides of gubernatorial vetoes, policy wins for the general assembly. The centerpiece program from Ehrlich's 2002 campaign pledge book, *101 Outstanding Ideas for Maryland*, slot machines at Maryland racetracks, failed in four consecutive legislative sessions despite the active support of State Senate President Mike Miller. All too often Governor Ehrlich seemed to prefer partisan confrontation over compromise, abandoning the moderate and pragmatic approach that he had touted in the 2002 campaign. Incumbent executives, governors, mayors, and presidents alike need substantial achievement records to promote and project. In Ehrlich's case, beyond the traditional Republican "no new taxes" mantra, there were only a handful of high-profile policy products. (See chapter 8 for an account of the Ehrlich administration.)

To most political observers the 2006 campaign began the day after Ehrlich defeated Townsend in 2002. Baltimore City's charismatic mayor Martin O'Malley let an opportunity pass that year when he decided not to challenge Townsend in the Democratic primary. No one expected him to defer again. He didn't. The resultant campaign was long, bitter, and expensive; O'Malley and Ehrlich raised and spent an all-time Maryland record of almost $34 million.

O'Malley announced his candidacy to a thousand cheering supporters at Patterson Park in southeast Baltimore on September 28, 2005. He was joined in the gubernatorial quest by Douglas Duncan, the Montgomery County executive, and a bitterly contentious Democratic primary appeared inevitable. Duncan posed a serious challenge to O'Malley. In his three terms as county executive of the largest subdivision in the state, he had a solid record of achievement. Montgomery County public schools ranked among the best in the nation, and Duncan oversaw the successful urban revitalization of Silver Spring. Half of the McKeldin formula, a divisive Democratic primary, seemed in place for Ehrlich, but the benefit was illusionary. Both challengers held significant leads over the incumbent governor in early polling matchups. According to a survey commissioned by Baltimore Sunpapers and released in November 2005, O'Malley had a fifteen-point lead and Duncan a five-point lead over the Republican. Pundits soon christened Ehrlich the most threatened incumbent in the country.[31]

Throughout the spring of 2006 Duncan took aim at the front-runner O'Malley, attacking his record as mayor, but he gained only modest traction. Polls showed Duncan trailing in the Democratic primary by ten to twenty points; even more important, he was well behind in fund-raising. He began television advertising in early June, posing between two cardboard cutouts of O'Malley and Ehrlich as the man in the middle, independent from partisan bickering and sniping. Then, on June 22, Duncan dropped a bombshell into the contest: he announced at a press conference that he was suffering from clinical depression and withdrew, wholeheartedly endorsing O'Malley. With Duncan's abrupt departure, the fall campaign began almost three months early and relieved O'Malley of the expense and inevitable ill feelings of a contested primary.

From Ehrlich's perspective, the name of the game was catch-up for the 2006 election. He had come from behind before, and his strategy focused on exposing the "horrific nature" of O'Malley's record as mayor.[32] This meant contrasting Baltimore's woes to Maryland's comparative prosperity. The governor's campaign slogan was "Changing Maryland for the Better," and he defined the contest as "about success versus failure, a successful state versus a failed city administrator."[33] He imported as his campaign manager Republican operative Bo Harmon, nationally known for his unrelenting attacks on former U.S. senator Max Cleland's patriotism in 2004. Beginning in August the assaults of the Ehrlich campaign on O'Malley's stewardship of Baltimore City were repetitive and fierce. Direct mail charged, "Under Martin O'Malley's failed leadership, crime is rampant in Baltimore" and echoed Roger Ailes's infamous 1988 "Willie Horton ad" against Michael Dukakis: "Do we really want to let Martin O'Malley do to Maryland what he did for Baltimore?" Television commercials focused on city schools and city crime. Baltimore schools were "out of control." In a *Law and Order* cadence an announcer intoned, "In the Baltimore criminal justice system, there's talk and there are facts," and described Baltimore as "the deadliest city in America." On the order of 4 to 1 Ehrlich attack ads outnumbered his positive spots that extolled his boyhood roots growing up in suburban Baltimore County or that boasted of state support for embryonic stem cell research that his administration officials had originally opposed.

The principal rule of political campaign communications is this: Offend reality at your own risk. Spinning is one thing; outright distortions are another. Few Maryland voters were shocked to learn that Baltimore City had dangerous neighborhoods and poor schools. O'Malley's record, compiled over seven years of largely glowing media coverage, could be damaged but not undone by a three-month Republican barrage. Polling data confirmed O'Malley's positive profile. In the final *Washington Post* survey, voters were asked if "O'Malley had changed Baltimore City for the better or worse." Only 9 percent of the respondents said "worse." The last pre-election *Sun* poll posed an "agree or disagree" statement: "Martin O'Malley should not be governor because he has left so many problems unsolved in Baltimore." The distribution was 52 percent disagree, 40 percent agree, and 8 percent undecided, results that closely mirrored the final vote.[34]

Furthermore some of Ehrlich's attacks undercut his own theme of "making Maryland better." In one commercial purported city residents complained, "When Governor Ehrlich with the independent board of education wanted to fix our schools . . . a few politicians stopped them." How the Maryland governor, one of the most powerful chief executives in the nation, was thwarted by "a few politicians" remained unexplained.[35]

In 2002 Ehrlich's selection of Michael Steele as his running mate was an unalloyed positive for the Republican effort, as Steele proved adept and adroit throughout the campaign. In 2006 Steele sought the U.S. Senate seat vacated by the retiring Paul Sarbanes, and Ehrlich again sought a statement in his choice for lieutenant governor. The governor waited until June 29, only a week before the filing deadline, to tap Kristen Cox from his own administration. Visually impaired from early childhood, Cox headed the nation's first state cabinet-level department of disabilities and had served in President George W. Bush's department of education. While the governor praised her selection as "historic," more cynical observers tied the Cox nomination to the obvious need to bolster support among suburban female voters.[36] Cox was certainly an innovative choice, but she added little to the Republican ticket. A complete unknown to Maryland voters, a resident of Ehrlich's own Baltimore County, her name was not included on campaign signs until September. Even the governor, in a radio interview, surprisingly conceded that Cox was selected because she was blind and probably not for her administrative or political skills.[37]

A front-running challenger, Martin O'Malley was not content to simply sit on his lead. O'Malley ran a disciplined "on message" campaign, designed to maintain expected Democratic majorities in the "Big Three" and challenge Ehrlich in suburban and rural jurisdictions that Townsend had effectively conceded in 2002. To a considerable degree that campaign served as a negative role model, a trove of what not to do four years later. In 2002 Kathleen Kennedy Townsend confounded Democratic insiders, especially African Americans, with her choice of Admiral Larson as her lieutenant governor. Four years later O'Malley geographically and racially balanced his ticket early with his selection of Delegate Anthony Brown, an African American attorney from Prince George's County. Brown, the majority whip in the house of delegates, possessed an impressive résumé, issue compatibility, and substantial political skills. A classmate of Barack Obama at Harvard Law School, Brown served in the Iraq War as a lieutenant colonel in the U.S. Army Reserve and was awarded a Bronze Star. Articulate and energetic on the campaign trail, he confirmed his prospects as a rising star in Maryland politics.

"Leadership that works" was the central O'Malley-Brown theme that provided positive, future-oriented promises, detailed in a ten-point plan entitled "Moving Maryland Forward," and sharp critiques of Governor Ehrlich's misdeeds. O'Malley himself proved a superb campaigner, earning accolades for his eloquence and rhetoric that combined a "sense of sweep, grandeur and popculture."[38] At rallies and receptions across the state he demonstrated his superb stagecraft, honed by his political experience and years of fronting his own Irish band, O'Malley's March, which played at festivals, auditoriums, and bars across the state. In his speeches he displayed an extraordinary ability to connect voters with Maryland history, communal concerns, and his own vision of a creative and inspiring future. In two gubernatorial debates a calm and contained O'Malley continually put Ehrlich on the defensive, once reducing him to complain about the Baltimore City budget, "I pay for you. Without us, you're done."[39] While state aid to the city is significant, Ehrlich's annoyed and sarcastic response seemed petulant and scarcely gubernatorial.

O'Malley's advertising campaign capitalized early on his personal strengths and family narrative. The initial production, "Mom," featured the challenger and his mother, Barbara, discussing his middle-class upbringing that was long on love, the value of a good education, and the importance of public service. In "My Dad," O'Malley's young son, William, spoke glowingly of an engaged father who, despite mayoral demands, still found the time to school his boy in baseball and help with homework. O'Malley's Baltimore record was highlighted in commercials entitled "Believe" and "Tough" that emphasized crime reduction and the much lauded CitiStat program that generates empirical data to identify problem areas in essential urban services. On balance O'Malley's media campaign was substantially more positive than Ehrlich's, but there were also sharp attack and reaction ads. What distinguished these from the Republican commercials was their linkage to the established O'Malley theme of working hard for Maryland families. Ehrlich's attacks on O'Malley settled on depicting "Baltimore as the seventh level of the netherworld," the classic "vote against" scenario.[40] The challenger's attack ads often focused on policy differences, such as Ehrlich's opposition to raising the minimum wage or expanding health care coverage for "Maryland's working families." The O'Malley spots distinguished the policy cleavages and placed Ehrlich on one side and O'Malley on the other. The incumbent governor supported "the special interests" or "big corporations"; the Democrat wanted government to help people attain the American Dream, not stand in their way.

O'Malley had worked closely with the leaders of Maryland's largest counties. The "Big Seven" (the county executives of Anne Arundel, Baltimore, Harford, Howard, Montgomery, and Prince George's counties and the mayor of Baltimore) has met regularly for decades to discuss shared problems of metropolitan governance. His positive relationships developed there delivered stunning political dividends in the most significant political commercial of the 2006 Maryland campaign. It began as a radio spot that complained of Governor Ehrlich's ignoring the telephone calls for help from Baltimore County Executive James Smith for the past three years. That became the basis for the television spot titled "Call," which featured a hanging telephone receiver visual and an announcer's voice asking "What kind of person takes calls from insurance companies during the Hurricane Isabel disaster but ignored calls for help from Baltimore County Executive Jim Smith?" In heavy rotation during the final weeks, this commercial attracted considerable free media coverage and discussion.[41] In the closing weeks the Smith campaign provided extensive volunteer support to supplement O'Malley's organization throughout Baltimore County.

The O'Malley effort and all Democratic campaigns throughout the state also benefited from an upgraded and expansive GOTV coordinated campaign conducted cooperatively by the Maryland Democratic Party, the Democratic Senate Campaign Committee, and the Democratic National Committee. This "no precinct left behind" approach featured thousands of volunteer and paid workers who telephoned, canvassed, and worked on Election Day as "flushers" (knocking on doors of citizens who hadn't voted), drivers, and poll workers or watchers. Literature that focused on drawing 2004 Democratic presidential voters to the polls was widely distributed and produced an upsurge (about 20 percent) in new gubernatorial voters in many heavily Democratic precincts. In addition four hundred lawyers were enlisted for an extensive voter protection program, designed to blunt anticipated Republican Election Day tactics and voter challenges.

The O'Malley campaign and related committees reported expenditures of over $14 million, while Governor Ehrlich, who had once been ahead in fund-raising by a 2 to 1 margin, spent close to $17 million. In the crucial stretch drive O'Malley actually outspent his rival on television ads by almost $1 million, thanks in part to a $500,000 campaign loan from a retired Washington attorney, John P. Coale.[42]

Polls were all over the lot in the final weeks. Fourteen days before the election a *Washington Post* survey showed a commanding ten-point lead for O'Malley. A week later the *Baltimore Sun* reported a narrow O'Malley margin of a single percentage point, well within the margin of sampling error. The two alpha males of Maryland politics faced an outcome marked by uncertainty after months of campaigning.

On Election Day Maryland Republican desperation, or at least an acute shortage of campaign volunteers, was apparent. Buses carried hundreds of poll workers, many recruited at homeless shelters, from Washington and Philadelphia to precincts in Baltimore City, Baltimore County, and Prince George's County. There they were paid $100 plus three meals to distribute a brochure labeled "Ehrlich-Steele Democrats Official Voter Guide," containing photographs of former congressman Kweisi Mfume and Prince George's County Executive Jack B. Johnson with the heading, "These are OUR Choices." In reality both Mfume and Johnson, lifelong Democrats, had endorsed O'Malley and Cardin. Inside, in ballot format, were the names of Ehrlich and Michael Steele, unidentified as Republicans, as well as Democrats for all lower offices. The brochures carried the authority line of both the Ehrlich and Steele campaigns. When questioned about the deception, Governor Ehrlich was unapologetic: "It's legal, and it's what the Democrats have done forever."[43]

O'Malley's statewide total of 942,279 votes was the highest ever recorded for a gubernatorial candidate in Maryland history. Like past Democrats, O'Malley tallied massive majorities in Baltimore City (75 percent), Montgomery County (61 percent), and Prince George's County (79 percent), the bedrocks of Maryland Democratic dominance. O'Malley's 120,385-vote margin in Prince George's County alone exceeded his 116,815-vote majority statewide. He also carried Charles and Howard counties and stayed at 40 percent or above in eight others. Townsend had lost ten counties by 2 to 1 or more in 2002; O'Malley was defeated by that lopsided margin in only four (Caroline, Carroll, Garrett, and Queen Anne's). His strategy of damp-ening Ehrlich's suburban advantage was stunningly achieved in the gover-nor's home Baltimore County, where O'Malley won 48 percent of the vote and ran fewer than 10,000 votes behind Ehrlich. Four years earlier Ehrlich had won Baltimore County by almost 65,000 votes. In Republican-leaning Anne Arundel, Ehrlich's 2006 margin was only 27,988 votes, compared to a healthy 53,215 in 2002.[44] Overall O'Malley's vote total was consider-ably less concentrated in the Democratic "Big Three" of Baltimore City and Montgomery and Prince George's counties than the totals of Townsend in 2002 or Glendening in 1994 or 1998. Slightly less than half of the to-tal O'Malley statewide vote came from those subdivisions, about the same proportion as William Donald Schaefer achieved in 1990 (see Table 3-4).

According to CNN exit polls, O'Malley attracted strong majorities from Maryland Democrats (85 percent), African Americans (84 percent), liberals (84 percent), Jews (76 percent), union households (64 percent), and voters with postgraduate degrees (62 percent). Voters with college degrees, ac-counting for over half of the total, broke decisively for O'Malley, 56 to 43 percent. In addition, of the 60 percent who disapproved of George W. Bush's presidential performance, O'Malley was preferred by a 78 percent margin. Among white Marylanders men opted for Ehrlich 59 to 39 percent; however, O'Malley edged the governor by a single point (50 to 49 percent) among white females. Ehrlich retained his Republican base (93 percent) and ran best among self-identified conservatives (82 percent), white Prot-estants (67 percent), high school graduates (54 percent), and those who ap-proved of President Bush (84 percent).[45]

DEMOCRATIC DOMINANCE EXTENDED

Ehrlich's 2006 defeat was decisive and broad-based. Despite a 10 percent increase in registered Maryland voters, the governor garnered 54,128 few-er votes than he had tallied in 2002. The Republican Party's "14/5 Plan," to pick up fourteen seats in the house of delegates and five state senate offices to sustain gubernatorial vetoes, also lay in tatters. The 2006 elec-tions returned the 70 percent Democratic majority to the state senate and produced a net gain of six seats in the house of delegates. State Repub-licans explained away the results as part of the national Democratic dy-namic. Ehrlich's communications director Paul Schurick observed, "It had nothing to do with the Governor's record."[46] In truth Maryland Democrats deliberately linked Ehrlich with President George W. Bush at every op-portunity. In 2006 Bush was extremely unpopular in Maryland, especially among Democrats. According to a *Washington Post* survey, 86 percent of state Democrats strongly disapproved of Bush, compared to a 74 percent national average.[47] Yet the stubborn fact remains that Ehrlich was the only incumbent governor in the country rejected by the voters in 2006. Republican governors withstood the Democratic onslaught in such blue states as California, Hawaii, Rhode Island, and Vermont. In every early survey Ehrlich trailed O'Malley by double digits well before the anti-Bush, anti–Iraq War dynamic was in place. No survey ever showed Governor Ehrlich with a lead. Certainly four years of intransigent leadership played a role, but so did the ingredients of the McKeldin formula for Republican success in Maryland. In 2002 Ehrlich ran to the center, and by virtue of his personality and Townsend's political missteps, edged her out. As governor Ehrlich seemed too often enamored with scoring partisan points rather than working with legislative Democrats for pragmatic solutions; the result was a thin record of achievement. In 2006 O'Malley, a self-described "pragmocrat," consumed the center and the left with a disciplined, well-organized, and well-financed campaign. In Maryland those voters outnumbered conservatives, and Democratic dominance was restored.

The restoration was solidified four years later as Ehrlich, competitive to the core, sought to reverse the 2006 election verdict. Following his first electoral defeat ever, he moved only three miles from the governor's mansion. He accepted a position with the business law firm of Womble Carlyle, opening a Baltimore branch. In addition Ehrlich and his wife, Kendel, began cohosting a two-hour Saturday talk radio program on WBAL, the same station that had provided Republican Ellen Sauerbrey a radio home and public presence between her two unsuccessful gubernatorial bids. On air he maintained a nostalgic government-in-exile tone as he answered calls from supporters and continually criticized the O'Malley administration.

Throughout the winter and spring of 2010 Ehrlich flirted with a "will he or won't he" storyline. Clearly intrigued by the potential for a Republican national surge, he inched ever closer to a formal announcement. This finally came on April 7, and the O'Malley-Ehrlich sequel officially began. While early polls showed a competitive race, with some pundits rating the contest a toss-up, one critical factor was often ignored. Governor O'Malley had fund-raised for 2010 throughout his entire term, and Ehrlich had not. O'Malley began the race with over $5 million in campaign money, compared to Ehrlich's $150,000. The disparity was soon evident, as the O'Malley campaign began a midsummer balanced media blitz that didn't subside until election day.

Following the familiar two-tier strategy of positive and negative advertising, the Democratic campaign focused on the specifics of the O'Malley theme "Moving Maryland Forward" (a reprise of O'Malley's 2006 ten-point platform). Radio and television spots extolled the governor's four-year tuition freeze for Maryland public colleges and universities, state tax credit programs and loans for small business start-ups, a Port of Baltimore expansion, and the *Education Week* ranking of Maryland public schools as number one in the country for the second consecutive year. Unlike many polyspots that provide vague and generalized positive abstractions, the O'Malley commercials were specific and fact-based, resonating with media coverage of the governor's record. In addition issues such as economic development were personalized with "man in the street" individuals extolling the governor and his policies (e.g., "This governor gets it").[48]

The negative advertising spots centered on Ehrlich's tenure as governor and his brief career at Womble Carlyle. The Republican was labeled a lobbyist for special interests, and his claim that he never raised taxes as governor was ridiculed. The television, radio, and Internet onslaught aimed to transform Ehrlich into a quasi-incumbent defending a precarious record in what proved, nationally, a decidedly nonincumbent year.[49]

Compounding Ehrlich's difficulties was Sarah Palin, who in early August injected herself into the Maryland gubernatorial campaign with a late and perplexing Facebook endorsement of Ehrlich's sole primary opponent, Brian Murphy. Calling the thirty-three-year-old Montgomery County business investor a "pro-life, pro–Second Amendment common-sense conservative," Palin's intercession provided an imperfect measure of pure Tea Party strength in Maryland. It wasn't much, but Murphy did attract almost one in every four Republican votes in the September 14 primary. Though the Palin factor seemed inconsequential, it did serve to detach the Ehrlich campaign effort from the rising tide of conservative Republican discontent in the country.[50]

Unlike in states where Democrats evaded any Obama connection, the president remained popular in Maryland, with a 59 percent approval rating. Obama's endorsement of O'Malley was carried in radio commercials, and he made a heavily publicized campaign appearance for the governor in vote-rich and majority African American Prince George's County. President Obama noted that he had shared his Harvard law classes with Lieutenant Governor Anthony Brown and hit the established O'Malley talking points ("Maryland schools are the best in America") with considerable enthusiasm.[51]

As the 2010 campaign moved into the fall, public opinion polls charted a growing O'Malley lead, and the tale of the two campaigns was reflected in their themes. O'Malley maintained "Moving Maryland Forward" throughout, while the Ehrlich effort seemed perpetually in search of a compelling logo. His initial "Taking Maryland Back" was quickly jettisoned and replaced by "More Jobs, Lower Taxes." Then "Proven Leadership, Real Results" had a turn, followed by the generic "We Can Do Better." As election day loomed and early voting began, Ehrlich was reduced to recycling the 1980 Reagan classic, "Are you better off today than you were four years ago?," claiming that the business climate in Maryland was poor, talking about illegal immigration, and attacking the federal Patient Protection and Affordable Care Act in an attempt to capture the national Republican tidal wave.[52]

The breadth and depth of O'Malley's victory were of historic proportions. Defeating Ehrlich by over fourteen points, 56 to 42 percent, Governor O'Malley amassed the greatest number of votes (1,044,961) for a gubernatorial candidate in Maryland history. He received massive majorities in the core Democratic subdivisions of Prince George's County (203,957 to Ehrlich's 26,156), Baltimore City (133,068 to 26,073), and Montgomery County (198,950 to 89,108). Those three locales delivered a 394,648–vote majority to the governor, substantially above his statewide margin of 268,642 votes. In addition O'Malley won majorities in Howard and Charles counties and edged his Republican rival in Ehrlich's former home, Baltimore County, by 1,326 votes. Ehrlich did carry sixteen suburban and rural counties that have steadfastly voted Republican in gubernatorial elections in the past twenty years.

In other statewide races results proved that the state was not America in miniature in any political sense. U.S. Senator Barbara Mikulski cruised to an easy 62 percent reelection victory for her fifth term. Attorney General Douglas Gansler was elected without opposition, extending the Maryland Democrat winning streak for that office to eighty-seven consecutive years. State Comptroller Peter Franchot handily disposed of his Republican opponent, William Campbell, by a 61 to 39 percent margin, preserving the Democratic winning streak for that office at 111 years. In U.S. House of Representatives contests Republican state senator Andrew Harris did unseat first-term incumbent Frank Kratovil in a rematch of their 2008 First Congressional District contest, but all other House incumbents (six Democrats and one Republican) retained their seats by comfortable majorities.

While Republicans gained six seats in the house of delegates, the 2010 general assembly results were something of a partisan tie because two state senate seats, held by Republicans since 1975 and 1987, were won by Democrats. Democrats also won every partisan election for state legislative and county government office in Baltimore City and Charles, Montgomery, and Prince George's counties. The Republicans did make significant gains on county commissions and councils in rural and outer suburban counties. The results of the 2010 gubernatorial election confirmed the Two Marylands model in polarized fashion and demonstrated the continuing strength of Democratic dominance in statewide elections despite countervailing national trends.

CHAPTER FOUR

Maryland Public Opinion

*Because of our diversity, because of our nearness to the national
and international crossroads, because of our tolerance and self-in-
terestedness, because of our mobility, we are among the least provincial of Americans.*
  George Callcott, Maryland historian

In political and policy preferences, Maryland is regarded as among the
most progressive states in the country. Government initiatives in environmental regulation, education, health care, abortion rights, gun control, and
other programs of a "liberal social contract" cannot long persist without
the approval of public opinion.[1] Public opinion on matters political serves
as both a support and a constraint on state policymakers. On highly visible
issues it defines the range and dimensions of which specific decisions are
tolerated or accepted or embraced.[2]

Maryland public opinion reflects the views and values of more than 4.4
million adults out of a total population of nearly 5.8 million. As reported
in the 2010 census, over half of Marylanders were born in the Free State,
40 percent moved to Maryland from another state, and 10 percent was foreign-born. The state is 58 percent white; black Marylanders constitute the
largest minority, at 29.4 percent, followed by Asian Marylanders at 5.5 percent. Hispanic Marylanders were counted at 8.2 percent. Almost every European ethnicity is represented in Maryland; the most numerous reported
as first or second ancestries are German (19 percent), Irish (12 percent),
English (11 percent), Italian (6 percent), and Polish (4 percent).[3] Popular
attitudes reflect a mentality that combines in diverse strands the tolerance
of the founding Calverts, the witty skepticism of Mencken, the idealism of

Justice Marshall, and the pragmatism of generations of Maryland political leaders. According to the historians Brugger and Callcott, Marylanders express a complex blend of sensible sophistication, "a middle temperament" that combines the best of progressive impulses with productive practical applications.[4]

Our primary source of data on state public opinion is the series *Maryland Policy Choices*. These are the reports on fifteen statewide surveys from 1992 through 2009 conducted by the William Donald Schaefer Center for Public Policy at the University of Baltimore. The random, representational samples of Maryland citizens averaged 856 respondents per survey, with a sampling error ranging from plus or minus 3.4 to 4 percent in individual surveys. Of course public opinion polls are snapshots of what citizens think at a specific point in time, but because the Schaefer Center surveys incorporated several standard questions from 1992 through 2009, they provide the advantage of a time line analysis for selected Maryland opinions.[5]

MARYLAND GOVERNMENTAL PERFORMANCE

When Marylanders are asked to rate the performance of state government in solving problems, the majority do not respond positively (see Table 4-1). In the fifteen referenced Schaefer Center surveys the average response for combined "excellent" or "good" assessments was only 30 percent, and judgments of "only fair" or "poor" combined for an average of 64 percent. Positive ratings began climbing in the early 1990s, but only in 2002 did the two positive evaluations (47 percent combined) approximate the "fair" and "poor" evaluations (51 percent combined).

The Maryland public is skeptical and critical of state government in an abstract and general sense, perhaps a reflection of President Ronald Reagan's "government is not the solution" rhetoric that has permeated political culture for decades.[6] When during an economic recession the 1992 sample faced the question of whether "the people in state government waste a lot of money, waste some of it, or don't waste much of it at all," a strong majority of 63 percent opted for the "wastes a lot" response; another 32 percent said the state government "wastes some." Only 3 percent felt the state government "does not waste much money at all."

When Marylanders are asked about specific components of state government a very different pattern of attitudes emerges. In the *Maryland Policy Choices: 2002* public opinion poll Marylanders were asked to evaluate the job performance of ten major state agencies. The Maryland State Police and the University System of Maryland topped the list with 83 percent

Table 4-1: Rating state government performance

	Excellent	Good	Only Fair	Poor
1992	1	12	47	38
1993	1	15	54	28
1994	1	21	54	21
1995	2	31	54	14
1996	1	20	55	21
1997	1	24	54	19
1998	3	36	46	11
2002	5	42	40	11
2003	2	33	42	20
2004	2	28	50	17
2005	1	28	53	16
2006	2	35	46	14
2007	3	41	43	12
2008	1	27	46	23
2009	1	31	48	15

Source: *Maryland Policy Choices, 1992–1998, 2002–2009*, Schaefer Center for Public Policy, University of Baltimore.
Note: This question was not asked in 1999 through 2001. The "year" designation refers to the year of publication. Most of the surveys were conducted in the late fall and early winter of the calendar year preceding the publication of *Maryland Policy Choices.*

and 80 percent positive ratings, respectively. The Department of Natural Resources and the State Highway Administration scored in the 60 percent positive range, and five departments received a majority of good or excellent responses. Only the Maryland Department of Education, at 48 percent, earned a positive rating (good and excellent ratings combined) of less than 50 percent.

Marylanders are also exceedingly reluctant to cut government spending for specific programs and purposes, even during a time of significant state budgetary constraints. In ten Schaefer Center surveys citizens were questioned about state government's spending preferences in seventeen program areas, ranging from aid to elementary and secondary schools to medical assistance to the poor. Respondents were asked to report if they felt more money, less money, or no change in the amount of money was needed. They were also cautioned "that spending increases come out of tax money paid by you." In every survey over a fifteen-year period an overwhelming number of Marylanders declared that there should be more spending for public education and public safety. Majorities responded in most surveys that spending should be increased in medical assistance for the poor and programs for the

Table 4-2: "Spend More" or "Spend Less" responses to program areas

Program Area	1992	1993	1994	1995	1997	1998	2003	2004	2005	2006
Public education	57–6	74–4	71–6	72–5	75–3	75–3	72–4	73–3	74–3	70–2
Higher education	41–15	48–9	44–11	43–12	46–8	44–8	42–10	43–12	49–8	38–9
Parks and recreation	15–33	21–22	25–18	21–22	29–11	27–10	31–12	23–17	27–10	23–13
Public assistance	36–16	54–12	38–23	28–27	39–17	36–11	41–12	45–9	51–8	51–5
Arts and culture	7–47	11–34	12–38	13–36	18–23	21–23	20–24	21–27	21–18	18–24
Local government	19–26	28–23	28–27	28–22	24–16	18–20	25–20	26–19	23–18	21–21
Baltimore City	23–30	35–21	29–31	25–29	32–15	25–22	28–20	30–19	30–15	29–19
Public transit	24–22	35–16	40–15	34–18	38–11	32–10	44–10	34–9	38–8	38–7
Protect environment	37–15	51–11	55–8	48–13	52–9	42–10	48–9	38–9	49–6	45–8
Police/public safety	55–3	75–4	81–2	74–3	73–3	70–3	60–3	55–4	58–3	62–2
Prisons/corrections	34–15	37–17	47–19	37–19	36–19	28–19	20–24	17–26	20–21	24–17
Roads/highways	20–24	34–16	32–16	31–15	39–9	28–10	37–12	40–9	38–9	38–9
Elderly programs	47–5	63–4	53–6	50–7	60–4	56–4	53–4	54–4	55–3	55–3
Medical aid to poor	51–7	66–4	56–8	44–13	56–10	53–5	60–6	64–5	64–5	62–3

Source: Maryland Policy Choices: 1992–1995, 1997–1998, 2003–2006.

elderly. In every survey more spending was favored over less spending by significant margins for higher education, public transportation, public assistance for the poor, and protecting the environment. The only program areas where more respondents chose "spend less" rather than "spend more" were aid to local government (two out of ten years), aid to Baltimore City (three out of ten years), prisons and corrections (three out of ten years), and arts and cultural activities (nine out of ten years; see Table 4-2).

This seemingly paradoxical pattern of attitudes toward government, bureaucracy, and public programs is indicative of what Lloyd A. Free and Hadley Cantril established in their landmark work, *The Political Beliefs of Americans: A Study of Public Opinion.* They found that almost a quarter of Americans are conservative in their political ideology but liberal in their positive support of specific government programs.[7] Many Marylanders seem to carry such an attitudinal package. They question the overall efficacy of state government but applaud the efforts of individual agencies and support the programs of those governmental units.

MARYLAND PROBLEMS AND PRIORITIES

In thirteen surveys since 1992 Schaefer Center pollsters have asked the open-ended question, "What would you consider to be the most important problem facing the state government (or state legislature) in the next year?" This form of survey question traditionally elicits the purest opinion and is regarded as an accurate barometer of what concerns the average citizen the most. Without prompting or provided categories, most Marylanders demonstrate that they are a vast "attentive public" on a variety of issues and pay attention to state governmental matters. When the state economy falters and tax revenues decline, Marylanders report that the most important problem facing state government is the state budget. This has happened six times in the past seventeen years; only in the survey conducted immediately after the late fall 2007 special session of the general assembly that raised taxes did the budget trail taxes in importance (22 to 23 percent). As Table 4-3 shows, public concern over budgetary affairs spikes during those periods when budget cuts and possible tax increases dominate the local news cycles. In 1992, when the Schaefer administration made deep cuts and raised taxes in response to that economic recession, an absolute majority, 51 percent, said the greatest problem was the state budget. Public budgetary concerns subsided but rose again as unfunded state mandates collided with declining revenues during economic slowdowns in 2002–3 and 2007–8. In the most recent survey the economy shot to the top of the

Table 4-3: "Most Important Problem Facing State" responses

Program Area	1992	1993	1994	1995	1996	1997	2003	2004	2005	2006	2007	2008	2009
Budget: state	51	38	14	25	23	10	34	26	16	9	11	22	16
Crime	3	7	34	20	14	23	6	5	5	9	9	8	4
Drugs		4							5				
Economy													46
Education: public	4	6	8	5	6	9	9	17	12	11	16	7	5
Environment							3			4			
Gambling								5	4	4			
Health care	3	11	9	6	6	4	4	12	14	12	9	9	4
Higher education	3	3					4	6	4	7	7	3	4
Taxes	11	6	5	13	12	14	6	5	19	9	9	23	4
Transportation							4		4	4	4		
Unemployment	11	11	7	4	5	3	5	4	4				
Welfare		4		4	4	7							5

Source: Maryland Policy Choices: 1992–1997, 2003–2009.

most important problems and was cited by 46 percent of the respondents; the state budget was a distant second at 16 percent.

Given Maryland's relatively high national rankings in violent crime and total crime during the past two decades,[8] it is not surprising that crime was cited twice as the most important problem, peaking at a high of 34 percent in 1994. It has declined to single digits since 2003. Most public crime is localized and concentrated in urban areas. *Maryland Policy Choices: 2003* reported that 76 percent of the statewide sample felt it was safe to walk in their immediate neighborhood at night; 53 percent of the Baltimore City subsample said it was unsafe. Forty percent of Baltimore City residents felt that crime was a major problem in their community, while only 11 percent shared that opinion statewide.

Maryland state taxes, public education, health care, and unemployment are the only other responses that have reached double-digit percentages to the open-ended question of the most important problem facing the state government or legislature. The public view of taxes as the major problem hit a sustained peak in the mid-1990s, when state budget issues became prominent news. Public education, impacted by Ehrlich administration budgetary reductions, tallied 17 percent in 2004 and remained in double digits until falling to 7 percent in the 2007 *Maryland Policy Choices* report. Unemployment worries hit a high of 11 percent during the recession of the early 1990s, and health care registered a 14 percent high in 2005. From 1992 to 2009 welfare was not identified as the major problem by more than 7 percent. Concerns over gambling reached 5 percent in 2004. The environment and transportation have never received more than 4 percent of the unprompted responses.

Six surveys in the *Maryland Policy Choices* series have asked respondents to evaluate policy priorities for the state and rate them in terms of whether each was "very important, just important, only somewhat important, or not important at all." The resulting distribution provides a profile of what Marylanders consider the most vital and central needs for the state. On the whole, an activist state government agenda is strongly validated. Improving public education and controlling crime regularly rank highest in the percentage of respondents choosing "very important." Developing and keeping jobs, protecting the environment, and improving colleges and universities have received the strongest support, with rankings above 80 percent. Since being polled after 9/11, preventing terrorist attacks has elicited very important responses, from 62 to 72 percent. Anti–big government issues such as taxes and downsizing government fared less well in the responses. "Very important" responses for avoiding tax increases and lower-

Table 4-4: "Very Important" responses to program areas

Program Area	1998	2002	2003	2007	2008	2009	Ave.
Controlling crime	87	82	na	83	82	82	83.2
Improving public education	85	81	70	80	71	82	78.2
Developing and keeping jobs	76	76	61	70	70	85	73.0
Preventing terrorist attacks	na	72	na	62	62	70	68.3
Protecting the environment	63	64	46	63	64	69	64.6
Improving colleges and universities	62	59	na	60	53	59	58.6
Managing growth and development	48	52	na	53	49	46	49.6
Avoiding tax increases	52	45	36	51	61	52	49.5
Preserving farmland	na	51	43	53	53	43	48.6
Attracting new businesses	55	52	42	44	43	52	48.0
Lowering taxes	48	43	31	46	58	44	45.0
Reinvesting in communities	36	38	40	44	43	52	42.2
Improving public transportation	36	32	32	42	38	40	38.0
Building more/better roads	28	35	25	37	37	31	32.2
Reducing size of government	37	22	20	29	34	27	28.2
Buying open space/parkland	na	26	21	23	18	18	21.2
Revitalizing downtown	na	na	20	23	20	21	21.0

Source: Maryland Policy Choices: 1998, 2002–2003, 2007–2009.
Note: The designation "na" means the question was not asked.

ing taxes have ranging from 31 to 58 percent, while the range for reducing the size of government has been a significantly lower 20 to 37 percent. Only two issues have received more "not at all important" than "very important" responses: buying open space and parkland (twice) and reducing the size of government (once; see Table 4-4).

TAXING MATTERS

As the old saying goes, "Don't tax you, don't tax me, tax the man behind the tree." Marylanders are generally critical of the taxes they pay, but their opinions are far from uniform on a variety of revenue-raising measures. On the 1992 Schaefer Center annual survey most Marylanders thought state taxes were inequitable and too high and provided less in service value than what taxpayers contributed. In a series of "agree or disagree" statements, majorities responded negatively to the tax and service system.

Another measure of Maryland opinion toward taxes is how citizens feel about specific forms of taxation. In the 1992 survey the sample was asked to evaluate four tax mechanisms—the state income tax, property taxes, the sales tax, and the gasoline tax—on whether each was too high, too low, or about right. As might be expected, 60 percent of the respondents felt that property taxes were too high, and 50 percent said the same of the Maryland gasoline tax. Only 45 percent believed the state income tax was too high, and only 19 percent said the state sales tax was too high. Fifty-one percent said the state income tax was too low or about right, and an astonishing 81 percent felt the sales tax was either too low or about right. These findings correspond closely to opinion research in other states and national surveys. The property tax is usually cited as the "least fair" tax; analysts surmise that the method of collection, an annual or semiannual tax bill, produces a tax "sticker shock" reaction among homeowners, generating public antagonism. Taxes that exact smaller and continual payments through withholding (income tax) or automatic incorporation (sales tax) are perceived as less offensive.

During the state budget crisis of the early 1990s many Marylanders supported higher taxes to close the revenue gap. When faced with the question "Would you prefer raising taxes or reducing services and programs?" 38 percent of the 1992 sample selected the "increase taxes" response, compared to 30 percent who wanted to reduce services; 23 percent preferred a mix of tax hikes and service cuts. When Marylanders were questioned further on what specific tax hikes they would favor or oppose, "sin" taxes, increased state excises on cigarettes and liquor, won overwhelming public support, with 87 percent favorable and 12 percent unfavorable. Only two other proposed revenue-enhancement measures gained majority support: increased taxes on business (59 percent favored, 35 percent opposed) and professional services (56 percent favored, 38 percent opposed). Increasing property and income taxes were opposed by substantial majorities. Only 52 percent opposed an increase in the Maryland sales tax, compared to 46 percent in favor of such a change.

A somewhat similar pattern appeared more than a decade later, again when state spending commitments exceeded projected revenues. In *Maryland Policy Choices: 2003* Schaefer Center pollsters asked whether citizens approved or disapproved nine items on a list of tax and policy proposals discussed within the Ehrlich administration or the general assembly. As Table 4-5 displays, Marylanders opted for increasing a "sin" tax and the taxes on the wealthy and corporations. Broad-based tax measures, such as a straight 1 percent sales tax hike or expanding sales tax coverage, were opposed by substantial majorities. In the 2004 survey public support grew

Table 4-5: Approval frequencies for tax proposals (percentages)

Tax Proposals	Approval 2003/2004	Disapproval 2003/2004
Increase tobacco tax	70/71	29/29
Increase corporate taxes	64/75	33/21
Increase tax rate on over $100,000 income	60/67	37/30
Legalize slot machines	57/57	41/39
Add sales tax to professional services	40/44	56/51
One percent increase in sales tax	32/43	67/56
Increase gasoline tax	27/na	73/na
Add sales tax to residential energy fuels	17/na	82/na
Add sales tax to medical supplies	11/na	88/na

Source: Maryland Policy Choices: 2003 and 2004.
Note: Approval represents a combination of "strongly approve" and "approve." Disapproval represents a combination of "strongly disapprove" and "disapprove." "Na" means the specific question was not asked of respondents in the report.

for tax increases on corporate taxes and high-income taxpayers, and there was less opposition to a 1 percent sales tax increase and a broadening of the sales tax coverage.

The fundamental question remains: How do elected officials respond to such an array of opinions? Maryland's combined state and local income tax as a percentage of personal income rose to the third highest in the nation, but because of a lower sales tax, the overall state and local tax burden ranked twentieth in 2004 as a percentage of personal income. With the exception of the 1994 gubernatorial campaign, when Republican candidate Ellen Sauerbrey made a 24 percent income tax cut her centerpiece theme, taxes have not served as a cutting issue in recent statewide elections. State tax policy has generally conformed to the basic parameters of public opinion. Maryland political leaders have generally opted for specialized tax measures or user fees to deal with revenue shortfalls. Cigarette taxes were raised during the administrations of Governor Schaefer, Governor Glendening, and Governor O'Malley. Governor Ehrlich, while maintaining a "no new taxes" posture, doubled state fees for vehicle registrations, initiated a "flush tax" to pay for water treatment facilities, tripled corporate filing fees, and triggered a 57 percent rise in the state's modest property tax rate through his budget proposals.

The intersection of public opinion and state tax policy was tested during the 2010 gubernatorial election cycle, when Governor O'Malley proposed, and the legislature approved, substantial tax increases during a fall 2007 special legislative session. There was no increase in the sales tax from 1977 until 2008, when it rose from 5 to 6 percent. The top rate of the state income tax was reduced 10 percent over five years beginning in 1998 but increased for high-income taxpayers in the 2007 special session and the 2008 regular session of the general assembly.

In response to recurring projections of budget deficits, the gambling industry persistently offered a portion of its revenues as a budget panacea. Gambling has had a long and checkered career in Maryland politics. Parimutuel betting on horse racing has been regulated by the state since 1920, when the Maryland Racing Commission was created after antigambling forces tried to ban the sport of kings.[9] Slots and other gaming devices were legal by local option in the counties of Southern Maryland for decades until closed down during the 1960s. After a constitutional amendment authorizing a state lottery was approved by voters in 1972, the State Lottery Commission has administered an increasing multitude of instant games, scratch-off cards, and lotto and keno devices designed to enrich state coffers.

Generally public opinion is moderately supportive of gambling issues but is often tempered with concerns over gaming locations and the individual consequences of expanded gambling opportunities. For example, the 1995 Schaefer Center survey found that 60 percent of the respondents agreed that legalized gambling "creates jobs and helps stimulate the economy," but almost the same percentage (59), believed it also "can make compulsive gamblers out of people who would never participate in illegal gambling." In that year 55 percent of the sample approved of Maryland's permitting casino-style gambling, while 42 percent disapproved. These frequencies were virtually reversed the following year, in the 1996 Schaefer Center survey, when 43 percent supported casino gambling and 54 percent opposed it.

A second question asked where casino gambling should be permitted. The only location that won majority support (51 percent) was horse racing tracks. Placing casinos in the Baltimore or Washington suburbs was strongly opposed (72 percent disapproval, 24 percent approval), as was such a venue in Baltimore City's Inner Harbor (66 percent disapproval, 32 percent approval). In 1997 the gambling question focused solely on citizen approval or disapproval of "slot machines at Maryland's horse racing tracks." In this instance 61 percent approved and 32 percent disapproved.

Years of lobbying and public campaigning by the Maryland horse racing industry and national gaming interests combined with the persistent push for slot machines by the Ehrlich administration did move Maryland public opinion somewhat on the issue. In 2004, 2007, and 2008 Schaefer Center pollsters again posed questions on slot machine legalization, revealing steadily favorable margins for approval. Marylanders who favored slots explained their support in two ways. Coding unprompted responses, the survey of 2004 found that 44 percent (46 percent in 2007) said the state needed the money generated by slots licensing and operation, which was the principal argument advanced by Governors Ehrlich and O'Malley, general assembly allies, and the ultimate basis for the 2008 advertising campaign in support of a constitutional amendment authorizing slot machines. Another 21 percent in both the 2004 and 2007 reports said they didn't want to see Maryland money going to Delaware and West Virginia racetracks that have vigorously promoted their slot machine operations. The reasons cited by opponents of slot legalization were more varied. The potential to harm the poor was cited by 33 percent in the 2004 survey and 31 percent in 2007. The fear of increased crime associated with gambling was expressed by 20 percent of the opponents in 2007 (only 13 percent in 2004), with another 19 percent reporting they were morally against gambling (again only 13 percent in 2004). The results reported in *Maryland Policy Choices: 2008* showed 56 percent in favor and 38 percent opposed to the constitutional amendment proposed during the 2007 special session of the general assembly to authorized slot machines. The ratification vote held during the 2008 presidential general election passed by a 58.7 to 41.3 percent margin.

ENVIRONMENTAL SENSIBILITIES

Given the historical and continued importance of the Chesapeake Bay to Maryland's development, consistent public support for strong and committed environmental policies is not surprising. Concern over the degradation of Maryland's natural resources is also nothing new. Mencken decried the drastic decline in the numbers and quality of Chesapeake crab and oyster stocks in 1918.[10] Since then Maryland has grown and boomed; as the environmental writer Tom Horton succinctly stated, "People keep on coming."[11] Pressures on Maryland's lands and rivers and the Bay have increased in both complexity and intensity. The Schaefer Center surveys over seventeen years have included a variety of questions about the environment in addition to the general issue inquiries.

A cluster of environmental questions in *Maryland Policy Choices: 1993* reflected mounting public anxiety. The state sample was asked to indicate the severity of nine environmental problems, such as "pollution of drinking water" and "cleaning up the Chesapeake Bay," from "a very serious concern" to "not a serious concern to you personally." Five of the selected items merited the highest concern from over two-thirds of the respondents; hazardous and toxic waste disposal ranked first, with 80 percent seeing it as a "very serious concern." This was followed by pollution of drinking water, threats to the Chesapeake Bay, and pollution of Maryland's rivers and streams. The only identified environmental problem that rated no concern among 50 percent of respondents was the danger of home radon exposure. Since 2003 a similar question has been asked about what activities pose "threats to the Chesapeake Bay"; respondents were asked whether the activity poses "a major threat," "a minor threat," or "not much of a threat." The results, presented in Table 4-6, have been consistent in revealing that an overwhelming number of Marylanders consider industrial discharge and sewage treatment plants as major threats, with growth and development and "farm runoff" ranking next highest.

A second question in 1993 employed the same list and asked Marylanders to identify "the most pressing environmental problem" in the state as a whole. Here the centrality of the Bay emerged; cleaning up the Chesapeake ranked first among 20 percent of the sample. Pollution of rivers and streams was second, with about 16 percent mentioning that issue. Various kinds of air pollution and toxic waste received 10 percent each. Lead poisoning, radon, and forests and natural areas each received 2 percent or less of the responses.

In addition the 1993 Schaefer Center survey revealed that a substantial majority of Marylanders were less than impressed with state governmental efforts to reduce environmental pressures, and most endorsed stricter rules and regulations, even when accompanied by significant costs. Majorities for "stricter environmental regulations" persisted even if it meant increased consumer costs for products (68 percent support, 26 percent opposed) and higher taxes (57 percent support, 38 percent opposed). However, once the ante of environmental protection was raised to include widespread negative economic consequences, approval of more stringent environmental protection declined abruptly in that survey. When Marylanders were asked if they supported or opposed stricter environmental regulations even if it meant it would "cost some workers their jobs" or would discourage "businesses from moving to Maryland," support fell to 31 percent in both cases. Obviously Marylanders hold protecting the natural environmental in high esteem, but not necessarily at any price. They will support efforts to preserve and protect their natural heritage, but not at the cost of employment or potential economic development. In that context the pragmatism of the pocketbook tempers the environmental impulse.

The environmental centerpiece of the Glendening administration was a far-ranging and ambitious series of Smart Growth initiatives designed to reduce suburban sprawl by channeling residential and economic development to existing developed or designated growth areas. A cooperative ven-

Table 4-6: "Major Impact" responses on threats to the Chesapeake Bay

Possible Threat	2003	2004	2005	2006	2007	2008	2009	Ave.
Industrial discharge	88	66	84	82	88	88	84	82.9
Sewage treatment plants	80	79	81	75	82	83	76	79.4
Farm runoff	61	62	60	60	65	69	59	62.3
Growth and development	58	60	61	63	63	66	50	60.1
Storm water runoff, urban areas	45	52	58	56	52	59	44	52.3
Automobile emissions	na	na	na	na	na	na	46	46.0
Residential runoff	na	na	na	na	na	na	31	31.0

Source: Maryland Policy Choices: 2003 to 2009.
Note: The designation "na" means the question was not asked.

ture between the state and local governing units, Smart Growth proceeded through state laws and budgetary decisions as well as local planning ordinances. Begun in 1997, the Maryland Smart Growth program won national acclaim and, with only one exception, sustained support from Maryland public opinion. Asked in the 1998 Schaefer Center survey whether they generally approved of "the state . . . trying to reduce sprawl type development by influencing where business and housing development take place," a substantial 66 percent majority approved. Seventeen percent were opposed, 7 percent offered conditional approval, and 10 percent reported that they had no opinion.

Public reaction to specific Smart Growth components were explored in both *Maryland Policy Choices: 1998* and *2002*. Marylanders were asked if they approved or disapproved of five legal provisions: laws that protect areas around the Bay and around rivers from development; laws that would require developers to include the costs of new schools, sewers, and roads in the cost of new homes; laws that will preserve farmland from development; laws that would allow future development only in areas where schools, roads, and other facilities already exist; and laws that require new houses to be built closer together to preserve open space in communities.

The results, shown in Table 4-7, show a level of sustained and substantial public approval for three of the Smart Growth initiatives. In addition, opinion moved in a modest but positive direction on four of the five items. Support for protecting the Chesapeake Bay and Maryland watersheds scored the highest, and the margin between approval and disapproval frequencies increased by 5 percent between the 1998 and 2002 surveys. The policy of requiring developers to include infrastructure costs in the price of new homes also saw its support margin expand by 4 percent. Farmland preservation showed a small decline (within the margin of error) in the percentage difference between respondent approvals and disapprovals from 1998 to 2002. Focusing development on areas of already established communities won a 47 percent plurality of support in both surveys, but opposition declined a modest 3 percent over the four intervals. Cluster or higher density housing remained the sole Smart Growth policy that experienced a higher disapproval than approval rate, but even here the degree of opposition decreased by 8 percent between the surveys. *Maryland Policy Choices* regularly tracks public support for farmland preservation; 88 to 96 percent of the respondents rated this policy "very important" or "somewhat important" in the 2005 through 2009 reports.

A MODERATED PROGRESSIVE PERSUASION

Many Marylanders refuse to classify themselves by ideology. When asked how they view themselves in *Maryland Policy Choices: 2004*, 22 percent identified as liberal, 29 percent moderate, and 20 percent conservative; 27 percent said they didn't "think in those terms," findings consistent with a series of public polls.[12] Clearly a considerable proportion of Marylanders define themselves as standing between established ideological extremes. But regardless of self-labeling, Maryland moderates and independent thinkers, more often than not, line up on the progressive side of assorted issues.

For example, according to Schaefer Center surveys, an overwhelming 80 percent majority supported "right to die" legislation (*Maryland Policy Choices: 1993*), a plurality of 48 percent believed that the federal government should administer a national health insurance program for all Americans (*Maryland Policy Choices: 1994*), and 50 percent agreed with Governor Glendening's decision to extend collective bargaining rights to state employees, compared to 24 percent opposed (*Maryland Policy Choices: 1997*). In addition, 61 percent think Maryland lobbyists have excessive influence, and 77 percent support more stringent regulation of lobbyists (*Maryland Policy Choices: 1995*). However, while 75 percent felt that campaign fund-raising promotes political corruption, a strong 67 percent majority disapproved of publicly funded campaigns as a replacement for the present system (*Maryland Policy Choices: 2003*). Although generally progressive, Maryland opinion is often moderated by a sense of practical realism. For example, most Marylanders believe that legalizing drugs would make the problems of crime and addiction worse.

Gun control has served as a perennial issue in the United States since the

Table 4-7: Smart growth opinion patterns (percentages)

Priorities	Approval/Disapproval 1998 survey	Approval/Disapproval 2002 survey
Bay and river protection	78 to 10	82 to 9
New homes should include infrastructure costs	63 to 17	69 to 19
Farmland preservation	71 to 14	68 to 14
Focused development	47 to 33	47 to 30
Clustered housing requirements	23 to 60	26 to 55

Source: Maryland Policy Choices: 1998 and 2002.

1960s in numerous electoral contests. Maryland opinion has predominantly supported expansive firearm restrictions, although there is considerable skepticism concerning the overall effectiveness of such policies. In the 1993 Schaefer Center survey 78 percent of the respondents favored stricter laws on the sale of handguns, 17 percent opted for retaining the present policy, and only 2 percent felt handgun restrictions should be reduced. When asked whether they supported or opposed specific gun control measures over 80 percent favored a seven-day waiting period, a total ban on the sale of military-style assault weapons, and a mandatory police permit for the purchase of a handgun. The opinion tipping point on gun control in Maryland would be laws moving from handgun regulation to outright prohibition, as Table 4-8 demonstrates. Banning the sale of all handguns was opposed by 59 percent of the respondents and supported by only 38 percent.

Maryland Policy Choices: 1996 revisited opinions on gun control and again found strong support for restrictive policies. Seventy-six percent approved of limiting all gun sales to registered gun dealers, and 64 percent supported a purchase limit of one handgun a month for all citizens. When asked "How effective do you think handgun regulation is in reducing crime and limiting violence?" a 59 percent majority of Marylanders believed such regulation is either "not very effective" (28 percent) or "not at all effective" (31 percent). Thirty percent felt such regulation was "somewhat effective," and a mere 9 percent opted for "very effective."

PROGRESSIVE OPINION CONTINUED:
THE ELECTORAL CONNECTION

Examining the cumulative responses to public opinion surveys helps us understand the attitudes of Marylanders, but the real consequence of public

Table 4-8: Support for handgun restrictions (percentages)

Proposed restrictions	Support/Oppose
Seven-day waiting period	92 to 6
Assault weapons ban	84 to 14
Police permit to buy	82 to 15
Handgun prohibition	38 to 59

Source: Maryland Policy Choices: 1993.

opinion resides in political behavior at the polls. Chapter 3 describes electoral behavior in terms of parties and candidates, and chapter 6 discusses
votes on constitutional amendments. Here we describe voting patterns on
contested ballot issues. In a number of states voters regularly decide major public policies through the direct democracy mechanisms of initiative
and referendum. Maryland is not one of them. Although Maryland citizens
have the right to referendum, it is a decidedly limited power. The Maryland
Constitution restricts the range of issues subject to public votes by excluding measures passed by the legislature that involve "any appropriation for
maintaining the State Government."[13] Laws relating to the manufacture or
sale of alcohol are also not subject to referendum. If passed and enacted
legislation may be challenged, the first stage is a petition drive by opponents of the legislation. Signatures of registered voters numbering at least 3
percent of the total votes cast for the office of governor in the previous gubernatorial election must be submitted on valid petitions within sixty days
after the passage of the questioned legislation. Once petitioned a law is not
effective unless approved by an affirmative majority vote in the next general election.

Petitioning laws passed by the Maryland General Assembly to referendum occurs very infrequently in Maryland. Through the 2010 general, election, there have been only eighteen referendums held since the constitutional amendment authorizing this form of direct democracy was passed in
1914. Subjects have covered a wide range; half have been approved by the
voters and half have been rejected. Voters rejected the creation of a fisheries commission and a term for the motor vehicles commissioner in 1940.
In 1962 a congressional redistricting plan was petitioned to referendum and
lost. From 1966 to 1974 a majority of votes were cast against all five laws
petitioned to referendum: providing for the construction of a second Bay
bridge in 1966, a modification to the housing discrimination laws in 1968,
the creation of a community development organization in 1970, and aid to
nonpublic schools in 1972 and 1974. Legislation that won approval includ-

ed changes in the state's Workman's Compensation Commission (1940), the creation of the Potomac River Compact (1960), and outlawing racial segregation in public accommodations (1964). The two measures that were petitioned to Maryland voters in 1988 and 1992 represented defining issues for the political character of the state. Both were challenges by more conservative and Republican groups to legislation passed by an overwhelming Democratic general assembly.

A 1988 referendum involved the creation of a handgun control roster board that would review the characteristics of all handguns manufactured or sold in the state.[14] Intended to target cheap firearms, the so-called Saturday Night Specials, the board was empowered to ban handguns it found of little use for sporting, self-protection, or law enforcement purposes. Pro-gun forces easily secured the necessary signatures to force a referendum, and the National Rifle Association poured resources into a $6 million campaign to persuade Marylanders to "vote no on Question 3." Gun control groups rallied in support of proposal. The Maryland electorate settled the issue decisively, and Question 3 passed by a comfortable 264,523-vote margin (927,947 votes for and 663,424 votes against), a 58 to 42 percent majority. Gun control won easily in the I-95 corridor's urban and suburban jurisdictions of Central Maryland, achieving lopsided majorities of 72 percent of the vote in Montgomery County and 69 percent in Baltimore City. Outside the six largest counties located in the Baltimore and Washington metropolitan areas, only Talbot County on the Eastern Shore supported Question 3, and there the margin was a mere six votes out of 10,824 ballots counted on the question. In Western Maryland, where hunting is long established and gun racks seem an integral accessory of every pickup truck, the measure failed by nearly a 3 to 1 margin, garnering only 13.7 percent in far western Garrett County.

Four years later, in 1992, voters confronted a second litmus test on referendum. This time it was abortion rights. In response to increasing national restrictions on abortion during the Reagan and Bush administrations, Maryland abortion rights activists attempted to codify the protections of *Roe v. Wade* into Maryland law. In the spring of 1990 an Omnibus Abortion Act passed the house of delegates but was blocked in the state senate by a group of pro-life legislators who filibustered for over a week. One Montgomery County senator, Frank Shore, a staunch opponent of abortion rights, dubbed the effort "the Super Bowl for Life" and showed up each day in a football uniform. Karyn Strickler, the director of the Maryland National Abortion Rights Action League PAC, recalled, "Many of the anti-abortion advocates in the Senate came from strong pro-choice districts in Montgomery and Prince George's Counties. We thought with the right candidates we could defeat them and help establish a pro-choice super majority."[15] As a consequence four prominent pro-life state senators were defeated by pro-choice challengers in the Democratic primaries held in September 1990. In the 1991 legislative session the Omnibus Abortion Act passed by comfortable margins in both chambers.[16]

Maryland right-to-life groups quickly petitioned the legislation to referendum. The Vote kNOw Coalition, an assemblage of anti-abortion groups, waged a grassroots campaign against Question 6, while Maryland for Choice, an umbrella association of pro-choice organizations, worked for its passage. In the end it wasn't very close. Question 6 passed easily, with a 61 to 39 percent majority, amassing 1,114,377 votes for to 690,542 votes against. The pro-choice measure won majorities in all but seven of Maryland's twenty-four subdivisions. Like Question 3 in 1988, the proposed law rolled up huge victory margins in the Baltimore and Washington metropolitan areas. Montgomery County recorded a 70 percent majority, and both Baltimore City and Prince George's County recorded 66 percent. In opposition were Allegany, Frederick, and Garret counties in Western Maryland. The measure was also defeated in Caroline, Cecil, and Somerset counties on the Eastern Shore and St. Mary's County in Southern Maryland.

SUMMARY

The electoral results of the referendums on gun control and abortion rights underscore Maryland opinion patterns at the beginning of the twenty-first century. Taken together with partisan election results and votes on proposed constitutional amendments, there is a consistency of progressive outcomes that convincingly demonstrate that a majority of Maryland citizens continue to support a perceived liberal social contract. Just as in election outcomes, the urbanized I-95 corridor defines the state's progressive tilt on public opinion. The rest of the state, which is more rural or lower density suburban, is considerably more conservative, as reflected in public opinion as well as electoral contests.

CHAPTER FIVE

Political Parties, Interest Groups, and Corruption

The end was the thing, and so that the end was accomplished the means mattered little.

Paul Winchester on Maryland's Democratic political machine, 1923

Strong political parties, combined with multiple and diverse interest groups, help promote and maintain stable democracies because they connect citizens with the process and institutions of self-government. Maryland has both. These institutions emerged early in state history and consistently demonstrated that Maryland trait, the politics of pragmatism. While the roles, functions, and sheer political power of political parties have declined, interest groups have grown more numerous, purposeful, and influential. This chapter examines the historical and contemporary dimensions of these institutions and an often troubling consequence: political corruption.

MARYLAND POLITICAL PARTIES: HISTORICAL DEVELOPMENT

Political parties have a long, sometimes distinguished and sometimes tarnished history in Maryland. Popular voting, the currency of competitive exchange in partisan politics, was well established early, and the elimination of property qualifications for voting in 1802 and 1810 provided the opportunity for a mass electorate. During the Age of Jackson, Maryland emerged as a national leader in party organization. Jacksonian Democrats, organized by Roger Brooke Taney, held their first state party convention on May 21, 1827, in Baltimore City and established a persistent, tenacious, and effective state central committee structure based on county representation that exists in substantially the same form today. This makes the Maryland Democratic Party one of the oldest political organizations in the world. Maryland also served as the national hub of party-building activities, with Baltimore City becoming the birthplace of the national political convention in 1831.[1]

The political fragmentation of the 1850s and the rise of the Know Nothing Party was especially pronounced in Maryland. At the start of the Civil War members of the declining Know Nothings joined with old-line Whigs and pragmatic Unionist Democrats to form the Constitutional Union Party in 1860. Fragments of Unionists and other anti-Democrats ultimately became the state Republican Party after the Civil War. Maryland Democrats, hampered by federal and state restrictions during the war years, quickly reassembled as the majority party once the war ended. In the second half of nineteenth century Maryland Democratic Party organizations made Maryland close to a one-party state in statewide elections. Coupled with the acceptance of patronage and governmental favoritism, one-party rule reflected and promoted machine politics and party bosses. Access to public office was tightly controlled, as candidates were endorsed on the county and state levels at party conventions and there were no primary elections. As detailed in chapter 2, the Maryland Democratic Party bosses were Arthur Pue Gorman from Howard County and I. Freeman Rasin of Baltimore City.

Progressive-era reforms such as the secret ballot, bipartisan administration of voter registration and elections, and direct primaries were intended to reduce partisan central power to control access to public office. In the second half of the twentieth century the advent of candidate-centered campaigns, television, and polling increased the ability of individuals to circumvent party hierarchies. Outsiders and insurgents such as Republicans Theodore McKeldin and Charles Mac Mathias and Democrats such as Paul Sarbanes and Barbara Mikulski appeared and prospered.[2] Over the past forty years winning candidates have frequently earned their primary election victories outside the official party structure or circles.

As Maryland state parties lost the ability to control access to public office and candidates for state offices became increasingly self-selected, the Maryland Democratic and Republican parties engaged in other important political functions. Today the competing state and local political parties are service organizations, repositories of campaign expertise, resources, and, increasingly, money for the winners of their respective party primaries.

CONTEMPORARY PARTIES: THE STATE CENTRAL COMMITTEE

State parties are sometimes described as stratarchies, or organizations of distinct and very separate levels with little coordination and communication between them.[3] This is not the case in Maryland, where cooperation and joint activities often characterize partisan campaigns and fund-raising efforts. At the state level there are the official state Democratic and Republican parties recognized in state law, headquartered in Annapolis, staffed with between three and five full-time professionals, and responsible for a variety of party-building and campaign functions. These include the maintenance and distribution of voter files that aid candidates in their canvassing and direct mail efforts; holding campaign training sessions for candidates, campaign staffers, and volunteers; creating persuasive messages to spin the Maryland media; targeting registration drives in high-performance precincts; coordinating a calendar of party and fund-raising events; and developing and implementing voter outreach programs to support groups in the electorate.

In Maryland state parties are creatures of the local party central committees. The executive directors of both the Democratic and the Republican state parties are approved by the respective executive committees of the Democratic and Republican State Central Committees. The state party operations and their personnel are dependent on the involvement of the local county central committees (including Baltimore City). This is predicated on far more than custom and tradition. As defined in Maryland statutes, the governing body of a recognized and official political party is the state central committee, comprising the members of the local central committees.[4] The members of these party committees are elected in gubernatorial primary elections in the twenty-three counties and Baltimore City. They may be elected from legislative, council, or special districts in suburban and urban areas or elected countywide in less densely populated jurisdictions. Especially in urban areas, candidates for these posts often run on tickets organized by incumbent state senators and delegates. The number of central committee members in each jurisdiction may vary from term to term, as the local central committee, or legislature, may determine prior to each election. After the suffrage amendment was ratified in 1920 the Democratic and Republican parties both added women in equal numbers to men to their local central committees. This practice faded in many jurisdictions over the years, only to be resurrected as part of national Democratic Party rule changes in 1984. Generally the contemporary Democratic State Central Committee contains about three hundred members, and the Republican

State Central Committee numbers approximately 240. State central committee members serve without monetary compensation, and turnover is relatively high, although it is not uncommon for some individuals to serve for decades on their local central committee.

By far the most significant power of local state central committees is their authority under the state constitution to fill any vacancies in the Maryland General Assembly. If a member of the general assembly retires, dies, or otherwise vacates office, the state central committee for that legislative district or county meets to determine a successor. Although the governor formally makes the appointment, gubernatorial approval is normally pro forma. If the state central committee members have a tie vote, fail to act in a timely manner, or recommend two different individuals in the event of a legislative district that crosses county lines, the governor can choose the new legislator; this occurred in 1995, 2005, and 2010. It is noteworthy that over the past few decades between 12 and 15 percent of the members of the state legislature first joined the general assembly as a result of their party state central committee exercising its power to fill a vacancy. For this reason election to the state central committee is often viewed as the initial step for a political career in Maryland.

The state central committees typically meet twice a year and provide an organizational base for state party participation in the national party committees and national conventions. Strong relationships with the respective national parties have often yielded political dividends in Maryland politics. Governors Ehrlich, O'Malley, and Glendening used strong national party ties to bolster their campaigns in cooperation with state central committees. Two former Republican gubernatorial nominees, Ellen Sauerbrey (1994) and Louise Gore (1974), both of whom upset better-known candidates in contested primaries, were aided by their active roles in state party politics and membership on the Republican National Committee. At the county level Democratic and Republican State Central Committees generally meet more frequently to organize party-building and maintenance events, such as Republican Lincoln Day banquets and Democratic Jefferson-Jackson dinners. In addition workshops for party activists are regularly conducted on a county or regional basis.

The state central committees also serve as important conduits for campaign contributions and expenditures. From 2003 through 2006 the Maryland Democratic and Republican parties engaged in a veritable fund-raising arms race that shattered all previous state records.[5] The Maryland Democratic State Central Committee received over $8.8 million in its federal account, which is regulated by the Federal Election Commission. Contributions to the federal account can come only from individuals and candidate or party committee transfers and can be spent in support of federal candidates, research, campaign personnel, voter contact, and party functions. Contributions to the Democratic State Central Committee's state account, regulated by the Maryland State Board of Elections, totaled $3 million and was largely spent on an extensive 2006 voter contact campaign. The federal account of the Maryland Republican State Central Committee collected $6.3 million in contributions and totaled $3.2 million in state fund-raising. With over $20 million in total contributions at their disposal, the Maryland parties were fully integrated into the campaign process at the federal, state, and local levels during the 2006 election cycle.

GRASSROOTS POLITICS: THE POLITICAL CLUBS

Political clubs, complete with established neighborhood headquarters and a full menu of social functions, once abounded in Maryland. One of the oldest, the Stonewall Democratic Club of South Baltimore, began its existence just after the Civil War and sponsored local baseball teams and organized a host of yearly bull roasts, crab feasts, and other public gatherings. Under the leadership of state senators George W. Della Sr., Harry "Soft-shoes" McGuirk, and George W. Della Jr., Stonewall was renowned for its control of patronage and influence on Democratic nominations within a substantial portion of the city. Thirty years ago the club met weekly; today it meets only as business arises, particularly during election years.[6] Other traditional clubs, such as Battle Grove Democratic Club in southeastern Baltimore County, remain vital political and social organizations hosting dances, bingo nights, crab feasts, and bull roasts as well as candidate forums and endorsement meetings.

Although the precise number of political clubs varies from year to year, according to state party records in 2006 there were ninety-five active Republican clubs and 108 Democratic clubs organized throughout Maryland, which is significantly lower than the hundreds that existed as recently as thirty years ago.[7]

Contemporary Maryland political clubs are active and engaged in the electoral process. Candidates often emerge from club membership, and virtually all serious candidates seek club endorsements and Election Day coverage when club members cover local polling places handing out sample ballots to prospective voters. Like other associations and interest groups, political clubs have adopted the advantages of technology by creating websites and using electronic communication to expand membership, communicate information, organize meetings and rallies, foster issue awareness, recruit volunteers, raise money, and provide forums for candidates.

Given Maryland's well-established economic, cultural, and demographic diversity, an influential and competitive interest group system is no surprise. What has dramatically changed over the years are the sheer numbers and types of groups engaged in the political process. A well-established pluralism, complete with countervailing groups competing over public policy goals, has emerged.

Historically the Maryland governmental system began as a preserve of economic power and privilege. During the American Revolution Samuel Chase, a founding father, congressman, and power in the house of delegates, helped his speculator friends and himself with currency legislation.[8] Maryland shared with other states an internal improvements mania during the early decades of the 1800s. From 1826 through 1840 it seemed the general assembly never encountered a railroad or canal proposal that it didn't like and funded them through state bonds.[9]

As the state grew and the economy diversified, more interest groups came to the Annapolis table for preferments, programs, and other governmental goodies. Few were turned away. Bay watermen "exerted heavy influence in Annapolis," and the general assembly reserved Chesapeake oysters for Marylanders who could only work under sail. In 1868 they established the Oyster Police, a state navy, to enforce the regulations against oyster pirates who flaunted state law and marauding Virginians.[10]

Unions also developed early, with Baltimore "a hotbed of labor organization." But periodic depressions, the early use of the state militia, and a conspiracy law to end strikes inhibited the ability of labor groups to compete with business interests on an equal footing.[11] It was not until passage of the federal Wagner Act in 1935 that Maryland unions secured a semblance of parity in the interest group process and also gained strength in the state's wartime manufacturing economy. Maryland is now considered pro labor, with unions that are active and influential within the Democratic Party and the general assembly. State policies reflect union power, especially the concerns of government employee and service industry unions such as the American Federation of State, County and Municipal Employees and the Service Employees International Union. Collective bargaining rights were formally established for state public employees in 1997 with the assistance of the governor and legislators who had received their strong electoral support.

Maryland's African American communities have an exemplary and historic track record of collective action, as discussed in chapters 2 and 3. In the long drive for civil rights Baltimore's Juanita Jackson Mitchell, an attorney with the NAACP, and her husband, Clarence Mitchell Jr., the NAACP's chief lobbyist, played vital roles, along with future U.S. Supreme Court justice Thurgood Marshall. Maryland public schools were companion cases to *Brown v. Board of Education*. Maryland was the first state below the Mason-Dixon Line to integrate its public universities.[12] The national headquarters of the NAACP moved to Baltimore in the 1986, and the president of the organization from 1996 to 2004 was Kweisi Mfume, who represented the state's predominantly African American Seventh Congressional District for ten years before assuming leadership of the NAACP.

Exponential growth in the 1950s and 1960s increased Maryland's already considerable sensitivity to environmental concerns. Under the leadership of Governor Millard Tawes, newly created agencies such as the Department of Water Resources, the Air Pollution Control Council, and the Department of Chesapeake Bay Affairs moved Maryland to the forefront of states in environmental protection.[13] Such groups as the Chesapeake Bay Foundation, the Maryland League of Conservation Voters, Save Our Streams, 1000 Friends of Maryland, and numerous others have contributed a significant counterbalance to established commercial and development interests on a range of public policy issues.

Virtually every type of interest group is represented in Maryland. The most numerous are economic interests, such as the Maryland Jockey Club (Pimlico Race Track), the Maryland Chamber of Commerce, and banking, insurance, and utility corporations. Other categories include occupational and professional organizations, such as the Maryland State Education Association (formerly the Maryland State Teachers Association until 2008), unions, the Maryland State Medical Society, and the Maryland Association for Justice (formerly the Maryland Trial Lawyers' Association); sociocultural groups, such as the NAACP, Maryland Catholic Charities, and Maryland Jewish Alliance; public interest groups, such as Progressive Maryland, Common Cause Maryland, and Maryland Public Interest Research Group; environmental groups, such as the League of Conservation Voters and 1000 Friends of Maryland; and single-issue interest groups, such as Planned Parenthood and Marylanders Against Handgun Abuse (now CeaseFire, Maryland).

Especially active are interest groups with progressive agendas that are often aligned with Maryland Democratic public officials. These include labor, teachers, environmentalists, civil rights, gun control, and abortion rights organizations. While not among the largest spenders in the Annapolis lobbying game, these progressive organizations have maintained a high profile and influence using traditional and nontraditional tactics. Interest groups with a more conservative or a Republican agenda are fewer in number; these include the National Rifle Association, Maryland Business for Responsive Government, and the Maryland Taxpayers Association.

MARYLAND INTEREST GROUP PROLIFERATION

The number of interest groups engaged in the lobbying process has more than tripled since 1980, the first year registration was required with the Maryland State Ethics Commission. Initially 305 groups filed and provided employment for 298 specialists in legislative liaison. By 2007 1,410 interest groups were formally represented by 714 professional lobbyists. The sheer growth in groups reflects several factors.

First and foremost, the agenda of Maryland state government in programs and policies has expanded considerably over the past few decades. The state budget, an imperfect but significant measure, amply reflects this expansion. In 1980 the overall Maryland budget was approximately $6 billion. By fiscal year 2008 it stood at over $30 billion, an increase of 500 percent. With such budgetary increases, more issues and policies are in play and more groups have a stake in and are involved with the political process. Second, the increase in partisan competition, especially the reality of divided government following the 2002 gubernatorial election, increased the incentives for group formation and action, both for those with Republican priorities and those with progressive goals.[14] Third, the extensive effort to expand legalized gambling added complexity and heightened scrutiny to the lobbying environment in Annapolis. Given these elements, it is likely that the Ethics Commission lobby registration list will continue to grow.

In Maryland most lobbyists serve a single interest group; however, the obvious trend is toward more contract lobbyists who represent multiple clients. In the 2003 reporting cycle 138 of the lobbyists (19 percent) were registered with two or more organizations, and sixty-one provided lobbying representation for eight or more registered organizations. As an examination of the annual disclosure documents filed with the State Ethics Commission reveal, not only do the more notable contract lobbyists regularly represent more than one client, but major business interests often hire more than one lobbyist to advance and protect their interests in Annapolis.

Table 5-1: Number of registered interest groups and lobbyists

	Interest groups	Lobbyists
1980	305	298
1987	449	332
1997	865	581
2007	1,410	714

Source: Annual reports of the Maryland State Ethics Commission.

In 2007 there were 2,809 lobbying registrations filed with the state commission. The actual number of lobbyists active in the legislative process is somewhat understated because those representing governmental agencies at any level and advocates for the Maryland Association of Counties and the Maryland Municipal League are exempt from registration. Ronald C. Lippincott and Larry W. Thomas estimated that there were at least 150 lobbyists in 1987; 166 were listed in the 2007 annual report of the State Ethics Commission (see Table 5-1).[15]

As the sheer number of groups has grown, so have lobbying costs. In American politics at every level power follows money, and Maryland is no exception.[16] The initial lobbying expenditure reports to the Maryland State Ethics Commission totaled $2,864,454 in 1980. By the 2007 cycle expenditures had increased more than fourteen times, to $40,607,750. According to the National Center for Public Integrity, Maryland placed eleventh highest out of the forty-three states recording such data in 2006.[17]

The lion's share of lobbying spending goes to the advocates themselves. Lobbyist compensation ($33,813,737) accounted for fully 83 percent of the overall total. Of that, professional contract lobbyists constituted the heavily rewarded elite, with 14 percent of all lobbyists receiving $100,000 or more in compensation. The top ten advocates averaged $772,707 and accounted for 23 percent of all compensation. All of these were contract lobbyists.

In the 2007 reporting cycle two well-connected lobbying firms received over 13 percent of the total reported compensation: Alexander and Cleaver reported $3,279,084.27 and Rifkin, Livingston, Levitan and Silver reported $2,114,496.[18] Gary R. Alexander was the former speaker pro tem of the Maryland House of Delegates, representing Maryland's Twenty-seventh Legislative District, and he ran on legislative district tickets headed by the current president of the state senate, Thomas V. Mike Miller Jr. The firm's registered lobbyists include the former speaker of the House of Delegates, Cas Taylor. The Rifkin firm is headed by Alan M. Rifkin, who served as a top assistant to former governor William Donald Schaefer and to the former president of the state senate and Schaefer's lieutenant governor, Melvin A. Steinberg. Both Rifkin and Alexander have extensive contact networks within both houses of the Maryland General Assembly. Alexander was the top individual lobbyist for the 2007 reporting period, with $1,151,314.47 in compensation; second place, at $972,017, was held by Joel D. Rozner, a well-liked Prince George's County attorney who had served as chief of staff to Governor Glendening when he was Prince George's county executive.

In their 1987 study of lobbyists in Maryland, Lippincott and Thomas noted that wining and dining "has validity in Maryland."[19] This remains essentially true because expenses for gifts and entertainment ranked second ($2,093,255) in the 2007 annual Ethics Commission report.[20] This sum funded 101 events in which all members of the Maryland General Assembly were invited. In addition lobbyists hosted ninety-seven receptions for Maryland House of Delegates standing committees and eight-nine for state senate standing committees. County legislative delegations were also fêted; Montgomery delegates and senators were treated to twenty-two receptions, Baltimore County representatives to nineteen, and Baltimore City and Prince George's County to sixteen each.

Establishing social bonds with legislators, transforming professional relationships into personal ones in congenial settings, is a talent well funded and practiced in Maryland. Simply put, it pays long-term dividends. The former head of the Ethics Commission, John O'Donnell, observed, "Usually, if bills don't directly affect their constituents or attract undue attention, most lawmakers are ambivalent about them. If that's the case, they are more likely to vote based on their personal relationship with a lobbyist."[21] Although it is often claimed that the single most important resource lobbyists provide is information, research costs are decidedly low, coming in at $469,838 for the 2007 reporting period, or only slightly more than 1 percent of expenditures. Interest group expenditures for grassroots lobbying, advocacy letters and e-mails, publications, telephone call campaigns, and circulating petitions to influence officials totaled $877,720, or slightly over 2 percent of expenditures.

DOMINANT INTEREST GROUPS

Earlier studies of interest groups in Maryland identified bankers, industrialists, the AFL-CIO, the Classified Employees Association, and alcoholic beverage companies as particularly influential in Annapolis.[22] Lippincott and Thomas found that in the 1980s banking, finance, and insurance institutions spent the most in the lobbying process, followed by health groups, trade associations, building and construction companies, various business organizations, health-related professional and occupational groups, and utilities.[23] When Lippincott and Thomas supplemented actual interest group expenditures with a reputational analysis based on a survey of legislators and lobbyists, they found that the two most effective groups were banking, finance, and insurance companies and business associations. Legislators added local governments, citizens groups, and labor unions to their list and lobbyists added unions, local governments, and health organizations.[24]

The Maryland State Ethics Commission annually ranks interest groups by their reported expenditures; the top twenty in total expenditures for the ten-year period 1998–2007 illustrate the continued primacy of economic groups. Table 5-2 displays the rank for each interest group or organization and its total reported lobbying expenditures for this period. The top spending interest group, Laurel Racing Association, represented horse racing interests seeking expanded legalized gambling and reported $3,668,594 in lobbying expenditures during the decade. Among other groups seeking expanded gambling, the Maryland Jockey Club ranked fourth ($3,576,477) and Allegany Racing ranked twentieth ($1,524,810). Ranking second was the Maryland State Medical Society, with $3,624,259 in expenditures; four other medical and health care–related groups ranked in the top twenty. The Maryland Association of Realtors ranked third, with $3,619,772. Ranking seventh and ninth were the state's two major utility power companies, and three groups in the top twenty represented the telecommunications industry.

Interest group spending patterns strongly reflect the realities of established and proposed public policies impacting education, health care, telecommunications, utilities, and the legal environment of business. The persistent presence of health-related interest groups is entirely understandable, pragmatic, and necessary given the heavy state regulation and the emerging importance of the biotechnology industry to Maryland's economy. Issues in this area often require professional expertise, provided by the groups themselves.

While medical care and health groups have long been active in the state's interest group process, gaming and gambling groups are more recent major players. Faced with dwindling attendance at its racetracks and increased competition from "slots-enhanced" tracks in neighboring West Virginia and Delaware, the Maryland horse racing industry began a concerted drive to add slot machines in the 1990s. Revenue from the slots would be employed to bolster horse race purses. Bill Boniface, owner of Bonita Farm, explained the rationale: "The larger our purses, the bigger the fields. The bigger the fields, the larger the handle. The larger the handle, the big-

Table 5-2: Interest group top spenders, 1998–2007

Rank	Interest Group	Total Spending
1.	Laurel Racing Association, Inc	$3,668,594
2.	Med Chi, MD State Medical Society	$3,624,259
3.	Maryland Association of Realtors	$3,619,772
4.	Maryland Jockey Club/Pimlico Race Track	$3,576,477
5.	Maryland Retail Merchants Association	$3,497,027
6.	Maryland Hospital Association	$3,197,244
7.	BG&E/Constellation Energy	$3,078,459
8.	Care First, Blue Cross Blue Shield	$2,989,402
9.	Pepco (Potomac Electric Power Co.)	$2,962,609
10.	Maryland State Teachers Association	$2,665,812
11.	Verizon Maryland, Inc.	$2,658,389
12.	Maryland Chamber of Commerce	$2,397,827
13.	The Johns Hopkins Institutions	$2,344,916
14.	Cable Telecommunication Association	$2,182,673
15.	Maryland Bankers Association	$2,099,411
16.	Med Star Health	$1,856,034
17.	AT&T and AT&T Wireless	$1,679,074
18.	Maryland Trial Lawyers Association	$1,546,318
19.	Mirant Mid-Atlantic, LLC	$1,537,808
20.	Allegany Racing	$1,524,810

Source: Annual reports of the Maryland State Ethics Commission, 1998–2007.

ger our Fund. People will pay more for a Maryland-bred horse if it can earn more. If it can earn more, everyone wins."[25] Former governor Parris Glendening rejected racing's entreaties for expanded legalized gambling, but Governor Ehrlich made legalizing slot machines at Maryland racetracks a centerpiece issue of his legislative agenda. Reflecting this change in gubernatorial priorities, the top three heaviest spenders in the 2003 State Ethics Commission report represented gaming interests. Governor Ehrlich's slots proposals failed, but not for lack of lobbying by such groups as Centaur, a privately held casino company, Magna Entertainment, which purchased majority positions in Pimlico and Laurel racetracks, and the Maryland Jockey Club, which operates those same tracks.

The slots issue subsided as the 2006 elections approached because Governor O'Malley publicly supported slots at Maryland racetracks. Gambling interests became intensive again in the fall of 2007, when O'Malley proposed, and the general assembly approved, a constitutional amendment to permit slot machines at five designated locations; the proposal was ratified during the 2008 general election. The companies seeking expanded gambling reported nearly $1 million in lobbying expenditures in 2007 and contributed over $6 million to the successful ratification campaign in the 2008 general election.

THE LOBBYIST CORPS

Adding the registered lobbyists to their agency colleagues, close to a thousand people lobby each year in Annapolis. The established divide in the profession is between those who lobby exclusively for one organization, called in-house lobbyists, and the "hired guns," the contract lobbyists. When Lippincott and Thomas surveyed Maryland lobbyists in 1987 they found that most of their respondents were white (97 percent), male (77 percent), and well-educated (61 percent held a graduate or professional degree); most (72 percent) were in-house lobbyists serving a single organization. There were considerable differences between the in-house and contract advocates: 58 percent of the contract lobbyists were attorneys, compared to only 9 percent of the in-house specialists. Almost half (49 percent) of the contract specialists had experience in legislative or public administrative areas, but only 28 percent of the in-house lobbyists reported such backgrounds.[26]

In 2002 M. James Kaufman conducted a survey of 111 Maryland legislators and staff that further explored distinctions among lobbyists.[27] He examined attitudes toward contract lobbyists and the three varieties of in-house lobbyists, defined as follows:

1. *Contract Lobbyist*: a person, usually an attorney, who represents multiple organizations or clients with different interests. Often they are members of a legal firm that specializes in government relations. Such lobbyists would include Gary R. Alexander, Joel D. Rozner, D. Robert Enten, and Paul A. Tiburzi. Several prominent Maryland law firms have created lobbying practices utilizing attorneys and former legislators, such as former Baltimore City state senator American Joe Miedusiewski.

2. *Association Lobbyist*: someone who represents an association or professional organization of a unitary industry or union. Examples include the representatives of the Maryland Hospital Association, the Maryland Chamber of Commerce, and the Maryland State Education Association.

3. *Corporate Lobbyist*: an advocate who is directly employed by a corporate entity (profit or nonprofit) and solely represents that organiza-

tion. Maryland examples include Potomac Electric Power, Verizon, MedStar Health, and the Chesapeake Bay Foundation.

4. *Government Lobbyist*: a representative of a state or local government, an administrative agency or department, or an organization such as the Maryland Department of Transportation, the governor's office, or the University of Maryland System.

Overall Maryland legislators and their staffs judged contract lobbyists as the best able to help with the process of legislation, developing a strategy and lining up votes. They were also regarded as the least likely to provide high-quality and reliable information on the issues, including the potential costs of a particular bill. In the area of impartial expertise, association lobbyists scored highest, closely followed by government lobbyists. Contract lobbyists, distantly followed by corporate and association lobbyists, were viewed as the most likely sources of campaign and fund-raising assistance, although extensive activities in this area have been substantially reduced by ethics legislation enacted in 2001. Government lobbyists, further constrained by law, were seen as basically useless in this area. When legislators were asked which type of lobbyist they were most likely to interact with during any given week during the legislative session, both government and contract lobbyists scored high, placing one and two respectively. Association and corporate lobbyists are more likely to "parachute" into the general assembly when issues emerge that impact their ongoing interests.[28] This places them at something of a disadvantage in dealing with the networks of personal relationships that often typify the legislative process. Unlike contract specialists, corporate and association lobbyists must rely heavily on their organizational position to legitimate themselves to legislators and staff.

Ease of access to legislators was an attribute most frequently ascribed to contract lobbyists, followed by government, association, and then corporate lobbyists. The high profile of many contract lobbyists produces a reputation for influence and playing the lobbying game close to the edge. Seventy-four percent of the sample felt that a contract lobbyist would be the most likely to appear in a newspaper story detailing a lobbyist's influence, and 83 percent saw the same type most likely to be reported for a violation of the state's ethics code. Government lobbyists were the least likely in both categories (see Table 5-3).

Access to legislators is the cornerstone of successful lobbying advocacy. Without access, no lobbyist, regardless of how persuasive, could make much headway in the legislative process. Kaufman's respondents were

Table 5-3: Lobbyist strengths and weaknesses

Lobbying area	Contract lobbyist	Association lobbyist	Corporate lobbyist	Government lobbyist
Legislative strategy	First	Second	Third	Fourth
Reliable information	Fourth	First	Third	Second
Campaign help	First	Third	Second	Fourth
Weekly interactions	Second	Third	Fourth	First
Legislator access	First	Second	Third	Fourth
Perceived influence	First	Third	Second	Fourth
Perceived corruption	First	Third	Second	Fourth

Source: M. James Kaufman, unpublished manuscript, 2002.

asked to rank the factors that promoted accessibility to Maryland lawmakers. By an almost 2 to 1 margin, existing personal relationships outscored expertise on a particular issue as the most important lobbyist attribute, followed by the personal character of the lobbyist and knowledge of the legislative process. The ability to assist in fund-raising and a lobbyist's work style were rated least influential.

Maryland contract lobbyists certainly earned both accolades and approbation as the high-profile tribunes of the legislative advocacy profession. Their ranks confirm the traditional stereotype of the influence-peddling attorney whose political contacts and Annapolis experience count for more than policy expertise and a reputation for objectivity. If compensation is a defining judgment, the contract lobbyists rank very high indeed. They dominate the Ethics Commission compensation schedules year after year.

Lobbying fees are not the sole determinant of influence in Annapolis. Such legislative advocates as Dru Schmidt-Perkins of 1000 Friends of Maryland and Sean Dobson of Progressive Maryland have achieved consistent success in representing liberal and environmental interests. A master of grassroots organizing and lobbying for progressive causes is Vincent DeMarco. A graduate of Johns Hopkins University and Columbia Law School, DeMarco was instrumental in turning back the National Rifle Association forces in both the 1988 legislation and the referendum that prohibited Saturday Night Specials. For this effort the *Baltimore Sun* designated him Marylander of the Year in the 1988. DeMarco's record in the 1990s included lobbying victories with the 1996 Maryland Gun Violence Prevention Act, which limits gun purchases to one a month, and an increase in the state tobacco tax designed to discourage smoking. As the head of Maryland

Citizens' Health Initiative DeMarco worked to expand health care benefits to the state's uninsured.[29]

INTEREST GROUP INFLUENCE: SITUATIONAL PLURALISM

With Maryland's social and economic diversity, a strong governor system, centralized leadership in the general assembly, and a large and professionalized state bureaucracy, the ability of elected officials to adopt an independent broker role amid conflicting interest group demands is well developed. In the past state leaders have defied the powerful Maryland State Education Association to enact pension reform and opposed construction and development interests to protect sensitive environmental areas. Despite the insistent demands of the Maryland horse racing industry, a massive influx of gaming money, and Governor Ehrlich's strong backing, slot machine legislation failed passage repeatedly from 2003 through 2006.

It is clear that lobbyists and the interests groups they represent are influential and their influence is growing.[30] Certainly members of Maryland's legislature feel that interest groups play a significant role in the policymaking process. In their 1987 study Lippincott and Thomas confirmed the "legitimacy" of the interest group influence in Maryland policymaking. A survey of both legislators and lobbyists produced almost identical results when the samples were asked of the "importance" of groups in determining legislative decisions. Eighty-six percent of the legislators and 93 percent of the lobbyists surveyed rated interest group influence as either "important," "very important," or "crucial."[31] The more recent Kaufman study reinforced those findings. When the composite sample of legislators and staff was asked if "the General Assembly works more efficiently because of lobbyists' participation," a huge 88 percent majority said yes.[32] Thus Maryland lobbyists work within a generalized cocoon of supportive legislative attitudes. Through their innumerable receptions, lobbyists underwrite much of the social environment during the ninety-day general assembly session. Through their testimonies and handouts, they also provide much of the substantive arguments for or against pending legislation.

One of the most elusive questions in state and local government is how much specific influence interest groups possess. The political scientist Betty Zisk cautioned all who bemoaned the power of the lobby, "The actual impact of interest groups is more asserted than really measured or documented."[33] Alan Rosenthal of Rutgers University pointed out that modesty is not a common character trait among lobbyists; a reputation for influence, deserved or overblown, is a valuable commodity in any politicized process.[34] To assess the overall power of interest groups one must consider the particular context of the issue at hand. In short, pluralism in Maryland is situational.

Often in Maryland a competitive interest group system operates on a broad variety of issues, with countervailing powers clashing straight out of the pluralist playbook. Business and labor groups have long ranked high in lobbying effectiveness, and debates over prevailing wage and collective bargaining issues have both interests arguing at the policy table. On some Chesapeake Bay matters, most notably a decade-long moratorium on fishing rockfish, organized recreational anglers provided a persuasive counterweight to traditional waterman interests, which tend to view restrictive governmental regulation as enemy action. An even more telling case of situational pluralism is illustrated by the lengthy battle over slot machines. Despite spending an average $12,500 per legislator in lobbying costs in the 2004 session, the deep-pocketed gaming interests were stymied for the second consecutive year by a loose but committed coalition of anti-slots groups that spent only $53 per lawmaker.[35] These groups provided both moral and political support for House of Delegates Speaker Michael Busch and his allies in blocking Governor Ehrlich's legislation that had gathered state senate support.

While pluralism does typify the group process on a gamut of issues, there are policy domains where specific group preferences dominate. Lippincott and Thomas identify banks and insurance companies as exercising considerable power, and there are other examples, such as the Maryland Association for Justice (formerly Maryland Trial Lawyers Association), a dominant group in its area of interest.[36]

Generally, liberal and environmental organizations are most active and influential in the initiation of state public policy. They develop ideas, find legislative champions to sponsor their proposals, and help lobby them to passage. In the 2004 legislative session Progressive Maryland was the spark behind a "living wage" bill that gained general assembly approval before Governor Ehrlich's veto. Maryland business groups, usually operating in a pro-labor and regulatory political context, often find themselves working to defeat legislation that threatens their interests.

THE ROOTS OF MARYLAND CORRUPTION

From its origins as a colony, Maryland has been about money and the culture of making government and its decisions pay for private interests. Political favoritism, whether in actual policy, contracting, or regulatory preferments, was deeply established on a quid pro quo, cash-and-carry basis; it was the price of doing business with the state. For much of its history Maryland politics inevitably had a seamier side and often operated with what the former *Baltimore Sun* editor Bradford Jacobs called "cash-register ethics."[37] Machine politics was sporadically disturbed by reformers from the Progressive era on, but it was never fully exposed and controlled until the 1970s. With the Gorman-Rasin Ring, organized fraud and corruption were expected, but charges of corruption even reached Governor Ritchie.[38] H. L. Mencken, surprised by little in human nature, once remarked, "The worst government is the most moral. One composed of cynics is often very tolerant and humane."[39]

The free and easy tolerance of political malfeasance began to fade with the rapid expansion of the suburban middle class after World War II. The developing expectations of solid, efficient, and honest government provided reformers, or, as party regulars dismissed them, "shiny-brights," with a solid base of support. Charges of corruption, long ignored, resonated loudly, and what were once accepted and protected practices now became suspect and indictable. In addition U.S. attorneys were encouraged and empowered by attorneys general from Robert Kennedy on to investigate political corruption at the state level. In Maryland the results were astonishing. The historian George Callcott charted the indictments from 1962 through 1979 and marveled at the sheer volume: "Two successive governors, a United States Senator, two congressman, a Speaker of the House of Delegates, eight other members of the General Assembly, and fourteen major state and county officials were indicted. . . . The time and place coincided . . . to establish [in] Maryland the most remarkable record of proven scandal for any state in any period of American history."[40]

Though corrupt officials have hailed from almost every region of the state, several jurisdictions produced the lion's share. In Baltimore City and Anne Arundel County, Baltimore County, and Prince George's County, "the entrenched corruption was stronger than the reformers," and practices of the Gorman-Rasin era remained operative.[41] Old school Maryland politicians, regardless of party, were prone to act as individual corrupt entrepreneurs, seizing opportunities for graft as they were presented. Those exposed by the ongoing investigations resigned, were fined, were imprisoned, or, in the sad case of Republican Eastern Shore congressman William O. Mills, committed suicide before trial. With the exception of Governor Marvin Mandel's nearly half a million in boodle, Maryland politicians came relatively cheap. U.S. Senator Daniel B. Brewster was indicted in 1975 on a $4,500 bribery charge, and Baltimore County executive Dale Anderson was convicted for accepting $38,000 in bribes.[42] For a time Maryland achieved the type of national recognition no state seeks. A national humor magazine sarcastically devised a state logo, "Cradle of Corruption," for a mock Maryland automobile license plate.[43] At football games between the University of Maryland and the University of Virginia in the 1970s "the Virginia student band had fun by announcing as a special guest 'the governor of Maryland,' whereupon a student dressed in a striped convict's suit ran onto the field."[44]

A TALE OF THREE GOVERNORS

The historian Robert Brugger identified 1973 as the pivotal year in the annals of Maryland political corruption. For a score of Maryland elected officials, from governor on down, "nothing sordid seemed impossible."[45] Drug dealing and carnal bribery now joined the list of corrupt practices that included the more mundane sins of tax evasion, unreported campaign contributions, and traditional bribery.

U.S. Attorney George Beall and his assistants uncovered a web of public works perversions extending from the administration of Democratic Baltimore County executive Dale Anderson to his immediate predecessor. Former governor Spiro Agnew, then Richard Nixon's vice president, was ultimately netted in a federal probe of kickbacks and bribery in Baltimore County local government. Agnew, whose newfound national standing afforded him scant protection from the widening probe, had been a ready and willing accomplice to the established traditions of corrupt governance.[46] In Baltimore County payoffs from contractors were a simple and self-explanatory perk of the system, similar to letterheads and secretaries. In October 1973, as part of his deal with the U.S. Department of Justice, Agnew resigned as vice president and pleaded nolo contendere (no contest) to a single charge of income tax evasion. Despite his self-serving statement that his actions were "part of a long-established pattern of political fund-raising in the State," his illicit actions had little to do with political campaigns and much to do with personal enrichment.[47]

The high-profile plummet of Agnew was a lesson that "went untaught, unlearned" by his successor, Governor Marvin Mandel.[48] In the summer of 1973 Mandel announced the end of his marriage to his wife, Barbara, his high school sweetheart and life partner for thirty-two years. She learned of his decision from local television news accounts. His divorce and subsequent remarriage made Mandel's case more complex and rooted in alpha male needs and the imperatives of midlife crisis than simple monetary avarice. Mandel was a product of Jack Pollack, an old-style urban boss, and his northwest Baltimore City political organization, the Trenton Democratic Club. Mandel, accustomed to backroom dealings, had a favorite expression: "We can work something out." His skills in the political arts helped propel him from the Democratic State Central Committee to the House of Delegates, the speakership of that body, and ultimately the governorship when Agnew resigned. Mandel continued to dominate the political and legislative process, but the gubernatorial salary of $25,000 fell far short of his needs.

This became glaringly apparent once Barbara Mandel, "Bootsie" to her friends and close associates, fixed a high price for the governor's freedom. She refused to move from Government House, the governor's official residence, for almost six months, relegating the governor to embarrassing and temporary quarters in a sublet apartment as he watched his 1974 reelection draw near. With lawyers' fees the ultimate divorce settlement cost Mandel over $400,000, a sum strikingly close to the accumulated bribes he stood convicted of in 1977.

As Bradford Jacobs, author of the definitive *Thimbleriggers: The Law v. Governor Marvin Mandel*, cautions, this was "only a part of the truth."[49] Mandel had long benefited from a close personal relationship with a group of businessmen and lawyers who owned Tidewater Insurance, a performance bonding company. Together they organized fund-raisers for the governor, solicited campaign contributions, and provided him with several lucrative money trees long before his marital problems became public. One was an estimated $300,000 interest in Security Investment that held the lease for the sprawling U.S. Social Security complex just west of Baltimore City in Woodlawn, Baltimore County. Another was Ray's Point Farm in Talbot County on the Eastern Shore, real estate valued at $350,000; the governor received a 15 percent interest in that for the paltry sum of $150.[50]

The crucial question was, what quid did Governor Mandel provide for the apparent quo of his cronies? According to federal prosecutors, Mandel applied his political powers to substantially expand the racing days for Marlboro Race Track, secretly owned by the governor's allies. In 1977 a federal jury agreed and convicted Mandel and five associates of mail fraud and racketeering. Ultimately the governor served nineteen months in federal prison before his conviction was overturned in 1987 by U.S. District Court Judge Frederick Smalkin following a U.S. Supreme Court decision that the federal mail fraud statute did not apply to the intangible right to honest and impartial state government.[51]

The 1978 Maryland gubernatorial election was won by Harry Roe Hughes, a former Eastern Shore attorney and state senator and the first state secretary of transportation. Three months before Mandel's conviction Hughes resigned from his cabinet post charging favoritism in awarding the Baltimore subway construction contract. With crucial support from the *Baltimore Sun* that ran front-page endorsements for his reformist candidacy in the closely contested, multicandidate Democratic primary, Hughes upset Lieutenant Governor Blair Lee III, who had served as acting governor for nineteen months during Mandel's legal struggles. Hughes then steamrolled former Republican U.S. senator J. Glenn Beall by a historic 425,000-vote margin. In his inaugural address Governor Hughes noted, "The people of Maryland have had enough political manipulation . . . scandal, shock, and shame." He pledged to be "an example of moral conduct which is beyond reproach" and that "the highest standard of ethical conduct will begin with the Governor and permeate throughout the state service."[52] He was true to his word. Ethics legislation, often mired in the legislature during the Mandel years, poured out of the general assembly. Stricter financial disclosure requirements, lobbyist registration and compensation disclosure, tightened procurement procedures, open meeting requirements, a ban on Election Day "walking around" money all passed. Most important, a state ethics commission was established in 1979 to interpret and enforce public ethics laws.

STATE AND LOCAL ETHICS INSTITUTIONS

At the state level, in addition to the State Ethics Commission, there are three other institutions that guard against corruption and official malfeasance, one for the entire government system, one for the state judiciary, and one for the general assembly. These mandates have produced a multilayered system of ethics watchdog agencies that are both broad and deep.

The Ethics Commission administers an extensive financial disclosure program for public officials, with more than 9,000 individuals filing reports. Commission staff also monitor the disclosure forms for potential or real conflicts of interest. Other duties include lobbyist registration, receiving compensation and expenditure reports for lobbyists and interest groups, issuing lobbyist conduct guidelines, lobbyist and general ethics training programs, and issuing advisory opinions on questions concerning the public ethics laws. In addition the commission reviews and formally approves the public ethics codes of counties, incorporated municipalities, and local school boards, which they are required by law to develop and administer.

Established by constitutional amendment in 1976, the office of state prosecutor investigates violations of election law, ethics, bribery, and other forms of official misconduct in all agencies of Maryland state and local government. The state prosecutor may undertake investigations on his or her own initiative or by request of the governor, the attorney general, the general assembly, the State Ethics Commission, or a local state's attorney. The state prosecutor has brought and won convictions against campaign contributors, candidates, and voters as well as public officials.

The Maryland Commission on Judicial Disabilities, created in 1966 by constitutional amendment, serves as the investigative arm of the Maryland Court of Appeals, the state's highest court, to monitor the conduct of judges. The commission is empowered to examine complaints made by parties to cases, attorneys, or the public against any Maryland state judge. The seven-member commission is authorized to hold complaint hearings and offer recommendations to the Maryland Court of Appeals if there is a finding for judicial retirement, removal, censure, or reprimand. The number of complaints averaged 120 a year between fiscal years 2000 and 2008.

The state legislative watchdog unit is the Joint Committee on Legislative Ethics, which was established by statute in 1972.[53] The twelve-member body is bipartisan and composed of six members of the state senate and six from the house of delegates. It is charged with the responsibilities of developing and administering rules pertaining to legislative conflicts of interests. The committee is authorized to hold hearings on violations and issue, if the case so warrants, an official reprimand. As part of its internal reform in 1999 the general assembly created a full-time ethics counsel with whom each member of the general assembly is required to meet at least once a year. At the local level there are more than 130 ethics panels for the twenty-four Maryland subdivisions and their school boards, eighty-three municipalities, and three multicounty agencies.[54] Despite these institutional commitments to ethics in government at the state and local level, corruption in Maryland politics continues to persist and cases remain pending.

A CULTURE OF CORRUPTION?

Since the wave of guilty verdicts during the 1960s and 1970s, high-profile instances of political corruption in Maryland have subsided, but cases have scarcely disappeared. State Senator Tommie Broadwater of Prince George's County lost his seat in 1984 after a conviction for food stamp fraud. After regaining his right to vote, he lost three primary election political comebacks for the state senate. In 1998 Baltimore City's Larry Young was the first state senator in Maryland history to be expelled from the legislature, although he was subsequently found not guilty of charges of extortion and bribery by a jury in the Anne Arundel County Circuit Court. Another Baltimore City state senator, Clarence Mitchell IV, was reprimanded in 2002 for conflict of interest when he concealed a $10,000 loan from several parties involved in pending legislation. Mitchell was defeated in his 2002 re-election bid. In 2007 former state senator Tommy Bromwell of Baltimore County was sentenced to seven years in the federal penitentiary for an elaborate scheme in which he received home improvements and money through a "no show" job for his wife from a prominent contractor company that did business with the state.[55] In early 2010, Baltimore City Mayor Sheila Dixon resigned in the aftermath of a guilty verdict in a state prosecution involving gifts from developers and misappropriation and on May 17, 2011, former Prince George's County Executive Jack Johnson pled guilty in U.S. District Court to corruption and bribery charges.[56]

Over the past decade two of the most notorious and publicized cases did not involve elected official, but rather two of Maryland's best-paid contract lobbyists. Bruce C. Bereano began his Annapolis career as a legislative aide and became the veritable king of the lobbyist clan during the 1980s and early 1990s. Bereano's approach combined high volume with high fees and a driven energy to push lobbying regulations to their breaking point. He represented dozens of clients during a legislative session, deluged legislators and their staffs with presents and gifts, and with a demonstrated mastery of the legislative process more often than not he won. His yearly reported lobbying compensation often topped $1 million. Then, in 1994, Bereano was charged and convicted of mail fraud for a complicated scheme of laundering illegal campaign contributions, masking them as lobbying expenses. Lobbying to the last, Bereano orchestrated a letter-writing campaign to sentencing judge William Nickerson that included a thick volume of pleas and testaments to Bereano's character from clients, friends, former judges, legislative leaders, and former governor William Donald Schaefer.[57] Bereano appealed the federal verdict, and the government appealed the sentence. His conviction was affirmed, and upon resentencing ordered by the Fourth Circuit U.S. Court of Appeals, he ultimately served five months of work release in a halfway house and five months of home detention.[58] Adding sanction onto penalty, the Maryland Court of Appeals ordered him disbarred in 2000.[59] Curiously Bereano has retained many clients and continues to rank among the best-paid Annapolis lobbyists.

The case that produced a defining phrase that continues to resonate in Maryland politics was not Bereano's. With earnings of $1,164,719 in 1999, Gerald E. Evans reached the pinnacle of compensated Annapolis lobbyists. In 2000 Evans was indicted and convicted of mail fraud, involving a supposed "bell-ringer" bill that would have generated financial losses for some of his clients if introduced and enacted. At his sentencing U.S. District

Court Judge J. Frederick Motz castigated not only Evans but the general assembly and state as well: "He took advantage of a culture of corruption that has been tolerated by lobbyists, legislators and the citizens of Maryland. . . . The evidence in this case has revealed there is a mess in Annapolis."[60] Perhaps surprising to some, but not to experienced observers of the state legislative process, four years after his release from the federal penitentiary Evans reported $631,000 in lobbying fees on his 2007 annual disclosure forms filed with the state ethics commission.

Stung by the criticism that received wide play throughout the Maryland media, the general assembly responded with a series of reforms in its 1999 and 2001 sessions that were intended to provide guidance for legislators and to constrain such lobbying practices as gift-giving, wining and dining, and campaign fund-raising as well as provide for training and potential sanctions for lobbyists.[61] Lobbyist-sponsored meals and receptions must be limited to "qualified legislative units." One-on-one and small group socializing paid by lobbyists is prohibited; if lobbyists wish to entertain, they must invite either the entire membership of the general assembly, the entire membership of either house, all members of a standing committee, or the whole membership of a county or a regional delegation. Written invitations are mandatory, together with an invitation disclosure form. After the event an expenditure disclosure form is required by the State Ethics Commission. Fund-raising limitations include prohibitions on lobbyists soliciting contributions, serving on fund-raising committees or as a treasurer for a candidate, establishing a political committee, and even forwarding tickets to a political fund-raiser to potential contributors. In addition the general assembly authorized the State Ethics Commission to revoke or suspend lobbyists' registrations for cause.

The commission rescinded Evans's registration in 2002, after he had served two and half years for mail fraud, and in 2003 Bereano's lobbying registration was suspended for ten months. The complaint against Bereano was based on an alleged 2001 contingency contract with Social Work Associates that paid the lobbyist 1 percent for state business that he personally secured for the company. Lobbying contingency fees had been prohibited by the general assembly since the Hughes-era reforms of 1979, and the ban was extended to state procurement in 1994. Evans successfully had his suspension voided by the Maryland Court of Appeals based on the retroactive application of the 2001 law changes to his case.[62] Bereano also sought judicial relief, but the state's highest court ultimately affirmed his suspension, notwithstanding another barrage of supportive letters from prominent Maryland politicians.[63] The augmented power of the State Ethics Commission to discipline lobbyists by withholding registration may well have a long-term deterrent effect, changing the game in Annapolis. Restrictions on wining and dining have hardly hobbled the lobbyist corps. Spending on entertainment took a small dip in the year immediately following the reforms and then escalated, leading the *Baltimore Sun* reporters Jeff Barker and Michael Dresser to note, "The figures suggest that legislators aren't eating less food, they're just doing it in the company of more people."[64]

In the 2002 Maryland gubernatorial election Republican candidate Ehrlich hammered the "culture of corruption" theme in attack media ads and campaign rhetoric, arguing that thirty-three years of uninterrupted Democratic dominance in Annapolis had permitted malfeasance and illegalities to flourish unchecked and unpunished. Democrats questioned Ehrlich's reform commitment and credentials, and two initial appointments rekindled criticism. First, Governor Ehrlich named former governor Marvin Mandel, a keystone of sordid state corruption in the 1970s, to the Board of Regents of the University of Maryland System and to chair a commission on governmental reorganization.[65] The governor also tapped the recently censured state senator Clarence Mitchell IV (who was defeated in a Democratic primary and endorsed Ehrlich for governor) to a newly created post as director of the Office of Urban Development, with a $92,000 annual salary. The Mitchell appointment encountered a firestorm of media and public criticism, and the former state senator relinquished his post within a week.[66] Although Ehrlich issued a revised state ethics executive order, no significant reform legislation was included in his legislative packages during his administration.

There was no reprise of "culture of corruption" in the 2006 and 2010 campaigns as both Ehrlich and O'Malley concentrated on other issues. The O'Malley victories neither validated nor vindicated the reform ethic. Future reform initiatives will probably emerge from three sources: legislators from reform-oriented districts, public interest groups such as Progressive Maryland and the Maryland branch of Common Cause, or future high-profile scandals.

SUMMARY

Within a highly pragmatic political system expectations of a corruption-free political zone are naïve at best. When resolving legislative issues means multiple millions to interest groups in costs or gains, they will spend millions in pursuit of such tangible goals. Maryland has created an extensive network of lobbying controls and restrictions. In the institution of the Maryland State Ethics Commission and Maryland state prosecutor there is a legitimate and respected enforcement mechanism. Corruption in Maryland politics has certainly diminished since the 1960s and 1970s, twin decades of relative statewide sham. But corruption will undoubtedly and unfortunately persist in new forms and venues, despite the proliferation of ethics panels, ever widening disclosure requirements, and lobbying reforms, for money will almost always find a way. Undoubtedly H. L. Mencken would feel vindicated.

CHAPTER SIX

The Maryland Constitution

We remain convinced that victory in Maryland could have been the
most significant advance in state government and in the federal
system in a decade.

John P. Wheeler Jr., on the 1968 Constitutional Convention

Drafting and securing the passage of a state constitution requires considerable political acumen and timing. Constitutions not only represent the
ideals and aspirations of a civil society, but also reflect the division and
delicate balancing of economic, social, and political power. Maryland has
operated under four constitutional schemes, adopted respectively in 1776,
1851, 1864, and 1867. Each tackled the fundamental issues of suffrage, the
allocation of representation in the legislature, the balance of power among
the branches and levels of government, and the relationship of the citizen
to his or her government in the context of the social, economic, cultural,
and political pressures of their respective eras. Maryland's political culture,
diversity, and essential political dynamics can be understood more fully by
examining the evolution of its Declaration of Rights and Constitution and
Form of Government.

The Maryland Constitution reflects the union of the two American constitutional traditions: a Whig "political covenant" of governance by the
consent of the people and a strong Federalist governmental structure with
a concurrent statement of enforceable individual rights. The state's basic
governing documents are also a mixture of the "commonwealth pattern"
and "commercial republic" pattern of state constitutions.[1] This is most dramatically manifested by a separate Declaration of Rights, which spells out
the longest list of specific and enumerated individual rights among all the

state constitutions. A separate Constitution and Form of Government details the authority, limitations, and structure of state and local government.

The present constitution, ratified by Maryland voters on September 18, 1867, is the twelfth oldest among the fifty states. As amended after the 2010 general election, it ranks twelfth longest among state constitutions, with more than 44,000 words. The Declaration of Rights, which precedes the constitution, contains forty-six articles.[2] It guarantees individual rights and outlines the relationship between the people and Maryland state government. The Declaration of Rights also provides express direction for and imposes prohibitions on the three branches of government. The Maryland Constitution contains twenty-eight articles,[3] which set forth the qualifications for voting and provide for the elections of and specify the duties and responsibilities of the executive, legislative, and judicial branches of government and other public offices. The articles also include provisions for public education, the militia and military affairs, the governance of Baltimore City, municipal and county government, public works, the formation of new counties, referendums on legislative actions, and making amendments to the state constitution. A new article, "Video Lottery Terminals," was added in 2008 following voter approval of an amendment authorizing video lottery terminals at five specified locations.[4]

HISTORICAL BEGINNINGS

The transformation of Maryland from an English colony to an independent state had its origin in the difficult economic times of the mid-eighteenth century. This was coupled with increasing frustration with various taxes imposed by the colonial British rulers and the overriding of actions taken by the provincial house of delegates.[5] Businessmen, landowners, and political leaders in Maryland, including the state's signers of the Declaration of Independence (Charles Carroll of Carrollton, Samuel Chase, William Paca, and Thomas Stone), participated actively in the events that produced the American Revolution. Like their counterparts in other parts of colonial America, they initiated a committee of correspondence, held meetings of a provincial convention, created a council of safety to manage the affairs of the nascent independent government, and sent representatives to the revolutionary Continental Congresses.

Responding to the request of the Second Continental Congress made on May 15, 1776, Maryland's revolutionary-era leaders began the process of drafting new governance documents for the soon to be declared independent state. Within the relatively compact time frame of less than six months, Marylanders saw their government formally changed to a constitutional republic. The series of political events was breathtaking, especially by modern standards.

On June 28, 1776, the Maryland Provincial Convention voted to instruct its delegates to the Second Continental Congress to join in the national declaration of independence. On July 6, 1776, the Provincial Convention adopted its own Maryland Declaration of Independence.[6] The Provincial Convention also declared itself prospectively dissolved effective upon the election on August 1, 1776, of seventy-six delegates to a constitutional convention created for the purpose of establishing a new form of government. The Maryland Constitutional Convention held its first meeting in Annapolis on August 14, and on August 17 a committee was designated "to prepare a declaration and charter of rights and a form of government."[7] On September 17 the convention ordered that a draft Declaration of Rights and Constitution be published and circulated in every county for public comment. The delegates met regularly during the early fall, engaging in occasional vigorous debate, especially over the question of property qualifications for voting and holding office.[8] The delegates completed their work with passage of a declaration of rights on November 3, the passage of the constitution on November 8, and the formal adoption of both governing documents for the new state of Maryland on November 10.

Section 61 of the constitution established equally rapid timelines for the formation of the new state government. Electors to choose the state senate were elected by qualified voters in the counties on November 25, 1776, and met on December 9 in Annapolis to select the first state senators. The initial members of the house of delegates and county sheriffs were elected on December 18. The first session of the legislature was held on February 10, 1777, and the selection of the first governor, Thomas Johnson, was made on March 21.

THE CONSTITUTION OF 1776

This remarkable, though imperfect document articulated the important basic concepts underlying the American Revolution, including the precepts that the source of governing power is the consent of the governed people; that there should be a separation of powers between the legislative, judicial, and executive branches; and that various checks and balances should exist among the parts of government. Maryland's constitutional drafters presented the convention delegates with a Declaration of Rights containing forty-two articles and a Constitution and Form of Government document containing sixty-one sections. The drafters of the first Maryland Constitution had all been active in the American Revolution.[9] Three were signers of the Declaration of Independence and five served as Maryland's delegates to the Second Continental Congress.

All of the drafters were representative of the mercantile and propertied elite. Not surprisingly they proposed maintaining the property qualifications for voting that existed during the previous colonial proprietary government. They also provided for stringent property qualifications for holding public office. To be a member of the house of delegates an individual needed to own real or personal property valued in excess of 500 pounds; a member of the state senate and a county sheriff needed to own 1,000 pounds; and the governor needed to own 5,000 pounds, including real property valued at least 1,000 pounds. The state's first constitution abolished the eighty-four-year-old prohibition on Catholics holding public office that had been first imposed in 1692, after the king of England broke with the Roman Catholic Church. Article 35 of the 1776 Declaration of Rights did require officeholders to express "a declaration of belief in the Christian religion," although Quakers, Dunkers, and Mennonites were permitted to take an alternative oath.

The framers of Maryland's initial state government were aware of practical and political necessities. Foremost among these was the recognition of the county's role in the administration of government and of the land division created by the Chesapeake Bay. Counties were recognized as the basis for representation in the house of delegates and as important for providing government services. Nineteen of Maryland's twenty-three counties existed at the time of the adoption of the 1776 constitution. The physical division between the Eastern Shore and the Western Shore was reflected in the distribution of state senators, the provisions for separate treasurers and registers of land offices on each shore, and a mandate for holding sessions of the general court on both sides of the Chesapeake Bay.

Maryland's first constitution contained a unique composition of the state legislature. Since 1650 the colonial general assembly had been a bicameral legislative body with a county-apportioned lower chamber, and that form was preserved. The lower house of delegates was to be elected every year, with four representatives from each of the then nineteen counties. In addition voters in Baltimore Town and Annapolis were each granted the right to elect two delegates. The upper chamber, designated as a senate to replace the previous proprietary council, had its forty members selected by electors, with each county electing two senatorial electors and Baltimore Town and Annapolis one each. These electors then met to choose fifteen "men of most wisdom, experience and virtue" to serve in the state senate.[10] Of the state senators, who could be chosen from among the electors or the public, nine were required to be residents of the Western Shore and six were to be residents of the Eastern Shore, a proportion roughly equal to the respective populations of the regions at that time. This use of an electoral college became a model for the selection of the president under the Constitution of the United States drafted eleven years later, in 1787.[11]

Mindful of the experiences of governance under the rule of English monarchs and proprietary governors, the legislature was definitively made the preeminent branch of government under the 1776 constitution. The legislature not only selected the governor but also limited the state's chief executive through a governor's council, consisting of fifteen members of the legislature, who had advice and consent power over the appointments and actions of the governor.

An amendment process to accommodate future government and social needs was included in the 1776 constitution. If a proposed constitutional amendment was passed by each chamber of the general assembly in one session, that amendment, in order to be effective, had to be ratified by the general assembly at the first session after an election for new members of the house of delegates.[12] The annually shifting political composition of the general assembly, and especially the disproportionate political results spawned by the method of selecting state senators, made significant changes difficult to achieve.

The 1776 constitution was amended sixty-six times before it was replaced seventy-five years later. Over half of the amendments (thirty-five) merely dealt with the arrangement of election districts within the various counties. The more noteworthy amendments made during its three-quarter-century life span included the relaxation of religious oath requirements for holding office, the elimination of property requirements for suffrage, the grant of additional delegates for a rapidly growing Baltimore City, and provisions for the direct election of the governor and the state senate.

The rigorous property requirements for voting in 1776, and the existence of a substantial slave population, meant that only approximately 20,000 Marylanders out of over 300,000 were eligible to participate in elections. Even fewer individuals were able to meet the higher property qualifications for holding public office. Attacks on these onerous limits intensified with a growing, diverse population and a changing economy.[13]

The more conservative Federalists lost control of both houses of the general assembly in 1801 to Jeffersonian reformers, paving the way for amendments abolishing the property qualifications for voting in state elections in 1802 and in federal elections in 1810.[14] Property qualifications for holding appointed and elected office were abolished in 1810. A new basis of discrimination was, however, concurrently imposed with the insertion of the word "white" in section 2 of the 1776 constitution between the words "free" and "male." Free blacks who owned sufficient property to qualify for voting and holding office were thus disenfranchised.

The clamor for a more representative state legislature and a more responsive governor persisted and was emboldened by the development of political parties and the Jacksonian reform movement. The final catalyst for change arrived with the state legislative elections in 1836.[15] Twenty-one Whig and nineteen Democratic electors for the state senate were chosen. Because the constitution required a quorum of twenty-four electors to choose a state senate, the Democratic electors refused to meet unless their demands for reform were satisfied. The recalcitrant electors were not wholly successful after holding out for nearly two and half months; the result was voter backlash and an overwhelming Whig legislature. But the boycott did result in agreements with Whig legislators to introduce constitutional amendments in the following session of the general assembly.[16] Among the reforms was the lengthy amendment providing for the direct election of the governor and of one state senator from each county (and Baltimore City), commencing in 1838. A new county, Carroll County, was formed out of parts of Baltimore and Frederick counties as part of the bargaining.

The electoral independence of the governor would prove critical to the administrative development of Maryland state government and to the evolution of state political dynamics. The allocation of state senate seats tied to county boundary lines rather than a population formula had political and policy ramifications that were undone only 128 years later by the reapportionment decisions of the U.S. Supreme Court in 1964 that included a challenge to Maryland's legislative body.[17]

THE CONSTITUTION OF 1851

The push for reform and greater democratization of government was not quelled despite the 1838 amendments to the 1776 constitution. During the 1840s Maryland experienced its largest population growth in the nineteenth century (over 24 percent), with large influxes of European immigrants. This wave of new residents coupled with economic difficulties added fuel to the demand for another change. Interest on the state bonds issued to pay for the legislature's direct investment in infrastructure improvements were not paid from 1841 through 1846. The election of a reform Democratic governor, Philip Thomas, in 1847, followed by changes in the partisan composition of the legislature in 1849, led to the passage of a resolution during the 1850 session of the general assembly providing for a special election on whether to call a constitutional convention. Critical to its passage was a limitation that the convention not disturb the existing master-slave relationship and the institution of slavery.

On May 8, 1850, the Maryland electorate overwhelmingly voted in favor of a constitutional convention, 83 to 17 percent, with only three Southern Maryland counties and one Eastern Shore county in opposition. The expectations of reform would be somewhat dampened by the election of a modest majority of Whig convention delegates. After six months of protracted discussion the convention adjourned on May 13, 1851, with a proposed new constitution that was quickly approved at an election held on June 4. Baltimore City and thirteen out of twenty counties favored the new constitution, which received 29,024 votes for and 18,616 against. Revealing regional, economic, and social differences, the new constitution was opposed by Kent and Somerset counties on the Eastern Shore, the three Southern Maryland counties, and Montgomery, Prince George's, and Allegany County on the Western Shore (see Table 6-1).

The 1851 constitution, made symbolically effective on July 4, contained forty-three articles in the declaration of rights, varying modestly from the 1776 provisions. The form of the constitution was restructured from sections to articles. The term of office for the governor was extended from three to four years, with the required rotation of the governor from among three geographic districts maintained.

The general assembly was enlarged by the creation of a new county (Howard County) out of the northern portion of Anne Arundel County, and Baltimore City was separated from Baltimore County in the body of the constitution. Each county and Baltimore City retained its single state senator, as established in 1838. The term of office for state senators was reduced from six years to four, and half of the senate were to be elected every two years. The house of delegates was apportioned with a minimum of two delegates and a maximum of four elected to two-year terms from each county based on population thresholds. Baltimore City was allocated four additional delegates, for a total of eight delegates.

The most politically significant achievement of the 1851 constitution was the creation of additional statewide and local public offices elected by a popular vote. The new constitution provided for the statewide election of a comptroller, a commissioner of land office, and four commissioners of public works, with four-year terms intended to ensure that the state

Table 6-1: Ratification votes on Maryland's constitutions

Subdivision	1851 For	1851 Against	1864 For	1864 Against	1867 For	1867 Against	1968 For	1968 Against
Allegany	948	1,113	1,839	964	2,059	1,779	3,732	12,531
Anne Arundel	1,333	703	281	1,360	1,282	199	15,880	31,033
Baltimore City	9,416	5,830	9,779	2,053	16,120	5,627	72,482	84,822
Baltimore	2,122	849	2,001	1,869	3,285	1,532	44,576	88,524
Calvert	174	333	57	634	348	153	1,153	2,001
Caroline	372	340	471	423	832	328	812	2,388
Carroll	1,473	1,094	1,587	1,690	2,187	1,920	2,855	9,124
Cecil	1,378	638	1,611	1,611	1,771	1,214	1,326	6,511
Charles	160	427	13	978	789	17	1,861	4,426
Dorchester	511	488	449	1,486	1,385	362	1,290	4,400
Frederick	3,179	943	2,908	1,916	3,397	3,028	3,984	10,148
Garrett	nf	nf	nf	nf	nf	nf	937	2,447
Harford	1,135	875	1,083	1,671	1,879	749	6,167	10,475
Howard	nf	nf	462	583	728	368	4,205	5,794
Kent	384	443	289	1,246	1,010	146	489	2,864
Montgomery	569	717	422	1,367	913	654	64,097	26,290
Prince George's	207	656	149	1,293	981	150	44,344	28,011
Queen Anne's	627	517	220	1,577	1,214	176	913	2,972
St. Mary's	165	533	99	1,078	746	119	2,073	3,066
Somerset	592	633	464	2,066	1,257	1,042	1,044	3,552
Talbot	618	340	430	1,020	1,075	255	1,735	3,651
Washington	2,913	688	2,441	985	2,658	2,527	4,121	12,317
Wicomico	nf	nf	nf	nf	nf	nf	2,939	6,861
Worcester	749	456	486	1,666	1,236	680	1,018	2,893
(subtotal)			27,541	29,536				
(soldier's)			2,633	263				
Total	29,025	18,616	30,174	29,799	47,152	23,036	284,033	367,101

Source: Prepared by John T. Willis from county and state election returns maintained by the Maryland State Archives.
Note: Shaded areas represent those years in which the majority vote in a jurisdiction was against ratification of the proposed constitution. The hash marks signify a tie vote in the county. "nf" means county not formed.

would not make unsound investments. The democratization of politics at the county level was firmly rooted with provisions for electing numerous public officials, including judges and justices of the peace, clerks of court, sheriffs and constables, registers of wills, state's attorneys, surveyors and road supervisors, and county commissioners (formerly called levy courts). Baltimore City was recognized in the 1851 constitution as an independent municipality, separate and apart from any county government, and granted the right to elect all of its own local public officials. Maryland had participated in the rise of political parties, and the extension of popular elections to county offices fostered, strengthened, and cemented partisan political party activity as part of the state's political culture and dynamics.

Drafted at the end of the Jacksonian reform movement, which democratized politics, and at the beginning of a tumultuous and bloody period in state politics, the 1851 constitution made strides in the state's ability to govern a more complex society. But the failure to deal with the slavery question mirrored the lack of a national solution and led to the constitution's becoming a documentary casualty of the Civil War.

THE CONSTITUTION OF 1864

The outbreak of the Civil War released enormous social, economic, and political tensions in Maryland and produced a series of events that culminated in a new state constitution that abolished slavery. Maryland's stormy politics preceding the Civil War yielded to pragmatism with the central theme of "Union" binding a clear majority of Marylanders and political leaders across a broad spectrum of ideology and interests. Governor Thomas Holliday Hicks, a slaveholder from Dorchester County on the Eastern Shore elected in 1857 as the nominee of the American Know Nothing Party, acted prudently and deftly in keeping the state legislature from passing a secession resolution.[18] Governor Augustus W. Bradford, elected in November 1861 as the candidate of the hastily formed Union Party, changed position on the slavery issue in less than a year, from outright opposition to Lincoln's 1862 Emancipation Proclamation to supporting the abolition of slavery without state compensation.

In the election held on November 4, 1863, the Unconditional Unionists ran on a platform of abolishing slavery and won a majority of the state senate and over 70 percent of the house of delegates. Shortly after the next legislative session began, the Unionist legislature issued a call for holding a constitutional convention. On April 6, 1864, the convention call prevailed by a vote of 62 to 38 percent, with strong support from the Baltimore region and Western Maryland. The Unconditional Unionists dominated the election for delegates to the convention, winning sixty-one out of the ninety-six seats.

The 1864 Constitutional Convention met throughout the last summer of the Civil War to transform state government and public policy. The proposed constitution maintained the structure of its two predecessors, with a declaration of rights and a separate constitution. Most provisions of the declaration of rights were left unchanged except for the important express abolition of slavery and the insertion of a statement acknowledging the supremacy of the federal constitution and laws. The basic form of state government was also unchanged, although there were modifications to the three branches of government, with noteworthy political implications.

The legislative branch was altered with a new formula for the allocation of members in the house of delegates among the counties based on "white population only" and the granting of three separate state senate districts to Baltimore City, with each allotted six members of the house of delegates. This increased representation for the urban center of Maryland and Western Maryland, where black population was a significantly lower percentage of the total population than it was in Southern Maryland and the Eastern Shore. Political considerations also led to the elimination of the geographic rotation of the governor and the creation of an independently statewide-elected lieutenant governor to preside over the state senate. The judiciary was changed slightly by increasing the judicial term of office from ten to fifteen years, increasing the number of circuit courts to thirteen, and increasing the number of elected judges on the court of appeals from four to five by adding a judge from the Baltimore region. These modifications to the three branches strengthened the hold of the Unionists over state government and increased the political influence of and representation from urban mercantile interests and areas.

A major achievement of the 1864 constitution was the resolution of the slavery question in Maryland. A new article (24) in the declaration of rights succinctly declared the abolition of slavery and involuntary servitude and a new section (36 of Article III) in the constitution expressly prohibited the legislature from passing a law or making an appropriation "to compensate the masters or claimants of slaves emancipated from servitude by the adoption of this Constitution." Often unnoticed in accounts of this era were new constitutional provisions mandating a statewide system for public education and authorizing the general assembly to provide for a uniform system of voter registration. The Unionist-dominated convention also provided for the disenfranchisement of southern sympathizers and loyalty oaths for voters and officeholders.

The 1864 Constitution was narrowly ratified by a margin of 375 votes out of 59,971 votes cast. The constitution received a substantial majority vote in Baltimore City and in the three westernmost counties but lost by wide margins in the remainder of the state (1,995 votes). It was only an overwhelming pro-constitution vote of 2,633 in favor to 263 against on ballots cast by

Union soldiers in various companies and regiments in the field on October 12–13, 1864, that supplied the margin of approval (see Table 6-1).

Opponents appealed to the governor and mounted legal challenges to the vote procedures, but the new constitution was declared properly approved by the state's highest court. Passed during the nation's most divisive era and with claims of a trampled ballot and federal interference, the 1864 constitution was destined to have a short life span, although its positive changes have endured into the twenty-first century.

THE CONSTITUTION OF 1867

The constitution of 1867 was adopted as part of Maryland's "self-reconstruction."[19] After the Civil War most Marylanders were eager to return to normalcy and to take control of their own affairs without the long arm of the federal government hovering over the state. The Unionist 1864 constitution, passed only three years earlier, had generated ill will, as much from who was responsible for its passage as for the relatively few provisions targeted for elimination. The clamor for a new constitution quickly gathered momentum, fueled by political leaders who had been swept away by the Unconditional Unionists in the elections held during the Civil War.

In the first legislative elections held after the Civil War, in the fall of 1866, a reinvigorated Democratic Party captured two-thirds of the seats in the general assembly. Almost immediately after assuming control in January 1867, a resolution was passed setting April 10, 1867, as the date for an election on whether to call a constitutional convention and simultaneously setting that date for the election of convention delegates. The convention call easily passed (34,534 to 24,136), carrying every subdivision. All 118 delegates elected to the convention represented the energized, conservative Democratic Party. The convention work began a month later, on May 8, and was completed on August 17. A prompt vote on the proposed constitution was held on September 18, and the 1867 constitution was overwhelmingly approved by over two-thirds of the statewide vote (47,152 to 23,036). It received a majority in every jurisdiction and huge margins in Southern Maryland and the Eastern Shore counties, a strong majority in Baltimore City and central Maryland, and narrower margins only in the three westernmost counties (see Table 6-1). The constitution went into effect on October 5, 1867, and with subsequent statewide and legislative elections on November 5 Maryland's "self-reconstruction" officially began.

The structure and form of the 1867 constitution are identical to its predecessors, with a separate declaration of rights and constitution. Reflecting pre-adoption political rhetoric, there was a restatement of the relationship between the state and federal government, emphasizing states' rights and state sovereignty, and the dreaded loyalty oath provisions were deleted. There were few other substantive changes to the state constitution. Thirty-five of forty-five articles in the 1867 Declaration of Rights were not altered; two articles were added and two previous articles were deleted. Important reforms in the 1864 constitution were maintained, including the mandate for public education, requirements for the registration of voters, and the prohibition on state compensation to former slaveholders. Motivated by political considerations, the authors modified some provisions pertaining to the three branches of government.

Apportionment of the house of delegates was again a central focus, with county representation changed to include the "whole" population of counties. This shifted some delegate seats back to rural agricultural counties with substantial black populations. Counties received one delegate for containing population up to 18,000; one additional delegate for population up to 28,000; one more for population up to 40,000; and additional seats for population up to 55,000, with a maximum of six delegates. Each county continued to have a single state senator, and Baltimore City retained its three state senators. Representation from the Eastern Shore was further enhanced with the creation of Wicomico County from parts of Somerset and Worcester counties, resulting in an additional state senator and two delegates.

The office of governor was strengthened with the grant of the power to veto legislation passed by the general assembly, subject to a potential override of a three-fifths vote in each chamber. The governor was also mandated to make reports to the legislature in recognition of the increasing complexity of the administration of state government. In a pointed rejection of the political coalition that controlled power during the Civil War, and critical of the performance of Lieutenant Governor Christopher Cox, the office of lieutenant governor was abolished.

The judiciary was weakened by eliminating the independently elected court of appeals and replacing its members with the chief judges of seven judicial circuits and a specially elected judge from Baltimore City. The governor was granted the power to designate the chief judge of the court of appeals subject to the advice and consent of the state senate. The clerk of the court for the court of appeals was changed from an appointed office to a statewide elected office. The number of judicial circuits was reduced from thirteen to eight, with seven serving the counties with an elected chief judge and two associate judges. Baltimore City was designated an eighth circuit, with six distinct courts having elected judges.

Seizing upon popular sentiment against the federal government, the 1867 constitution was a symbol and a vehicle for reordering Maryland politics and government. As the historian Jean Baker concluded about this volatile era of state government, "By 1868, the politics of the past had become, for Maryland, the politics of the future."[20]

THE PRESENT, AMENDED MARYLAND CONSTITUTION

An amendment to the state constitution and declaration of rights can be made by a legislative proposal approved by three-fifths majorities of each house of the Maryland General Assembly. A constitutional amendment becomes effective upon the affirmative vote of the electorate at a subsequent general election. Through the 2010 general election there have been 271 proposed amendments considered by Maryland voters;[21] the electorate has approved 227 (83.8 percent) and rejected forty-four (16.4 percent). The nature of the proposed amendments, and respective ratification votes, help narrate the story of Maryland politics and government since 1867. The degree of approval or rejection illustrates the regional political differences within the state, reflects the voting patterns and behavior of statewide partisan elections, and demonstrates the contemporary "two Marylands" perspective.

As set forth in Table 6-2, few modifications were made to the 1867 constitution during the nineteenth century, and a modest number of changes were made in the first four decades of the twentieth century. Constitutional reform accelerated during the next four decades, peaking with a flurry of amendments proposed and adopted in the 1970s. Thirty-one amendments were considered by voters in the 1940s and twenty-six voted upon in the 1950s. From 1946 through 1960 Marylanders approved fifty-two proposed amendments and rejected none. Forty-three amendments were proposed for approval in the 1960s. From 1970 to 1978 seventy-one constitutional amendments were submitted to the voters, with the sixty-two ratified representing over 27 percent of the total amendments approved in 142 years. The pace of constitutional change has diminished in the three recent decades, with forty proposed amendments adopted and five rejected from 1980 through the 2010 general election.

The leading subject matter of proposed constitutional amendments has been the authority, compensation, composition, operation, and procedures of the state legislative, with seventy-five proposed amendments, about 28 percent of the total. Sixty-four of these proposals were approved and eleven were rejected. The structure, composition, compensation, and operation of the judicial branch of government ranks second, at fifty-seven proposed

Table 6-2: Constitutional amendment votes by decade

	Proposed	Ratified	%	Rejected	%
1868–1899	11	8	72.7	3	27.3
1900–1909	6	3	50.0	3	50.0
1910–1919	16	13	81.2	3	18.8
1920–1929	12	8	66.7	4	33.3
1930–1939	10	7	70.0	3	30.0
1940–1949	31	24	77.4	7	22.6
1950–1959	26	26	100.0	0	0.0
1960–1969	43	36	83.7	7	16.3
1970–1979	71	62	87.3	9	12.7
1980–1989	15	13	86.7	2	13.3
1990–1999	18	16	88.9	2	11.1
2000–2009	10	9	90.0	1	10.0
Totals	269	225	83.6	44	16.4

Source: Prepared by John T. Willis from official records maintained by the Maryland State Archives.

amendments (almost 21 percent), with fifty approved and seven rejected. The duties and powers of the governor have been amended sixteen times. Public official salaries have been the subject of thirty-one proposed amendments; seven were defeated. Baltimore City has been the subject of thirty-two proposed amendments, with twenty-nine ratified and three rejected. Provisions affecting county and municipal government have been the subject of twenty-two proposed amendments. Increasing or clarifying the condemnation powers of state or local government has been proposed in twenty-six amendments, half of which were defeated.

Among the most significant amendments to the Maryland Constitution have been the creation of the executive budget process (1916), the reapportionment of the general assembly (1901, 1922, 1956, 1970, and 1972), the right of citizens to petition for referendum laws passed by the general assembly (1915), the authorization of charter government and home rule for counties (1915, 1960, and 1966),[22] and the restructuring of the Maryland judiciary (1944, 1966, 1970, 1978, and 1980).

The Maryland Declaration of Rights has proven durable and been altered less than the constitution. Thirty-four of the original forty-five articles have not been amended. There have been only two additions. In 1972 Maryland voters approved Article 46, providing that "equality of rights under the law shall not be abridged or denied because of sex." In 1994 Article 47, a "victim's rights amendment," was overwhelmingly passed with 93 percent of the vote. Only one article has been deleted; Article 38, which placed restrictions on the transfer of state property to religious organizations, was removed in 1948. There have been thirty proposed amendments to the declaration of rights, and all but two have been ratified. The defeated proposals were attempted modifications of Article 15, dealing with the method of taxation. Of the eleven articles that have been modified, four have been altered more than once. Article 23, defining the conditions for trial by jury, has been amended six times; the latest was approved by voters in 2010 to raise the limits for a right to a civil jury trial to amounts in controversy exceeding $15,000. Article 35, limiting the holding of dual public offices, has been amended three times to permit general assembly members to serve in the military reserves, in law enforcement agencies, and in fire departments. Article 5 was amended three times to permit a jury in civil cases to have fewer than twelve members. Article 15, dealing with taxation, has also been amended twice.

The forty-four proposed amendments that were rejected offer another insight into the character and temperament of the Maryland electorate. Reflecting a healthy skepticism of government and a high regard for property rights, nearly 30 percent of the rejected proposed amendments sought to expand the state's or county's authority to take or dispose of private property. In 1996 and 2000 proposed amendments to grant Harford County and Prince George's County "quick take" authority to confiscate private property were soundly defeated. The Maryland electorate occasionally opposed judicial restructuring, defeating four proposals (in 1940, 1942, 1966, and 1968). A 1994 proposal to increase the mandatory retirement age for judges from seventy to seventy-five was also rejected.

Fiscal conservatism has been expressed in the frequent disapproval of pay raises for public officials. Increases for the legislature were voted down six times (1920, 1928, 1934, 1940, 1962, and 1966), twice for members of the judicial branch (1920 and 1923), and once for the governor (1974). An alternative to approval of constitutional amendments for changing the salaries of elected officials by creating salary commissions was approved by the voters for the legislature in 1970 and for the governor and lieutenant governor in 1976.[23]

Differences in voter attitudes and behavior between and among the regions of Maryland are readily apparent in the votes on constitutional amendments. The more progressive the proposed amendment, the more likely the urban core counties, especially Montgomery and Prince George's, will vote in favor of change. The rural, outer-boundary counties support constitutional changes much less enthusiastically or have voted in opposition. The voters of staunchly conservative, rural Garrett County in Western Maryland have never supported a proposed constitutional amendment that expressly gave Baltimore City more representation in the general assembly or additional authority for any purpose. Garrett County was also the only county to oppose the state's equal rights amendment when it was approved overwhelmingly with 75 percent of the vote in 1972.

ATTEMPTS AT CONSTITUTIONAL REVISION

A student of government may properly wonder why a purportedly progressive state like Maryland has one of the oldest state constitutions. The answer resides in the flexibility and the pragmatism of the governing documents adopted in 1867 and in the political difficulties of achieving wholesale changes, especially in periods of significant social and cultural unrest.

Maryland voters are required by the state constitution to decide every twenty years whether to call a constitutional convention for the purpose of drafting a new state constitution. The Maryland electorate clearly rejected the convention call four times (1887, 1907, 1970, and 1990). On three occasions (1930, 1950, and 2010) more votes were cast in favor of calling a constitutional convention than were cast in opposition. But after those results the general assembly did not pass the appropriate enabling legislation providing for the election of delegates to a convention because the vote in favor was not "a majority of voters at such election," as expressly stated in the constitution.[24] Maryland historians and political analysts concur that the predominantly rural members of the general assembly did not wish to call a convention after the 1930 and 1950 elections out of fear that a convention would lead to a legislative reapportionment altering the balance of power between the urban and rural regions and interests of the state.

Responding to increased political and public pressure for change fueled by impasses and extensive litigation over reapportionment, demands on government services generated by population growth, and a flurry of state constitutional reform efforts sweeping the nation, Governor Millard Tawes appointed a constitutional convention commission in 1965 to study the need for a new Maryland constitution. In 1966 the general assembly passed legislation authorizing a vote on whether to call a constitutional convention to be held on the date of the 1966 gubernatorial primary election, four years in advance of the next constitutionally required vote, scheduled for 1970. This legislative call for a convention stipulated that a majority of those voting on the question would be considered a favorable vote. A divided Maryland Court of Appeals upheld this procedure, and the only constitutional convention of the twentieth century was subsequently convened.[25]

The Tawes constitutional convention commission was an elite group of business, political, education, and professional leaders who met for over two years in advance of the 1967 convention. The commission conducted a thorough review of the state's constitutional history, made a detailed analysis of state government, set forth a comparative constitutional study, and prepared a proposed draft constitution.[26] The convention delegates elected on June 13, 1967, had the benefit of the commission's work during their six months of deliberation and debate. On January 10, 1968, the constitutional convention approved a comprehensive, dramatically altered constitution for a ratification vote. The new constitution won critical acclaim and support from academics, political scientists, major media organizations, and an all-star collection of contemporary and former political, business, and community leaders. It was hailed as a model for all the states.

In a shock to the proponents of constitutional reform, and most of the state's political elite, voters turned out in unexpected force to cast ballots against the proposed model constitution. In a special election held on May 14, 1968, the highly touted governing document was soundly rejected by Marylanders, with 367,101 voting against (56 percent) and 284,033 for (44 percent). Only the voters in Montgomery County and Prince George's County voted to approve the proposed constitution. It received less than 35 percent support in seventeen counties, including the large suburban counties of Anne Arundel and Baltimore. The model reform constitution also lost narrowly in Baltimore City, which had experienced significant civil disturbances five weeks earlier in the aftermath of the assassination of Dr. Martin Luther King.

In retrospect the reasons for rejection of the proposed 1968 constitution are clear. The proffered constitution called for too many changes affecting too many politically attuned constituencies in an era of social and political upheaval. Major governmental and political changes included abolishing the board of public works; altering some of the duties of the statewide elected comptroller and attorney general; creating a new four-tiered judiciary with new names and jurisdictions for the respective courts; eliminating the local elected offices of county commissioner, clerk of court, sheriff, surveyor, and register of wills; authorizing the creation of regional governments, with another layer of elected officials; mandating home rule for county governments; replacing multimember legislative districts with single-member districts; and merging the declaration of rights with the constitution.

These major changes sparked opposition across a broad public and political spectrum. Hundreds of locally elected officials opposed the new constitution with an attitude the *Washington Post* labeled "political blackmail" in a scathing editorial: "The arrogance with which the courthouse functionaries around Maryland are approaching the writing of the state constitution is almost unbelievable. One by one, representatives of these old courthouse gangs have arrived in Annapolis with ultimatums. Boiled down into simple language their statements say that if the new constitution proposes to change their offices in any way, they will do whatever they can to defeat the constitution at the polls. . . . This attitude is one that can only be described as political blackmail."[27]

Despite the decisive negative ratification vote, the comprehensive work of the constitutional convention commission and the delegates to the convention did help pave the way for the modernization of Maryland state government. Notable recommendations of the commission and convention were subsequently adopted piecemeal as individual constitutional amendments passed by the Maryland General Assembly and separately approved by the voters.[28] These suggestions included the reinstitution of the office of the lieutenant governor, the creation of a four-tiered judicial system, the removal of some judges from the partisan election process, and the expansion of the governor's authority over executive branch agencies.

SUMMARY

Maryland's declaration of rights and the constitution of 1867 may be old, it may be wordy, and it may be flawed—but it has been generally effective in serving the citizens of Maryland during more than 140 years of social, economic, and political change. Marylanders have shown willingness to make improvements in the state's governing documents, although perhaps with greater caution than their contemporary political leaders. They have consistently expressed a high regard for property rights and clearly manifested a healthy respect for civil rights and social justice.

CHAPTER SEVEN

The Maryland General Assembly

The right of the People to participate in the Legislature is the best security of liberty.
Article 7, Maryland Declaration of Rights

State legislatures often seem like the Rodney Dangerfield of American political institutions. In an executive-oriented age of media- and poll-driven personalities, our state assemblies typically receive public indifference or ridicule—in short, little or no respect. Yet despite the condemnations and critiques, state legislatures are among the most durable political institutions on the planet. They labor on, year after year, session after session, approving multibillion-dollar budgets, enacting or rejecting changes in state legal codes, overseeing and sometimes investigating the conduct of state administrative systems, and providing significant constituent services that range from awarding legislative scholarships to approving notary public commissions. Even if they serve as touchstones for popular discontent, they continue to perform their fair share of the heavy lifting that defines self-governance in representative democracies.[1] The Maryland General Assembly is no exception. From its colonial beginning it has demonstrated qualities of independence and initiative that have confounded proprietors, governors, the media, interest groups, and sometimes the public.

The Maryland General Assembly, which held its initial meeting in 1635, has changed profoundly, especially within the past fifty years, moving from an imperfect reflection of the dominant elite to a far more accurate representation of the complex demographic diversity of Maryland. As a law-making body it has moved from a collection of largely part-time citizen-legislators to a legislature of semiprofessional politicians, supported by a qualified and extensive staff of legal and fiscal experts.

The general assembly meets in the imposing and elegant Annapolis State House, distinguished nationally as the oldest state capitol building continuously employed as a legislative meeting place. Construction of the present state house was begun in 1772, when the last colonial governor, Robert Eden, tapped the foundation stone. The state house was considerably enlarged between 1902 and 1905, and the house of delegates and state senate chambers are located in what is termed the Colonial Revival section, which more than doubled the size of the building.

The trappings of tradition loom large in Maryland legislative proceedings. The house of delegates mace, a two-foot-long ebony and silver rod dating back to the late 1600s, is displayed before every session. Paintings of past Maryland political and legislative leaders adorn the walls of the chambers, coexisting with electronic voting boards and contemporary members' laptop computers. Professionalization of the state legislature (higher percentages of full-time legislators, expanding professional support staff, and skyrocketing costs of legislative campaigns) has permanently changed the style of Maryland representation. The historic Maryland legislature was typically a gathering of white, middle-aged men who met every other year in Annapolis during the slow winter season for farmers. Because of pervasive malapportionment, rural interests, unsympathetic and unresponsive to urban concerns, often dominated the sessions and helped confine state government to matters of small cost or importance. Diversity came slowly to the legislature. The first woman elected to the house of delegates in 1922, and to the state senate in 1934, was Mary Risteau from Harford County. The first African Americans were elected to the state senate and house of delegates in 1954 from the Fourth Legislative District of Baltimore City. As late as 1966 only thirteen women and four blacks served in either the house or senate out of a total of 185 legislators. That general assembly is long gone, replaced by a far more representative, diverse, and activist body.

THE MARYLAND GENERAL ASSEMBLY:
HISTORICAL DEVELOPMENT

On February 26, 1635, a short eleven months after Lord Baltimore's *Ark* and *Dove* first dropped anchor in the Chesapeake, the freemen of the fledgling colony first assembled in St. Mary's City, the original capital of Maryland. A contentious group, their legislative initiatives were opposed by Governor Leonard Calvert and ultimately refused by the proprietor himself, Cecil Calvert. Another assembly was not convened until 1638. With the governor presiding, the assembly produced a set of rules that provide "convincing evidence of the continuity of the legislative process in Maryland."[2] They included orders for debate decorum, quorum requirements, designation of presiding officers, recognition of speakers, and three readings on three separate days for legislative proposals. Derived from British parliamentary proceedings of the time, many of the procedures remain in force to this day.

The conflict between the British-based proprietor and the assembly continued for over a century. One bill from 1638 titled "For the liberties of the people" asserted that Marylanders had the same rights as English citizens.[3] By the thirteenth session, conducted in April 1650, a bicameral solution was reached. An upper house, a governor's council of landed, mostly Catholic gentry, represented the Calverts' interests, while members in the lower house of the assembly served as representatives of the Maryland citizenry.

Following the British "Glorious Revolution" of 1688, Maryland became a crown colony, and the assembly gained political and policymaking power. A standing committee system established a counterweight to executive encroachments. Representation was enlarged to four delegates for each county, and the power of the purse, control over all money bills, was acquired.

Despite extensive property qualifications for both holding state office and voting, a somewhat more democratic and representative general assembly emerged from the American Revolution and the 1776 Maryland Constitution. With the governor and a five-member "council to the governor" both elected by the legislature, there was really no question which branch was dominant. The lower body, the house of delegates, had seventy-six members popularly elected to one-year terms. Representation was based on county unit, with each of the eighteen subdivisions allotted four delegates. In addition Annapolis and Baltimore City were granted two delegates each. The fifteen-member state senate was removed from direct popular control. Senators, who served five-year terms, were selected by a senatorial electoral college, whose members, two per county, were elected by the voters. Senate representation was based on region: nine members were selected from the Western Shore and six from the Eastern Shore. James Madison praised "the salutary operations" of the Maryland Senate in Federalist Paper Number 63 as a model for the proposed federal version.[4]

The nineteenth-century Maryland legislature wrestled with issues of internal improvements, regulating oyster stocks, distributing patronage to the party faithful, and myriad local issues that the counties forwarded for resolution. Expanding the basis of popular governance became a perennial topic as the population of Baltimore City swelled and the democratic impulse of the Age of Jackson gained momentum. Responsive constitutional amendments in 1837 provided for the direct popular election of state senators, apportioned one per county and one for Baltimore City, and representation in the lower house moved closer to popular apportionment. After the 1840 federal census any county with a population greater than 35,000 citizens was allotted a maximum of six delegates. Counties with fewer people were entitled to representation on a sliding scale of three to five delegates each. Baltimore City was accorded the same status as the most populous counties, but Annapolis lost its separate delegation. A constitutional amendment in 1846 extended the terms for the house of delegates to two years and established biennial sessions. Baltimore City gained additional representation with the passage of the 1851 and 1864 constitutions and through amendments passed in 1900 and 1922.

As the populations of the suburban counties soared following World War II apportionment became more and more biased in favor of the smaller rural counties. By 1960 Baltimore City and Anne Arundel, Baltimore, Montgomery, and Prince George's counties contained over 75 percent of the Maryland citizenry but were represented by only ten of the twenty-nine state senators (34 percent) and sixty of the 123 delegates (49 percent).[5]

Along with escalating malapportionment, the twentieth century also brought the rise of strong governors and the administrative state. For the Maryland General Assembly this meant a sharply diminished role. As the Maryland historian George H. Callcott observed, the legislature was "left almost without function, except doing favors for the people back home and vetoing governors' unwarranted initiatives."[6] Both the house and the senate were fragmented, poorly led, and decentralized bodies, each with a bewildering array of committees. The house of delegates had thirty-nine committees as late as 1947, including such titles as aviation, militia, railroads and canals, public records, insolvency, printing, and public hygiene. The twenty-nine members of the state senate were scattered across thirty-one committees with such jurisdictions as inspections, pensions, roads and highways, insurance, federal relations, and sanitary condition of the state. Legislative salaries were only five dollars per day during the biennial ninety-day sessions until 1943; most general assembly staffers earned more than the delegates and senators they served.

The professionalization of the Maryland legislature began in 1939 with the creation of the legislative council. A de facto standing committee composed of the general assembly leadership, the council met regularly, hired full-time staff and auditors, and monitored state government operations. Over time the legislative council more than doubled its membership ranks, from an initial fourteen (seven from the house and seven from the senate) to thirty by 1967. The council has strengthened the institutional identity of the legislature and formulated an agenda of leadership bills, often independent and contrary to gubernatorial desires. The council was renamed the Legislative Policy Committee in 1976. In addition committee consolidation began. In 1945 the senate eliminated seven committees, and in 1947 the house of delegates cut eighteen.

The executive budget system of Maryland, adopted in 1916, greatly diminished the fiscal power of the general assembly. In Maryland the legislative branch does not exercise the power of the purse. As described by Alan Rosenthal, the preeminent scholar of state legislatures, the Maryland legislature "is constitutionally proscribed from increasing items in the governor's budget, or even switching funds around. All the legislature can do is cut."[7] Initially the executive budget was developed on a biennial basis, matching the regular legislative sessions, but the economic depression of the 1930s frequently forced special sessions because of revenue shortfalls. On the advice of a gubernatorial commission the state switched to annual budgeting, and a 1948 constitutional amendment provided that the general assembly meet every year, ninety days in odd-numbered years and thirty days in even-numbered years, to consider the annual budget. A constitutional amendment passed in 1964 equalized the length of each annual session to seventy days. Another amendment lengthened sessions to ninety days commencing in 1970. It remains at ninety days, with the annual regular session beginning on the second Wednesday of January and ending at midnight on the second Monday in April.

Legislative leadership was substantially upgraded in the early 1960s by the elections of William S. "Billy" James to president of the senate in 1962 and Marvin Mandel to speaker of the house of delegates in 1964. James, a gentleman farmer from then rural Harford County, had a reputation for conscientious service and unwavering rectitude. He brought to the post both institutional respect and a personal desire to restore balance to the state's governmental system. Mandel was of a very different background. He rose from a northwest Baltimore City political machine to become "a lawmaker's lawmaker; he exercised caution, kept promises, and got results."[8] Together James and Mandel represented the most competent, sophisticated, and strong leadership the Maryland General Assembly had enjoyed in decades.[9]

THE MAKING OF THE MODERN MARYLAND LEGISLATURE

As happened to every state legislature with the exception of Massachusetts and Wisconsin, the U.S. Supreme Court rulings swept out the malapportioned Maryland districts of the past. Indeed Senate President James welcomed the rulings, noting in his *Recollections*, "In the area of fair representation, the general assembly flunked all tests."[10] In the first state election held under the "one person, one vote" standard in 1966, a full 80 percent of the delegates and state senators, 106 in all, were newcomers to Annapolis. The old rural hierarchy, its ranks greatly depleted, did not go gently, but go it did. State Senator Frederick C. Malkus of Dorchester County, chair of the judicial proceedings committee for three terms, complained, "The fact that I am from the Eastern Shore should not be held against me."[11] Reflecting the power shift to metropolitan Maryland, Senator J. Joseph Curran Jr. of Baltimore City replaced Malkus as chair.

A perfect storm of reforms emerged from the 1967–70 sessions that produced something of a "legislative renaissance" in Maryland.[12] A bipartisan Citizens Commission on the General Assembly produced forty-six recommendations, and ninety-two proposals emerged from a Rutgers University Eagleton Institute study funded by a $20,000 appropriation from the general assembly and headed by Alan Rosenthal.[13] The Rosenthal study noted, "If states are generally negligent in supporting their representatives, Maryland is particularly remiss." While the state ranked tenth in per capita personal income in 1965, it was thirty-eighth in per capita legislative expenditures.[14]

Guided by Senate President James and House Speaker Mandel, committees were consolidated, with the senate decreasing from twenty committees to four and the house from nine to five. Interim committee meetings between regular legislative sessions were established, the prefiling of bills permitted for all members, and a consent calendar adopted for noncontroversial measures. In addition the professional, full-time, nonpartisan staff of the general assembly increased dramatically. In 1968 the Department of Fiscal Services was established, with capabilities of reviewing and analyzing the executive budget and providing fiscal notes detailing the long-term budgetary consequences for all pending legislation. This agency complemented the department of legislative services that began as the Baltimore City research agency with shared city and legislative functions. Legislative services became a strictly Annapolis agency in 1966. The costs of the legislative branch increased as well. In 1960 the operating budget for the general assembly was only $675,000. Ten years later this had increased to $3.9

million, and ten years after that to $14.5 million. Thirty years later, in 2010, the cost of maintaining the general assembly had grown to $76.5 million, or $406,915 per legislator.

The transformation of the general assembly also extended to the pay of legislators. After constitutional amendments to substantially increase legislative salaries failed ratification in 1966 and 1968, legislative leaders turned to a more pragmatic mechanism. In 1970 the voters approved the creation of a compensation commission that would recommend the "appropriate" level of legislative pay. The mechanism works in nineteen other states, and succeeded in Maryland as well. The pay of legislators for a succeeding term of office is recommended by a nonpartisan committee, a nine-person board appointed jointly by the governor and the legislative leadership. No member of the general assembly may sit on the commission. The commission forwards a salary resolution to the general assembly on a four-year cycle, coinciding with the legislative term. This resolution becomes law unless the legislature votes to reject or modify it. Such was the case in 2002, when the commission set the base salary of $34,500 for 2003, with annual $3,000 per year raises through 2006. The pay scale until the 2015 session is $43,500 per year, and the speaker of the house and the president of the senate receive $13,000 more each year for their additional duties and responsibilities.

In addition to salary general assembly members are also reimbursed for meal, lodging, and travel expenses incurred during the regular ninety-day session as well as during the interim while performing official business. In 2008 meal and lodging expenses were limited to $164 per day for in-state costs. Compared to other states, Maryland ranks in the upper quarter for legislative compensation.[15]

The Miller and James Senate Office Buildings and the Lowe House Office Building in Annapolis are the base of operations for Maryland legislators. Legislators are also provided an annual appropriation for maintaining and staffing a district office: $18,265 for fiscal year 2007, a funding level higher than all but four other states.[16] Over half of Maryland's legislators have a separate district office; the remainder use their Annapolis office for interim constituency service.

REPRESENTATION AND REDISTRICTING

With the eighth largest legislature in the country, the Maryland State Senate numbers forty-seven and the Maryland House of Delegates 141 legislators. Compared to other states, the state senate is thirteenth in membership size and the house of delegates ranks eleventh.[17] Senators are elected from single-member legislative districts. These forty-seven districts also contain the house of delegates districts. Over two-thirds (thirty-two out of forty-seven) are multimember districts, with three delegates elected at large, although in district 36 on the Eastern Shore, each of the three elected delegates must be from different counties. Twelve legislative districts are divided into two subdistricts that send either two or one delegate to Annapolis. The remaining three legislative districts contain three separate subdistricts for single-member delegate seats. The fifteen divided legislative districts are found in generally rural areas of the state, where retaining separate and individual county representation in Annapolis is viewed with considerable historical and contemporary importance. With a mix of Democratic and Republican legislators, about a fifth of the districts, ten in total, sent partisan split delegations to Annapolis after the 2010 elections. This is sharply reduced from fifteen such districts produced by the 2002 elections and demonstrates the growing partisan polarization in the state.

The ideal population of a legislative district in Maryland is 122,842 for the redistricting process after the 2010 census. This number places the Maryland senate districts twenty-third in size nationally and the at-large house district eleventh in population size. Maryland is nationally unique in its retention of multimember districts. While six other states (Arkansas, Idaho, New Jersey, North and South Dakota, and Washington) have two-member districts, Maryland is the only state in the nation with all three-member legislative districts.[18]

The basis for representation has proven an issue of historical protracted political conflict in Maryland as advocates of county-based representation struggled against those who wanted legislators apportioned by population. While the U.S. Supreme Court "one person, one vote" decisions brought constitutional closure to the apportionment debate, the question of where district lines would go and who would draw them remained. A substantial political asset, the authority to redraw legislative district lines after every federal census, was added to the gubernatorial arsenal by a constitutional amendment ratified in 1972. In the second year following the census the governor is responsible for submitting a redistricting plan to the general assembly. That plan prevails and becomes law unless the legislature passes an alternative redistricting plan of its own design, an option the general assembly has never exercised. On three occasions gubernatorial maps have been revised by the Maryland Court of Appeals after legal challenges, which are permitted under constitutional provisions to be made directly to the state's highest court.[19] The major consequence of redistricting in the past twenty years has been a loss of representation in the Baltimore metropolitan area and a corresponding gain predominantly in the Washington metropolitan area.[20]

MEMBERSHIP CHARACTERISTICS

Constitutional qualifications for the Maryland General Assembly are simple and direct. A person first must be a state resident for at least one year before election, with six months residency in the district. Delegates must be at least twenty-one years of age upon election, and state senators at least twenty-five. There are no term limits placed on legislative service in Maryland.

Seventy-one percent of the general assembly elected in 2010 were Democrats. Republican legislative strength has increased and declined during the past forty years, constituting only 12 percent of the general assembly in four consecutive elections from 1974 through 1986. Republicans gained ten seats in the state legislature in the 1990 election cycle and twenty-two in 1994, when Ellen Sauerbrey nearly won the governorship. They lost six seats in 1998 state elections, picked up seven in 2002, dropped six in 2006, and regained six in 2010 (all in the lower house). After the 2010 general election Republicans hold fifty-five of 188 seats in the Maryland legislature. There are twelve Republican state senators and forty-three Republican members in the house of delegates. As the legislative district map 7-1 depicts, the base of the Democratic majority is centered along the urban and suburban I-95 corridor, where Republican strength is concentrated in the more rural and peripheral areas of Maryland.

Consonant with its tradition of tolerance and reflective of its contemporary progressive political inclinations and the diverse pluralistic population of the state, Maryland displays high levels of female and minority representation in the general assembly.[21] According to the Women's Legislative Network of the National Conference of State Legislatures, in 2006 Maryland ranked first nationally, with women accounting for almost 35 percent of the general assembly, which dropped to 31 percent after the 2010 election. The overwhelming majority of female legislators are elected from Central Maryland districts, especially Baltimore City and Prince George's County, where women account for nearly half of those two combined delegations. Women legislators also represent more conservative, suburban, and rural districts in Central Maryland, the Eastern Shore, and Southern Maryland. But while the number and status of female legislators have improved considerably, men continue to occupy most of the formal leadership positions.[22] There has never been a female house speaker or state senate

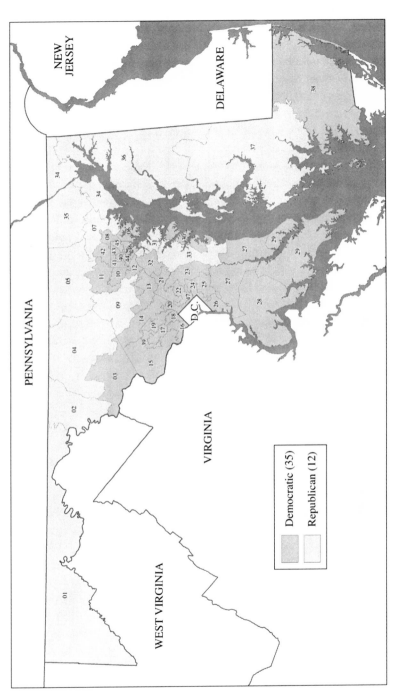

Map 7-1. State senate districts by party, 2011–2015

president, although Delegate Maggie McIntosh served two years as Democratic house majority leader (2001–2), and Delegate Ellen Sauerbrey was Republican house minority leader from 1987 until her unsuccessful run for governor in 1994. State Senator Rosalie Abrams served as senate majority leader from 1978 to 1982, and Delegate Adrienne A. Jones began serving as speaker pro tem in 2007. Of the ten legislative standing committees in the 2011 legislative session, three were chaired by women and three served as committee vice chairs.

African Americans won forty-two seats in the general assembly, or 22 percent of the total membership, during the 2006 election cycle. Maryland placed third in 2009, just behind Mississippi and Alabama, in the percentage of black legislators (23). Seven legislative districts, three in Baltimore City, three in Prince George's County, and one in Baltimore County, elect all-black delegations, and nine districts are biracial. In 1970 the Legislative Black Caucus was formed and is often a critical voting bloc in the general assembly. Maryland's African Americans have served as legislative leaders: State Senator Clarence W. Blount of Baltimore City was senate majority leader for almost twenty years (1983–2002); former delegate Anthony Brown, elected lieutenant governor in 2006, served as house majority whip and was succeeded by Baltimore City Delegate Talmadge Branch; and two major standing committees, one in the senate and one in the house, were chaired by black legislators in the 2011 regular session of the general assembly.

A strong undercurrent of pragmatism is reflected in who voters send to Annapolis. Nativism, support for homegrown sons and daughters, is not a predominant influence, as it is in less cosmopolitan states. Nationally 66 percent of all state legislators are native sons or daughters.[23] In contrast only 50 percent of the Maryland General Assembly members were born in the state they represent; 11 percent were born in the neighboring District of Columbia, and others come from a wide distribution of twenty states and seven foreign countries (Dominican Republic, El Salvador, India, Iran, Italy, Jamaica, and Ukraine). Birth origins may conceal a considerable life commitment to the district.

In a profile of the general assembly members produced after the 2010 elections, over 37 percent were sixty or older, 24 percent were fifty to fifty-nine, and 23 percent were forty to forty-nine.[24] Only 13 percent of the general assembly were in their thirties, and only four (2 percent) were under thirty. Although three-quarters of senators and delegates are married with children, Maryland has elected openly gay and lesbian legislators. The religious affiliations of legislators are significantly split: 48 percent are Protestants, with Methodists, Baptists, and Episcopalians making up 66 percent of that contingent, 28 percent are Catholic, and 9 percent are Jewish. As in other urbanized states, Maryland's legislators score well above average in educational attainment and income: 50 percent hold advanced degrees and 33 percent graduated from college. Twelve members reported at least some college, six (3 percent) only graduated from high school. Twenty percent of the general assembly are attorneys, a number sharply diminished from 1968, when 47 percent of the state senate and 33 percent of the house of delegates both practiced and made law.

A HYBRID LEGISLATURE: TILTING TOWARD FULL TIME

Almost all state legislatures have become stronger institutions over the past few decades by increasing session lengths, adding staff, and enhancing compensation for legislators to lessen the noblesse oblige aspect of the profession. The most significant factor that continues to divide these bodies is whether the legislative membership is comparatively full time or part time. The issue is effectively settled in states that meet in virtually continuous year-long sessions, such as California, Massachusetts, New York, Ohio, and Pennsylvania. Other states, with abbreviated or biennial sessions, are the polar opposite. Maryland falls in between, a hybrid legislature; however, the trend line is decidedly toward the full-time model, with 21 percent reporting their occupation as full-time legislator in the 2011 session of the general assembly.

The amount of legislative activity during every annual session is substantial. As Table 7-1 shows, well over 2,000 bills are filed each legislative session. Although each piece of legislation varies drastically in import, substance, and outcome, bills are the basic product of state legislative lawmaking. Sandy Rosenberg, a twenty-six-year veteran of the Maryland House of Delegates, observed, "A bill is not the only way a legislator can change things, but it's the most visible way."[25]

Making public policy is only one of multiple legislative functions. Maryland legislators review the state budget, provide legislative oversight of state agencies, and serve as district ombudsmen. Because most legislators have district offices, Maryland citizens are accustomed to contacting their delegate or state senator with local, state, and even federal problems. Effective casework is a significant part of a legislator's workload, during both the legislative session and the interim. In Rosenthal's 2001 survey of Maryland legislators, 63 percent of the sample reported that they spent sixty or more hours performing their official duties during the ninety-day session. Dur-

Table 7-1: Average annual legislation outcomes

	Filed	Passed/%	Vetoed/%
1960–69	1,448	652/45	25/4
1970–79	2,887	939/32.5	77 /8
1980–89	2,712	907/33	95/10.5
1990–99	2,325	815/35	114/14
2000–9	2,478	793/32	154/19

Source: Prepared by authors with information obtained from the Department of Legislative Services, Maryland General Assembly, Annapolis.

ing the May through December interim, when standing committees meet at least once a week in Annapolis, a 53 percent majority said they spent at least twenty-five hours a week on their legislative job; 22 percent reported an average of thirty-five hours or more consumed by their political role.[26]

LEADERSHIP AND COMMITTEES

In a compressed ninety-day session the overall success or failure of a state legislature is influenced by two factors: the competence of its committees and the skill of its leadership. For a legislature to serve as a significant, if not coequal partner to the governor in the policymaking process its leaders must command respect and direct a decentralized process, a "circus with hundreds of rings," to reasonable and productive outcomes.[27] The effective legislative leader knows when to hold and when to fold, when to compromise, when to stand firm, and, just as important, who to appoint to party and committee posts. Leadership in the Maryland legislature over the past thirty-five years has been generally stable, with orderly successions and little factional in-fighting, unusual for a political body so dominated by one party. These are characteristics of strong and accepted leadership with high degrees of legitimacy and credibility among the members. Speakers of the house and presidents of the senate, Democrats all, are first selected in party caucus and then elected by straight party-line votes in their respective chambers. They are empowered to appoint the members of all committees, from chairs on down; they control the schedule of legislation; and they serve as coleaders of the powerful Legislative Policy Committee.

Since 1970 the state senate has had five presidents and the house of delegates six speakers. While the Baltimore metropolitan area has produced most contemporary governors and other statewide officeholders, the same cannot be said for general assembly leaders. Two house speakers have come from Eastern Shore counties, one from Southern Maryland, one from Western Maryland, one from Baltimore City, and one, Michael E. Busch, from an Annapolis-area district in Anne Arundel County. All six speakers moved up from chairing one of the six substantive standing committees of the house of delegates. Two speakers left office to become state judges, one departed to run successfully for the U.S. House of Representatives, one retired voluntarily to spend more time with his family, and one, Casper R. Taylor Jr., was defeated by his Republican challenger in 2002. Taylor, as were most house speakers before him, was a group-oriented, collaborative leader who depended on influential committee chairs such as the late delegate Howard "Pete" Rawlings of the appropriations committee to marshal support for leadership legislation. Busch, according to a number of experienced delegates, seems more staff-driven, although he has retained inner and outer circle leadership meetings every Monday during the session.[28]

The five presidents of the state senate since 1962 have not hailed from rural areas; all have represented districts in the Central Maryland region, with one each from Baltimore County, Harford County, and Howard County. Two presidents, including the longest tenured senate president in the history of Maryland, Thomas V. "Mike" Miller Jr., represented Prince George's County. Two of the previous senate presidents left the legislature to run for lieutenant governor. President James retired from the senate in 1974 and was subsequently elected by the general assembly to serve three consecutive terms as Maryland state treasurer.

A successful leadership coup occurred in the state senate at the beginning of the 1983 session, when Senator Melvin A. Steinberg organized a coalition of Baltimore City, Baltimore County, and Prince George's County senators to oust Senate President James Clark Jr., an old-school, low-key gentleman farmer from Howard County. Steinberg rewarded his allies by conveying three committee chair posts to Prince George's County senators, including the judicial proceedings committee to Senator Mike Miller. Support from the legislative black caucus was acknowledged by replacing as senate majority leader Rosalie Abrams, a Baltimore City senator who stuck with Clark, with Senator Clarence W. Blount, the first African American to hold a major Democratic Party legislative leadership post. Three years later Steinberg relinquished his seat to run successfully for lieutenant governor with Governor William Donald Schaefer; Senator Miller succeeded him as president of the state senate.

Miller's success is a tribute to both his energy and his political skills. He is politics driven, and has been since childhood. The oldest of ten children,

Miller grew up in Clinton, Maryland, well aware of the dominant Democratic machine politics of the area. As part of the Prince George's County Democratic organization led by Peter O'Malley and Steny H. Hoyer, himself a senate president from 1975 to 1978, Miller learned the value of the team approach and pooled campaign fund-raising. He pays close attention to the electoral process and the fortunes of his fellow Democratic legislators. Personable and gregarious, he does not hesitate to aid his legislative allies through the Democratic Senatorial Committee Slate and Maryland and Marylanders for Mike Miller, two campaign committees that raise hundreds of thousands of dollars each election cycle. His appointed committee chairs regularly receive maximum contributions from these fund-raising entities. Some longtime Annapolis observers credit Miller with escalating partisan tensions in the senate by his reliance on the Democratic caucus to maintain discipline and cohesion. Still, his service to his core constituency, his support group of Democratic state senators, especially during campaign season, explains his continued tenure.

For the vast majority of issues Maryland legislative leaders depend on the committee system of expertise and institutional memory to resolve disputes and conflicts and to process prospective legislation. Once the committees were consolidated in the 1960s imbalances in member workloads lessened. Every delegate and senator had a meaningful committee assignment, and the influence of committees in the legislative process escalated considerably.[29] Within general assembly committees the general rule is to "follow the chair's lead," although leadership styles of chairs can differ from democratic and collegial to somewhat more arbitrary and authoritarian approaches.[30] Because they are appointed by the presiding officer of their chamber, committee chairs are subject to change. Of the ten standing committee chairs in the session of the Maryland General Assembly that met in 2011, only two, Delegates Joseph F. Vallario Jr., chair of the judiciary committee, and Sheila E. Hixson, chair of the ways and means committee, have served for longer than seven years. Both began their tenures as chairs in 1993. Although seniority and experience play some role in chair selection, the relationship a delegate or senator has with the leadership is the single most important factor. As might be expected, the core Democratic subdivisions of Baltimore City, Montgomery County, and Prince George's County contain the home districts of most standing committee chairs.

Party ratios in committees generally reflect the overall partisan percentages of Democrats to Republicans in both the house and the senate. Partisanship in committee behavior is typically contextual, dependent on the issues, the governor, and the members. Traditionally, money committees such as budget and taxation in the senate and the appropriations committee in the house, tend to attract fiscal conservatives from both parties, and nonpartisan executive budget cutting is the norm. However, increased Republican representation and the election of Governor Ehrlich produced partisan acrimony in a number of committees. One former veteran Democratic state senator, George Della observed, "Ten years ago Republican senators were always part of everything we did. There was mutual respect for one another and it showed in committee deliberations, debate, and voting. That's changed. The old Senate is gone."[31]

Because committee chairs serve as part of the inner circle of leadership in both the state senate and the house of delegates and because there are so few major standing committees, these work groups do not serve as an institutional decentralizing force. Overturning an unfavorable committee report is rare. In Maryland a committee's recommendation almost always determines the fate of legislation.

In the senate there are only four substantive policy standing committees, each with extensive jurisdictional scope and coverage:

1. *The Budget and Taxation Committee* is the fiscal jewel in the crown, combining the functions of two house committees, appropriations and ways and means. The committee reviews the state operating and capital improvement budgets, state and local bond authorizations, pension policies, and taxation.

2. The broad jurisdiction of the *Senate Education, Health, and Environmental Affairs Committee* encompasses the licensing and regulation of a wide variety of economic activities, including business, health, and related occupations and professions. It also reviews legislation in such areas as alcoholic beverages, natural resources, agriculture and land preservation, environment, energy, ethics, election procedures, veterans affairs, secondary public school policy, public health, governmental procurement, and state government organization and procedures.

3. *The Senate Finance Committee* has jurisdiction over banks and other financial institutions, credit regulation and consumer financing, economic and community development, insurance, horse racing and lotteries, social programs, transportation, labor and employment, unemployment insurance, utility regulation, workers' compensation, and state government personnel issues.

4. *The Judicial Proceedings Committee* is responsible for the civil and criminal code of Maryland as well as judicial administration and court structure and regulations governing the legal profession.

The Maryland House of Delegates has six substantive policy committees:

1. *The House Appropriations Committee* reviews the state operating and capital budgets as well as bond authorizations for the state and counties. It is also responsible for state and local agency procedures and state personnel, pension, and collective bargaining agreements.

2. The jurisdiction of the *Economic Matters Committee* extends over banks and other financial institutions and includes commercial law, licensing and regulation, economic development, electronic commerce, unemployment insurance, utility regulation, workers' compensation, and alcoholic beverages.

3. *The Environmental Matters Committee* considers legislative proposals in the fields of agriculture, natural resources, and environmental issues as well as mass transit and motor vehicles.

4. The jurisdiction of the *Health and Government Operations Committee* includes health facilities and insurance, public health concerns, long-term care, Medicaid, and health occupations and professions. The committee also oversees a variety of state governmental matters such as organization, procurement, procedures, and administrative law.

5. The concerns of the *House Judiciary Committee* are Maryland criminal and civil law, judicial administration and structure, the legal profession, public safety and corrections, and juvenile justice.

6. *The Ways and Means Committee* reviews legislative proposals concerning state taxation, property assessments, tax credits, education financing, primary and secondary education programs, elections, transportation funding, and the lottery and horse racing.

In addition to the standing committees, the general assembly maintains sixteen joint statutory committees, and each house has rules and executive nominations committees. Some statutory committees have broad and general jurisdictions, such as the leadership's legislative policy committee, whereas others are more specialized, such as the joint committee on Chesapeake and Atlantic Bays Critical Area. Along with commissions, task forces, and other committees that may vary from year to year, these work groups serve to augment the institutional resources of the general assembly and provide a wider distribution of legislative responsibility to the membership.

In military terms, both strategically and in a tactical sense, the Maryland governor almost always holds the high ground when matched against the legislative powers of the general assembly. Formal gubernatorial assets include the powers and priorities of the executive budget, the authority to call special sessions, control of governmental appointments, and the veto. Informally the governor commands far more media attention and serves as the very definition of state government for many Maryland citizens. This imbalance in institutional resources has provoked a legislative response.

Since 1973 the general assembly has frequently strengthened its institutional role, especially in the area of budgetary and fiscal matters, often relying on amendments to the state constitution, which cannot be vetoed by the governor. In 1973 the legislature passed a constitutional amendment mandating a balanced budget, which was approved by the voters in 1974. Previously there had been an expectation but no constitutional requirement that revenues and expenditures matched in the executive budget. Five years later, in 1978, the legislature passed another amendment approved by the voters that gave the general assembly the authority to mandate certain expenditures in the annual budget subject to funding sources. Because Maryland assumed full financial responsibility for new school construction in 1971 and later took on the past school debt service of local jurisdictions, state indebtedness skyrocketed in the early 1970s, rising from $159 million in 1971 to $484 million in 1975. This prompted the legislature to establish the Capital Debt Affordability Committee in 1978, which provides both the governor and the general assembly with an annual debt authorization ceiling.[32] In 1982, on the recommendation of the legislative policy committee, the general assembly established the Joint Spending Affordability Committee, which provides a spending target for the operating budget designed to stabilize state expenditures at a level consistent with the statewide growth of personal income. The general fiscal goals are prudence, measured growth, and above all retention of Maryland's coveted triple-a credit rating. Politically these institutional structures tend to deflate Republican claims that the legislative Democratic majority is the reckless "tax and spend" party.

In addition the department of legislative services was given statutory authority to conduct oversight of the executive budget. Although the general assembly cannot "legislate in the budget bill," the legislature has regularly taken advantage of a 1978 Maryland Court of Appeals decision that upheld the right of the assembly to impose conditions or limitations on an appropriation relating to the expenditure of funds.[33] Overall the Maryland legislature, though certainly not having fiscal equality with the governor, established a significant degree of institutional independence and influence that provides an operative meaning to the principle of separation of powers.

Democratic governors Marvin Mandel, William Donald Schaefer, and Parris Glendening combined ambitious and far-ranging policy agendas with considerable legislative success. Often issues such as the Baltimore subway (Mandel), Orioles Park at Camden Yards and an emergency income tax surcharge (Schaefer), and two NFL stadiums, vehicle emissions testing, and gun control (Glendening) were controversial and threatened Democratic Party cohesion within the legislature. But with the skillful use of executive powers they were all enacted. Mandel, having been house speaker and elected by the legislature, was quite popular with most of his former colleagues and relied on both personal and positional powers. Schaefer and Glendening were of a different temperament. Neither was particularly well liked by a majority of legislators, but both understood the necessity of working with the legislature even if they were somewhat distant from the members and sometimes aggressive and combative. Both recognized the worth of gubernatorial largesse in dealing with the legislature; for example, Delegate Sandy Rosenberg observed that "quite a few road construction projects became worthier in Governor Glendening's estimation after certain members voted for Ravens Stadium."[34] Furthermore, akin to Mandel before them, Schaefer and Glendening also knew when to resolve issues through give and take and mutual accommodations, the essence of the legislative process. Most Maryland governors practiced what former U.S. senator Robert Dole called "honest compromise," a recognition of and respect for positions other than one's own. They cocreated policies and programs with the general assembly. Glendening usually saw his legislative priorities enacted, and the general assembly often served as more of an "enabler" than a competing adversary.[35] When he exercised his veto the rejection was absolute: no Glendening veto was overridden during his two terms, a claim no other modern Maryland governor can make.

A governor's veto produces the ultimate institutional confrontation between the executive and legislative branches (see Table 7-2). The conflict contains a strong partisan determinant in Maryland. Democratic governors almost always get their way: Hughes suffered nine overrides (1.13 percent), Schaefer two (0.3 percent), Glendening none, and O'Malley one (0.5 percent). Overrides of the vetoes of the last two Republican governors occurred with far greater frequency; Agnew suffered eleven (16.7 percent) and Ehrlich thirty-seven (5.1 percent). It takes a three-fifths vote in each legislative chamber to reject a veto. Assuming high party voting cohesion, that threshold is well within reach of normal Democratic general assembly majorities. A flurry of high-profile overrides at the opening of the 2006 session provoked charges of "a partisan witch hunt" from Governor Ehrlich's press secretary, and legislative leaders complained that the executive failed to compromise. House of Delegates Majority Leader Kumar P. Barve observed, "Previous governors would work with us during the interim to try a find a middle ground and this governor doesn't."[36]

Certainly a Republican who campaigned against Annapolis could expect a hard slog through the legislative process dominated by Democrats, but Ehrlich had served two terms as a delegate, he was popular with his colleagues on both sides of the aisle, and he knew the process. Many of his defeats verged on self-inflicted. His primary legislative goal, legalizing slot machines at Maryland racetracks, failed four years in a row. His 2003 proposal came in two versions, and the initial offering was riddled with conflicting statistics that earned the ridicule of the Democratic leadership. House Speaker Busch complained, "The plan they had was a bad plan, and it failed because the governor didn't have a bill 50 days into the session."[37] Senate President Miller, a supporter of slots, castigated the Ehrlich administration's lobbying effort: "It is like a band of wandering gypsies."[38]

Even Ehrlich's appointments came under legislative and media fire. Lynn Y. Buhl, a former attorney for the Chrysler Corporation and the governor's choice to head the Maryland Department of the Environment, was rejected by the state senate. Former Democratic state senator Clarence M. Mitchell IV, who endorsed Ehrlich in 2002, was named director of the office of urban development despite a crescendo of criticism for his ethical lapses as a legislator. He seemed a curious choice for a governor who proclaimed his dedication to rid Annapolis of a "culture of corruption." Mitchell resigned quickly from his $92,000-a-year post after public legislative and media protests.[39]

The Ehrlich administration's plans to sell "surplus properties" and some of the state's previously preserved land was exposed by the *Baltimore Sun*, provoking a hostile legislative response.[40] In the 2005 session the general assembly passed by a wide bipartisan majority a proposed constitutional amendment restricting the authority of the board of public works to sell state open space or recreational, preservation, or conservation land without

Table 7-2: Gubernatorial vetoes and legislative overrides

Governor	Bills passed	Vetoed/%	Overrides/%
Agnew			
1967–69	1,159	66/4.1	11/16.7
Mandel			
1969–78	8,186	529/6.5	7/1.3
Hughes			
1979–86	7,252	799/11.0	9/1.1
Schaefer			
1987–94	6,643	813/12.2	2/0.3
Glendening			
1995–2002	6,787	1177/17.3	0/0.0
Ehrlich			
2003–6	2,984	724/24.3	37/5.1
O'Malley			
2007–10	3,154	316/10.0	1/0.3

Source: Prepared by authors from information supplied by the Department of Legislative Services, Maryland General Assembly, Annapolis.

legislative approval. Two other statutory restrictions on gubernatorial power were passed, vetoed by Ehrlich, and overridden in the 2005 session; one limited his power to name members to the Maryland State Board of Elections, and the second required the governor to obtain legislative consent prior to announcing Maryland's position on international trade agreements.

Institutional and partisan combat between the Republican governor and the Democratic-dominated general assembly intensified steadily beginning with a special session called by the governor on medical malpractice. In the special three-day session during the holiday season in December 2004, the Medical Injury Compensation Reform bill proposed by the governor received unfavorable reports from committees in both chambers, and the legislature crafted its own bill. Governor Ehrlich vetoed the general assembly bill only to have it overridden and enacted at the beginning of the 2005 regular legislative session. This pattern of conflict and contention persisted throughout Ehrlich's term on a variety of issues, including a special session to deal with utility regulation in June 2006, shortly before the filing deadline for state and local candidates and legal challenges to legislative authority.[41]

PARTISAN POLARIZATION

With overwhelming majorities Maryland Democrats could routinely ignore Republican challenges for most of the twentieth century. Some Republicans, through diligent hard work and the force of their personalities, did achieve considerable influence. One was the minority leader and state senator John A. Cade of Anne Arundel County, a fixture on the decidedly bipartisan senate budget and taxation committee. Cade was a veritable walking encyclopedia of legislative detail and history. When he talked the entire state senate listened and often agreed. But Republicans such as Cade were very much the exception. For most of the twentieth century GOP legislators, their rhetoric, and their legislative agendas signified little of enduring substance in the Annapolis system.

With the election of Delegate Ellen Sauerbrey to the post of minority leader in 1987 the tone of the Republican efforts in the Maryland General Assembly began to change. Although faced with insurmountable Democratic majorities, Sauerbrey worked to energize the Republican house minority by presenting budget and policy alternatives to Governor Schaefer's agenda. These challenges were consistent in conservative ideology and persistent. Slowly a cohesive partisanship among Annapolis Republicans emerged. The theme that Maryland had suffered grave consequences from Democratic domination was often voiced; for Maryland Republicans one-party rule meant wasteful spending and machine-style corruption. Gubernatorial candidate Robert Ehrlich emphasized these issues in 2002, arguing that a "culture of corruption" could best be eliminated by meaningful two-party competition.

Once elected in 2002, Ehrlich and the Republican house and senate minorities did indeed change the Annapolis culture, but in a different way than was implied by their campaign rhetoric. During the general assembly sessions of his administration, legislative politics in the Maryland capitol became, as the Sunpapers columnist C. Fraser Smith observed, "a far more partisan, a more divided and more contentious place."[42] The Republican general assembly leadership encouraged confrontational floor tactics that were a far cry from the "get along, go along" days, when Republicans were routinely ignored. One tactic was forcing votes on hot-button social values issues by sponsoring floor amendments unrelated to the legislation under consideration. For example, during the 2004 session Republicans forced votes on gay marriage and the rights of illegal immigrants. Both amendments were quite similar to Republican-sponsored bills that had failed in committee, and Democrats charged that the tactic violated the informal rules of the legislative game.[43]

Another example of polarized politics was gridlock on the racetrack slots issue from 2003 through 2006. With public opinion divided and the gubernatorial Democratic nominee, Baltimore City mayor Martin O'Malley, an announced advocate of slots at the racetrack, the prospect for its passage in the pre-election 2006 session was effectively doomed. In a 2007 fall special session of the general assembly convened to deal with fiscal issues, Governor O'Malley moved the slots issue forward by proposing a constitutional amendment that allowed the voters the final say in the November 2008 general election.

Legislative politics in Maryland has become far more partisan as Republicans elected to the legislature have often been more conservative, and Democrats often more liberal, than their predecessors, making the ideological gulf between the parties wider and sharper. With a reduced Republican contingent after the 2006 elections, the legislative role of the minority party was again more limited, but the climate remained politically charged, as exemplified by the judicial challenge filed by Republican legislative leaders to the 2007 special legislative session.[44]

SUMMARY

In Maryland the state legislature is decidedly not the first branch of government in either a constitutional or a political sense. In state constitutional order, the first two articles deal with suffrage and the executive department, with the general assembly coming third. Politically, since the administration of Albert Ritchie the drive wheel of Maryland government has remained firmly fixed in the governor's office on the second floor of the state capitol building.

During Democratic administrations, almost without exception, the legislative priorities for the annual sessions are largely determined by the governor and the general assembly leadership. When the speaker of the house, the president of the senate, and the governor agree on a proposal, it is inevitably enacted. With Republican governors, the governing dynamic changes. Governor Ehrlich and the general assembly clashed repeatedly, and less than a third of his administration's legislative agenda was enacted, demonstrating the strength of the progressive base in Maryland politics as reflected in the state legislature. Democratic legislators have little to fear from a Republican governor. As Montgomery County state senator Brian E. Frosh said in reaction to an Ehrlich threat, "What's he going to do, short-sheet my bed?"[45]

Only a handful of legislative districts are competitive, and the dominance of strong, cohesive, and well-led Democratic legislative majorities is assured for both the short and the long term. With a Democratic governor once again in office after the 2006 gubernatorial election, the institutional combat faded, as evidenced by the thirty-five-year low in the number of bills vetoed by the governor after the 2008 regular session of the Maryland General Assembly. Legislative importance in the state's policymaking process was renewed, with cooperation, compromise, and majoritarian consensus replacing confrontation.

CHAPTER EIGHT

The Maryland Governor and the Executive Branch

The responsibility for good government has gravitated to the governor. It is to him that the people look for salutary laws, it is to him that they look for economical and efficient administration.
Charles James Rohr, *The Governor of Maryland*, 1932

The twenty-first-century governor of Maryland possesses significant and broad executive powers, making the institutional powers of the office among the strongest of all chief executives in the nation's fifty states.[1] The governor enjoys envied budget power, wide-ranging administrative power, extensive appointment power, veto power over acts of the legislature, a unique legislative redistricting power, and limited competition from other statewide elected officials.

The constitutional qualifications to be governor are few: a person must be a state resident, a registered voter for five years, and at least thirty years old.[2] The constitutional restraints on the Maryland governor are also few; the most consequential are a two-term limit on service in office and restrictions on lame duck appointments made in the last months of the final term.[3]

With extensive duties, responsibilities, and powers, Maryland's politically dominant chief executive stands in sharp contrast to the original conception and design of the executive branch of state government. The over 230-year development of the office of governor provides an excellent guide to the evolution of Maryland government. In many respects it parallels, if not foreshadowed, the growth of executive power in other states and the strengthening of the presidency at the federal level of government.

The modern Maryland governor is truly a chief executive and chief operating officer presiding over the most complex and largest organization in the state. With an annual budget exceeding $30 billion and approximately 80,000 employees, the governor controls substantial resources and wields significant political power. It is a public office from which much can be accomplished through the administration and management of the large executive branch and by establishing a direction and vision for the state.

THE OFFICE OF GOVERNOR: HISTORICAL DEVELOPMENT

In 1776 the delegates to Maryland's first constitutional convention approved Article 8 of the Maryland Declaration of Rights, which boldly proclaimed, "The Legislative, Executive and Judicial powers of Government ought to be forever separate and distinct from each other." The landed gentry and mercantile-minded drafters of Maryland's initial governing documents severely limited the role of the governor. This structure was an unmistakable response to the arbitrary actions of Maryland's colonial and proprietary governors as well as the decisions of King George.[4] Under the 1776 constitution the governor was elected by the legislature for a single-year term and was allowed only three successive single-year terms. In addition gubernatorial appointments were subject to approval of a governor's council selected by the general assembly.[5]

The Maryland governor gained independence from direct legislative control with the 1837 ratification of a constitutional amendment providing for the direct popular election of governor.[6] Legislative concerns about a revival of strong executive power and the potential dominance of a statewide gubernatorial election by voters in the growing urban center of Baltimore fostered the inclusion of a provision that the governor was to be elected from one of three regions (Eastern Shore, Southern, and Northwest) on a rotating basis every three years. This was intended to prevent successive terms as governor by one person and to mandate geographic relevance and diversity.

After the Civil War the role of the governor was strengthened considerably by the 1867 constitution, in part because a reunified Democratic Party was confident of winning statewide elections. The most important power gained by the office of governor was the right to veto legislation passed by the general assembly. The mandated geographic rotation of the office was eliminated, increasing the political power of the constantly growing and vote-rich Baltimore City and its surrounding area.

Throughout the nineteenth century and into the early twentieth century the selection of governors was tightly controlled by the political leadership of the Democratic and Republican parties. An individual was nominated through a state party convention process dominated by political insiders and party bosses.[7] Not until election reform legislation was enacted providing for statewide party primaries did the governor have the potential for political and electoral independence by being able to appeal directly to voters.

The foundation for the transformation of the office of governor and the executive branch into the most powerful of Maryland's three branches of government was solidified with the ratification of the Executive Budget Amendment in 1916.[8] As state comptroller before his election in 1915, Emerson C. Harrington had repeatedly warned of the perils of deficit spending in his official reports.[9] After his election Governor Harrington accepted the recommendations of the Goodnow Commission and championed the quick passage of a constitutional amendment to create the executive budget process.[10]

After his close election in 1919 Governor Albert C. Ritchie not only used executive budget powers to strengthen the office of governor, but he also initiated a reorganization of state government into nineteen administrative departments and created a gubernatorial advisory council, the predecessor to the modern state cabinet system.[11] The political influence of the governor was further enhanced in 1922 by the passage of the Fewer Elections Amendment, which made the terms of all state elected officials, and most county officeholders, coterminous with the four-year term of the governor. This created a political environment in which the governor could establish political dominance as the head of the party and as the candidate at the top of the political party ticket during the gubernatorial election cycle.

Gubernatorial powers were again enhanced in the late 1960s and early 1970s in the fourth wave of executive branch reorganization that swept through the country. Responding to calls for improvement and streamlining the state's administrative organization, Governor J. Millard Tawes appointed a commission for the modernization of the executive branch of state government in the summer of 1966. Six months later this commission made three principal recommendations: (1) strengthening of the governor's staff; (2) calling for executive reorganization to be a continuing responsibility under an agency accountable to the governor; and (3) authorizing the governor to initiate reorganization plans to be effective if not disapproved by the legislature.[12] The work of this commission was embraced by the constitutional convention commission appointed by Governor Tawes in 1967 and by the elected delegates to the 1967–68 constitutional convention. Both proposed a stronger state executive and a greater role for the governor in the organization of the executive branch and administrative operations.[13] Some of the reform suggestions were adopted through statutes passed by the Maryland General Assembly and some by constitutional amendments ratified by voters.

There were three notable limitations placed on the office of governor during the twentieth century. First, paralleling the enactment of presidential term limits, and having experienced a strong-willed, four-term chief executive in Governor Ritchie, the voters approved a constitutional amendment in 1948 imposing a limit of two consecutive gubernatorial terms.[14] Second, the ability of a governor to pocket-veto a bill by failing to sign a duly passed bill was eliminated in 1960.[15] Third, reacting to instances of dubious late-term executive action, the legislature passed and voters approved modest limitations in 1996 on the governor's authority to make appointments after the primary or general election in which a sitting governor could not be reelected to office.[16]

Over the past century the Maryland electorate approved constitutional amendments to increase the salary of the governor in 1954 and 1966 but rejected an increase in 1974, during Mandel's tenure. To avoid the constitutional mandate of popular voting on specific pay increases, a constitutional amendment was passed in 1976 establishing the Governor's Salary Commission to review and recommend the pay level for the governor and lieutenant governor for each succeeding term of office. If the commission recommends an increase in pay, the approval of the Maryland General Assembly is still required for final approval. Under this authority the pay for the office of governor has been increased five times, from the $25,000 paid during the 1975–79 term to $150,000 for terms commencing in 2007. This has moved the pay for Maryland's governor from last among the nation's fifty governors in 1978 to the tenth highest in 2007.[17]

STRUCTURE OF THE EXECUTIVE BRANCH

Modern state government interacts with nearly every aspect of the daily lives of its citizens. Along with the governor, lieutenant governor, and secretary of state, there are twenty cabinet departments that comprise the executive council responsible for the administration and management of state government. The departments are headed by a secretary, who is appointed by the governor and initially subject to confirmation by the state senate, with two exceptions: the state superintendent of education is appointed by the state board of education, and the secretary of higher education is appointed by the Maryland Higher Education Commission. The members of those boards are, however, appointed on a staggered basis by the governor with the consent of the state senate. The cabinet secretaries are responsible for the operation of their respective departments and the implementation of the policies of the governor and those policies mandated by the legislature. In addition to the cabinet-level departments there are fifty-three independent agencies exercising state authority over particular subject matters. Figure 8-1 depicts the organization of the executive branch of Maryland state government.

The cabinet departments and independent agencies vary greatly in size and the scope of their duties and responsibilities. As detailed in the governor's 2010 budget documents, the cabinet departments with the largest numbers of full-time employees are the Department of Public Safety and Correctional Services (11,307), the Department of Transportation (9,012), the Department of Human Resources (6,742), and the Department of Health and Mental Hygiene (6,584). The University System of Maryland had 21,901 authorized positions in fiscal year 2010. The highest annual budgets in fiscal year 2010 belonged to the Department of Health and Mental Hygiene (over $8.1 billion), the State Department of Education (over $6.9 billion), the University System of Maryland (nearly $4.4 billion), the Department of Transportation (nearly $3.5 billion), the Department of Human Resources (nearly $1.9 billion), and the Department of Public Safety and Correctional Services (nearly $1.3 billion). The other cabinet-level departments range in size from twenty-six to 2,400 employees, with budgets between $4.4 million and $300 million. The independent agencies with the most employees in fiscal year 2010 were the State Department of Assessments and Taxation (593 employees), the Maryland Insurance Administration (282 employees), and the State Lottery Agency (186 employees). Only six other independent agencies have more than one hundred employees.

EXECUTIVE BUDGET POWER

Foremost among the powers of the Maryland governor is control over the state budget. The governor must submit an annual budget detailing revenues and expenditures to the general assembly on or before the third Wednesday of January. Because the legislature cannot increase expenditures (except through a supplementary bill containing specified new revenues), this means, in practical terms, that nearly everything to be spent by or on behalf of the state requires the governor to include a request for such an appropriation in the annual budget. The governor may also submit supplemental budgets during a legislative session, providing that total appropriations do not exceed the total estimated revenues for any given fiscal year. The careful use of this supplemental power has proven useful for gov-

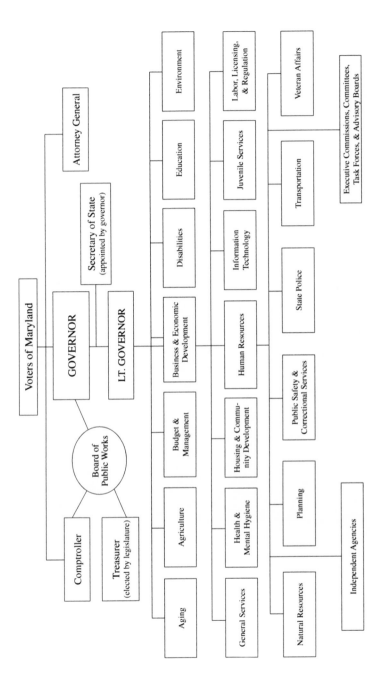

Figure 8-1. The executive branch. Source: Maryland State Archives, *Maryland Manual On-line*, 2009.

ernors in convincing legislators to support administration initiatives as well as the annual budget bill.

As discussed in chapter 10, the legislature possesses noteworthy procedural and political influence over the budget, but the governor is clearly the dominant agenda setter and principal policy actor on state fiscal matters. In addition to shaping the state budget, Maryland's governor has the ability to reduce expenditures after approval by the general assembly. This power derives from the administrative and management control exercised by the governor over departments and agencies and from statutory authority to reduce discretionary appropriations up to 25 percent with the approval of the board of public works.[18] This authority was used six times by Governor Schaefer during fiscal years 1991–93 to address state fiscal issues; by Governor Glendening in fiscal years 2002–3; by Governor Ehrlich in fiscal years 2003–4; and by Governor O'Malley in fiscal years 2007–10.

THE POWER OF APPOINTMENT

The governor of Maryland is endowed with significant powers of appointment that add substantially to the capacity and strength of the office. The heads of all executive departments and agencies (or their appointing authority boards) are appointed or designated by the governor. The governor possesses the power to initially appoint, with the consent of the state senate, all of the judges that serve on the trial and appellate courts of the state's judicial system. The governor also fills vacancies in the Maryland General Assembly, normally upon the recommendation of local party central committees but having discretion to choose in the event of tie votes, conflicting recommendations from multicounty districts, or a lapse in time. The governor even holds the power to select the attorney general and the comptroller in the event of vacancies in those statewide elected offices. This occurred in 1998 with the death of Comptroller Louis L. Goldstein less than seven months before the end of his tenth term of office.

On the second Thursday of every February during the regular annual session of the Maryland General Assembly the governor's appointments secretary delivers in a green leather bag to the president of the state senate and to the speaker of the house of delegates those appointments made by the governor to various offices, boards, and commissions that require approval by the respective legislative chambers. The "greenbag appointments" are anxiously awaited every year by the legislature. The greenbag often reflects the nature of the relationship between the executive and legislative branches of state government. By the inclusion or exclusion of certain individuals in the greenbag the governor can express his agreement or disagreement with members of the legislature who may have sought appointment for one of their constituents or associates.

The governor enjoys the opportunity to appoint numerous members of the nearly three hundred advisory boards, commissions, task forces, and committees that have been created by legislative action or by executive order and that often do not require the approval of the legislature. The governor has the ability to exercise the direct appointment of nearly six thousand individuals, giving the Maryland governor extensive reach into statewide constituencies and into local government affairs.

THE MODERN GOVERNOR'S OFFICE AND STAFF

The personnel and resources of the contemporary governor's office are substantial and would hardly be recognized by the early governors, who labored with little administrative assistance. For fiscal year 2010 there were eighty-six positions authorized by the legislature for the office of governor, with an annual budget in excess of $9.5 million. The governor has a chief of staff to coordinate implementation of policy with the executive departments and agencies. Other senior staff are devoted to policy development and to working directly with the general assembly on administration priorities. A professional communications office assists the governor in media relations and message development and delivery. A Washington office is maintained by the governor's office to coordinate relations with the federal government and the U.S. Congress. In addition the governor has personal administrative staff to assist with scheduling and correspondence as well as intergovernmental relations. Finally, professional staff are assigned to the operation of Government House, the official residence of the governor, for official state functions as well as for the personal needs of the gubernatorial family.

The staff positions authorized for the governor are supplemented by persons detailed from other departments or agencies. For example, the governor is assigned a full complement of state police officers who provide around-the-clock executive protection services. From time to time individuals are assigned from the cabinet departments and executive branch agencies to work on specific projects or policy initiatives with the governor's staff.

ADDITIONAL POWERS OF THE GOVERNOR

The governor possesses singular personal power in discharging the role of the state's chief executive. Gubernatorial authority to represent and negotiate on behalf of the state has been asserted and upheld with respect to interstate agreements and intergovernmental affairs. In addition the governor has rule-making and policymaking authority through the issuance of executive orders. The governor has the sole, broad power to grant executive clemency, pardons, and commutations (with or without conditions). The number of pardons granted varies with the criminal justice philosophy of each governor.

Under Article IX of the Maryland Constitution the governor appoints an adjutant-general for the Maryland National Guard subject to confirmation by the state senate. Power over the state militia and military affairs permits the governor to respond to emergency situations caused by natural forces or man-made disasters.

Unique to Maryland, the governor plays the central role in legislative redistricting every ten years under the state constitution.[19] Governors have appointed redistricting committees to assist in the formulation and development of legislative district plans but personally retained their prerogative to shift state legislative boundary lines for constituent and political objectives.

OTHER EXECUTIVE BRANCH CONSTITUTIONAL OFFICES

The Lieutenant Governor

The office of lieutenant governor of Maryland was first created under the constitution of 1864. However, Lieutenant Governor Christopher Cox alienated the members of the Maryland General Assembly to the extent that the office was abolished under the 1867 constitution, before his term expired. With the approval of a constitutional amendment in 1970 it was reestablished after Governor Spiro Agnew became vice president of the United States.[20]

Secretary of State Blair Lee was elected independently as Maryland's first twentieth-century lieutenant governor in the same general election that ratified the constitutional amendment restoring the office and also providing for the election of a lieutenant governor on a joint ticket with the governor commencing in 1974. A gubernatorial candidate must now designate a running mate at the time of filing to run for the office of governor.

Once elected, the duties specified in the state constitution provide that the lieutenant governor "shall have only the duties delegated to him by the governor." Maryland's lieutenant governor is a person in waiting for the disqualification, resignation, or death of the governor. On those occasions when the governor will be out of the state for an extended period of time, it has become the custom to designate the lieutenant governor as the acting governor. The role of lieutenant governor in Maryland continues to evolve, with increasing recognition that the complexity of modern state government make the office important, relevant, and useful for an administration.

Maryland's lieutenant governors have participated as active members of their respective governor's administration, with one exception. Blair Lee provided legislative acumen and a gentlemanly demeanor to the Mandel era and assumed the role of acting governor in 1977. Governor Hughes's lieutenant governor during his first term, former Prince George's County councilman Sam Bogley, was chosen in the haste of a filing deadline and proved ideologically incompatible with the governor and was given little responsibility.[21] State Senator Joe Curran was chosen by Governor Hughes to be his second-term running mate because of his legislative experience, political compatibility, and prior relationship with the governor. Lieutenant Governor Curran carved out substantive policy areas to handle for the Hughes administration, which laid the groundwork for Curran's election as attorney general in 1986. Governor Schaefer's lieutenant governor, former state senate president "Mickey" Steinberg, was selected because of his legislative skills and relationships. A serious rift developed between them during Schaefer's second term as Steinberg sought independence in fashioning his own run for governor in 1994.

Governor Glendening chose Kathleen Kennedy Townsend to be lieutenant governor in 1994 and gave her significant responsibility over criminal justice matters in their first term and over economic development in their second term. He allowed her to chair meetings of the board of public works and routinely shared the spotlight with her in public appearances. Governor Ehrlich gave his lieutenant governor, Michael Steele, a prominent role as a spokesperson and representative for the administration on issues ranging from criminal justice to public education. At the 2004 Republican National Convention it was Lieutenant Governor Steele, not Governor Ehrlich, who made a nationally televised convention floor speech. Maryland's current lieutenant governor, former Prince George's County delegate Anthony Brown, selected by Governor O'Malley for his political compatibility and to balance the ticket, was given the responsibility of coordinating state readiness for the impact of the federal Base Realignment and Closure Act and of helping to shepherd health care reform issues through the legislature.

With a single exception, Maryland's lieutenant governors have not been successful in utilizing the office as a springboard for future electoral success. Blair Lee (Mandel's lieutenant governor) in 1978 and Mickey Steinberg (Schaefer's lieutenant governor) in 1994 failed to capture their party's nomination for governor after serving two terms as lieutenant governor. Although avoiding serious primary opposition, Lieutenant Governor Kathleen Kennedy Townsend failed in her general election bid to become governor in 2002. Sam Bogley, (Hughes's lieutenant governor) was dumped from the Hughes ticket in 1982 and instead ran on an opposition ticket in the primary election, losing decisively to the incumbent governor and his new running mate. Lieutenant Governor Michael Steele lost a high-profile race for a vacant U.S. Senate seat to Congressman Ben Cardin in the 2006 general election but remained active in party politics, becoming chair of the Republican National Committee in 2009. The only lieutenant governor to serve in a subsequent political office was Joe Curran, who ran successfully for Maryland attorney general in 1986 and served a record five consecutive four-year terms.

The Comptroller of Maryland

The Maryland Office of Comptroller is a nationally unique, statewide elected office first established under the 1851 constitution; the comptroller holds a two-year term with responsibility for "general superintendence of the fiscal affairs of the State."[22] Beginning in 1926 the term of office was extended to four years. There are no express qualifications for the office set forth in the Maryland Constitution and no limit on the number of terms that can be served.

The comptroller has numerous constitutional and statutory duties. Article IV of the state constitution sets forth broad supervisory and management mandates and makes the office responsible for the collection of all taxes and revenues. These constitutional directives have been supplemented by extensive duties and responsibilities assigned under statutes passed by the general assembly. Consequently the comptroller's office is a prime point of citizen contact and for the state's political subdivisions through the collection of revenue from a multitude of sources. The comptroller sits as a member of the powerful board of public works. Other statutory positions include the board of revenue estimates, the capital debt affordability commission, the commission on state debt, the state board of canvassers, and the hall of records commission. In fiscal year 2010 the office of comptroller had more than 1,140 employees and an annual budget of over $136 million.

The individuals who have served as comptroller have been central to the political and governmental history of the state. Three were elected governor after completing terms as comptroller (Goldsborough, Harrington, Tawes), and two (Lee and Goldsborough) subsequently served in the U.S. Senate. In the past eighty-seven years there have been only six persons elected comptroller. William S. Gordy Jr. was elected five times (1921–34). J. Millard Tawes was elected four times (in 1938, 1942, and again in 1950 and 1954 before being elected governor in 1958). James J. Lacy was elected for a single term in 1946 between the Tawes terms.

The legendary Louis L. Goldstein began nearly forty years of service as comptroller with the first of ten successful elections in 1958, before his death only a few days before the candidate filing deadline in July 1998. Comptroller Goldstein's remarkable career earned him the title "Mr. Maryland" out of respect for his being the quintessential public servant who oversaw the transformation of the office of comptroller to an efficient, modern, technologically advanced fiscal public office.[23] During his four decades as comptroller Maryland was the first state to share computerized data with the Internal Revenue Service and in 1976 was one of the first states to implement a central computerized accounting and reporting system. The comptroller's office building in Annapolis is named after Goldstein, and the National Association of State Comptrollers presents its Leadership Award in his honor to recognize "extraordinary excellence and leadership in state financial management."

Former governor William Donald Schaefer, elected in 1998, became the first former governor to resume a political career as comptroller under the 1867 constitution. Schaefer was reelected to a second term in 2002 but finished third in a closely contested 2006 Democratic primary won by Peter Franchot, a member of the house of delegates from Montgomery County. The only Republicans elected comptroller were Robert P. Graham in 1895 and Phillips Lee Goldsborough in 1897, who was also elected governor in 1911.

The Attorney General

Under Section 48 of the 1776 Maryland Constitution the attorney general was appointed by the governor, with the advice and consent of the legislative governor's council. The office of the attorney general was abolished and expressly prohibited under the 1851 constitution but was reestablished under the 1864 constitution, when it became a statewide elected office serving a four-year term. The attorney general is the legal counsel to all three branches of government and, with few exceptions, to all state departments, boards, and commissions.

In fiscal year 2010 the attorney general directed the work of 249 lawyers, managed a budget of over $27.3 million, and represented the state in litigation before Maryland and federal courts. The attorney general's office also represents the clerks of court, the registers of wills, the sheriffs, and the state's attorneys of the twenty-three counties and Baltimore City. The attorney general renders opinions to the general assembly, the governor, and any state department or agency. The administrative rules and regulations of the state departments and agencies must be reviewed by the office of the attorney general before becoming effective. The attorney general enforces the antitrust, consumer protection, and securities laws of the state and directs the Medicaid Fraud Control Unit in the investigation and prosecution of program fraud.

Under the Maryland Constitution the attorney general must be a citizen of the state and a qualified voter and must have resided and practiced law in Maryland for a period of ten years preceding the election. In 2006 the Maryland Court of Appeals disqualified a candidate for attorney general only a few weeks before the 2006 primary election, holding that he had not practiced law for ten years in the state.[24] There are no term limits for the office of attorney general.

The nominee of the Democratic Party has been elected attorney general in thirty-five out of the thirty-seven general elections held from 1867 to 2006. The only Republicans elected were Harry M. Clabaugh in the 1895 Republican sweep and Alexander Armstrong, who won a narrow 589-vote victory in 1919. Democrat Douglas F. Gansler, the former two-term state's attorney for Montgomery County, the state's most populous jurisdiction, won the contested 2006 primary and general elections with comfortable electoral margins and was unopposed in the 2010 election.

In the first half of the twentieth century three attorneys general became governors (Ritchie in 1919, O'Conor in 1938, and Lane in 1946). Four other attorneys general have sought the governor's office in the past century, but three were unsuccessful in primary elections (Thomas B. Finan in 1966, Francis B. Burch in 1978, and Stephen H. Sachs in 1986) and one lost in a general election (Armstrong in 1923).

The State Treasurer

Elected on a joint ballot by the two houses of the Maryland General Assembly, the past four state treasurers since 1975 have been, not surprisingly, former members of the general assembly. The current treasurer, Nancy Kopp, served nearly twenty-seven years in the state legislature before her first selection as treasurer in 2001. Her immediate two predecessors, Richard N. Dixon and Lucille Mauer, had long tenures in the house of delegates, and the former president of the state senate, William James, served as treasurer from 1975 until 1987.

The treasurer of Maryland is responsible for the accounting of all deposits made on behalf of the state in financial institutions authorized by the treasurer and for preparing and signing all checks disbursing state funds, which are countersigned by the comptroller. The treasurer is also the custodian of all stocks, bonds, and other investments of the state. The treasurer is, in essence, the state's banker. In fiscal year 2010 the office supervised a professional staff of sixty-one with a budget in excess of $41.6 million.

Along with the governor and the comptroller, the treasurer is one of three members of the important board of public works. The treasurer is also a member of the board of revenue estimates, the board of trustees of the Maryland State Retirement and Pension Systems, the state board of canvassers, the Maryland Industrial Development Financing Authority, and the capital debt affordability committee.

The Secretary of State

The office of secretary of state was created by constitutional amendment in 1837 simultaneous with the constitutional change providing for the direct election of the governor. Common to the mid-Atlantic region of the original thirteen states, from Virginia to New York, Maryland's secretary of state is appointed by the governor, subject to the approval and confirmation by the state senate of the Maryland General Assembly.[25] The secretary of state performs numerous constitutional, statutory, regulatory, and customary and traditional functions, including certifying documents, producing and publishing the voluminous Code of Maryland Regulations, and registering and regulating charitable organizations and serves on the state board of canvassers that certifies all state elections. The secretary is a member of the governor's cabinet and attests to the governor's signature on all public papers and documents as required by law for intrastate, interstate, and international purposes. The secretary is also the chair of the governor's sub-cabinet on international affairs.

BECOMING GOVERNOR

The roadmap to becoming the governor of Maryland has changed significantly during the course of the state's history. From 1776 until the first popular election of governor in 1838 the legislature selected the governor annually. Not surprisingly all of the Maryland's early governors either had prior service in the state legislature or close personal relationships with the members of the general assembly. The first elected governors also had legislative experience, and given the limited powers of the office, service as governor was often merely a stepping stone to another public office or private business position. From the Civil War until the first party primary elections in 1915 the nominees for governor were selected at state party conventions. Consequently the individuals nominated were firmly connected to party politics, which was essential for forging the coalitions necessary to receive the nomination at the statewide party conventions.

With the implementation of gubernatorial primary elections in 1915, the roadmap for becoming governor was dramatically altered. The Maryland route varies from the national pattern, in which most governors have had some legislative experience.[26] No sitting member of the Maryland General Assembly has been elected governor since the nineteenth century. Service in the statewide offices of comptroller and attorney general and as the chief executive of a large urban jurisdiction has been the dominant recruitment pattern.

Beginning in 1946 a former attorney general, one comptroller, three mayors of Baltimore, and two county executives from large suburban jurisdictions have been elected governor. Governor Mandel was first chosen by the legislature to fill a vacancy in the office before running as a sitting governor in 1970. Governor Ehrlich has been the only person elected without local executive or statewide office experience since World War II and the first sitting member of Congress to be elected governor since 1899. By occupation and training, fourteen of the sixteen governors elected under the primary system have been lawyers. The other two were a former businessman (Tawes in 1958) and a college professor (Glendening in 1994; see Table 8-1).

ELECTORAL PATTERNS

There have been forty-six gubernatorial general elections in Maryland, from the first popular election of governor in 1838 through 2010. The first elections were highly competitive races between Democratic and Whig candidates, with the winner never receiving more than 52 percent of the vote. The American Know Nothing Party captured the governor's office in 1857, during the tumultuous pre–Civil War era, and the nominees of a new, pragmatic, centrist, and loosely formed Union Party garnered the majority of votes in 1861 and 1865, during the Civil War.

Thirty-seven gubernatorial general elections have been contests between major party Democratic and Republican candidates since 1867. The Democratic candidate has won twenty-nine of these elections; only six Republican candidates have won seven elections (in 1895, 1911, 1934, 1950, 1954,

Table 8-1: Profile of Maryland governors (elected 1946 through 2010)

Term	Residence	Name	Occupation	Prior position	Prior public offices
1947–51	Washington County	William Preston Lane	lawyer	private business	attorney general, 1931–35
1951–59	Baltimore City	Theodore R. McKeldin	lawyer	mayor, Baltimore City, 1947–51	(none)
1959–67	Somerset County	J. Millard Tawes	businessman	comptroller of Maryland, 1951–59	comptroller, 1939–47
1967–69	Baltimore County	Spiro T. Agnew	lawyer	county executive, Baltimore County, 1962–66	(none)
1969–79	Baltimore City	Marvin Mandel	lawyer	speaker, house of delegates,1964–69	house of delegates, 1952–69
1979–81	Baltimore City	Harry R. Hughes	lawyer	private law practice	state senate, 1959–70; house of delegates, 1955–59
1987–95	Baltimore City	William Donald Schaefer	lawyer	mayor, Baltimore City, 1971–87	Baltimore City Council, 1955–67; council president, 1967–71
1995–2003	Prince George's County	Parris N. Glendening	college professor	County executive, Prince George's County. 1982–94	Prince George's County Council, 1974–82; Hyattsville City Council, 1972–74
2003–7	Baltimore County	Robert L. Ehrlich Jr.	lawyer	U.S. House of Representatives, 1995–2003	house of delegates, 1987–95
2007–	Baltimore City	Martin O'Malley	lawyer	mayor, Baltimore City, 1999–2007	Baltimore City Council, 1995–99

Source: Prepared by John T. Willis from official records.

1966, and 2002). The closest gubernatorial election in Maryland history (by vote margin and percentage of margin) occurred in 1919, when Democrat Albert C. Ritchie defeated Republican Harry W. Nice by 165 votes out of 228,778 votes cast (0.07 percent). Since the Second World War gubernatorial election voting patterns have merged with the partisan outcomes evident in presidential election results in Maryland.

GUBERNATORIAL STYLE AND LEADERSHIP

Although the Maryland governor's considerable formal powers provide the capacity for a strong executive, the success of a governor is ultimately determined by the individual's administrative, management, and political skills. These include the effective exercise of appointive powers, persuasive advocacy capabilities, mastery of the media and public relations, the substantive content of a policy agenda, a compelling vision for the state, and achieving productive relationships with other public, party, and legislative officials. The personality and professional orientation of the person occupying the office of governor can augment or diminish the formal institutional powers. The style and leadership skills of each governor are often the most critical factors affecting policy and program outcomes.

In the modern era of state politics all of Maryland's governors have displayed unique personal skills and styles, first politically, to win office, and subsequently in discharging their duties and responsibilities as the state's chief executive.

THE CONSUMMATE INSIDER: MARVIN MANDEL

Governor Mandel ascended to the role of governor in 1969 from his position as speaker of the house of delegates, which elected him in a joint ballot with the state senate to succeed Spiro Agnew.[27] During the first half of his tenure, drawing on his considerable legislative experience, Mandel "dominated the legislature by dint of his insider's skill in bargaining, persuading, and using patronage."[28]

Governor Mandel's extensive knowledge of individual legislators and of the legislative process helped him achieve nearly universal approval of his initiatives in his first two years as governor, when ninety-three out of ninety-five of his legislative proposals were enacted. Mandel successfully steered the reorganization of state government in accordance with the recommendations that flowed from numerous commissions and reform efforts of the 1960s.[29] It was during his administration that the structure and form of modern Maryland state government were fashioned and long-sought reforms and restructuring of the judicial branch of state government were substantially accomplished. With the governor's support, Maryland enacted significant progressive legislation in the 1970s related to consumer protection, environmental protection, health care and aging, public school construction, mass transit, public education, and, ironically, campaign finance and ethics reform.

Governor Mandel's political skills extended to maintaining personal control of the Maryland Democratic State Central Committee, which he chaired in 1968. In 1970 he encountered nominal opposition in the primary election and cruised to victory with a substantial (66 percent) majority in the general election. Mandel always had allies in charge of the Maryland Democratic Party and maintained a firm grasp on state and local party affairs. On the national level he was active in the National Governor's Association and chaired the National Caucus of Democratic Governors in 1971.[30]

Mandel's 1974 reelection was likewise never in doubt, despite some hints of darkening personal and political clouds. In the spring of 1973 his supporters organized a unified Democratic ticket for the four statewide offices and raised a then unprecedented $1 million for the campaign at a single event labeled the "Four Star Salute."[31] Less than seven weeks after this politically powerful event, during the July fourth holiday weekend, Governor Mandel announced a very awkward separation from his wife. He moved out of the official governor's residence for five months while a resolution of his domestic situation was negotiated.[32]

Governor Mandel's policy accomplishments were overshadowed by an investigation by the U.S. Attorney's Office for the District of Maryland that was following leads of alleged corruption in county and state government.[33] In November 1975 he and several of his longtime associates were indicted by a federal grand jury on charges of mail fraud and racketeering, sending shock waves through the Maryland electorate and political establishment. For nearly six years the story of Mandel's two trials, various appeals, a civil lawsuit by the state to recover furniture and personal property removed from the governor's mansion by the Mandels, his fifteen months in a federal prison, and sentence commutation by President Reagan were a persistent backdrop to the state's political environment.[34] The historian George H. Callcott reflected on the Mandel administration's conduct: "Circumstantial evidence of the governor's wrongdoing was overwhelming: huge gifts, huge conflicts of interest, huge benefits to the givers of gifts, were all facts. Perhaps the exact nature of the quid pro quo, the peculiar charges, and the court's bungling hardly mattered. A costlier re-

sult for society, in the Mandel case as in Watergate, was the growing dis-
taste for government itself."[35]

THE GOVERNOR OF REFORM: HARRY R. HUGHES

Six days after Governor Mandel relinquished power to Lieutenant Governor Blair Lee due to his pending corruption trial, Harry R. Hughes resigned
as Maryland's secretary of transportation in protest over what he termed
unethical and improper interference with the selection process for management consultant services for the new Baltimore subway system.[36] In a
closely contested Democratic primary election in September 1978 Hughes
won a come-from-behind victory, and after winning 71 percent of the vote
in the general election over former Republican U.S. senator J. Glenn Beall
was sworn in as governor.

Tall and handsome, reserved, calm, and cool, Hughes looked the part of
a governor. His administration was marked by a cooperative relationship
with the Maryland General Assembly, where he had served one term as a
member of the house of delegates and three terms as a state senator representing Caroline County. He served as state senate majority leader and was
chair of the Maryland Democratic Party from 1969 to 1970.

Governor Hughes is often credited with restoring integrity to and confidence in the office of governor. His pronounced governmental philosophy,
that the legislative branch was "the policy-making arm of government,"[37]
was an unprecedented admission for a modern Maryland governor. His first
term was marked by an aggressive economic development program, tax relief measures, expansion and modernization of correctional facilities, conformity of the Baltimore City court system with the rest of the state, increased and modified state aid to public education, and new environmental
programs for the disposal of nuclear and toxic waste. His second term saw
the passage of the state's acclaimed Critical Area Act, which imposed restrictions on building and farming activity within 1,000 feet of the Chesapeake Bay.[38] In a personal interview Hughes proudly noted that his two
biggest accomplishments were landmark progress on environmental issues and breakthroughs in achieving diversity in the Maryland judiciary.
Hughes's judicial appointments included the first African American to be
appointed to the court of special appeals and the first women to serve on
the district court and circuit court in several jurisdictions.

Active in politics since law school and a former chair of the Maryland
Democratic Party, Governor Hughes embraced his role as party leader.
He championed a former legislative colleague as chair of the party, State

Senator Rosalie Abrams (the first woman in the top state party post), and he opened the door for participation by young party activists throughout the state. Through personal attendance at party functions and encouragement given to party leaders at all levels, he supported party-building efforts throughout the state. He similarly enjoyed his role as the state party leader at national conventions and on the campaign trail.

Hughes's tenure as governor ended with disappointment and a failed election bid for the U.S. Senate. In the winter of 1985 two state-chartered savings and loan institutions failed, leaving tens of thousands of Marylanders without access to their savings and business accounts. A combination of lax state regulatory oversight, a delayed response, and the magnitude of the crisis placed responsibility (fairly or unfairly) on the Hughes administration.[39] The governor and the general assembly fashioned a bailout and a state guarantee to depositors of their principal in special legislative sessions held in the spring and fall of 1985. These efforts did not help Governor Hughes reach his political goals. A seeming shoo-in for the U.S. Senate seat being vacated by the retiring liberal Republican Charles Mac Mathias, Governor Hughes saw his commanding lead in the polls one year before the election evaporate into a third-place finish behind two popular Democratic congresspersons in the 1986 Democratic primary election.

"THE 800 POUND GORILLA": WILLIAM DONALD SCHAEFER

In 1986 Marylanders turned to another style of leadership in the highly charged, magnetic personality of William Donald Schaefer, who gained respect and fame during his fifteen-year tenure as mayor of Baltimore for his energy, drive, determination, and "do it now" attitude toward government services. After a period of public courting by his numerous supporters, Mayor Schaefer entered the gubernatorial race as "the 800 pound gorilla of Maryland politics."[40] He overwhelmed Attorney General Steve Sachs in the Democratic primary and obliterated the token Republican opposition in the general election with a record-shattering 82.4 percent of the vote.

Schaefer brought to the statehouse his expansive and quirky personality, his flair for media, and his "big city mayor" mentality. In his political biography of the governor the journalist C. Fraser Smith aptly observed, "He ran on the highest octane human fuel: self-doubt, anger and the clarity of those who believe in their own vision."[41] From support for a "Maryland You Are Beautiful" campaign to efforts to deal with the state's outdated tax structure, there was no issue, big or small, that could not, would not be tackled once Governor Schaefer decided to make it part of his agenda.

The list of accomplishments trumpeted by the Schaefer administration is long and varied.[42] In addition to the customary general statements of support for education, economic development, health care, public safety, and the environment, specific mentions include the reorganization of the higher education system, mandatory kindergarten attendance, a new department of environment, an expanded Baltimore Convention Center, Maryland's first light rail system, the nation's first state outreach effort for AIDS patients, a ban on "Saturday Night Special" handguns, and construction of a premier baseball stadium, the world-renowned Oriole Park at Camden Yards.

During his first term Governor Schaefer averaged double-digit increases in state spending, with significant expansion of transportation projects and state buildings as well as program increases in education and public safety. His second term proved more difficult, with a national recession sharply curtailing state revenues. Special sessions of the Maryland General Assembly were called in 1991 and 1992 to handle budget shortfalls.

Schaefer's governance style and personality, hampered by the sluggish economy and recovery, generated negative notoriety during his second term. When he inquired of a delegate from Worcester County, "How's that (expletive)-house of an Eastern Shore?" as he made his way onto the floor of the Maryland General Assembly to attend the swearing-in of the state treasurer during the 1991 legislative session, Schaefer offended an entire region of the state.[43] Responses included a parade of outhouses aboard pickup trucks circling the statehouse in Annapolis and packages of corn cobs wrapped in toilet paper mailed to the governor.[44] Citizens who complained about Schaefer's actions were startled to receive untempered handwritten letters and photographs of themselves in envelopes from their governor.[45] His solid job performance ratings at the beginning of his tenure in office dropped sharply in 1993 to decidedly negative ratings before recovering to below 40 percent ratings at the end of his second term in January 1995.[46]

Although a "big city mayor" in terms of his style, policies, and belief in an activist role for government, Schaefer was not firmly rooted in Democratic Party affairs. Throughout his career, even during his tenure as governor and titular head of the party, he frequently supported and encouraged Republican candidates, sometimes quietly and indirectly through allies and sometimes, though less often, openly and loudly. His tacit support of Republican Anne Arundel County executive Robert Pascal in the 1982 gubernatorial election against incumbent Democrat Harry Hughes foreshadowed his appointment of Pascal to be his appointments secretary in charge of patronage during his first term as governor. He utilized his influence on the congressional redistricting process in a special legislative session in 1991 to protect the district of his friend, Republican Congresswoman Helen D. Bentley. This was to the detriment of Democratic Congressman Tom Mc-Millan, who lost reelection after being placed in a new and unfamiliar First Congressional District against incumbent Republican Congressman Wayne Gilchrist. His 1992 endorsement of President George Bush for reelection drew anger, frustration, outrage, and shock from many Democrats, and he barely eluded a formal rebuke by the Democratic State Central Committee.[47] Schaefer openly encouraged his longtime friend Bentley to enter the race to succeed him as governor in 1994. In the 2002 gubernatorial election his former chief of staff was the campaign manager for the Republican candidate for governor, Robert Ehrlich, and significant, close friends and associates of Schaefer strongly supported Ehrlich. Because of his government program and policy initiatives, Governor Schaefer is properly considered a Democrat, but his personal politics and style made him a party unto himself.

Unquestionably William Donald Schaefer's strong-willed personality and heartfelt desire to use the resources of government for the public good make him one of the most dominant and important Maryland public officials of the twentieth century. However, his quixotic personality, gruff demeanor, and temper tantrums, combined with the staunch loyalty of his supporters, sometimes conjured a cult image surrounding his extraordinary career.[48] After his death in April 2011, the three-day funeral arrangements typified his public life with a viewing held at the state capitol building in Annapolis followed by a procession around Baltimore City landmarks, another resting in state at city hall, and church services where he was lauded by political leaders, supporters, and former staff.[49]

Indeed Schaefer has had more public buildings and places named after him than any other politician in the history of Maryland. On the occasion of the naming of a municipal office building in Frederick in his honor, Schaefer remarked, "I don't know if you know it, but I am so pleased if you name a matchstick after me."[50] In response to the flurry of recognitions orchestrated by the Schaefer staff and loyalists prior to his leaving office, former Baltimore City state senator Julian Lapides noted in the same article, "The only thing left to change is the state's name."

THE ANALYTICAL AND PRAGMATIC PROFESSOR: PARRIS GLENDENING

As the country was grappling with economic turmoil and a global wave of political changes in the early 1990s, Marylanders again turned to a gubernatorial candidate with a different style from his predecessor. Professorial, calculating, cool, and determined, Prince George's County Executive Parris N. Glendening fashioned a convincing 1994 primary election victory based on a carefully assembled long-range plan. Seizing the opportunities of being a chief executive of a mini-state for an unprecedented three terms, Glendening honed his personal and political skills with his sights firmly on the statehouse. He captured a narrow 5,993-vote general election win over a surprise Republican nominee as the only newly elected Democratic governor east of Oregon in a decidedly Republican year. Fully utilizing gubernatorial powers during his first term to broaden and deepen his political support, Governor Glendening easily withstood a primary election challenge in 1998 to a second term and comfortably repelled, by ten percentage points, a repeat Sauerbrey challenge in the general election.

A student and practitioner of government and politics, Glendening came to the statehouse with a unique set of qualifications and experiences. He also arrived in Annapolis in an unexpected and challenging environment. His conservative Republican opponent did not cease her election challenge until two days before the inauguration.[51] The outgoing temperamental predecessor held on to power resolutely, even submitting his own version of the next fiscal year's budget that proposed spending all available revenue.[52] One of Glendening's county political antagonists was firmly entrenched as president of the state senate, and the speaker of the house of delegates, a close ally of the departing governor, had aspirations to be governor and was considering a 1998 primary challenge. Barely two weeks after his inauguration Glendening and several members of his staff from Prince George's County were embroiled in allegations of receiving inappropriate and early pension benefits from county government.[53]

Undaunted, Governor Glendening began pursuing a substantive agenda consistent with the "Vision for Maryland's Future" pamphlet published at the beginning of his campaign. While addressing the concerns of the electorate and his opponents with targeted tax cuts, tax incentives, and fiscal pruning, he began work on the education and environmental initiatives that constitute the hallmarks of his administration. In his first term he boosted state aid to public education and negotiated a settlement of Baltimore City's lawsuit for increased education funding with a $256 million-a-year disparity grant and a reconstituted, jointly appointed school board. Governor Glendening changed the formula for public school construction to favor schools in older communities and spent a total of $1.2 billion on public school construction. After he approved another $650 million for construction of higher education facilities, higher education saw its annual general fund revenue increased by nearly 23 percent, to $948.7 million.

Governor Glendening fashioned his Smart Growth policies during his first term, featuring five major components. Most significant was the establishment of priority funding areas throughout the state as a mechanism to target state expenditures. The Smart Growth initiatives earned Maryland a national reputation and were copied by twenty-five states in only a few years.[54] Critical to the successful implementation of Smart Growth endeavors were other program and policy changes, including the creation of a neighborhood revitalization program and office in the Department of Housing and Community Development and transportation priorities.

The Glendening years were marked by a progressive policy agenda on a range of issues running counter to the national trends. While the U.S. Congress and other states were retrenching on gun control measures, Glendening won approval of two gun violence measures: the 1996 Gun Violence Act, limiting handgun sales to one a month and outlawing straw purchases, and the 2000 Gun Safety Act, requiring ballistics testing and fingerprinting of new handgun sales.[55] While labor rights were being diminished elsewhere, Governor Glendening secured and won collective bargaining rights for state employees that had not been previously allowed in Maryland. When Congress enacted a law restricting Medicaid funds from being used to pay for the care of undocumented immigrants, the Glendening administration replaced the deleted federal funds with state dollars.[56] As anti-gay sentiment rose elsewhere in the country, the Glendening administration successfully amended state employment laws in 2001 to prohibit discrimination based on sexual orientation.[57] As affirmative action programs were being dismantled in other states and at the federal level, the Glendening administration enhanced minority contract opportunities through legislation and executive orders.

Governor Glendening exercised his appointive powers to produce a veritable litany of firsts in state government, in the composition of the state judiciary and on boards and commissions. Highlighting these appointments were the selection of Judge Robert Bell as the first African American chief judge of the Maryland Court of Appeals, the state's highest court; the first African Americans appointed as circuit court judges in Anne Arundel, Howard, Baltimore, and Montgomery counties; the first woman judge appointed among the nine counties on the Eastern Shore; and the first Hispanic and Asian American circuit court judges in the state's history. Over 25 percent of his judicial appointments were minorities and 38 percent were women. Administratively Glendening chose the first African American in Maryland to be a governor's chief of staff, Major F. Riddick Jr. One-third of the Glendening cabinet were African Americans, and nearly half were women.

Governor Glendening assumed the role of leader of the Maryland Democratic Party as soon as he secured the nomination in the 1994 primary election. At the fall organizational meeting of the Democratic State Central Committee he had nominated and elected a slate of party officers to assume control of the party operations. These included former governor Hughes as party chair. Glendening continued to exercise firm control over party activities during his tenure, with the successful recommendation of party officers, party staff, and representatives to the Democratic National Committee and the selection of delegates, alternates, and committee members to the 1996 and 2000 national conventions. He was also active in the affairs of the Democratic Governor's Association, becoming its chair in 2000 and the head of its fund-raising arm for the 2002 election cycle.

Prompted by a downturn in the economy that sharply curtailed state revenues in 2001 and 2002, the Glendening administration came under attack for its fiscal policies from the Republican Party and from his predecessor in office, the state comptroller. Governor Glendening was also injured in the public eye and press for having separated from his respected political spouse shortly before the 2000 Democratic National Convention and marrying a younger member of his staff in early 2002. After eight years of pragmatic, progressive policies successfully adopted and implemented, the failure of the Democrats to hold power in the statehouse left the legacy of the Glendening administration somewhat unsettled.

THE REPUBLICAN OPPORTUNIST: ROBERT EHRLICH

In the 2002 gubernatorial election Marylanders again chose a governor with a style and career experiences very different from his predecessor's. Robert Ehrlich was the first Republican governor to be elected in thirty-six years and brought with him a political perspective acquired as a member of a minority party from 1987 to 1994 in the Maryland state legislature and as a member of a Republican majority party in Congress from 1995 to 2003.

Ehrlich's winning political coalition differed from those assembled by the previous five Republican governors, who had won their elections as the more liberal candidate in their respective races. They had won with majority support from voters in the state's more progressive urban areas, including Baltimore City. Although prominently featuring the moderate label in campaign advertising and speeches, Ehrlich often described his government philosophy, before and after assuming office, as "conservative with libertarian leanings."[58] His governing style was marked by conflict, confrontation, and seeming contradictions.

Consistent with the priorities expressed by his predecessors, the Ehrlich gubernatorial website continually promoted commitments "to the five pillars of my Administration—budget, education, public safety, healthcare and the environment, and commerce."[59] Saddled with significant increases in health care costs, early revenue shortfalls to meet legislatively mandated increases in public education funding, and statewide demands for increased transportation funding, Governor Ehrlich endeavored to navigate a delicate course between political ideology and government necessity. As a consequence his administration's policies and practices contained apparent contrasts and contradictions.

His 2002 campaign mantra, "No new taxes," stood in contrast to a 2004 fiscal year budget proposal that triggered a 57 percent rise in the state property tax rate. Repeated assertions of fiscal conservatism conflicted with a plethora of increased fees and charges for government services totaling over $1 billion proposed by Governor Ehrlich and approved by legislation or administrative action. These included a 35 percent hike in car title registration fees and a tripling of the annual franchise fee paid by all business entities, regardless of size. The lack of a substantive long-term budget solution prompted the *Baltimore Sun* and the *Washington Post* to label these fiscal efforts "irresponsible budgeting practices" and "a lot of borrowing from Peter to pay Paul."[60] Claims that the administration turned projected deficits into surpluses were at odds with a persistent billion-dollar structural deficit at the beginning and end of Ehrlich's term in office.[61]

Governor Ehrlich created a similarly bipolar record on other public policy issues. He won praise for budget support for disability services and drug treatment programs but garnered criticism for Medicaid cutbacks affecting prescription costs for the elderly and suffered legislative setbacks and received a judicial rebuke for cutting funds extending health care benefits to immigrant women and children.[62] He found support among environmental organizations and activists for a thirty-dollar-a year flush tax to generate money for failing sewer plants but generated harsh criticism over severe cutbacks to land preservation and open space programs. An attempted sale of state land led to a protracted First Amendment fight with the *Baltimore Sun* after Ehrlich issued an order banning state employees from talking to two journalists.[63]

Governor Ehrlich won praise for selecting an African American to be his running mate, but he often irritated Maryland's diverse population with statements like "There is no such thing as a multicultural society that can sustain itself."[64] While he repeatedly blamed the prior administration for the state's alleged budget woes, his budget submissions exceeded the budgets of the previous administration by billions of dollars; his proposed fiscal year 2007 budget of $29.7 billion exceeded his proposed fiscal year 2006 budget by a record $3.765 billion and exceeded the last budget presented by his predecessor by 33 percent, or $7.49 billion.

Although borrowing heavily from the administration of Governor Schaefer and relying on former legislative colleagues for members of the cabinet, the Ehrlich administration did not hesitate to make personnel changes reaching far into state government departments and agencies. These actions went beyond the normal transition turnover in Maryland, provoking several legal challenges and settlements.[65] As a consequence the Maryland General Assembly launched a legislative investigation into state personnel policies in the fall of 2005, focusing on the antics of a longtime Ehrlich political associate and the actions of the appointments office.[66]

Governor Ehrlich was the dominant political force for Maryland Republicans after the second defeat of Ellen Sauerbrey in 1998. At the 2001 winter convention of the Republican State Central Committee, Congressman Ehrlich sharply called for unity and observed that his party at the time lacked "the discipline, the cohesion and the understanding of what it takes to win."[67] Governor Ehrlich's close association with national Republican leaders and lobbyists yielded unprecedented resources for the Maryland Republican Party.

Ehrlich's style and legislative priorities generated battles with the Democratic-controlled legislature, some natural and others unusual for Maryland executive-legislative relationships. Governor Ehrlich unsettled the normal budgeting process of previous administrations by not sharing information in the same manner and on the same timetable with legislative leaders and their staff in the Department of Legislative Services. In statements and press releases following legislative sessions he frequently attacked the Democratic-controlled legislature and its leaders while proclaiming funding increases and policy changes as solely his own accomplishments.[68] Another example of the strained relationship was the manner in which Governor Ehrlich used the procedure of permitting a bill to become law without his signature or veto. In March 2004 he did not sign the bill that cleared the way for additional public education funding under the Bridge to Excellence in Public Schools Act, but in press releases and campaign statements he subsequently touted record increases in public education funding. In the last year of his term he permitted an extraordinary and unprecedented 155 bills to become law without his signature or veto, sending transmittal letters in April and May 2006 to legislative leaders noting "time constraints."[69] Previous and subsequent governors used this procedure only sporadically and in instances of policy disagreements.

Atypical of historical problem solving in Annapolis, but exemplary of Governor Ehrlich's relationship with the legislative branch, was the special session of the Maryland General Assembly called by the governor during the 2004 holiday season to address the issue of medical malpractice insurance. Without the normal consultation and concurrence of legislative leaders, the governor summoned the legislature to its first special session in over twelve years to deal with an issue that had been brewing for several years. He presented a bill to the legislature that was not acted upon; instead the legislature passed its own bill, which was promptly vetoed by the governor and subsequently overridden by the legislature prior to the commencement of the next regular session, on January 10, 2005. This chaotic gridlock was symptomatic of protracted partisan conflict that had not existed in Maryland during most of the twentieth century.

As a reaction to this term of the first modern Republican governor, legislative efforts to reassert power were more open and pronounced. In 2004 the Maryland General Assembly overrode three vetoes of the governor (more overrides than in the preceding twenty years combined) and passed a bill to limit the ability of the governor and board of public works to reduce expenditures without the approval of the general assembly. In 2005 the legislature overrode nine additional gubernatorial vetoes and passed a resolution placing on the 2006 general election ballot a proposed constitutional amendment that would limit the governor's ability to sell state land without the approval of the general assembly.[70] During its 2006 regular session the Maryland General Assembly overrode a record twenty-one policy vetoes on issues ranging from high-profile, precedent-setting measures such as the state minimum wage and requiring Walmart to provide health care coverage or contribute a surcharge to the state's Medicaid program to lower profile legislation related to election procedures and juvenile services.

For Governor Ehrlich confrontation with the Democratic Party and its leaders, as well as with the media and anyone who disagreed with an administration position, was a default option in handling matters of public policy and politics. For example, Ehrlich's refusal to talk to certain reporters from the *Baltimore Sun*, and his order banning state officials from talking to them, led to high-profile federal court litigation.[71] Tired of Governor Ehrlich's governance by conflict and confrontation and his policy contradictions, in the 2006 general election Maryland voters chose his equally telegenic and resourceful opponent.

THE TWENTY-FIRST-CENTURY PRAGMOCRAT:
MARTIN O'MALLEY

The election of Martin J. O'Malley as Maryland's fifty-third governor restored the state's political norm to policymaking and the operation of state
government. In his inaugural address O'Malley touted the theme "One
Maryland, where we move forward together." His experiences as Baltimore
City mayor not only prepared him for the role of chief executive of the state
but also enabled him to forge relationships with the leadership of the general assembly and with fellow municipal and county officials throughout
the state. The *Baltimore Sun* welcomed the reunified government with the
headline "Tone Changes in Annapolis."[72]

But governing the state would not be as easy as winning the election.
In 2007 Maryland was still dealing with fiscal challenges caused by burgeoning health care costs, education program commitments, and a sluggish economy. During O'Malley's initial term the national recession and
its drag on the state's economy and tax revenues would only worsen. After
a relatively calm first legislative session, fiscal realities prompted Governor O'Malley to call for a special session in the fall of 2007 to address the
state's fiscal needs. This controversial session led to an increase in the state
sales tax from 5 to 6 percent and a state income tax increase for higher income taxpayers. The special session also passed a proposed constitutional
amendment, with the governor's assent, to authorize the expansion of legalized gambling at five designated locations in the state. O'Malley's actions garnered praise from various interest groups as well as the media. The
Washington Post columnist E. J. Dionne called him "a governor unafraid of
government."[73] On the other hand, the tax increases passed during the special session rekindled the ire of opponents and provided a foundation for
policy and political dissent.

In tackling the administration of state government O'Malley brought
with him lessons and techniques learned from his award-winning Baltimore City programs. The template of CitiStat was used to create BayStat,
to track progress on cleaning up the Chesapeake Bay, and StateStat, to coordinate policies, programs. and budgets among state agencies. The use of
technology and data to measure performance and monitor progress was one
of the reasons Governor O'Malley garnered a "Public Official of the Year"
award from *Governing* magazine in 2009.[74]

O'Malley's relationship with the Maryland General Assembly stood in
marked contrast from that of his Republican predecessor and even recent
Democratic governors. After the second legislative session the president of

the state senate observed, "He's got a personality where he reaches out to people and says: This is a team effort. Help me get the job done."[75] Reflecting this approach, after the 2008 session Governor O'Malley vetoed only forty-five bills passed by the general assembly, the fewest vetoes issued by a governor in thirty-five years. During his initial four-year term he issued fewer vetoes than any governor since Mandel's first full term (1971–74).

During the 2007–11 term Governor O'Malley's policy agenda was decidedly progressive. His ideology and willingness to take political risks were demonstrated in his appearance before a legislative committee to support the repeal of the death penalty.[76] The governor's website lists education, environment, families, opportunities, public safety, and progress as his policy initiatives. The headings are consistent with the priorities of previous Maryland governors, but the links to videos, speeches, reports, legislation, and other data illustrating administrative success reflect his embrace of twenty-first-century technology.

With respect to core government functions, Maryland continued to rank high under the O'Malley administration. Environmental protection received a boost when initiatives on clean energy, greenhouse gases, and energy efficiency earned the administrative an A from the League of Conservation Voters.[77] Public education received program funding increases, and a vigorous public school construction program was maintained. *Education Week Magazine* ranked Maryland's public schools number one in the nation in 2008, 2009, and 2010.[78] In July 2010 Governor O'Malley received the "Governor of the Year" award from the National Education Association.[79]

Within his own party Governor O'Malley easily assumed the role of leader and has kept the state party engaged in the promotion of Democratic initiatives and in the essentials of party activity. He led the delegation to the 2008 Democratic National Convention and he actively participated in the Democratic Governor's Association and other national organizations. State party chairs recommended by O'Malley have been successful fund-raisers, and the party apparatus fully embraces the new campaign technologies and techniques.

Confronting significant fiscal challenges and a changed national political environment, Governor O'Malley found himself with declining approval ratings and an energized opposition party at the end of his initial term. In 2010 he easily withstood a challenge to a second term from the opponent he defeated in 2006, former Republican governor Robert Ehrlich, which was a test of personalities as well as a measure of the state's traditional political tendencies. It was the first time in state history that a former governor sought reelection after having been previously defeated.

SUMMARY

All of the modern Maryland governors ultimately focus on (and proclaim in self-appraisals of their respective administrations) the basic functions of state government—education, transportation, health care, human services, and public safety—which comprise the bulk of the state's budget. In addition Maryland's chief executives always publicly promote the health of the Chesapeake Bay, although such appeals have been accompanied by varying degrees of personal commitment and financial support. A strong governor has generally served the citizens of Maryland well, as there has been consistently sound financial management for the past sixty years and a general responsiveness to the needs of the citizens and the state.

There have been, and there are now, signs that the strong office of governor is not always appreciated. The other branches and levels of government, as well as the general public, exhibit occasional unease over the powers and performance of Maryland governors. Every governor in the past half-century has left office at the end of his term or terms with less public support than he enjoyed at the beginning or midpoint of his tenure in office.

In response to gubernatorial extensions of power the legislative branch of government has asserted greater authority in mandating programs and influencing the budget and regularly expresses dismay over the powers of the Maryland governor. The judicial branch of government has more frequently demonstrated its independent authority by circumscribing or rejecting decisions of the Maryland governor on issues ranging from land use to redistricting.

The seeds of this interbranch disenchantment are rooted not only in the exercise of independent governmental power but also in a reaction to the sophisticated use of executive power by the experienced and strong-willed personalities that have served as governor. Yet conflict with the legislative and judicial branches has not fundamentally diminished the power and policy potential of the governor's office. Maryland's governor remains among the most powerful in the nation, and future governors will undoubtedly be the central, dominant political and governmental actors in the Old Line State.

CHAPTER NINE

The Maryland Judiciary

We must never forget that the only real source of power that we as judges can tap is the respect of the people. We will command that respect only as long as we strive for neutrality.
U.S. Supreme Court Justice Thurgood Marshall, 1981

Maryland's diversity is manifested in multiple forms. The life history of Robert Mack Bell is an illustrative case. On June 17, 1960, the sixteen-year-old president of the student body at the all-black Dunbar High School in Baltimore City was arrested as he led a busload of students to join the sit-in of a segregated downtown restaurant one block from the city courthouse. His conviction was upheld by an all-white male Maryland Court of Appeals in 1962, later to be overturned by the U.S. Supreme Court.[1] Nearly thirty-eight years after this civil rights protest Robert Mack Bell was sworn in as the chief judge of the Maryland Court of Appeals and became the head of the state's judicial branch of government.[2]

The judiciary is often simultaneously considered the weakest and the strongest among the three branches of government. Judges do not pass laws, raise taxes, administer large agencies, or deliver services. The judiciary does not ordinarily dominate the popular press or the political process. It can, and does, exercise its powers to check and balance the legislative and executive branches of government. Acts of the general assembly and governors have been declared invalid under the state constitution or in violation of state law. Maryland courts handle more than 2.3 million cases a year and are the daily arbiter of thousands of disputes between and among residents, businesses, associations, and organizations in the state.

If the judiciary did not function as designed, much of what is assumed in a civil society would fracture.

In common with the other branches of government the judiciary reflects the state's geographic and demographic diversity. All four levels of the state judiciary are divided into geographic judicial districts reflecting a commonality of interest or historical connections. Maryland has produced an impressive list of jurists and lawyers. In addition to Justices Taney and Marshall, Maryland has been the home state of three other Supreme Court justices, six attorneys general, and three solicitors general of the United States.[3]

THE MARYLAND JUDICIARY: HISTORICAL DEVELOPMENT

The 1776 Maryland Constitution proclaimed the judiciary an independent and separate branch of government, but the role of the early judiciary was limited.[4] Judges were appointed by the governor and approved by the legislature's governor's council. Judicial functions were performed by justices of the peace, county courts, a general court (the former colonial provincial court), the court of chancery, the court of admiralty, and a court of appeals. The general court was required to "sit on the western and eastern shores for transacting and determining the business of the respective shores, at such times and places as the future legislature of this State shall direct and appoint."[5]

A growing population led to a constitutional amendment, ratified in 1805, that divided the state into six judicial districts (or circuits), each containing three judges.[6] This reorganization replaced the county courts and reconstituted the court of appeals (the state's highest court) as the chief judges of the six districts.

The 1851 Maryland Constitution brought substantial change to the judiciary, highlighted by the popular election of judges for ten-year terms by the voters of their respective jurisdictions. Circuit court judges were elected in eight judicial circuits. Each judge of a revised court of appeals was elected from one of four newly designated appellate judicial districts. A distinct court system was established for Baltimore City consisting of four courts (superior court, court of common pleas, criminal court, and the circuit court), with an elected judge for each.

The democratization of the judiciary in 1851 extended to other courthouse officials, as clerks of court, registers of wills, and judges of the orphans' court also were elected. Although there have been sporadic attempts to have these courthouse offices abolished or made appointive, all of these positions remain elected with the exception of that of orphans' court judges in Montgomery County and Harford County, which were abolished in 1964 and 1972, respectively.[7]

The 1864 constitution only slightly altered the Maryland judiciary by adding a one-year residency requirement for circuit court judges, increasing the annual pay from $2,000 to $2,500, raising the value limits for exclusive civil case jurisdiction, and enlarging the number of circuit court districts from eight to thirteen. Membership on the court of appeals was increased from four to five by adding a fifth appellate district comprising Baltimore County, Harford County, and the first seven wards of Baltimore City.

The post–Civil War 1867 constitution changed the judiciary as part of the state's "self-reconstruction" and political reformulation. Circuit courts were reconstituted back into eight circuits. The legal system for Baltimore City was divided into six courts with specific subject matter jurisdictions. The direct election of judges for the court of appeals was abolished, and the court returned to being composed of the chief judges from the eight circuit court districts. The clerk of court for the court of appeals was made a statewide elected office, influenced by the political process for nominating candidates.

Beginning in 1867 the judicial structure of Maryland remained essentially intact for more than seventy years. Pressing workloads did prompt occasional amendments, increasing the number of circuit court judges. Twentieth-century demands on the judicial system from an expanding and more complex society eventually led to midcentury judicial reform. The business and legal community persistently agitated for the reestablishment of an independent, full-time court of appeals in order to upgrade the quality and professionalism of the Maryland judiciary. Although strongly resisted by the rural-dominated state senate, a constitutional amendment reestablishing the independently elected five-member court of appeals finally passed during the wartime legislative session of 1943 with the help of Governor O'Conor and was ratified in 1944.[8] Maryland was the next to last state to establish structural independence for its highest court, which is widely credited among Maryland's legal scholars and practitioners as being of utmost importance to the development of the state's modern judicial system.

Judicial reform remained a frequent subject of constitutional revision after World War II. Sweeping changes to the judicial branch of government (including the renaming of the various courts and the removal of courthouse offices from partisan elections) were rejected in 1968, along with a proposed state constitution. Subsequently several recommendations of the constitutional convention were adopted. The state's lower-level trial court, the district court, was created by a constitutional amendment ap-

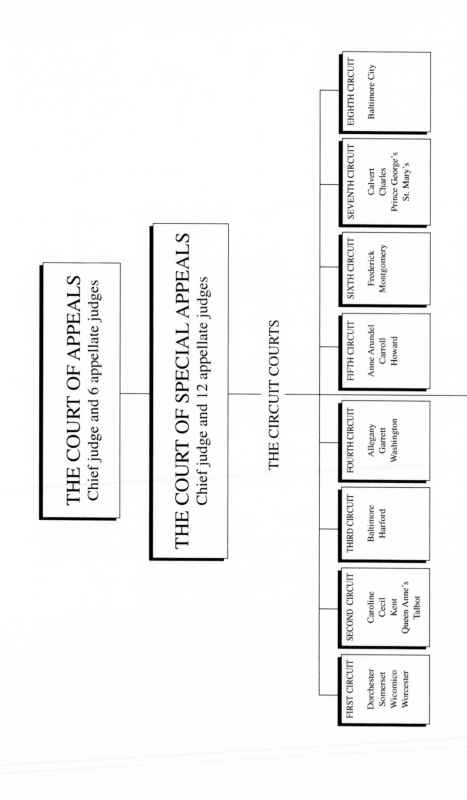

THE COURT OF APPEALS
Chief judge and 6 appellate judges

THE COURT OF SPECIAL APPEALS
Chief judge and 12 appellate judges

THE CIRCUIT COURTS

FIRST CIRCUIT	SECOND CIRCUIT	THIRD CIRCUIT	FOURTH CIRCUIT	FIFTH CIRCUIT	SIXTH CIRCUIT	SEVENTH CIRCUIT	EIGHTH CIRCUIT
Dorchester Somerset Wicomico Worcester	Caroline Cecil Kent Queen Anne's Talbot	Baltimore Harford	Allegany Garrett Washington	Anne Arundel Carroll Howard	Frederick Montgomery	Calvert Charles Prince George's St. Mary's	Baltimore City

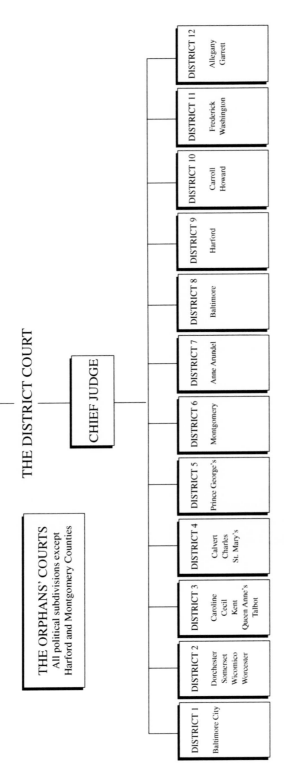

Figure 9-1. The Maryland judicial system. Source: Maryland Judiciary, *Annual Statistical Abstract*, Annapolis, 2007.

proved in 1970. The commission on judicial disabilities, first created in 1966 and strengthened in 1974, provides for the discipline of judges under the authority of the court of appeals.[9] The Maryland General Assembly was granted the power to determine the number of judges in each circuit and county by a constitutional amendment approved in 1976.[10] The Baltimore City courts were consolidated and made to conform to the judicial structure existing in the twenty-three counties through a constitutional amendment approved in 1980.[11]

STRUCTURE OF THE MARYLAND COURT SYSTEM

The judicial branch of government in Maryland has four levels: two trial courts and two appellate courts (see Figure 9-1). At the time of appointment judges must be at least thirty years old and must have been a state resident for not less than five years. Judges serve specified terms and are subject to mandatory retirement at age seventy. In 2010 there were 289 men and women serving as judges. Diversity of gender and race in the Maryland judiciary began slowly; the first woman was appointed to the circuit court in 1955 and the first African American was appointed in 1969. In the twenty-first century diversity on the trial and appellate courts is a source of state pride.

All Maryland judges are initially appointed by the governor and subject to confirmation by the Maryland State Senate. Since 1975 judges have been screened, interviewed, and approved by countywide or statewide judicial nominating commissions. Created by executive orders of the respective governors, the commissions submit a list of qualified applicants to the governor, who makes a selection for each appointment. This is a modified "Missouri Plan" system of judicial selection. The size and composition of the nominating commissions have varied under the executive orders of the different governors; the number of lawyers compared to public nonlawyer members has been a distinguishing factor.[12]

THE DISTRICT COURT

The lowest level court in Maryland is also the newest court. Created by a 1970 constitutional amendment, the district court began its operations on July 1, 1971. The district court was formed to unify and replace various county and municipal courts of limited jurisdiction (formerly the people's court, magistrate court, and municipal court) and to relieve the caseloads of the circuit courts. The district court has jurisdiction over landlord-tenant cases and concurrent jurisdiction with the circuit courts in cases involving motor vehicle offenses, misdemeanors, and civil claims up to $30,000. There is no right to a jury trial in the district court. In cases guaranteed a jury trial under the state constitution, the defendant in a criminal case, or the plaintiff or defendant in a civil case, may elect to have a case filed in district court heard in the circuit court.

The district courts are organized for administrative purposes into twelve judicial districts with at least one district court judge serving in each of Maryland's twenty-three counties and Baltimore City (see Figure 9-1). The judges of the district court are appointed by the governor and subject to confirmation by the Maryland State Senate. They serve a ten-year term and can be reappointed. District court judges are not subject to a contested election or an approval election by the voters. The district court is headed by a chief judge who is appointed by the chief judge of the court of appeals from among the district court judges. The chief judge of the district court designates an administrative judge for each of the twelve districts. The chief clerk of the district court and a chief administrative clerk in the twelve districts are appointed by the chief judge of the district court.

The workload of the district court is substantial and steadily increased during its first thirty years. In its first year the district court handled nearly 800,000 cases, which grew to 1,275,800 cases by its tenth year. During fiscal years 2005–10 it averaged nearly 2 million cases annually (see Table 9.1). In fiscal year 2010 the district court received 681,589 motor vehicle violation cases, 604,514 landlord-tenant cases, 359,955 civil actions, and 187,341 criminal cases.[13] The First District Court, comprising Baltimore City and twenty-seven judges, handles approximately 21 percent of the landlord-tenant cases filed in the state and 30 percent of the criminal cases filed in the district court.

THE CIRCUIT COURT

The court of general jurisdiction in Maryland is the circuit court, which conducts jury and nonjury trials involving major civil cases and the more serious criminal cases. The circuit courts are also responsible for overseeing and deciding family matters and juvenile cases. Appeals from state and local administrative agencies as well as the district court and the orphans' court are handled by the circuit courts. The circuit courts averaged in excess of 299,900 cases annually in 2005–10. In fiscal year 2010 the 324,657 cases filed in circuit courts were divided among civil cases (33 percent), criminal cases (27 percent), family law cases (31 percent), and juvenile cases (10 percent).[14]

Table 9-1: Maryland judiciary caseloads

Court of Appeals	FY2003	FY2004	FY2005	FY2006	FY2007	FY2008	FY2009	FY2010
Filed	140	157	137	146	148	165	176	143
Disposed	133	136	153	139	176	135	98	140
Writs of Certiorari	700	651	604	651	633	611	651	624

Court of Special Appeals	FY2003	FY2004	FY2005	FY2006	FY2007	FY2008	FY2009	FY2010
Filed	1,960	1,856	2,041	2,040	2,121	2,242	2,012	1,980
Disposed	1,901	1,936	1,796	1,875	1,887	2,009	2,111	2,140

Circuit Courts	FY2003	FY2004	FY2005	FY2006	FY2007	FY2008	FY2009	FY2010
Filed	282,673	282,211	278,083	278,511	293,940	309,352	314,884	324,657
Terminated	255,734	256,698	279,263	264,482	278,225	294,933	285,747	308,549

District Courts	FY2003	FY2004	FY2005	FY2006	FY2007	FY2008	FY2009	FY2010
Filed	1,982,742	2,133,484	2,141,601	2,128,690	2,086,826	1,842,925	1,890,545	1,828,399
Terminated	2,149,129	2,323,770	2,302,813	2,307,646	2,302,961	2,088,303	2,089,915	2,093,676

Source: Compiled by John T. Willis from Administrative Office of the Courts, *Annual Statistical Abstracts*, Annapolis.

The circuit court judges are organized into eight judicial circuits for administrative purposes. After their appointment circuit court judges must stand for election after completing at least one year of service, at which time other qualified lawyers may run against them in contested, partisan elections. Circuit court judges elected by the voters serve fifteen-year terms and may run for reelection to successive terms until reaching the mandatory retirement age of seventy. In circumstances of heavy caseloads, conflicts, or vacancies, retired judges are eligible to be designated to serve on circuit courts by the chief judge of the court of appeals.

THE COURT OF SPECIAL APPEALS

There is one intermediate appellate court in Maryland, the court of special appeals. A constitutional amendment ratified in 1966 authorized the general assembly to "create such intermediary courts of appeal, as may be necessary."[15] The court of special appeals was established in the next legislative session, with five judges to handle the increasing appellate criminal caseload of a growing state population.[16] Its jurisdiction was expanded in 1970 to include the hearing of appeals in civil cases and other matters.

The judges of the court of special appeals are initially appointed by the governor and subject to confirmation by the state senate. In 2010 there were thirteen members of this court, including four women and three African American judges. Seven of the judges must come from one of seven appellate judicial districts, and the remainder may reside in any part of the state. Since 1976 the judges of the court of special appeals are subject to an election of affirmation or rejection, without opponents, after completing at least one year of service. After voter approval the judges serve a ten-year term and are subject to a popular vote of approval or rejection every ten years until reaching the mandatory retirement age. The chief judge of the court is designated by the governor.

The court of special appeals hears appeals of civil and criminal cases from the circuit courts. The court normally sits in three-judge panels and renders written decisions based on the record of the proceedings below after receiving written and oral arguments from the parties. The court may also sit en banc to hear a case or review a case decided by a panel. In its 2008–9 term the court docketed 818 criminal appeals and 1,265 civil cases and filed 1,500 opinions in fiscal year 2010. These decisions are binding precedent on issues of law for lower trial courts and become part of the common law of Maryland. The clerk of the court of special appeals is appointed by the chief judge of that court.

THE COURT OF APPEALS

The highest court in Maryland is the court of appeals, created by the original 1776 state constitution.[17] Since 1961 the court has consisted of seven judges initially appointed by the governor, subject to confirmation by the state senate.[18] Each judge represents one of seven geographically distinct judicial districts or circuits. Previously required to run in contested partisan elections, since 1976 the judges of the court of appeals have been subject to an election of affirmation or rejection by the voters of Maryland after completing at least one year of service.[19] They then serve a ten-year term and are subject to elections of affirmation or rejection every ten years until reaching the mandatory retirement age of seventy. In 2010 three of the seven judges on the court of appeals were women, two were African American men, and two were Caucasian men. The chief judge of the court of appeals is designated by the governor and is the official head of the Maryland judiciary.

The court of appeals and its chief judge exercise authority over the operation of the judicial system and the practice of law in Maryland. The court is responsible for regulating the practice of law and the conduct of more than 35,000 lawyers, for adopting the rules of procedure applicable to the conduct of trials and appeals, and for the administration of courts. This power is exercised through various judicial entities, including the Administrative Office of the Courts, the State Board of Law Examiners, the State Law Library, the Client Protection Fund of the Bar of Maryland, the Mediation and Conflict Resolution Office, and the State Reporter. The judges of the court of appeals are also members of numerous commissions, committees, and task forces related to the administration, supervision, and improvement of the state court system. The clerk of the court of appeals is appointed by the judges of the Maryland Court of Appeals and has extensive administrative duties.

In its 2005–10 terms the court of appeals averaged 152 cases. Another 600 to 700 petitions for certiorari are filed every year. Between 15 and 25 percent of these petitions are accepted by the court; the remainder are rejected, thus affirming the decisions of the lower court of special appeals. The court disposed of eighty-seven attorney grievance proceedings in fiscal year 2010.

Pursuant to a unique state constitutional provision, the court of appeals has original jurisdiction "to review the legislative districting of the state."[20] By statute the court of appeals must hear all cases involving the imposition of the death penalty and the removal of certain public officials and must respond to requests for certification of questions of law.[21]

SPECIALIZED COURTS AND ADJUDICATORY ENTITIES

In Maryland there are several specialized courts that have been established by constitutional provisions and legislative action in order to handle the adjudicatory needs of the public.

In twenty-one counties and Baltimore City three individuals are elected in partisan political elections to serve as judges of the orphans' court. Except in Baltimore City, these judges do not have to be lawyers or members of the bar association. The orphans' courts process, hear, and decide matters relating to wills, estates, and probate. The judges also have jurisdiction to appoint guardians of the persons and to protect the estates of minors who are under parental authority.[22] Although there have been attempts to abolish the orphans' courts, all counties (except Harford and Montgomery) and Baltimore City retain this specialized institution. The judgments of the orphans' courts can be appealed to a circuit court or, in certain cases, to the court of special appeals.

The general assembly created the Maryland Tax Court in 1959 to perform the quasi-judicial functions of the former State Tax Commission.[23] The tax court hears appeals from individuals and business entities on matters relating to the valuation, assessment, or classification of property; the imposition of a tax; the requests for the abatement or reduction of an assessment, tax, or exemption; the allowance or disallowance of refund claims for taxes; and certain licenses. The tax court consists of five members appointed by the governor for terms of six years, subject to their confirmation by the state senate. Geographical and political considerations impact the tax court. One of the judges must be a resident of the Eastern Shore, one a resident of the Western Shore, and one a resident of Baltimore City. There can be no more than three members of one political party on the court. Each judge must be a taxpayer and a qualified voter of Maryland, and two must be members of the Maryland State Bar Association. The chief judge of the court is designated by the governor.

A Board of Contract Appeals was created in 1970 to hear cases involving disputes between the State of Maryland and the vendors and companies doing business with the state.[24] This three-member board hears approximately twenty to thirty complex contract cases a year. Its decisions can be appealed to the circuit courts in Baltimore City and the twenty-three counties.

In 1989 the Maryland General Assembly created the Office of Administrative Hearings to coordinate the hearing of various appeals from the administrative actions of state departments, agencies, and entities and to alleviate the caseload that was growing in the twenty-four circuit courts.[25] This quasi-judicial body consists of a chief administrative judge, appointed by the governor and confirmed by the state senate for a six-year term, and up to sixty administrative law judges who are appointed by the chief administrative law judge. Administrative law judges must be members of the Maryland State Bar Association with a minimum of five years of legal experience before becoming a judge. In 2010 the Office of Administrative Hearings received 45,288 new cases. Hearings in contested cases involved more than thirty state agencies, more than two hundred different programs, and more than five hundred types of hearings. Among the twenty-seven states with a centralized administrative hearing entity, Maryland's is among the largest, with the broadest subject matter jurisdiction. Decisions of administrative law judges can be appealed to the circuit courts.

OTHER COURT OFFICIALS IN MARYLAND

Reflecting the political history and culture of Maryland, various courthouse officials are elected by a popular vote during gubernatorial election years in every county and Baltimore City. Candidates for these offices are nominated by the Democratic and Republican parties in primary elections. Other individuals may run for these offices as independent candidates or as selected by other political parties. These local elected officials often play a significant role in county and city politics.

The sheriff of every county and Baltimore City has been an elected official since the 1776 constitution. The sheriff was granted public safety and election integrity duties and assumed the English common law functions of the county sheriff. The contemporary duties and responsibilities of the county sheriff may include law enforcement, transporting prisoners, operating local detention centers, providing courtroom security, and performing the important functions of serving circuit and district court papers and enforcing the various orders of the circuit and district courts. In the five most populous Maryland counties and Baltimore City a local police department performs the principal law enforcement functions, leaving the sheriff's office with the primary duties of courtroom security and assisting the courts. In the remaining counties the sheriff exercises full police powers.

Essential to the operation of any judicial system is a clerk's office. Under the first state constitution court clerks were appointed by the judges of their respective courts. Since the 1851 constitution the clerk of the circuit court in each county and Baltimore City has been an independently elected office. The general assembly has given the circuit court clerk's office additional duties and responsibilities; these include the issuance of licenses, collection of fees, and maintenance of official records. The monies collected by the clerks of court are in excess of $425 million a year, 95 percent of which is returned to county and city governments for local programs and expenditures.

Since 1851 every Maryland county and Baltimore City has elected its own prosecutor, the state's attorney. Responsible for the prosecution of crimes, the state's attorney possesses significant discretion and occupies a very visible public office. Service as the state's attorney has often been a springboard to other elected public office or a judicial appointment; some state's attorneys have settled into long careers as public prosecutors. The elections for state's attorneys are open to all qualified lawyers residing in the county and are frequently contested in primary and general elections. The successes of Milton Allen as the first African American state's attorney in Baltimore City in 1970 and of Alex Williams in Prince George's County in 1990 in heavily contested elections were heralded at the time and can properly be considered harbingers of political change in their respective jurisdictions. Allen's success was followed twelve years later with the election of Kurt Schmoke, a graduate of Harvard Law School, as state's attorney for Baltimore City. Schmoke's electoral success in 1982 and 1986 set the foundation for his three successful elections for mayor of Baltimore in 1987, 1991, and 1995. After Williams's appointment to the federal bench he was succeeded by Jack Johnson, who served two terms as state's attorney before becoming Prince George's County executive in 2002. Maryland Attorney General Douglas F. Gansler, elected statewide in 2006, served two high-profile terms as the state's attorney for Montgomery County.

A register of wills is elected by the voters in each of Maryland's twenty-three counties and Baltimore City. The register of wills provides administrative support for the orphans' court and is responsible for the collection of state inheritance taxes and the fees related to the administration of decedent estates. The offices of the register of wills are funded by a portion of the revenues they collect, and if insufficient, by additional state funding.

CONTEMPORARY ISSUES FOR THE MARYLAND
JUDICIARY BUDGET AND WORKFORCE NEEDS

As the third branch of government in a growing, diverse state, the Maryland judiciary confronts numerous challenges in the delivery of judicial services. The need for additional court facilities and judges often engages the judiciary in the legislative process, as the annual budget of the judiciary is subject to the approval of the general assembly. The chief judge of the court of appeals submits a budget request, which the governor must place in the budget bill, but the legislature has the authority to approve or disapprove of proposed expenditures.

In Maryland the expenses for the judiciary are shared by the state government and the jurisdiction in which the courts are located. The expenditures for the Maryland judiciary in fiscal year 2010 exceeded $407 million for the costs of operation of court facilities and the personnel costs for judges, more than 4,000 clerks, and other individuals who help administer the judicial system.[26] The state portion was approximately 69 percent and the local government share approximately 30 percent of the funds required to deliver judicial services in Maryland. A small fraction of the state judicial expenditures (1 percent) comes from federal government programs.

Expenditures relating to the number of judges and the jurisdictions in which they serve often form the basis for disagreement between the legislature and the judiciary. Although judges do have the constitutional protection that their salaries cannot be diminished during their term of office, increases in pay for the judiciary are subject to approval or disapproval by the general assembly. A judicial compensation commission was established in 1980 to make recommendations about the base salaries for the judges serving on each of the four levels of the state judiciary.[27] Between 1983 and 2010 the commission recommended no increases in judicial pay in eleven of those years. The general assembly rejected the commission's recommendations for salary increases on eight other occasions including 2010. Judicial salary increases were approved seven times, although judges have received cost-of-living increases granted to other state employees. Maryland's judicial salaries have ranked slightly above the national averages for trial and appellate judges over the past two decades, but are well below federal judicial salaries.

JUDICIAL DISABILITY AND MISCONDUCT

Under the Maryland Constitution judges are subject to removal by the governor "on conviction in a Court of Law, of incompetence, of willful neglect of duty, misbehavior in office, or any other crime."[28] In addition the general assembly possesses the power of impeachment of judicial officers.[29] The governor and the general assembly rarely use these powers. The commission on judicial disabilities, created in 1966, has the power to investigate complaints against judges, conduct hearings, issue reprimands, and recommend to the Maryland Court of Appeals the removal, censure, retirement, or other appropriate discipline of a judge.[30] In 1996 the composition of the commission was increased to eleven members (one judge each from the appellate, circuit, and district courts, three attorneys, and five laypersons) nominated by the governor and confirmed by the state senate.[31] The proceedings of the commission are open in those instances where formal charges are made against a judge.

JUDICIAL ELECTIONS

Under the 1851 constitution all judicial offices in Maryland were made subject to partisan elections. A 1976 constitutional amendment removed the judges on the court of appeals and court of special appeals from a partisan, competitive election process but reduced their terms in office from fifteen to ten years.[32] Since that amendment all appellate judges have been retained in office by receiving an affirmative vote of at least 80 percent from Maryland general election voters.

Circuit court judges in Baltimore City and the state's twenty-three counties remain subject to partisan competitive electoral contests. Although it is unusual for newly appointed or incumbent judges (often referred to as sitting judges) to lose contested elections, it does happen. Out of the 444 circuit court judges that were subject to open, partisan elections from 1970 through 2010, eleven (or 2.5 percent) were defeated. Four judges lost their judicial seat by losing both the Democratic and Republican primary elections. Another six circuit court judges lost in the general election, although they won both or one of the political party primary elections. Since 1970 there have been successful challenges to sitting judges in only four jurisdictions: three in Anne Arundel County (2004 and 2010), five in Baltimore City (1968, 1980, 1982), two in Baltimore County (2000 and 2002), and one in Howard County (1996).

Contested judicial elections are supported as a method for ensuring the opportunity for participation in the judiciary by minorities and others who were overlooked by the backdoor processes by which lawyers had received their nomination from a governor to become a judge. African American lawyers made successful challenges to become judges in Baltimore City in 1968, 1980, and 1982. In 2008 a newly appointed African American woman in Harford County successfully won election to a full fifteen-year term on the circuit court. The first black judge appointed in any of the twenty-three counties was James H. Taylor, who was named by Governor Marvin Mandel in 1969 to the circuit court for Prince George's County. Judge Taylor retained his circuit court judicial seat in a contested election in 1970.

However, since 1996 four of the last six judges defeated in contested partisan elections were African Americans residing in the suburban counties of Anne Arundel, Baltimore, and Howard.

The specter of partisan politics has resurfaced in Maryland judicial elections, along with increased concerns over judicial campaign fund-raising and tactics. In 2006 Maryland became one of fourteen states to have an official volunteer judicial campaign oversight group. Chief Judge Robert Mack Bell of the court of appeals created the Maryland Judicial Campaign Committee, cochaired by a former Republican U.S. attorney for Maryland and a former Democratic Maryland attorney general, which issued voluntary "standards for the conduct of judicial elections" for the 2006 election cycle.[33] Removing circuit court judges from partisan elections and reducing the role of money in judicial elections have been recommended by a variety of commissions and studies and will likely continue to be recommended until circuit court judges are removed from the rigors of partisan elections in Maryland.[34]

THE COURTS AND PUBLIC POLICY

The Maryland Court of Appeals, the state's highest court, has steadfastly preserved its independence from the other branches of government and not shied away from overturning executive and legislative actions determined to be in conflict with the state constitution. As early as 1802 the court of appeals embraced the important jurisprudence doctrine of judicial review, which makes the judicial branch of government the final arbiter of meaning and interpretation of the Maryland Declaration of Rights and Constitution.[35] The exercise of this judicial function has drawn the state courts into the public policy arena. Circuit court judges regularly make decisions regarding county and municipal land use policy. The lengthy proceedings in circuit court with regard to the education funding prompted action by the state and local government. The appellate courts routinely render decisions affecting a wide array of public policy matters, from individual rights and criminal procedure to land use, personal injury, and taxation.

At various times throughout its history the court of appeals has exercised its discretion to draw conclusions different from those of the other two branches of government. The court has interpreted acts of the general assembly differently than have leading members of the legislature. The court of appeals has similarly manifested independence from the governor and the executive branch. Immediately after the Civil War the court of appeals held that while "the Governor has political and discretionary powers he is not immune from judicial process."[36]

During the past decade the court's activism has increased, alarming some members of the legislative and executive branches of government. Exercising its original jurisdiction, the court of appeals modified the 2002 legislative redistricting of the Maryland General Assembly.[37] The court's decision and line drawing resulted in the reduction of the number of state senators representing Baltimore City from eight to six and the number of delegates from twenty-three to eighteen. The minor judicial line drawing outside the Baltimore metropolitan area changed the outcome of a few notable legislative races. The seeds of defeat of the incumbent speaker of the house of delegates, Cas Taylor of Allegany County, were sowed by the inclusion of precincts in neighboring Washington County that voted overwhelmingly against him and provided the seventy-six-vote margin of victory for his opponent. The chair of the state senate's budget and tax committee was defeated as a result of combining Baltimore City legislative districts. An African American Democratic state senate candidate, former Howard County council member, and past president of the National Association of Counties, C. Vernon Gray, lost because of the court's inclusion of two precincts in State Legislative District Thirteen that had been the locus of controversial county land use decisions.

In a 2001 decision the court of appeals charted new ground in judicial-executive relations by requiring the governor to turn over telephone records from his personal office and scheduling information in response to a request filed by the media unrelated to any pending court proceeding.[38] The court raised the ire of the legislature by a ruling in 2003 that weakened the shoreline protection of the Critical Area Act and the authority of the Maryland Health Care Cost Commission.[39]

The court of appeals has also rendered decisions affecting the election process. In 2003 the court struck down the state law granting ballot access to the Green Party and Ralph Nader for the 2004 presidential election.[40] In 2004 the state's highest court affirmed a Prince George's County Circuit Court ruling that declared unconstitutional the legislative prohibition on "walking around money."[41] Less than four weeks before the 2006 primary election the court declared the legislature's effort to craft a statute permitting "early voting" in violation of the state constitution and declared a candidate for attorney general ineligible to hold office under Article VI of the Maryland Constitution.[42]

During the single term of Governor Ehrlich the court of appeals found itself refereeing institutional and policy battles between the legislative and executive branches of government. The court decided a separation-of-powers dispute over the termination of members of the public service commission, siding with the governor's executive power of appointment over the legislative power to create independent agencies.[43] In another case the court ruled against the governor, holding that his administration improperly denied health care benefits to the children of legal immigrants.[44]

SUMMARY

The judicial branch of government in Maryland is strong and independent. Sound institutional structures have evolved to ensure that the judges can perform their essential functions and maintain the "respect of the people" sought by Chief Justice Thurgood Marshall. As future social, economic, and political conflicts emerge in Maryland the state's judiciary will undoubtedly be called upon to calm, or disturb, the waters and provide guidance for Marylanders and their government leaders.

CHAPTER TEN

The Politics of Taxation and Spending

Maryland proudly provides services from the cradle to the grave.
Louis L. Goldstein, Comptroller of Maryland, 1959–1998

Self-government inevitably leads to differences of opinion over the proper role of government. There is constant debate over the appropriate revenues to fund governmental operations and how much to spend on what, where, and how. As in every state, Maryland's annual budget reflects the choices and compromises, preferences and priorities of the state's political actors in the formulation, adoption, and implementation of public policy. By examining the processes and substance of the state budget, the politics of taxation and spending become readily apparent. Contained within the annual state budget are not just the programs and policies highlighted in the current year's headlines, but also the expectations of Marylanders and the policy priorities of generations of Maryland policy actors responding to their respective constituencies and to a multitude of policy advocates.

The annual state budget process exposes the tensions between the branches of government and the levels of government. The budget process also plainly reveals the political divisions and differences among the various subdivisions, regions, and constituencies in the state. Maryland, with its broad-based economy and diverse, well-educated populace, consistently ranks among the most wealthy and highest wage-earning states. The state proudly boasts of forty-eight consecutive years of triple-A bond ratings from national financial institutions. These institutions regularly grant Maryland their highest rating. Standard & Poor's observed, "Maryland has consistently had well-defined financial management policies."[1] In July 2010 Moody's referred to "Maryland's strong financial management policies and economy."[2]

In Maryland the linkage of state affluence and government fiscal responsibility has been generally bipartisan and persistent over decades, making Maryland one of the most financially stable states in the country. Yet inevitably the raising of revenues and the expenditures of public money are fraught with political overtones. The fiscal and budgetary realities of Maryland are also often disconnected from the political discourse and media reports; even in periods of economic recession Maryland consistently ranks in the top tier of states with positive cash balances at the end of every fiscal year.[3] Nevertheless the annual public debate over taxation and spending in Maryland is spirited and often contentious, even if rhetorically distorted and exaggerated. Except in periods of significant economic downturn, the fiscal debate in Maryland revolves primarily around "projected" expenditures and revenues in future years.

THE MARYLAND BUDGET: A DESCRIPTION

The annual Maryland Budget is large and complex. The state's fiscal year runs from July 1 of one calendar year to June 30 of the following calendar year. For the 2010–11 fiscal year the total operating budget for the state exceeded $33 billion. Fifty years ago the state budget was less than 1 percent of the current fiscal year budget. The annual operating budget passed the $1 billion mark in fiscal year 1967, the $10 billion level in fiscal year 1989, and the $20 billion mark in fiscal year 2002. In addition to the annual operating budget, the governor proposed and the general assembly approved a capital budget in excess of $3 billion for fiscal year 2011.

To understand the Maryland budget it is important to distinguish between the types of budgets. A *proposed budget* is prepared by the governor and submitted to the general assembly; the *approved budget* represents the appropriations made by the general assembly; and an *actual budget* reflects the final accounting of revenues and expenditures at the close of a fiscal year. There are *supplemental budgets* that a governor may submit during a legislative session, and there are *supplementary budgets* that may be passed at the initiative of the legislature if specific taxes or revenues are dedicated or passed to pay for the program or service. In addition there are budget reconciliation acts and deficiency acts that may be passed at subsequent legislative sessions that make changes to an already approved current fiscal year budget. The annual operating budget receives the most public attention, although the yearly capital budget is also important to the vitality of the state and attracts considerable interest.

There are significant distinctions among the various sources of state revenues. *General funds* represent revenues received by the state that are not directed by law to be used for any specific purpose and are not required to be placed in a designated fund category. Public discussion, media reports, and professional analysis often focus on general fund revenue and expenditures even though such revenue now constitutes less than half of the monies available for expenditure by the state government. *Special funds* are revenues dedicated by law to specific governmental activities, programs, or projects. The largest examples are highway user funds (gas tax and revenues from motor vehicle titling and transfer), which are primarily dedicated to transportation needs. During economic downturns the transportation trust funds have been tapped to balance the annual state operating budget. *Federal funds* are monies received from the federal government to pay for designated programs, services, and projects.

Since 1986 *higher education funds* have been reported separately in the budge under two categories. There are unrestricted higher education funds (such as tuition, fees, and the general fund allocation contained in the state budget) that can be used for any higher education purpose and restricted higher education funds (such as grants and contracts from federal, state, and local governments as well as from private sector sources) that can be used only for the purposes required by the terms of the grant or contract.

THE BUDGET PROCESS

There are multiple individual and institutional actors in the annual state budget process. As reflected in Figure 10-1, work on the state budget is a continual, cyclical process that has a rhythm of its own. A primary reason for the relative financial health of Maryland rests with the constitutional budget provisions and the institutional framework constructed by statute for the budget process. They are often cited as a model and yield frequent high national rankings from bond rating agencies, academics, and government practitioners.

Under the executive budget system adopted in 1916 the governor has the responsibility for the preparation of the annual budget and is the most significant policy actor in the process. In 1950 the governor was also given the right of a line-item veto over expenditures placed in a supplementary budget bill passed by the legislature. The governor sets budget priorities, issuing guidelines to and reviewing the proposed budgets from all of the state agencies, boards, commissions, and departments and other public and private entities seeking state funds. The key component of this budget power is that, with few exceptions, no single item can become

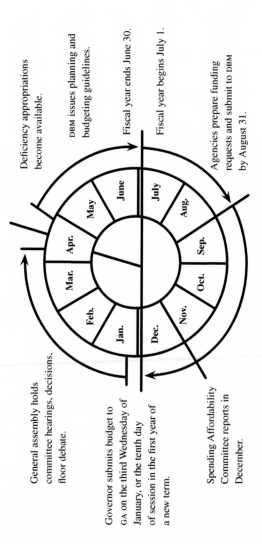

Budget is enacted upon adoption of the conference committee report. The governor does not sign the bill and may not line-item-veto any part of the bill.

Deficiency appropriations become available.

DBM issues planning and budgeting guidelines.

Fiscal year ends June 30.

Fiscal year begins July 1.

General assembly holds committee hearings, decisions, floor debate.

Governor submits budget to GA on the third Wednesday of January, or the tenth day of session in the first year of a new term.

Spending Affordability Committee reports in December.

Agencies prepare funding requests and submit to DBM by August 31.

Governor and DBM hold budget hearings to review agency requests.

DBM: Department of Budget and Management
GA: General Assembly

Figure 10-1. The budget cycle. Reproduced by permission from Department of Legislative Services, *Legislative Handbook Series*, vol. 4, Annapolis, 2006, 5.

part of the budget, or a supplemental budget, without the consent of the governor.[4]

The governor is aided in budget work by personal staff, the cabinet-level Department of Budget and Management (DBM), and the fiscal officers of state agencies and departments. Planning and budget guidelines are developed for the following fiscal year shortly before the beginning of an upcoming fiscal year. All state entities forward budget requests during the summer months to the DBM, which prepares the budget documents and assists the governor in the making of policy decisions and specific program decisions. At the end of every calendar year the DBM and the governor's staff, in strict confidentiality, begin drafting the budget bill that will be presented to the Maryland General Assembly. Typically, with choreographed announcements and press fanfare, the governor's budget is released to the public simultaneously with (or shortly before to the press) its submission to the legislature.

The second most important policy actor in the budget process is the Maryland General Assembly, which must approve all taxes and fees and must appropriate the funds for all programs and projects. The legislature cannot (with few exceptions) add to the executive's proposed budget but can delete items. Through the use of a supplementary appropriation bill, the general assembly may add a single work or purpose to the annual budget if a tax or new revenue source is identified.[5] This is rarely done for operating expenditures (only eight times since 1974) but is regularly used in the passage of bond bills for capital expenditures. Supplementary appropriation bills are subject to veto by the governor. A constitutional amendment, ratified in 1978, granted the general assembly the power to mandate in legislation that funds be allocated in the future annual budget bills for specific programs at specific minimum funding levels.[6] Once formulated the budget must be approved by the general assembly by the eighty-third day of its annual ninety-day legislative session.

In addition the general assembly has the authority to impose conditions or limitations on an appropriation relating to the expenditure of funds.[7] The legislature regularly utilizes this power, as exemplified by language in the approved 2006 fiscal year budget bill providing for twenty-eight items dependent on legislative enactments, thirty items contingent on legislative committee review, and 227 other budget items containing restrictions and contingencies or mandating reports.[8] It is the legislature, rather than the governor, that reviews and approves the budget for the judicial branch of government. The legislature also controls its own budget without gubernatorial involvement or oversight.

The general assembly has sought to enhance its influence over the state budget process as both a reaction to the more sophisticated use of executive branch power by governors and a desire to be a more important policy actor. Critical to the ability of the legislature to analyze and assess the mammoth state budget is the oversight authority over the executive budget granted to the department of legislative services by statute. This legislative entity employs an extensive professional staff to conduct reviews of budget requests, prepare reports for the legislature, and perform regular audits of state agencies and departments and other entities.

In 1978 the general assembly asserted a role in the capital budget process in response to dramatic increases in Maryland's outstanding debt by creating the Capital Debt Affordability Committee.[9] This committee consists of the comptroller, the treasurer, the secretary of the DBM, and a member of the public appointed by the governor and makes an annual report to the legislature.

To give legislators a benchmark to assess the annual proposed executive budget, the general assembly created the Spending Affordability Committee in 1982.[10] This committee issues a report prior to the legislative session, setting guidelines for the growth of state spending. In the twenty-eight years since the creation of the Spending Affordability Committee the legislature has approved a budget below the spending affordability guidelines in all years except 1984 and 1992.[11] The legislature has also enacted laws to modify the state's ability to discount bonds, finance projects and procurement relating to county road projects, and to borrow against the receipt of future federal funds.[12]

A third, sometimes overlooked, but significant budget entity is the Board of Revenue Estimates. Composed of the comptroller, the treasurer, and the secretary of the DBM, the board's projections not only impact the governor's proposed budget and the legislature's actions but also influence the public discourse about the state budget. The board makes a report in mid-December estimating revenues for the fiscal year beginning July 1 of the following year. Revised estimates are made in March, before the budget is adopted, during the annual legislative session. Revenue estimates can cause public and political alarm or provide governmental and political relief. A not uncommon 1 percent margin of error in general fund estimates can compute to over $130 million and can quickly lead to claims of fiscal responsibility and success or assertions of fiscal irresponsibility and overtaxation by administration detractors.

For fiscal years 2000 through 2006 the estimates of general fund revenue made by the Board of Revenue Estimates varied between 1.3 percent below and 2.7 percent above actual revenue corrections.[13] Projections of revenue extending beyond one or two years are inherently uncertain, as revenues and the demand for government services are caused primarily by the changes and cycles of the national, regional, and state economies and other external factors beyond the control of state government.

The final important policy actor in the state budget process is a governmental institution, unique to Maryland among the fifty states. The Board of Public Works, composed of the governor, the statewide-elected comptroller, and the legislatively elected state treasurer, have extraordinary fiscal authority.[14] The specific duties of the board as set forth in Article XII of the Maryland Constitution are to "exercise a diligent and faithful supervision of all Public Works in which the State may be interested as a Stockholder or Creditor" and "to sell the State's interest in all works of Internal Improvements . . . and . . . in any banking corporation." The state's direct investments in infrastructure improvements (roads, canals, railroads) and banking corporations plagued the state's financial vitality for over forty years in the mid-nineteenth century. It took the board nearly fifty years to accomplish its constitutional directive of divestment.

The duties, functions, and responsibilities of the Board of Public Works have evolved and grown substantially, especially with regard to the procurement of goods and services, out of the generic constitutional language that provides that the board "shall hear and determine such matters as affect the Public Works of the State, and as the General Assembly may confer upon them to decide" and "shall perform such other duties as may hereafter be prescribed by law." Pursuant to legislation passed since 1867 the board exercises a wide array of duties and responsibilities. These include approving the sale of bonds and expenditure of bond funds; approving the sale, lease, or transfer of state property; adopting procurement regulations and policy; approving contracts in excess of $200,000; approving the allocation of funds for school construction; and approving the capital expenditures of the state, except for certain transportation matters.

It is the Board of Public Works that establishes annually, by May 1, the state property tax rate.[15] Any proposed reductions in legislative appropriations during a fiscal year considered by the governor to be unnecessary or required by a budget bill must also be approved by the board.[16] The governor chairs the board and controls the bimonthly agenda but needs a vote from either the comptroller or the treasurer to prevail on any given agenda item.

TAXES AND REVENUE

The major sources of revenue for the state budget are depicted in Figure 10-2. Funds for the state operating budget are classified as general, special, federal, and higher education (restricted and unrestricted). Funds received from the federal government typically range between 22 and 24 percent of the total state funds but rose to approximately 30 percent in fiscal year 2010, almost $9.8 billion, as a result of federal stimulus funds proposed by the president and appropriated by Congress.

The largest source of state tax revenue is an income tax that was first adopted in 1937 and restructured in 1967. In a special session called to address the state's structural budget problems in the fall of 2007, the general assembly created top-tier rates of 5.0 percent, 5.25 percent, and 5.5 percent for high-income taxpayers. In the 2008 regular legislative session a top rate of 6.25 percent was created for net incomes in excess of $1 million. The income tax revenue has increased nearly fourteenfold in the past thirty-five years and generated nearly $6.2 billion for the state general fund in fiscal year 2010. Maryland's combined state and local income tax rate came under sharp political attack in the late 1980s and into the 1990s for being one of the highest in the country. After the top rate for the state income tax was reduced to 4.75 percent in 2002, the state top bracket ranked ninth lowest among the forty-one states taxing all income.[17] This ranking changed to the seventeenth highest after the 2008 regular legislative session.

The second largest source of state tax revenue is a sales and use tax on designated goods and services, first adopted in 1947 at 2 percent. It was raised to 3 percent in 1959, 4 percent in 1969, 5 percent in 1977, and most recently 6 percent during the 2007 legislative special session. Sales and use tax receipts were nearly $3.8 billion in fiscal year 2010. A substantial number of transactions are exempted from Maryland's sales tax, including sales of food at grocery stores, sales of medicine and medical supplies, sales of agriculture and seafood harvesting equipment and supplies, sales of tangible property used in research and development and used directly and predominantly in a production activity, and sales to nonprofit, charitable, education, and religious organizations that possess a tax exempt certificate and account number from the office of comptroller.[18]

The third largest source of tax revenue is the gas and fuel taxes, with the current rate of 23.5 cents per gallon of gas set in 1992. These taxes generated over $722.6 million in fiscal year 2010. Gas tax revenues are considered special funds and are placed in the transportation trust fund.

Maryland first enacted a corporate income tax in 1937 with a 0.5 per-

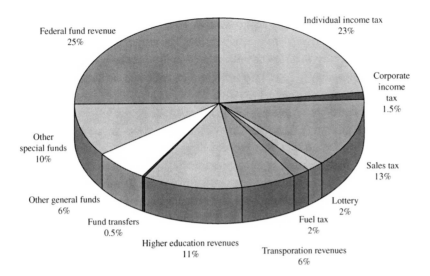

Revenues ($ millions)

	FY 2008	FY 2009	FY 2010	% change 2010 over 2009	% Total revenues
Indiviudal income tax	6,940	7,111	7,181	1.0	23.0
Corporate income tax	735	743	776	4.3	1.5
Sales tax	3,749	3,943	3,924	-0.5	13.0
Lottery	577	535	575	7.5	2.0
Fuel tax	755	741	749	1.1	2.0
Transportation revenues	1,980	1,852	1,880	1.5	6.0
Higher education revenues	3,092	3,302	3,408	3.2	11.0
Fund transfers	1,098	842	250	-70.3	0.5
Other general funds	1,866	1,808	1,756	-2.9	6.0
Other special funds	2,369	2,811	3,022	7.5	10.0
Federal fund revenue	6,561	7,102	7,663	7.9	25.0
Total revenues	**29,723**	**30,790**	**31,184**	**1.3**	**100.0**
Changes in general fund balances and reversions	(153)	245	504		
Total available	**29,569**	**31,035**	**31,688**	**2.1**	

Note: Totals and percentages may not add due to rounding.

Figure 10-2. Proposed revenues, FY 2008–2010. Source: Department of Budget and Management, *Maryland Budget Highlights*, Annapolis, 2009, 6.

cent rate. A 7 percent rate, established in 1968, was raised to 8.25 percent during the 2007 legislative special session. The corporate income tax yield was enhanced by the closing of a related entity loophole in 2004 by the general assembly.[19] Over $689 million was collected in fiscal year 2010 for the general fund (see Table 10-1).

The state levies a 2 percent tax on life insurance premiums, which yielded $301.8 million in fiscal year 2008, and a 2 percent tax on the gross receipts of public utilities that yielded $133.5 million. The tobacco tax in Maryland, first imposed in 1913, remained at only thirteen cents per pack until 1991. The rate has since been raised five times. It was set at $1.00 per pack in 2002 as a health measure and raised again to $2.00 per pack in the 2007 special legislative session, tied for the fourth highest in the country. Nearly $406 million was raised from the tobacco tax in fiscal year 2010.

Inheritance taxes, first established in 1844, were eliminated for all lineal descendants of Marylanders who died after mid-2000. There is a 10 percent tax rate for collateral heirs that yielded $50 million in fiscal year 2006. Estate taxes, first imposed in 1929, were decoupled from the federal estate tax in 2004. Total death taxes generated $173.5 million for the general fund in fiscal year 2010.

Alcohol taxes are quite modest in Maryland; the current rate for liquor of $1.50 per gallon was set in 1955 and the present rates of nine cents per gallon for beer and forty cents per gallon for wine were set in 1972. Justifying its anti-Prohibition slogan, "The Free State," Maryland's excise taxes on liquor in 2007 were the lowest of all the thirty-two states that do not directly control the sale of distilled spirits, and the state's taxes on beer and wine ranked eighth and twelfth lowest in the country, respectively. During the 2011 regular legislative session, the general assembly raised the sales tax on alcoholic beverages from 6 percent to 9 percent complicating comparative rankings with other states.

Like other states, Maryland relies on other sources of revenue not generally considered to be taxes. The state institutions of higher education generated in excess of $2.4 billion in unrestricted higher education funds revenue from tuition and fees charged to students and users of state public college and university facilities in fiscal year 2010. Tuition and fees were raised an average of 41 percent from 2002 through 2006.[20] After a significant increase in fees and rates in 2010,[21] the Department of Motor Vehicles generates over $1.3 billion a year in revenue from the imposition of vehicle registration, titling and license tag fees, driver's license renewals, and other motor vehicle fees and surcharges. The judicial branch of government re-

Table 10-1: Primary sources of state tax revenue

Type of Taxation	First passed	Current rate	Year set	FY 2010 revenue (millions)
Income/personal	1937	4.75% ($100,000) to 6.25% ($1 million)	2008	6,185.2
Sales/use	1947	6.0%	2007	3,753.7
Gasoline	1922	23.5 cents/gallon	1992	729.7
Income/corporate	1937	8.25%	2007	891.4
Vehicle titling	1933	5.0% of value	1978	543.4
Real property	1777	11.2 cents/$100	2008	897.3
Tobacco	1958	$2.00/pack	2007	405.9
Insurance	1941	2.0% of premiums	1941	277.0
Death taxes				173.5
(estate)	1929	16% ($1 million)	2006	
(inheritance)	1844	10% (nonlineal only)	2000	
Real property transfer	1970	0.5% value of conveyance	1970	123.4
Franchise (public utilities)	1972	2.0% gross receipts	1972	124.1
Alcohol				29.9
(liquor)	1933	$1.50/gallon	1955	
(beer)	1936	$.09/gallon	1972	
(wine)	1935	$.40/gallon	1972	

Sources: Comprehensive Annual Financial Reports of the Comptroller of Maryland; Annual Reports of the Treasurer of Maryland; "Tax Article," Annotated Code of Maryland; Legislative Handbook Series, vol. 3.

ceives over $160 million a year in court costs, fines, fees, and commissions collected by the various clerks of court.

One of the largest remaining revenue sources is the Maryland State Lottery. After passage of a constitutional amendment in 1972 the Maryland State Lottery began operations in July 1973 with a weekly game. With the expansion of daily, biweekly, special, and multistate games, the Maryland State Lottery generated between $473 million and $508 million for the state's general fund on annual total revenues of approximately $1.7 billion during fiscal years 2008 through 2010. A small portion of certain lottery games was dedicated to sports facilities constructed by the Maryland Stadium Authority.

Led by the owners of Maryland's horse racing tracks and the broader horse racing industry, there were sustained efforts over the past twenty years to bring slot machines and other forms of gambling back to the state. Once extensive in southern Maryland, slot machines were banned after July 1, 1968, under legislation passed by the general assembly in 1963.[22] A declining attendance and interest in horse racing combined with the introduction of slot machines (or video lottery terminals) at racetracks in the neighboring states of Delaware and West Virginia sparked a renewed effort to expand legalized gambling. During his administration Governor Glendening announced a "No Slots, No Casinos" policy, which forestalled expansion of legalized gambling in the state.[23] Governor Ehrlich offered administration bills legalizing slot machines in every legislative session from 2003 through 2006, but no bills passed both chambers of the legislature during his term. During the 2007 special legislative session, the general assembly, supported by the Governor O'Malley, succumbed to the push for expanded gambling by passing a proposed constitutional amendment to authorize slot machines at five designated locations. In the 2008 general election this amendment cruised to 58 to 42 percent statewide approval and won in every county and Baltimore City. Gambling opponents were outspent seven to one as "Vote Yes on Question 2" commercials flooded the Maryland airwaves and proponents were aided by a faltering economy. The first video lottery location opened in Cecil County in September 2010 and the second in Worcester County in January 2011.

Revenue is also generated by state-created entities conducting specific activities. These enterprise revenues include the Maryland Transportation Authority (created in 1971) that, in fiscal year 2009, generated total revenues of $403 million and net revenues of $125 million from toll collections imposed on bridge and road traffic. The Maryland Environmental Service, an independent quasi-state agency created in 1970, operates more than two hundred water and waste treatment facilities and generates and provides technical services related to water supplies, wastewater treatment, and solid waste management to public and private entities in every Maryland county. One of the largest of the quasi-independent entities is the Injured Worker's Insurance Fund, created in 1988, which provides workman's compensation insurance to governments and to private businesses unable to secure private insurance; it now covers nearly 25 percent of the workers in the state. In fiscal year 2009 this fund had revenues of $254 million, a net income of nearly $12 million, and ended the year with assets in excess of $1.6 billion.

Another important annual source of revenue is money generated from the sale of state-backed bonds that are used to pay for capital expenditures authorized every year by the general assembly. The annual level of borrowing by the state fluctuates with the economy as well as state needs and is influenced by the annual report of the Capital Debt Affordability Committee. The Maryland Constitution mandates that the state's debt be paid by an annual tax solely dedicated to the payment of interest and principal and that the principal of any state debt be paid within fifteen years.[24] The state property tax on real estate is dedicated by statute "to the debt service requirements" of the state's bonded indebtedness.[25] After being stable at only 8 cents per $100 of valuation for twenty-one years (since 1982), the state property tax rate was raised by 57.14 percent in 2003 to 13.5 cents per $100 of assessed value, but was reduced to 11.2 cents in 2009. Unique to Maryland, since 1973 all real and personal property has been assessed by a state entity, the State Department of Assessments and Taxation, rather than by local government tax assessors.[26] Real property is assessed on a staggered basis every three years in each of the state's counties and municipalities.

The total level of state general obligation debt as of June 30, 2010, was $6.52 billion, representing less than 1 percent of the valuation of the state real property assessable base and approximately 3.3 percent of the total personal income of Marylanders. Borrowing for transportation projects is not considered backed by the full faith and credit of the state and is accomplished through consolidated transportation bonds and certificates of participation that are paid for with transportation trust fund monies derived from a variety of sources. The total amount of the transportation indebtedness was $1.65 billion at the end of fiscal year 2010.[27]

Independent evaluations of Maryland's tax structure generally rate the state far more favorably than do state residents and some political actors. Consistent with the relatively high income and wealth of its residents, the state ranks high on measures using per capita income and significantly lower using a percentage of personal income. A 2002 study by the Maryland Budget and Tax Policy Institute found that, in 1999, "Maryland ranked thirty-eight among the fifty states in tax revenues as a percentage of personal income and forty-eight among the fifty states in total revenue as a share of personal income."[28] A legislative staff report in 2002 found Maryland ranking twenty-sixth in total state revenues per capita, and thirty-eighth in tax revenues as a percent of personal income.[29] These rankings have been affected by recent changes in Maryland's tax structure, with a composite ranking in the middle of states considering all tax revenue and individual or corporate income.

A final source of revenue also relies on fee-based or cost-recovery revenue. In an effort by state public policymakers to avoid general tax increases, fee for service became an attractive alternative, with substantial increases in corporate filing fees, license renewal fees, motor vehicle fees, and state park campground fees being imposed. Virtually every cabinet department and state entity charges for something—a license fee, permit fee, filing fee, application fee, construction fee, or copy costs. Even the Maryland Department of Public Safety and Corrections is a revenue generator, earning millions of dollars by employing inmate labor to produce and sell goods and services.

The nature of government expenditures has changed in the past fifty years as the role and responsibility of state government have evolved. The changing percentages of the state budget allocated to major program areas over the past several decades is presented in Table 10-2. Transportation consumed the largest share of the state budget in the 1950s and early 1960s. Education ranked number one in the late 1960s and 1970s. In the twenty-first century health care has become the largest single category of state expenditures.

The annual Maryland budget expends over 85 percent of its revenue in six major areas: public education, higher education, health care, human resources, transportation, and public safety. As depicted in Table 10-2, for the 2010 fiscal year, expenditures were approved for over $6.5 billion for public elementary and secondary education, over $4.8 billion for higher education, over $8.3 billion for health and mental hygiene, nearly $3.7 billion for transportation, over $1.8 billion for human resources, and $1.8 billion for public safety. As the dominant portions of the state budget, each of these multibillion-dollar public policy areas warrant elaboration (see Figure 10-3).

A substantial portion of the state budget consists of funds transferred to the county and municipal levels of government for program implementation and service delivery. These intergovernmental transfers constitute nearly 20 percent of the total state expenditures and were $6.2 billion in fiscal year 2010. Public education accounts for nearly three-quarters of the state funds allocated to the twenty-three counties and Baltimore City; community colleges, libraries, and public health account for notable single-digit percentages.

Public Education

Public education budgets receive annual, intense political attention and public discussion. There were 848,412 students enrolled in 1,450 public elementary and secondary schools during the 2009–10 school year.[30] Another 135,722 students were enrolled in 1,483 private schools under the jurisdiction of the Maryland State Department of Education. In fiscal year 2010 the state expended over $7 billion for public education, and the twenty-three counties and Baltimore City spent over an additional $6 billion.

Table 10-2: Approved major expenditures, 1950–2010 (in $ millions)

Fiscal Year	Education	Higher Education	Health	Human resources	Transportation	Public safety	Total
1950	29.3	16.0	15.7	6.8	37.2	5.4	135.6
	21.6%	11.8%	11.6%	5.03%	27.8%	4.0%	
1960	95.6	36.2	45.8	29.8	124.2	12.1	448.2
	21.3%	8.08%	10.2%	6.7%	27.7%	2.7%	
1970	351.9	131.5	183.1	135.0	224.3	51.1	1,336.5
	26.3%	9.8%	17.5%	10.1%	16.8%	3.8%	
1980	836.4	606.0	725.0	409.6	986.0	119.2	4,778.0
	17.5%	12.7%	15.2%	8.6%	20.6%	2.5%	
1990	2,858.8	1,384.2	1,937.7	782.2	2,130.7	579.8	10,957.8
	26.1%	13.5%	19.0%	7.1%	20.8%	5.7%	
2000	3,377.8	2,688.4	3,716.0	1,378.6	2,515.8	1,154.7	17,579.0
	19.2%	15.3%	21.1%	7.8%	14.3%	6.6%	
2010	6,542.8	4,855.5	8,306.6	1,860.1	3,698.9	1,804.0	32,287.6
	20.3%	15.0%	25.7%	5.6%	11.5%	5.6%	

Source: Department of Budget and Management (previously Department of Budget and Fiscal Planning), *Fiscal Digest of the State of Maryland for the Fiscal Years 1970–2010;* Department of Legislative Services, Maryland General Assembly. Table prepared by John T. Willis from official sources.

Note: Efforts have been made to adjust prior year allocations to the 2010 classifications.

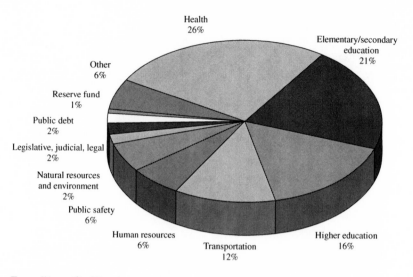

Health
26%

Elementary/secondary
education
21%

Other
6%

Reserve fund
1%

Public debt
2%

Legislative, judicial, legal
2%

Natural resources
and environment
2%

Public safety
6%

Human resources
6%

Transportation
12%

Higher education
16%

Expenditures ($ millions)

	FY 2008	FY 2009	FY 2010	% change 2010 over 2009	% total expenditures
Health	7,347	7,984	8,391	5.1	26
Elementary/secondary education	6,406	6,615	6,675	0.9	21
Higher education	4,672	4,969	5,100	2.6	16
Transportation	3,625	3,744	3,698	-1.2	12
Human resources	1,768	1,775	1,857	4.6	6
Public safety	1,797	1,789	1,833	2.4	6
Natural resources and environment	756	665	656	-1.3	2
Legislative, judicial, legal	614	677	697	3.0	2
Public debt	693	746	785	5.3	2
Reserve fund (all but Sunny Day)	263	212	176	-16.9	1
Other	1,629	1,862	1,820	-2.3	6
Total	**29,569**	**31,035**	**31,688**	**2.1**	**100**
Planned Board of Public Works reductions (unallocated)		(98)			
Budget bill reductions			(86)		
Estimated reversions		(85)	(40)		
Net Total	**29,569**	**30,853**	**31,562**	**2.3**	

Note: Totals and percentages may not add due to rounding.

Figure 10-3. Proposed expenditures, FY 2008–2010. Source: Department of Budget and Management, *Maryland Budget Highlights,* Annapolis, 2009, 7.

State support for public education in Maryland was first mandated by the 1864 constitution with detailed provisions authorizing a property tax for funding and specifying distribution of funds to counties proportionate to the population between the ages of five and twenty.[31] The 1867 constitution replaced the detailed requirements for the funding and administering of public education with the following, still controlling, short, and seemingly simple, statement: "The General Assembly, at its First Session after the adoption of this Constitution, shall by Law establish throughout the State a thorough and efficient System of Free Public Schools; and shall provide by taxation, or otherwise, for their maintenance."

The general assembly subsequently created a two-tier structure for the provision of public education in Maryland, with responsibility for management and funding split between the state and county (and Baltimore City) governments. This basic structure remains in existence today, having evolved over the past 140 years as a result of legislative, executive, and judicial initiatives and actions. An eleven-member state board of education appointed by the governor is responsible for the development and oversight of public education policy, the standards for student performance, the certification of teachers, and the supervision of schools and school systems. The state board of education appoints the state superintendent of schools, who manages the Maryland State Department of Education, with its five divisions, multitude of functions and duties, and nearly 1,800 employees. The state board of education and the state superintendent do not have direct administrative control over the local boards of education, the local superintendents, or the locally hired teachers and support personnel.

Unlike most school districts in the country, Maryland's twenty-four school districts are coterminous with the boundary lines of the twenty-three counties and Baltimore City. Maryland has fewer school districts than all other states except Hawaii and Nevada. While 90 percent of the nation's school districts are served by elected board members, public education in Maryland's counties and Baltimore City is governed by five boards of education whose members are appointed by the governor (or jointly with the mayor for Baltimore City) and nineteen elected county boards of education. The local school boards hire a local superintendent of schools and exercise management authority over the administration of public education in their jurisdiction.[32]

The county and Baltimore City school boards in Maryland are considered state entities with limited powers. Again unlike most school districts in the country, local school boards in Maryland do not have independent fiscal authority and are wholly dependent for their funding on the budget authorizations and appropriations by state and county government. The local boards of education, aided by their appointed superintendents, must prepare and submit annual budget requests to their county or city government. In turn the county or city government must provide local tax revenue to meet the operating budgets and school facilities needs of the local school system and seek state funding from the governor and general assembly. This separation of fiscal authority and responsibility from the administration and management of school systems complicates the annual education funding battles, creating conflict between and among the local boards of education, the county governments (and Baltimore City), the state board of education, the state legislature, the governor, and teachers, parents, and all other parties concerned about public education.

The ambiguity of language in the state constitution has led to periodic lawsuits filed on behalf of local governments, parents and students, and interested parties. In 1979 a lawsuit was brought by the governing school boards in Baltimore City, Caroline County, St. Mary's County, and Somerset County alleging federal and state constitutional violations in the funding of public education. After an extensive four-month trial the plaintiffs received a favorable ruling from the Baltimore City Circuit Court but were unsuccessful when the case was appealed to the state's highest court. Holding that the constitutional requirement for a "thorough and efficient System of Free Public Schools" does not mandate uniformity in per pupil funding and expenditures among the state's school districts, the Maryland Court of Appeals overturned the lower court decision in 1983.[33] The state's highest court also rejected state and federal equal protection claims in deferring to the legislative efforts to address equity, fairness, and quality issues in Maryland public education. The court's decision, along with continuing public and political pressure, did prompt a legislative response in 1987 that created a new formula for the distribution of state aid for public education known as the APEX formula (Action Plan for Educational Excellence).

In 1994 another circuit court lawsuit, initiated by the Board of School Commissioners for Baltimore City, along with two cases filed by individual plaintiffs in federal district court sought changes to the state's education funding formulas. A negotiated settlement of these lawsuits resulted in some funding increases, the creation of the Aging School Program, and a new board of school commissioners for Baltimore City to be jointly appointed by the governor and the mayor.[34]

The current state funding formulas for public education are the product of the Commission on Education Finance, Equity and Excellence (known as the Thornton Commission), established by the general assembly in

1999.[35] After the release of the commission's final report in January 2002 the Maryland General Assembly passed the Bridge to Excellence in Public Schools Act.[36] Numerous public education funding programs were restructured into four basic components. Targeted funding levels to be reached by fiscal year 2008 were established, increasing the state share by an annual total of $1.3 billion with the goal of approximately total equal funding between the state and the twenty-four locally funded school districts. The political consequences of this legislation were significant as the education program enhancements were passed without an established future funding source. This led to well-publicized projections of billion-dollar state budget deficits that provided a backdrop for the 2002 gubernatorial election and aided in the push for legalized gambling as a potential source of state revenue. In 2004 the general assembly reaffirmed the state's commitment of the increased funding targets.[37]

Another highly visible, headline-grabbing portion of the annual education funding debate in Maryland revolves around monies for school construction, rehabilitation, and repair. Following the 1971 recommendations of the Commission to Study the State's Role in Financing Public Education, the general assembly established the state school construction program and authorized the board of public works to adopt rules, regulations, and procedures to manage the program.[38] Since the program's inception through fiscal year 2010, the state has expended over $2.4 billion for public school construction projects, with all but 5 percent of the funds deriving from the sale of state general obligation bonds. Every year local government requests for school construction funds substantially exceed the monies approved and appropriated, generating headlines in local papers lamenting the lack of funds.[39] Wealthier and fast-growing jurisdictions often build new schools with local funds (forward funding) and then sometimes make retroactive requests for state reimbursements.

The level of state funding for school construction has ebbed and flowed, in part in response to the economy and state fiscal health and in part in response to policy priorities and changes. When the program commenced, the state assumed 100 percent of the cost of construction of new schools. Financial and growth pressures led to a series of program modifications, including a state-county share formula that currently ranges from an equal division of costs to a 97 percent state share, depending on the tax base and relative wealth of a local jurisdiction. The legislatively created Task Force to Study Public School Facilities recommended in its 2004 report spending $3.85 billion over eight years to bring school facilities in Maryland in line with minimum standards.[40] In 2010 over $260 million in new construction was recommended for approval.

Although there is continual debate about the quality of education and the appropriate level of funding, Maryland consistently ranks high among the fifty states in public education accountability, assessment, and achievement.[41] Along with funding formula adjustments and school construction requests, a recurring education issue in Maryland public education is the recruitment of, retention of, and compensation for teachers. A persistent complaint from the teachers and their organized bargaining units involves pension benefits, which rank among the lowest in the country. Public education will remain a dominant public policy issue in Maryland as state and local political actors pursue solutions.

Higher Education

In contrast to the constitutional mandate for public elementary and secondary education, higher education in Maryland lacks specific supportive provisions in the state constitution. Until the creation of the advisory council on higher education in 1963 and the board of trustees of the state colleges, there were no statewide entities or authorities responsible for the development, management, and implementation of higher education policy. State support for public higher education, community colleges, and private colleges was ad hoc and divided among individual institutions and specific programs.

After decades of studies and several reorganizations, the current structure of public higher education in Maryland was established in 1988 with the creation of the Maryland Higher Education Commission (MHEC) and the merger of eleven state public higher education campuses and two research and public service institutions into the University System of Maryland.[42]

MHEC is responsible for coordinating the programs of the public higher education institutions, administering the state student financial aid programs, overseeing academic matters, and supervising state support for community colleges and private institutions.[43] The state's sixteen community colleges were placed under the administrative oversight of the MHEC in 1981. Each of the sixteen community colleges has a board of trustees, appointed by the governor.

The University System of Maryland is governed by a state board of regents (appointed by the governor and confirmed by the general assembly) that selects a chancellor with overall administrative responsibility and presidents of each of the eleven campuses and two research institutions. Morgan State University (a historic black college dating to 1867 that became a state school in 1939) and St Mary's College in Southern Maryland (founded in 1840 as a nonsectarian women's seminary that became a state institution in 1927) were permitted to remain outside the university system and have their own governor-appointed board of trustees.

In 1984 legislation was passed to make the University of Maryland Medical System, which educates and trains health care providers as well as provides direct medical services, a private, nonprofit corporation with a board of directors appointed by the governor that must include members of the board of regents and the Maryland General Assembly.[44]

Maryland has a modest grant program dating to the mid-nineteenth century that provides state funds to qualified private institutions of higher learning. These grants were formalized in 1971 and withstood a constitutional challenge in the U.S. Supreme Court.[45] Grants to the seventeen qualifying colleges and universities totaled over $38 million in fiscal year 2010 and are based on a formula of full-time student equivalents and a percentage of general fund support for public four-year institutions.

Lacking specific constitutional and statutory funding requirements, expenditures for higher education in Maryland have often been subject to wild swings in the level of state support, dependent on the health of the state economy and state budget. Generous increases accompanied the reformulation of the governance structure of the state's colleges and universities in the 1980s, followed by double-digit losses of state funding during the recession of the early 1990s. Another round of historic funding increases in operating budgets and capital construction funding during the middle and late 1990s was followed again by significant decreases in general fund support in fiscal years 2003 and 2004. The consequences of the cuts in higher education funding were hefty increases in student tuition and fees from fiscal year 2002 to fiscal year 2006, in some instances climbing as high as 44 percent.[46] A special legislative committee in 2004 found that the state's public institutions of higher education were the sixth most expensive for state residents in the nation.[47] In seeming contradiction to Maryland's high ranking among the fifty states in the educational attainment and achievement of its residents, state support for higher education in Maryland lags behind national averages as a percentage of the state budget and a percentage of income.[48] A dedicated source of funding for higher education in Maryland was established during the 2007 special legislative session, with a portion of the increase in corporate income taxes directed toward the new Higher Education Investment Fund.[49] In fiscal year 2010 total spending for higher education was over $4.8 billion, comprised nearly 15 percent of total state expenditures, and served over 349,000 full- and part-time students.

Health Care

Over the past several decades there has been an explosion in health care costs, impacting annual state budgets. Maryland is no exception. With a predominantly urban population and progressive policy tendencies, the state has seen cost increases due to state initiatives as well as the expansion of federal programs. In past eras state health care expenditures were dominated by facility operations and traditional public health issues. Now the vast majority of current expenditures pay for health care services for individuals.

In fiscal year 2010 the Maryland Department of Health and Mental Hygiene was allocated over $8.3 billion, making it the largest single category of state expenditures in the state budget, consuming over 25.7 percent of total state expenditures. Health care expenditures have more than tripled in fifteen years, increased nearly nine times in twenty-five years, and thirty times in thirty-five years (see Table 10-2). The department regulates the state's health care system and private health care providers, coordinates public health programs, and provides direct health care services.

Nearly two-thirds of the health care spending in Maryland (over $4.9 billion) is for the federally created, but state-administered, Medicaid and Children's Health Insurance programs. Medicaid provides payments to health care providers for services rendered to persons of lower income eligible under federal and state guidelines. Medicaid enrollment in Maryland covered over 830,000 people in fiscal year 2010, with state optional benefits exceeding the federally mandated coverage. Approximately half of the Medicaid payments are covered by reimbursements from the federal government. Medicaid spending increased a budget-busting 28 percent in only four years from fiscal years 2000 to 2005 and dwarfs the spending for other health care–related matters. Following the federal law passed in 1997, Maryland expanded programs for children's health care in 1998 and again in 2000.[50] Under the current program Medicaid coverage is available for children up to age nineteen whose family income is up to 300 percent of the poverty level and for pregnant women with income up to 250 percent of the poverty level, limits that rank at the top among all the states.[51] During fiscal year 2006 an estimated 115,000 children and 800 pregnant women received benefits.

Other significant components of health care costs in Maryland are the mental hygiene administration, the developmental disabilities administration, and traditional public health matters. The mental health administration operates state psychiatric hospitals and residential treatment centers and manages community-based programs that account for almost 13 percent of the health department's annual expenditures. The Developmental Disabilities Administration serves more than 21,000 individuals and accounts for approximately 10 percent of the department's expenditures. Traditional public health programs provided in cooperation with local health departments consume approximately 7 percent of the department's annual budget. Maryland was the first state to allow local health departments in each of its major local subdivisions to receive state funding. The original 1956 case formula was revised in 1993 and is now titled the Targeted Funding Program; it supports services in nine broad areas specified by statute.[52] State funding levels rose dramatically from 1993 to 2003 and were approved at over $66 million for fiscal year 2007.

The progressive policy tendencies of Maryland are reflected not only in the expanded benefit coverage and higher income eligibility limits for federal programs but also in a variety of state initiatives. For example, Maryland began a pharmacy assistance program, covering nearly 44,000 adults who did not qualify for Medicaid, before the federal government began assuming 50 percent of these costs in July 2002.[53] A senior prescription drug program for low-income seniors receiving Medicare in medically underserved counties was created in fiscal year 2001; it provides $1,000 a year in benefits to up to 30,000 individuals.[54] In July 2002 Maryland implemented a pharmacy discount program for Medicare beneficiaries with incomes between 116 and 175 percent of the poverty level, extending coverage to another 44,000 individuals at an annual cost of $8 million.

Maryland was a leader at the state level in AIDS awareness, diagnosis, evaluation, and treatment with the creation of an AIDS administration office in 1987 and expanded prescription drug coverage. With the lack of a national health care system or plan, a consistently large population segment without private health insurance, the upcoming retirement age arrival of the state's baby boomers, and progressive policy tendencies, Maryland's health care budget is likely to remain the highest category of state expenditures.

Human Resources

Although social welfare public policy developed slowly in the United States and in Maryland, after the Great Depression in the 1930s it became generally accepted that one function of government is to provide for the basic needs of those individuals who cannot provide for themselves—the poor, the seriously ill, persons with disabilities, children, and the elderly. In the late 1960s state leaders embraced the War on Poverty. By the twenty-first century Maryland had emerged as a national leader in several human services areas. Recognition of different needs among the regions of the state have led to special allocations in state funding formulas for a variety of programs.

Among the state departments and agencies responsible for the delivery of human resource services the largest is the Maryland Department of Human Resources, which administered a budget in excess of $1.8 billion in fiscal year 2010 with 6,816 employees. The department works closely with counterparts at the county and city level to provide a variety of social services. The social service director in every county and Baltimore City is jointly appointed by the governor and the highest elected official in each jurisdiction.[55] The Department of Human Resources manages direct public assistance (welfare), the federal food stamp program, and a full range of services for children and adults with disabilities. Enrollment in human resources programs fluctuates with the state of the economy; increases have occurred during the most recent recession.

Successful implementation of the 1996 federal welfare reform act (the Personal Responsibility and Work Opportunity Act) brought dramatic drops in welfare caseloads. Maryland had the seventh largest percentage drop (65 percent) in families receiving Temporary Assistance to Needy Families among all fifty states, even though it was also one of only five states that increased net benefits during the same comparable period.[56] From a peak of 227,887 individual recipients of Temporary Cash Assistance in January 1995, caseloads fell to fewer than 65,000 in fiscal year 2001, which was the seventh greatest percentage decrease in welfare caseload among the fifty states. More progressive than other states, Maryland did allow recipients to fulfill eligibility requirements through enrollment in approved education programs.

The Maryland Department of Juvenile Services is also involved with the provision of human resources, as it works not only with delinquent youth but with children in need of assistance and children in need of supervision. Concern about the special needs of certain population cohorts has prompted the granting of cabinet-level departmental status to the Department of Aging (1995), the Department of Veterans' Affairs (1999), and the Department of Disabilities (2004).

Transportation

The construction and operation of transportation infrastructure has always been a significant topic in Maryland politics and government. The structure of state government itself was influenced by the failure of state transportation investments, leading to the creation of the board of public works in the middle of the nineteenth century and later to enhanced budget powers of the governor in 1916. The advent of the automobile brought the creation, in 1908, of the independent state roads commission, a vivid illustration of the intersection between state government and politics in a growing America. Transportation funding accounted for approximately 27.8 percent of the total state budget in fiscal year 1950. Although down from earlier eras as a percentage of the state budget, the state transportation budget has steadily increased and was nearly $3.7 billion in fiscal year 2010 (see Table 10-2).

The revenue for the operation of the Maryland Department of Transportation are placed in a transportation trust fund created in 1971. Sources include dedicated taxes, bond proceeds, federal funds, and all other special fund fees and charges derived from the operation of the department. Unlike for other state entities, transportation's unexpended budgeted monies at the end of a fiscal year are permitted to remain in the transportation trust fund for future needs. Federal grants account for approximately 24 percent of the transportation department's annual operating budget and nearly 40 percent of its annual capital budget. Portions of the fuel, titling, and corporate taxes, along with registration fees, are placed in a gasoline and motor vehicle revenue account known as the Highway User Fund. These funds are allocated by statute to the transportation department, which receives approximately 70 percent, the state's counties and municipalities, and recently to the general fund.

The key planning document for the Maryland Department of Transportation is a six-year rolling capital projects plan. Capital projects may be funded from the trust fund and from the issuance of consolidated transportation bonds and are payable only from the transportation trust fund. The department of transportation has also been granted the authority to issue certificates of participation that allow investors to participate in a share of future revenue from the road or facility to be constructed. In 2002 the Maryland General Assembly authorized the Department of Transportation to participate in the federal Transportation Infrastructure Finance and Innovation Act and to issue bonds in anticipation of federal revenues.

The substantial ongoing transportation needs and demands create tensions between state and local governments over funding levels and priority projects. Annual debates occur about the allocation of monies between mass transit and road construction, as well as urban versus rural needs. The construction of a major, multibillion-dollar highway project between Rockville and Laurel (known as the Intercounty Connector, or ICC) will strain the state's transportation budget for at least a decade. At the same time there is increasing pressure to develop more mass transit in the Baltimore metropolitan region (an east-to-west "red line") and to upgrade mass transit systems in the populous Washington DC suburbs.

Public Safety and Corrections

A fundamental and essential function of government in a civil society is to provide for the security of its citizens. Historically the state role in public safety was limited to the passage of criminal laws by the legislature, proscribing individual conduct, and the housing of prisoners sentenced by the state courts. In response to changing patterns and perceptions of crime, the state's role and costs have increased for crime fighting and public safety.

The number of incarcerated persons has risen dramatically as a result of tough-on-crime public policies, the expansion of criminal laws, and other social factors; correspondingly the state expenditures for public safety have grown tremendously. The number of prisoners in state institutions more than tripled from 1970 to 22,481 as of June 30, 2010.[57] The number of persons under the supervision of parole and probation officers similarly increased, from 24,000 in 1970 to over 68,000 at the end of June 2010.

Prison construction was a public policy priority and resulting big business in the 1970s and 1980s. Large correctional facilities were built in Somerset County and Washington County, and the facilities in Baltimore City were modernized. In 1970 the state expenditures for public safety were slightly more than $51.1 million; in fiscal year 2010 the budget for public safety comprised almost 5.6 percent of the total state budget and stood at over $1.8 billion (see Table 10-2).

The Maryland Department of Public Safety and Correctional Services is a large cabinet-level agency with nearly 11,700 employees that operates twenty-seven correctional facilities for adult criminal offenders, manages alternative sentencing programs, and performs other, related duties. More than 90,000 arrestees are processed annually through the department's central booking facility; a daily average of 28,000 individuals are housed in the department's correctional facilities and more than 60,000 are supervised by the Division of Parole and Probation. The department receives substantial special funding from the "911" surcharge on telephone bills, but its operational and management demands continue to need general fund support.

A separate cabinet-level department of juvenile services administers a variety of programs to assist youths as well as prevent and punish delinquent acts. More than 50,000 youths are subject to the jurisdiction of the department annually, with 43 percent of cases resulting in a formal petition of a delinquency, 22.5 percent handled through informal supervision, and over 32 percent resolved at the initial intake process. Management of the nineteen state-owned facilities, with a rated capacity of 839 places for the care and custody of delinquent children or young adults, has been a persistent problem for successive gubernatorial administrations.

The Maryland State Police, with roots dating to the early 1900s, became a separate state entity in 1935 and a cabinet-level department in 1994. With 2,488 civilian and uniformed employees in fiscal year 2010, the state police have primary responsibility for the enforcement of highway safety and statewide jurisdiction over criminal activity, except for nonnarcotics offenses within incorporated municipalities. The state police operate a crime laboratory and training facilities for law enforcement personnel. The state fire marshal and the state fire prevention commission are also under the administration of the department of state police. The state provides only a little more than 2 percent of the total funding for fire and rescue services; county and municipal governments spend nearly a half-billion dollars annually on these necessary public safety services.

Even in a post-9/11 global environment with a focus on homeland security, the bulk of routine law enforcement remains the duty and responsibility of county and municipal police and sheriffs. County and municipal governments collectively spend over $1 billion dollars annually on local police activities; less than 7 percent of that is contributed by state government. Crime rates vary dramatically among the state's twenty-three counties and Baltimore City, creating very different challenges for law enforcement and the criminal justice system. Although crime rates have dropped dramatically in the past five years, Baltimore City remains among the national leaders in the rate of homicide. Prince George's County, bordering the eastern and southern boundaries of the District of Columbia, also has a disturbingly high homicide rate and significant urban crime. Suburban and rural counties in Maryland are not immune from crimes related to drug trafficking and drug abuse as well as property crimes.

The responsibility for law enforcement is handled differently among Maryland's subdivisions. There is the classic big city police department in Baltimore City, as well as full-service countywide police departments in the large metropolitan and urban counties. Other suburban and rural counties rely on the county sheriff and municipal police for public safety functions. The state police was authorized to enter into contracts with local government to provide law enforcement. This unique resident trooper program operated in several jurisdictions and extensively in Carroll County, for thirty-seven years with up to forty-five officers but will terminate on July 1, 2013.

The state's twenty-three counties also operate local detention centers that house individuals awaiting trial, persons sentenced and preparing for transfer to state facilities, and those receiving sentences of less than eighteen months of confinement. The financial strain on the criminal justice system led to the state takeover of the Baltimore City jail in 1993. County governments do receive a formula-based reimbursement from the state for the costs of housing inmates after sentencing. The state also adopted a construction program for local detention centers that pays for either half or all of the construction costs of detention facilities.[58] Community adult rehabilitation centers have been constructed with state support in Baltimore City, Cecil County, and Montgomery County that allow offenders to maintain a job or perform community service work. The average daily number of individuals residing in county detention facilities was over 12,800 in fiscal years 2004 and 2005.

The public safety challenges for local and state officials will continue to increase, with a constant need for more resources to meet the demands and expectations of the public. The working conditions in correctional facilities and in active law enforcement are inherently dangerous and make staffing and personnel issues constantly challenging. Levels of staffing are routinely below ideal or standard, and the pay scales are well below the average income of Marylanders. County and municipal governments will continue to seek increased state aid for public safety services and courthouse operations. In the twenty-first century intergovernmental cooperation will become even more important in public safety administration and policy.

SUMMARY

In 2006 Governor Robert Ehrlich, who was elected in 2002 amid allegations of an unhealthy state fiscal condition, proposed the largest single-year spending increase in the history of the state for fiscal year 2007, an increase of over $3.7 billion, representing 12 percent more in total expenditures from the prior fiscal year and 33 percent more than the last fiscal year budget proposed by his predecessor four years earlier.[59] Maryland Comptroller Louis L. Goldstein used to say regularly in public speeches, "The state proudly provides services from the cradle to the grave." Even contemporary Maryland Republicans subscribe, at least in an election year, to this sentiment.

CHAPTER ELEVEN

"Pleasant Living" Policies and Politics

We have wasted our inheritance by improvidence and
mismanagement and blind confidence.
> William A. Brooks, *The Oyster*, 1891

As we turn the watershed increasingly to human use, we
permanently foreclose valuable options for reversing pollution.
> Tom Horton, *Bay Country*, 1987

These critical observations, made nearly one hundred years apart by two
esteemed environmentalists, reflect a deep, abiding concern for Maryland's
greatest natural resource and defining geographic feature: the Chesapeake
Bay. Brooks and Horton are certainly not alone; most Marylanders believe
the Bay must be nurtured and protected. The Bay is North America's largest estuary and an important ecological and economic asset for the nation
and the state. The Chesapeake Bay and its tributaries comprise almost one-
third of the state's area. Fourteen of the state's twenty-three counties, along
with Baltimore City, together have over 11,000 miles of Bay shoreline. All
of the remaining nine Maryland counties contain land that is part of the
wider regional drainage basin. The significance of the Chesapeake Bay to
the dynamics, structure, and policy content of the state's government and
politics is undeniable.

From colonial times to the present, countless observers have marveled at
this great body of water and savored the bounty of the Bay. H. L. Mencken
observed that the Chesapeake Bay was an "immense outdoor protein facto-
ry."[1] Indeed the seafood trapped, dredged, caught, and netted from the Bay
has provided a livelihood and lifestyle for generations of watermen. The
Bay is esteemed not only for its natural beauty and resources but also for

its economic and transportation importance. In addition the Bay has been an inspiration for poets and writers, a backdrop for painters and photographers, a living laboratory for scientists, a training ground for the U.S. Naval Academy, a testing site for the Defense Department, and a recreational haven and delight for boaters, sailors, swimmers, canoeists, fishermen, hunters, and adventurers.[2]

Approximately one in ten motor vehicles registered in Maryland display the Chesapeake Bay specialty license plate, with its logo "Treasure the Chesapeake."[3] Since 1985 Maryland taxpayers have donated a portion of their state income tax return to the Chesapeake Bay Trust, raising millions of dollars. It is therefore not surprising that Maryland political and governmental leaders, across party lines and otherwise opposing political ideologies, embrace the rhetoric of the Bay in their campaign advertising, public statements, and policy initiatives.

At the beginning of the twentieth century the platforms of the Maryland state Democratic and Republican parties proclaimed support for legislation to replenish the depleted oyster beds and bars of the state and "to foster and increase the supply of the natural products of our great inland sea."[4] Echoes of the same refrain continue to reverberate throughout the state's body politic into the twenty-first century. Just as their counterparts proclaimed in the 1903 and 1907 gubernatorial elections, the Democratic and Republican candidates for governor in the most recent gubernatorial elections expressed their support for the restoration of oysters in the Chesapeake Bay.

The natural bounty of the Bay has provided a substantial source of food and income for the inhabitants of the region. With railroad expansion providing a reach into markets in the Ohio Valley and points west as well as to the more populous northern states, exports of oysters from the Bay averaged 7 million bushels a year from the establishment of packing houses in 1834 until the publication of the classic study, *The Oyster*, after the 1890 dredging season.[5] Determining the appropriate balance between environmental concerns, economic necessity, and individual land use preferences has provided the grist for hundreds of years of public policy debates, discussions, and actions. Contemporary Maryland, as well as historical Maryland, can be understood by examining the processes and outcomes of these balancing efforts.

Population growth and a changing state economy persistently exert pressures on the Bay and its tributaries. The billions of dollars spent on interstate, state, and local road projects have been a convenience to motorists seeking access to their place of work and home. But the state's modern road network has resulted in significant environmental and land use degradation. The natural environment that is treasured by Marylanders is threatened by their transportation needs, expectations, and demands. This conflict often stretches the governmental and political dynamics of Maryland in competing public policy directions.

Public officials and political candidates in Maryland are confronted with a public demand for less traffic congestion, more roads, and easier commuter access at the same time that they are subjected (particularly in election years) with a public demand for environmental protection and land preservation. Numerous publications and books have highlighted these competing political and policy pressures.[6] Marylanders from varying perspectives often display dissatisfaction with the balances that are struck by public officials among environmental, land use, and transportation public policies.

ENVIRONMENT AND LAND USE PROGRAMS AND POLICY

Since the nation's environmental consciousness was raised by Rachel Carson's *Silent Spring*, which sparked action in the halls of Congress and state legislatures, Maryland has been consistently ranked among the "green states."[7] A timeline of the state's major environmental and land use actions, legislation, and initiatives is presented in Table 11-1.

The state's environmental and land use policies and programs began in the late 1960s with the creation of the Maryland Environmental Trust, intended to promote the conservation of open space, and the passage of Program Open Space, which dedicated a portion of the state transfer tax on real estate to the acquisition of land for public purposes.[8] Before, and especially after federal environmental initiatives in the 1970s such as the Clean Air Act and Clean Water Act were enacted, Maryland fully embraced a progressive environmental public policy agenda. The 1980s brought action as well as attention to the Chesapeake Bay with the multistate Chesapeake Bay Agreements and Maryland's acclaimed Chesapeake Bay Critical Area Protection Act.[9]

The 1990s witnessed the creation of Maryland's Smart Growth policies, which endeavor to use the resources of the state to influence the direction of future growth through a combination of financial incentives, land use limitations, and market mechanisms, with implementation responsibility spread across departmental and agency jurisdictional lines. The executive director of the Michigan Land Use Institute called Maryland's Smart Growth policies "arguably the most important policy initiative of the past decade: and the most important social policy of the 21st century."[10] The syndicated columnist Neal Peirce observed, "Finally one American state has done a reality

Table 11-1: Timeline of major environmental laws and actions

1967	Maryland Environmental Trust
1968	Scenic and Wild Rivers Program
1969	Program Open Space
1970	Environmental Services Act
	Maryland Council on the Environment
	Departments of Agriculture and Natural Resources
1973	Shore Erosion Control Program
1974	Coastal Zone Protection Program
1977	Maryland Agricultural Land Preservation Program
1980	Chesapeake Bay Commission
1982	State Development Task Force executive order
1983	First Chesapeake Bay Agreement signed by Maryland, Delaware, Pennsylvania, Virginia, the Chesapeake Bay Commission, and the Environmental Protection Agency
1984	Chesapeake Bay Critical Area Protection Act
1987	The Second Chesapeake Bay Agreement signed
1989	Non-Tidal Wetland Protection
1992	Economic Growth, Resource Protection and Planning Act (2000, amended, adding eighth state policy vision)
1993	Forest Conservation Act
1995	Neighborhood Business Development Program
1996	Neighborhood Stabilization Preservation Act
	Maryland Heritage Preservation and Tourism Program
1997	Smart Growth and Neighborhood Conservation Act
	Priority Funding Areas Act
	Rural Legacy Program
	Live Near Your Work Program
	Job Creation Tax Credit Act and Program
	Brownfields Voluntary Cleanup and Revitalization Program
	Historic Rehabilitation Tax Credit
1998	Water Quality Improvement Act
2000	Third Chesapeake Bay Agreement signed
2001	Greenprint Program
	Office of Smart Growth codified
2002	Atlantic Coastal Bays Protection Act
2004	Chesapeake Bay Restoration Fund
2006	Healthy Air Act
2007	Clean Cars Act
2008	Chesapeake and Atlantic Coastal Bays Critical Area Protection Program (amending Critical Area Act)
2009	Greenhouse Gas Reduction Act
2010	Sustainable Communities Act

Source: Compiled by John T. Willis from public document sources.

check, recognized sprawl development's incredibly heavy costs, and started thinking about potential savings—fiscal, social, environmental—from curbing state subsidies."[11]

The environmental public policy issues generated by concern for the Chesapeake Bay are multifaceted and complex. The Bay is a complex ecosystem and possesses a delicate food chain that needs to be understood, balanced, and protected. Accordingly concern about the health and supply of finfish, crabs, and oysters inevitably leads to concerns about water and air pollution and Bay grasses and habitat. The sources of pollution are both readily identifiable (point sources such as industrial and wastewater treatment plants) and not readily observable (nonpoint sources such as contaminated runoff from agriculture, suburban lawns, and impervious surfaces, such as roads, parking lots, and buildings). These pollutants not only flow into the vast number of streams and tributaries in Maryland but can also degrade groundwater seepage and underground water flows.

The state's environmental and land use policies extend beyond the Chesapeake Bay and generally embrace progressive initiatives. The state air quality standards, for example, exceed the federal guidelines. In 2006 the Maryland General Assembly passed the Healthy Air Act, requiring the state's seven coal-fired power utility plants to reduce four specific emissions: carbon dioxide, mercury, sulfur dioxide, and nitrous oxide.[12] The 2006 Healthy Air Act also required the governor to participate in the multistate Regional Greenhouse Gas Initiative.

Maryland governors and the general assembly have supported, to varying degrees, energy conservation. The Maryland Energy Efficiency Standards Act of 2004 established efficiency standards in excess of federal standards for nine products with the intent of reducing energy demand, and hence air pollution, while providing savings for consumers.[13] The Maryland General Assembly passed legislation in 2004 requiring the state government to derive 7.5 percent of its energy from renewable energy sources.[14] With a new, supportive gubernatorial administration, the 2007 session of the general assembly produced a cascade of environmental legislation, including the Maryland Clean Cars Act, mandating increased fuel efficiency by 2011, a ban on the sale of dishwashing detergent containing phosphorus, a mandate for environmental site-design techniques, and the addition of solar energy to the state's renewable portfolio standard.[15] These initiatives were followed in the 2008 session by legislation strengthening the state's Critical Area Act that had been narrowed by judicial interpretation and bills passed increasing energy efficiency and the use of renewable energy sources.[16]

Responsibility for the implementation of environmental public policy in Maryland resides with several cabinet-level departments and other agencies. The Department of Environment issues approvals, certifications, licenses, permits, and rules and regulations for more than forty different environmental standards, including water quality, air quality, wetlands protection, waste disposal (regular, hazardous, and toxic), radiation, noise, and mineral resources.

The Maryland Department of Natural Resources is the administrative home of the State Forest and Park Service, which has management responsibility for approximately 260,290 acres in ninety-seven different parks, forests, and other areas. The Wildlife and Heritage Service, within the Department of Natural Resources, manages 130,000 acres of state-owned land. The Maryland Fisheries Services assesses and assists the fish, crabs, shellfish, aquatic reptiles, and their habitats that comprise the Chesapeake Bay ecosystem.

The environmental responsibility of the Maryland Department of Agriculture includes oversight of agricultural nutrient management plans, support of agricultural land preservation and rural legacy programs, and supervision over pest management and pesticide control.

The Critical Area Protection Commission, created in 1984, has planning and approval authority over land within 1,000 feet of the edge of tidal water in the Chesapeake Bay watershed, which brings approximately 650,000 acres, or 10 percent of the state's land area within sixteen counties and Baltimore City, under its jurisdiction.

Maryland Environmental Services was created in 1970 as a public corporation to finance, construct, and maintain liquid and solid waste treatment and disposal facilities for the Chesapeake and Coastal Bays Restoration Fund. Since 2004 it has imposed a thirty-dollar annual charge on every residence to support the modernization and upgrading of the state's wastewater treatment facilities.[17]

The Maryland Department of Planning provides extensive technical assistance to state, county, and municipal governments on land use issues. Coordination among state departments and agencies was first mandated by executive order in 1998 and later mandated through the Office of Smart Growth.[18] The Maryland Sustainable Growth Commission was established in 2010 to ensure representation of a wide range of stakeholders in promoting smart and sustainable growth policies.[19] The Smart Growth Subcabinet includes cabinet members from departments not normally associated with the environment, such as the Department of Health and Mental Hygiene and the Department of Labor, Licensing and Regulation.[20]

Maryland's educational institutions are also heavily engaged in environmental and land use projects. Within the University of Maryland System is the Center for Environmental and Estuarine Studies, with more than a hundred full-time faculty members. Located in three laboratories in different regions of the state, the center conducts research on the ecology of the Bay and its watershed, coastal oceanographic processes, the effects of human activity on natural resources, and the ecology of wildlife and freshwater fish. Environmental research is conducted and services are provided statewide through the Maryland Agricultural Experiment Station, the Maryland Cooperative Extension Service, and the Maryland Biotechnology Institute, which are part of the University of Maryland System. In 2002 the National Center for Smart Growth Research and Education was established within the University of Maryland at its main College Park campus to conduct research on land use policies and to assist state and local governments in improving the effectiveness of their programs. In October 2007 the center sponsored the conference "Smart Growth @ 10," which presented a rich source of commentary and information about Maryland's leading environmental initiative.[21]

The conceptual foundation of Maryland's Smart Growth and sustainable communities policies does not rest simply on the preservation and conservation of green space. These landmark public policies include the use of the state's financial and other resources to direct growth activity into targeted priority funding areas. Maryland's programs and policies are designed to create the supply and channel the demand for developable space on which economic and population growth can occur.

TRANSPORTATION PROGRAMS AND POLICY

Almost from its inception Maryland has enjoyed a competitive advantage in transportation (see chapter 2). Transportation changes from sail to steamship and from horse power to rail power and the automobile's ascendency have all generated needs and demands that impacted Maryland's economy and its people. The transition from a manufacturing economy to a service economy put its own stresses on the state transportation networks in the second half of the twentieth century, requiring billions of dollars in highway, rail, port, and airport improvements. In twenty-first century Maryland the transportation infrastructure will continue to be challenged by a growing and shifting population in the nation's fifth most densely populated state.

Transportation policy is developed and implemented under the auspices of the Maryland Department of Transportation, which was created in

1970 to bring together previously separate transportation components. This made Maryland one of the few states that placed all modes of transportation under a single department and makes the implementation of policy initiatives such as Smart Growth and sustainable communities more manageable and effective. Recent governors have creatively used the resources of the Department of Transportation to enhance priority funding areas, bolster neighborhood revitalization, obtain open space, and even preserve the battlefield at Antietam in Washington County.

The Maryland Department of Transportation is organized into five modal administrations with specific areas of responsibility, each of which impacts land use and the environment.

The Motor Vehicle Administration licenses passenger and commercial vehicles, registers and titles vehicles, regulates vehicle sales, administers highway safety programs, and has general responsibility for motor vehicle services, including emissions testing.

The State Highway Administration is responsible for more than 5,200 miles of highways and 2,300 bridges that comprise the state highway system. There is an additional 24,662 miles of highway maintained by county and municipal governments that serve the general public. The 485 miles of interstate highway in Maryland provide key economic linkages within the state and facilitate interstate commerce. Given Maryland's relatively small physical size, significant portions of the interstate highway system are also used as commuting routes, creating growth pressures and aiding sprawl. Central to the transportation public policy debates is a rolling six-year capital improvement plan developed by the department and influenced by public hearings throughout the state, taking comments from citizens, local governments, and public officials.

The Mass Transit Administration (MTA) is responsible for the capital improvements and operation of a 15.5-mile subway system, a thirty-mile light rail system, and bus services in the Baltimore metropolitan area. The Baltimore Metro Subway first opened in 1983 and now consists of fourteen stations running from the Owings Mills designated growth area in western Baltimore County to the Johns Hopkins Hospital complex in east Baltimore City, with an annual ridership of nearly 15 million passenger trips. The Central Corridor Light Rail began operations in 1992. The system runs from a designated employment center in Hunt Valley in north-central Baltimore County south through Baltimore City to Glen Burnie, with a spur to the state's international airport in Anne Arundel County. Bus service in the Baltimore metropolitan area is provided on more than fifty basic routes operating throughout Baltimore City, Baltimore County, Anne Arundel County, and Howard County, with connections to other portions of the state. The MTA runs the MARC commuter rail, which carries approximately 6 million passengers a year on three separate lines covering 201 miles of track to and from the Baltimore and Washington central train stations. The MTA also oversees the grants for transit programs operated by county, municipal, and private sector companies throughout the state.

The Maryland Aviation Administration has general responsibility for the development and support of aeronautics policy. The administration operates the Baltimore-Washington International Thurgood Marshall Airport (BWI), located twelve miles west of Baltimore with convenient access to interstate highways. The airport was originally constructed and owned by the City of Baltimore. In 1972 the state purchased the airport for a modest $36 million. Major expansions of terminals and runways over the past three decades have propelled the airport to national prominence. It is now among the most active and fast-growing airports in the country. The surrounding area serves as an important access point for numerous sectors of the Maryland economy and is a major economic engine for the state, host counties, and region. A former Anne Arundel County executive, Janet Owens, labeled the BWI corridor her county's "Gold Coast," with skyrocketing land values and significant new business ventures.[22] The BWI Business Partnership, Inc., with more than eight hundred members, is among the most active and strongest business organizations in the state. In addition the Maryland Aviation Administration operates the Martin State Airport in eastern Baltimore County (purchased in 1975) and provides assistance to the eighteen airport facilities owned by local governments that are open to the public throughout the state. The Maryland Aviation Administration also licenses and regulates the thirty-five public use airports located in the state.

The Maryland Port Administration is charged with ensuring commercial navigation and promoting international and domestic markets for the Port of Baltimore. The administration owns and operates six public marine terminals and manages the dredging of shipping channels, which requires a delicate balancing of commercial interests and environmental protection. It also owns and operates the World Trade Center, a prominent thirty-story office building, located in the Inner Harbor of the Baltimore downtown business district.

There are additional transportation-related agencies and entities that are not under the direct control of the Maryland Department of Transportation but are vital to serving the transportation needs of the public. The state's seven toll facilities (four toll bridges, the Harbor Tunnel Thruway, the Fort McHenry Tunnel, and the John F. Kennedy Memorial Highway in northeastern Maryland) are managed and operated by the Maryland Transportation Authority, an enterprise agency of the state, created in 1971. The authority has six members appointed by the governor, subject to confirmation of the state senate, and is chaired by the secretary of the Department of Transportation. The authority has the power to issue revenue bonds for the costs of its projects and for other revenue-producing transportation projects, such as the Seagirt Marine Terminal and parking facilities at the state's airport and near mass transit stops. Toll receipts are used to pay the principal and interest on revenue bonds and for the administration and operation of facilities. The Maryland Transportation Authority has its own police force for public safety at its toll facilities, which also provides law enforcement services at the Port of Baltimore and Baltimore Washington International Airport. It is also the funding vehicle for the controversial Intercounty Connector, which will be the state's most expensive transportation project at over $2.6 billion.

The Washington Metropolitan Area Transit Authority (WMATA) is an interstate compact between Maryland, Virginia, and the District of Columbia originally formed in 1967 to development a rail transit system for the Washington metropolitan area. Bus service was added to its responsibility in 1973 with the purchase of the major private area carriers. The 106-mile Metrorail system serves the state's two largest population counties, Montgomery and Prince George's, with lines running north, south, and east from the center of the nation's capital. Maryland's share of the cost was $215.7 million for fiscal year 2010. Maryland's interests in WMATA are represented by the Washington Suburban Transit Commission, whose members are appointed by the governor. Plans for a proposed "purple line" running between inner beltway Metro stations in densely populated Montgomery and Prince George's counties have been initiated, cooled, and restarted in recent years.

BALANCING ENVIRONMENT, TRANSPORTATION, AND LAND USE POLICIES

Every gubernatorial administration in Maryland's modern era has wrestled with the perceived and actual tensions created between environmental and land use policy and transportation policy. The agendas of every gubernatorial administration have included programs or initiatives to "save the Bay." Every administration has also sought to improve the transportation infrastructure to meet the demands and needs of the public.

Often conflict between transportation improvements and sound environmental and land use public policy is presumed as inevitable. Sometimes in the implementation of a specific project conflicts do arise and efforts are made to mitigate the environmental degradation. For example, the dredging of shipping channels for the Port of Baltimore invariably raises concerns from environmental advocates, while maintaining the economic vitality and competitiveness of one of the state's economic engines is deemed an urgent necessity by port-related businesses and government officials.

Since the 1960s there has been a general recognition and consensus among most public policymakers in Maryland about the need for a proper balance between the seemingly contradictory goals and objectives of environmental, land use, and transportation policies. The Maryland Department of Transportation's first cabinet-level secretary, Harry R. Hughes, became a governor who initiated a bold, progressive environmental program. The former secretary of transportation under Governor Schaefer observed, "Transportation should be a servant of community development, not its master. . . . We must develop transportation systems that preserve and enhance community development goals."[23] The concept of Smart Growth is predicated on the claim that the apparent or presumed conflicts between prosperity and environmental sensitivity have created a false dichotomy and that environmental protection and economic growth can be mutually consistent goals in the implementation of state public policy.

COUNTY AND MUNICIPAL PUBLIC POLICY

In Maryland counties exercise primary responsibility for land use decisions over particular parcels of land. Within counties and municipalities land use and transportation issues rank perhaps only second to public education in governmental and political salience as they directly impact the quality of life in a jurisdiction. *Farmland Preservation Report* ranked five Maryland counties among the top ten in the country at the end of 2009 in protecting farm acreage.[24]

Fifteen Maryland counties have certified local agricultural land preservation programs that collectively have preserved more than 100,000 acres of farmland through a variety of programs. Central Maryland's rich farmland counties in the Piedmont plateau have significant acreage in preservation programs. Carroll County landowners have actively participated in agricultural preservation programs for more than thirty years, and by 2007 51,296 acres were permanently protected from development, nearly one-third of its agricultural use land.[25] Frederick County has supplemented the state's agricultural land preservation program with the Critical Farms Program, first adopted in 1994, that lends money to farmers during the period of time they are waiting for acceptance into the state program.[26] Harford County has protected 27,257 acres through a local agricultural preservation program in place through 2009 and limits residential density in agriculture zoning districts to one unit for every ten acres. With more than 22,000 acres of agriculture land permanently preserved under various programs, Washington County passed a right-to-farm ordinance in 2003 and an agricultural reservation district ordinance in 2009 that has another 10,000 acres under ten-year temporary easements.[27]

Laudatory land preservation programs and growth control measures have also been enacted in some of Maryland's central core, urban, and suburban counties. The state's most populous county, Montgomery, has earned national acclaim for its agricultural zoning restrictions, preservation programs, and related housing policies. The county's density in rural zones of one unit per twenty-five acres, combined with a transferable development rights program, has aided significantly in the preservation of more than 113,000 acres in the northern and western portions of the county. This places the state's most populous county first among all counties, with nearly 36 percent of its land preserved from development.

Baltimore County, a large urban county surrounding Baltimore City, established the Urban Rural Demarcation Line in 1967; it limits density and development predominantly in the northern areas of the county and endeavors to direct development into targeted growth areas served by public water and sewer systems.[28] Baltimore County has more than 51,000 acres of publicly owned and easement-protected land.

Prince George's County, a geographically large and populous county adjacent to the nation's capital, adopted a progressive woodland conservation program in the 1980s, ahead of the state law, aggressively supported recycling, and designated a large swath of land on the east side of Route 301 as a nongrowth area in an effort to protect the Patuxent River watershed.

Howard County, centrally located midway between the two large urban core cities of Baltimore and Washington, had 20,390 acres of land in agriculture preservation in 2007. The outgoing county executive in 2006 successfully proposed doubling from $20,000 to $40,000 the amount per acre the county would pay to preserve some of the remaining farmland from the onslaught of development pressures in order to keep pace with rising land costs in one of the nation's wealthiest counties.[29] During his first year in office Howard County Executive Ken Ulman created a county commission on the environment and sustainability and pushed for increased environmental standards and energy efficiency.[30]

Baltimore City, along with the state's other 156 incorporated municipalities, benefits from the state's Smart Growth policies by their automatic designation as priority funding areas. These older, developed places are the flip side of land preservation efforts. As the supply of undeveloped land is diminished by state and county preservation programs, other state programs make the redevelopment of existing urbanized areas more economically feasible and desirable.[31] The annexation of land by municipalities changes the decision-making authority over land use, and if perceived as creating unwanted growth or sprawl, is followed closely by environmental organizations as well as local citizens.[32]

BALANCING PUBLIC POLICIES IN
THE TWENTY-FIRST CENTURY

In 1999 the Sierra Club ranked Maryland first in the nation in protecting open spaces, third in land use planning and community revitalization, and twelfth in transportation planning.[33] Those and similar rankings are frequently placed in jeopardy. There is a virtual race between the development of land for business, commercial, industrial, and residential use fueled by the state's strong economy and the preservation of farmland and open space in Maryland pushed by growth concerns and environmental sensitivity. From 1993 to 2002 an average of 13,301 acres of farmland per year was lost to other land uses, while an average of 11,845 was simultaneously being preserved under one of the state's exemplary conservation and preservation programs.[34] From 1998 through 2002 the amount of land preserved in Maryland actually exceeded the number of acres that were developed. That positive trend was reversed in 2003–5, but turned positive again in 2006–9, aided by a weakened economy.

The once seemingly inexhaustible supply of fish and shellfish has become severely strained as expanding populations, increasingly intense land use, and overharvesting continue to impact the quality and productivity of the Bay. Oyster and crab harvests have languished dramatically over the decades, prompting the state to set new limits on catching and dredging.[35] In 2007 the Atlantic States Marine Fisheries Commission ordered a 50 percent reduction in the harvesting of rockfish.[36]

The fate of the Chesapeake Bay, the preservation of farmland and open space, and other environmental issues are public policy concerns that cross the geographic and political divides of contemporary Maryland. Environmental advocacy groups like the Chesapeake Bay Foundation, the League of Conservation Voters, and 1000 Friends of Maryland are strong, well organized, and firmly rooted in the public policy process.

Politicians of both major parties have worked to protect the Bay. Former Maryland Republican U.S. senator Charles Mac Mathias (1969–87) garnered federal funds from the Environmental Protection Agency in 1975 for a study of the health of the Chesapeake Bay and championed the creation of the Chesapeake Bay Commission in 1980 for the purpose of providing professional policy analysis to federal and state legislatures. Congressman Wayne Gilchrest (1st, 1991–2009) was consistently rated among the most environmentally sensitive Republican congressmen in the nation and regularly spoke out in the halls of Congress, in legislative hearings before the Maryland General Assembly, and in his district on issues related to water and air quality. Every Democratic governor, U.S. senator, and congressman regularly touts his or her environmental record.

Local elections have been, and will be, won and lost over issues relating to land use, growth, traffic, and environmental protection. These transcend party identification as both Republican and Democratic candidates have been successful or defeated based on their actions and positions on these quality-of-life issues. In the 2002 and 2006 elections slower growth and environmentally sensitive candidates of both parties won local offices in counties as diverse as Carroll, Queen Anne's, Howard, and Montgomery. Proposed large tract developments in rural Allegany County in Western Maryland and rural Dorchester County on the Eastern Shore brought statewide attention as well as local opposition and protest.[37] A proposed sale of previously preserved land in St. Mary's County provoked the general assembly to place a proposed constitutional amendment on the 2006 general election ballot limiting the power of the board of public works to sell open space, conservation, preservation, outdoor recreation, forest, or park land.[38] The amendment overwhelmingly passed with nearly 85 percent statewide approval and with margins in excess of 80 percent of the vote in every county and Baltimore City.

SUMMARY

The symbolism and spirit, as well as the physical reality, of the Bay are deeply embedded in Marylanders and ingrained in the state's political consciousness and rhetoric. The University of Baltimore's annual public opinion survey, *Maryland Policy Choices*, consistently finds that 90 percent or more of Marylanders agree that it is "very important" or "somewhat important" that the state preserve land for farming.[39] As Dru Schmidt-Perkins, the executive director of the environmental nonprofit group 1000 Friends of Maryland, astutely observed, "Everyone's green in an election year."[40] This is true especially in Maryland, where it is likely that a tradition of progressive environmental and land use public policy will continue even as transportation infrastructure needs expand and population growth persists in the "Land of Pleasant Living."[41]

CHAPTER TWELVE

Maryland in the Federal System

Section 1. Be it enacted . . . that a district of territory, not exceed-
ing ten miles square, to be located as hereafter directed on the
river Potomac, at some place between the mouths of the Eastern
Branch and Connogochegue, be and the same is hereby accepted
for the permanent seat of the government of the United States.
Chapter XXVII, Acts of Congress, July 16, 1790

Maryland's role in the federal system was destined and defined by a single significant act of the First Congress of the newly formed United States. Congressional representatives generally agreed on the importance of a central location for the seat of the new federal government, but finding a specific location proved difficult. After a year and a half of wrangling and proffers of land ranging from New York to Virginia to become the nation's capital, it was, appropriately for Maryland, a pragmatic political compromise between Alexander Hamilton and Thomas Jefferson that finally led to the congressional votes needed to create the nation's permanent capital on July 16, 1790. In exchange for southern support for the federal assumption of certain unpaid state Revolutionary War debts, President Washington was empowered to choose the location for the permanent seat of government on the east side of the Potomac River in Maryland.[1] This landmark legislation authorized the appointment of three commissioners "to purchase or accept such quantity of land as the President shall deem proper for the use of the United States" and to "provide suitable buildings for the accommodation of Congress, and of the President, and for public offices of the government of the United States."[2] After selecting an area consisting predominantly of tidal swampland in Prince George's County, George Washington engaged the services of Charles L'Enfant to design the city that would bear his name. This land transaction formed an obvious, unique, and significant basis for Maryland's role in the federal system.

Surrounding the nation's capital for more than two centuries on its east, north, and south boundaries for twenty-six miles has had, and continues to have, an enormous impact on the government and politics of Maryland. It certainly boosts the state's economy. Every era that brought growth in the size and scope of the federal government has meant population increases and enhanced economic opportunity for Maryland.[3] Encasing the seat of federal power made keeping Maryland in the Union during the Civil War a strategic imperative for the federal government.[4] The expansion of the federal government as a result of the New Deal, the Second World War, the cold war, President Johnson's Great Society, and 9/11 all boosted the intergovernmental connection between Maryland and the national government on multiple levels. Although not all the owners of the land that became part of the nation's capital realized their individual hopes for prosperity from the sale of their property, Maryland has reaped enormous long-term dividends from the willingness of the state in 1790 to surrender part of its sovereign land to the national government.

MARYLAND'S POLICIES AND POLITICS
IN THE FEDERAL SYSTEM

The political consequences of Maryland's intimate proximity to the nation's capital are multifaceted and make the state's collective perspective of the people, policy, and politics of Washington very different from most other states. From dual federalism through cooperative federalism, creative federalism, new federalism, and devolution, Maryland has played an active role in the federal system. Despite the decidedly pro–states' rights stance of most of its political leadership from the Revolutionary War through the Great Depression, Maryland has always pragmatically benefited from the existence of the nation's capital as its neighbor and has generally placed its economic interests over political ideology. Since the New Deal of President Franklin D. Roosevelt Maryland has consistently accepted federal social and economic initiatives.

Maryland's modern-era public officials have generally understood that the public, in clamoring for government services, does not differentiate precisely between the source of public funds and the legal responsibilities of levels of government. Marylanders expect government to play a role in their daily life. Whether it is a natural disaster, a man-made accident, economic downturns, homeland security, environmental protection, or school resources, Marylanders expect an appropriate government response. This public attitude, combined with pragmatic political leadership, has kept Maryland opportunistic in the federal system.

A candidate for federal office in Maryland must be wary of complaining about bureaucracy, given the large percentage of Marylanders employed, directly or indirectly, by the U.S. government. Particularly in the suburbs adjacent to the nation's capital, community audiences and neighborhood meetings are likely to contain federal government employees who either drafted the nation's rules and regulations or who work daily implementing them. Therefore the "running against Washington" campaign rhetoric loudly employed by candidates of all parties in many states is muted and rarely practiced in contemporary Maryland.

Maryland's representation in Congress generally reflects the state's electoral voting patterns and political sentiment and performance as pragmatically progressive. The state's two U.S. senators have been Democrats since 1987. Although considered among the most liberal pair in the U.S. Senate, Ben Cardin and Barbara Mikulski are pragmatically associated with and strongly support the state's defense, science, and technology industries, as did Maryland's longest serving U.S. senator, Paul S. Sarbanes (1977–2007). Republicans last won a U.S. Senate seat in 1980 with Charles McC. Mathias of Frederick County, who had a solidly progressive record on civil rights and enjoyed unusual labor union support for a member of his party.

The state's members of the House of Representatives largely reflect the party preferences of their region. The First Congressional District has been held by Republicans since 1990 except for two years when Queen Anne's County state's attorney Democrat Frank Kratovil won a close race in 2008. Before that election Republican Congressman Wayne Gilchrest, who was defeated in the 2008 primary, held the seat for eighteen years as a throwback to previous moderate, pro-environment state Republicans. The Western Maryland counties and the suburban and exurban areas along the northern boundary of the state, which make up the Sixth Congressional District, have been represented by Republican Roscoe Bartlett since 1992. The other six districts contain the large, sprawling urban and suburban areas of the central core of the state and have Democratic representatives. In the 2008 general election Maryland's seven incumbents received between 59 and 98 percent of the vote, manifesting the political polarization that divides the state.[5]

Even though the majority of the state's congressional delegation was politically estranged from the second Bush administration, Maryland's repre-

sentatives have been effective in protecting state interests. The members of
the House of Representatives and U.S. Senate are well positioned on congressional committees and use their legislative skills effectively. Maryland's
federal influence was significantly strengthened when the Democrats regained control of Congress in the 2006 election cycle. Congressman Steny
Hoyer (Dem: 5th), the longest serving member of the House of Representatives from Maryland in state history, was elected by his peers to be majority
leader. Nancy Pelosi, a native of Baltimore City, where her father and brother
both served as mayor, was elected Speaker of the House of Representatives
in 2007 and minority leader in 2011. Congressman Chris Van Hollen (Dem:
8th, Montgomery County) assumed leadership of the Democratic Congressional Campaign Committee for the 2008 election cycle. The election of
President Barack Obama strengthened the state's federal relationships, especially with a return to a more urban agenda and familiar appointments.

Maryland's congressional delegation has consistently enjoyed meaningful personal, professional, and political relationships with the state legislature. These relationships provide a solid foundation for federal-state legislative cooperation. U.S. Senator Ben Cardin served in the Maryland House
of Delegates for twenty years and rose to become speaker of the house.
Congressman Steny Hoyer served in the state senate, including a term as its
president (1975–78).

In recognition of the new dynamic in federalism that shifted some program responsibilities to the states, the Maryland General Assembly created
in 1983 a statutory legislative committee, the Joint Committee on Federal Relations, to replace the Maryland Commission on Intergovernmental
Cooperation that had been formed in 1937.[6] The Joint Committee on Federal Relations meets several times a year to receive briefings from federal
and state agency heads and policymakers and to monitor and review federal public policy initiatives and actions having implications for the state.
The subjects range from transportation and Amtrak to Medicaid and Medicare and from homeland security to welfare reform. The committee is also
charged with proposing or facilitating the adoption of interstate compacts
and the enactment of uniform or reciprocal statutes and rules or regulations. Two members of the state's congressional delegation served on this
committee when they were members of the state legislature.

Maryland's governors have also generally had close personal, professional, and political relationships with the congressional delegations. Many
of these relationships spanned several decades and were formed prior to
service in state or federal office. The current governor, Martin O'Malley,
was a campaign fieldworker and driver for Senator Mikulski in her first

successful statewide campaign in 1986. Governor Ehrlich served eight
years in the U.S. House of Representatives before becoming governor.

The governor's office has maintained a fully staffed, permanent Washington office since 1967 to monitor federal legislation and to work cooperatively with the state's congressional delegation. Major state entities such
as the Maryland Department of Transportation and the University of Maryland System also have staff dedicated to working with Congress. The governor routinely meets and communicates with the state's members of Congress on fiscal and program issues. Announcements of federal grants and
projects are normally an occasion for bipartisan ribbon cutting, with state
economic interests and transportation infrastructure kept paramount.

During the past two decades Maryland has benefited from positive relationships between its governor and the president of the United States. Governor Schaefer had a personal bond with President George H. W. Bush that
was highlighted by his endorsement of Bush's reelection in 1992.[7] Governor Glendening developed a cooperative working relationship with President Clinton, exemplified by the first ever attendance of a U.S. president at
a bill signing of a state law in Annapolis after the 2000 legislative session.[8]
Governor Ehrlich was an early supporter and friend of President George W.
Bush before the 2000 presidential election. This relationship paid dividends
for candidate Ehrlich during the 2002 gubernatorial campaign and for Governor Ehrlich in obtaining federal cooperation on a number of state government priorities, including the fast-tracking of environmental reviews for the
Inter-County Connector, a proposed major highway initiative, and the important base realignment and closure process. It always helps the state when
the governor can call the White House and speak directly to the president.

THE FISCAL IMPACT OF THE
FEDERAL GOVERNMENT ON MARYLAND

The enormous financial impact of the federal government on Maryland
extends well beyond the transfer of funds from the federal government to
state, county, and municipal governments and the direct payment to Maryland residents of government program benefits such as Social Security. The
more than 132,000 federal employees residing in Maryland use state and local public services and are consumers of private sector goods and services.
Federal employees generate state and local taxes, fees, and other government revenues and help fuel the state's economy. The over 13.2 billion in
salaries and wages paid in federal fiscal year 2009 to federal employees residing in Maryland was the fifth highest total and fourth highest per capita

among the fifty states.[9] Federal civilian and military jobs accounted for 7.5 percent of the total state workforce in 2006, more than twice the national average of 3.4 percent.[10] Often overlooked in assessing Maryland's economy and workforce is the impact of the military and defense industry. More than 480,000 Marylanders are military veterans, representing 11.2 percent of the state's civilian population over age eighteen and ranking Maryland twenty-ninth among the fifty states and above the national average.[11]

Flowing naturally from its proximity to the seat of the federal government, there are over fifty federal agencies, facilities, and installations located in Maryland with important and diverse missions. As partially detailed in Table 12-1, these range from the presidential retreat at Camp David in rural Frederick County to the behemoth National Security Agency, located at the intersection of the Baltimore Washington Parkway (I-295) and Maryland Route 32 in Anne Arundel County, and the headquarters of the Social Security Administration, located at the terminus of Interstate 70 intersecting with the Interstate 695 (the Baltimore Beltway) in Baltimore County.

Major health and research agencies such as the National Institutes of Health and the Food and Drug Administration are located in Maryland, providing employment for highly skilled physicians, scientists, and technicians. The state hosts major federal science and technology government agencies such as NASA's Goddard Space Flight Center in Beltsville and the National Oceanic and Atmospheric Administration. The U.S. Census Bureau and the Internal Revenue Service are also headquartered in Maryland.

Maryland hosts national defense installations such as Andrews Air Force Base, Aberdeen Proving Grounds, Fort George G. Meade, the National Security Agency, the Naval Surface Warfare Center, the Patuxent Naval Research Laboratory, and the U.S. Naval Academy, founded in 1845. Under the 2005 Base Realignment and Closure Act defense-related facilities in Maryland are being enhanced. The state's impact analysis estimates that more than 45,000 federal and private sector jobs will be created at Aberdeen Proving Grounds in Harford County, the Fort Detrick biological warfare laboratory in Frederick County, Fort Meade in Anne Arundel County, the National Naval Medical Center in Bethesda, Montgomery County, and Andrews Air Force Base in Prince George's County.[12] During the 2007 legislative session the O'Malley administration proposed and the general assembly approved the creation of a Base Realignment and Closure Subcabinet to plan and coordinate the impact of the anticipated increase in federal employment.[13]

As reported in the 2009 federal fiscal year Consolidated Federal Funds Report issued by the U.S. Census Bureau, the $92.2 billion of federal gov-

Table 12-1: Selected federal agencies and installations

Department/Agency	County/City
Department of Agriculture	
Beltsville Agricultural Research Center	Prince George's County
Department of Commerce	
U.S. Census Bureau	Prince George's County
Internal Revenue Service	Prince George's County
National Oceanic and	Montgomery County
Atmospheric Administration	
National Weather Service	Montgomery County
Department of Defense	
Aberdeen Proving Grounds	Harford County
Andrews Air Force Base	Prince George's County
Army Research Laboratory	Montgomery and Prince George's Counties
Coast Guard Yard	Baltimore City
Fort Detrick	Frederick County
Fort George G. Meade	Anne Arundel County
Navy National Medical Center	Montgomery County
Naval Surface Warfare Center	Montgomery and Prince George's Counties
National Geospatial-Intelligence Agency	Montgomery County
U.S. Naval Academy	Anne Arundel County
Patuxent Naval Research Laboratory	St. Mary's County
Department of Energy	
Office of Biological and	Montgomery County
Environmental Research	
Department of Health and Human Services	
Centers for Medicare and Medicaid Services	Prince George's County
National Institutes of Health	Montgomery County
Independent Agencies	
Camp David	Frederick County
Consumer Product Safety Commission	Montgomery County
Food and Drug Administration	Montgomery County
National Institute of Standards	Montgomery County
and Technology	
NASA Goddard Space Flight Center	Prince George's County
National Security Agency	Anne Arundel County
Nuclear Regulatory Commission	Montgomery County
Social Security Administration	Baltimore County

Source: Prepared by authors from official sources.

ernment expenditures made in Maryland computes per capita to the fourth highest among all fifty states (behind Alaska, Virginia, and Hawaii).[14] Maryland businesses are substantial recipients of the federal government's largesse. Over $34 billion of federal government procurement of goods and services were paid to Maryland entities in fiscal year 2009. This placed Maryland fourth in total dollars among all the states (behind only California, Texas, and Virginia) and over $14 billion ahead of fifth-place Masschusetts. In fiscal year 2009 businesses located in one Maryland county (Montgomery County, a large urban county north of Washington DC) received more than $17.5 billion in federal government procurement expenditures—a sum greater than similar expenditures made in forty-three states.[15] Maryland businesses such as Lockheed Martin, Northrop Grumman, Computer Sciences Corporation, and Hughes Aerospace benefited from increased defense appropriations under the Bush administration and from new federal spending for homeland security in the post-9/11 federal government priorities.[16]

The central core of the state receives the bulk of the total federal expenditures in Maryland. Three jurisdictions (Baltimore City and Montgomery and Prince George's counties) accounted for 63.5 percent of the five-year growth of federal expenditures in the state, from 1999 to 2004.[17] Total federal spending in Montgomery County exceeded $27.9 billion in fiscal year 2009. Other Maryland jurisdictions have received significant boosts to their local economies. In Frederick County, along the northern boundary of Montgomery County and home to Fort Detrick, the military's biotech laboratories, federal spending more than doubled in the past decade to almost $2.4 billion in fiscal year 2009. The important defense research facilities located on and near the Patuxent Naval Research Laboratory in St. Mary's County and the chemical research facilities at Aberdeen Proving Grounds and Edgewood Arsenal in Harford County generate considerable amounts of economic activity for their local areas.[18]

Higher education institutions in Baltimore City (the University of Maryland, Baltimore and Johns Hopkins University) and Prince George's County (the University of Maryland, College Park) benefit enormously from federal largesse. Annually the Johns Hopkins University System ranks near the top of all the colleges and universities in the country in the total amount of federal grants, and the University of Maryland System ranks in the top fifty. Johns Hopkins has ranked first in grants received from the National Institutes of Health for more than ten consecutive fiscal years. In fiscal year 2005 it received $607,222,589 in NIH grants, and the University of Maryland, Baltimore, ranked thirty-second and received $181,548,023.[19]

Geographically small and constrained, Maryland has had land and natural resource conflicts with its neighbors. The land granted to Cecilius Calvert by King Charles of England under the 1632 Charter included all land "which lieth under the Fortieth Degree of North Latitude for the Equinaoctial, where New England is terminated . . . unto the true Meridian of the firft Fountain of the River of Pattomack, thence verging towards the South, unto the further Bank of faid River . . . and thence by the fhortest Line unto the aforesaid Promontory or Place, called Watkin's Point."

Unfortunately for Marylanders, its seemingly specific boundaries were eroded and negated by adverse interpretations, negotiations, and rulings of subsequent royal governments. On its northern border, shared with Pennsylvania, the Calverts were ordered to abide by the general terms of a 1732 agreement between Charles Calvert and William Penn's sons. Accordingly between 1763 and 1767 the famous Mason-Dixon Line was drawn to settle the conflict between the colonial charters of Pennsylvania and Maryland and to resolve the boundary of the Delaware colony. The fortieth parallel referenced in Maryland's charter is roughly twelve miles farther north of the current state boundary line and would have included Philadelphia, Gettysburg, and other significant Pennsylvania settlements.[20] A dispute over whether Maryland's westernmost border was marked by the southern or northern forks of the Potomac River was not settled until the U.S. Supreme Court ruled against Maryland in 1910 in favor of West Virginia.[21]

Along its southern border with Virginia, which includes open waters across the Chesapeake Bay, Maryland has had territorial battles from the founding of the colony and sometimes lost land and the exercise of state sovereignty to its geographically larger neighbor. Efforts by Virginians to take control of Kent Island and other parts of the Chesapeake Bay in defiance of the Calvert family rule, as well as a battle by Virginia Puritans to settle along the Severn River, finally ended with the affirmation of Lord Baltimore's claim to the land contained in Maryland's charter in 1657.[22] Decades of disputes were resolved by the Compact of 1785, ratified by the Maryland General Assembly and the Virginia Assembly, setting forth an agreement covering navigational and fishing rights on the Potomac River and in the Chesapeake Bay.[23]

In 2003 Maryland lost another boundary and natural resources dispute to Virginia when, in a 7-2 decision, the U.S. Supreme Court granted Virginia the right to withdraw water from the Potomac River free from Maryland's long assumed regulatory authority.[24] This unprecedented decision leaves state officials in a quandary over the environmental and water resources impacts of growth patterns in Virginia as well as the extent of Maryland's jurisdiction.

Other contemporary disputes and competition between Maryland and its neighbors have centered on economic issues. The intense development of the Norfolk-area port and railroad infrastructure by Virginia in the 1970s seriously impacted the economics of the Port of Baltimore. It took decades for Maryland to adjust to this intense, ongoing competition between the respective ports for cargo and, more recently, for cruise ship passengers.[25] Virginia's comparatively lax regulatory environment and its different tax structure gave it a perceived competitive advantage over Maryland for new businesses in the 1980s and 1990s. Northern Virginia remains a constant competitor over the location of federal facilities with the Maryland counties adjacent and near to the District of Columbia. Politicians campaigning for office in Maryland (usually statewide Republican candidates) frequently cite Virginia as more business-friendly in an effort to boost their candidacies in Maryland.

Delaware's favorable corporate laws have been a persistent challenge for state economic and business public policy. The threatened relocation of bank operations from Maryland to Delaware led to a special session of the Maryland General Assembly to modify state corporation laws in 1983. The use of Delaware holding companies to siphon income from corporations doing business in Maryland generated successful litigation by the state to recover lost tax revenue and spurred legislation intended to close corporate tax loopholes on transactions between related corporate entities.[26] The absence of a Delaware sales tax was a major factor in the enactment in the 2000 legislative session of a one-week "back to school" sales tax exemption in Maryland for clothing and footwear costing less than one hundred dollars. After the exemption expired in 2006 it was renewed during the 2007 special legislative session for future years beginning in 2010.[27]

The existence of legalized gambling in Delaware, Pennsylvania, and West Virginia was a major factor in the ultimate approval of limited gambling facilities in Maryland by a constitutional amendment in the November 2008 general election.

Maryland has consistently demonstrated leadership dealing with its neighboring states and the District of Columbia on issues of vital importance to the Chesapeake Bay. The 64,000-square-mile Chesapeake Bay drainage basin stretches from the headwaters of the Susquehanna River in central New York near Ithaca through central Pennsylvania; from the origin of the Potomac River in the Alleghany Mountains of West Virginia; from the westward tributaries of the James River along the southern boundary of Virginia; and the numerous rivers and streams of the tidewater region of Delaware, Maryland, and Virginia. An aerial view of the Potomac River reveals a marked difference between land use patterns on the Virginia and Maryland sides of the Potomac River. In northwest Montgomery County and southwest Frederick County on the Maryland side of the Potomac thousands of acres have been permanently protected from development by state and local programs, in contrast to the negative effects of sprawl plainly visible on the Virginia side.

INTERSTATE COMPACTS, AGREEMENTS, AND COMMISSIONS

The ability of states to coordinate public policies and programs is facilitated by Section 10, Article I of the U.S. Constitution, which provides in pertinent part that "no State shall, without the Consent of Congress, . . . enter into any Agreement or Compact with another State." Maryland has been a party to numerous interstate compacts (see Table 12-2). In addition the state has entered into other agreements and joined other interstate commissions and organizations on subjects ranging from air quality and poultry farming to transportation planning and crime-fighting. The work of these interstate entities often guides legislative initiatives in the Maryland General Assembly. Working with neighboring states and interstate organizations provides opportunities for the governor and legislative leaders to exhibit leadership on important public policy issues. In addition to elected public officials, other representatives, appointed by either the governor or the Maryland General Assembly, serve on these interstate entities.

Interstate compacts, agreements, and commissions reflect Maryland's conflicted geographic identity as well as its public policy concerns. The Old Line State is pulled in at least four geographic regional directions because of these intergovernmental relations. Maryland participates in the *Appalachian* Region Commission and the *Appalachian* States Low-Level Radioactive Waste Commission; the *Atlantic* States Marine Fisheries Commission, the *Mid-Atlantic* Fishery Management Council, the *Mid-Atlantic* Poultry Advisory Council and the *Mid-Atlantic* Regional Community Policing Institute; the *Southern* Regional Education Board and the *Southern* States Energy Board.

Among its bordering states Virginia is a party to twelve interstate compacts, Delaware a party to ten, Pennsylvania a party to eleven, West Virginia a party to ten, and Washington DC a party to five. Two of the compacts are bilateral (one each with Virginia and West Virginia), and two others are

Table 12-2: Interstate compacts

Title	Year enacted	Parties
Adult Offender Supervision	2001	national
Appalachian States Low-Level Radioactive Waste Commission	1986	MD, DE, PA, WV
Atlantic States Marine Fisheries Commission	1942	15 states
Education Commission of the States	1966	national
Mining Compact Commission	1973	19 states
Oil and Gas Compact Commission	1973	30 states
Potomac Highlands Airport Authority	1998	MD, WV
Potomac River Basin Commission	1960	MD, DC, PA, VA, WV
Potomac River Fisheries Commission	1958	MD, VA
Southern Regional Education Board	1949	16 states
Southern States Energy Board	1963	16 states
Susquehanna River Basin Commission	1967	MD, PA, NY
Uniform State Laws	1892	national
Washington Metro Area Transit Authority	1965	MD, DC, VA
Washington Metro Area Transit Commission	1988	MD, DC, VA

Sources: Department of Legislative Services, Maryland General Assembly; Maryland State Archives, Annapolis.

solely with Virginia and the District of Columbia. Eleven of the interstate compacts are directly related to environmental and natural resources issues. The Chesapeake Bay is the primary subject for four of the interstate compacts, and transportation the subject of three.

Maryland's relations with its immediate neighbors have improved with the necessity for coordinated transportation planning, economic development, and environmental action becoming more apparent to public policy decision makers. In 1998 Congress ratified the compact between West Virginia and Maryland to resolve the needs of the Cumberland area with improvements to an airport located across the Potomac River in West Virginia. In 2005 Maryland, Virginia, and the District of Columbia joined forces to promote the region's research and technology potential by signing a memorandum of understanding to establish the Chesapeake Nanotech Initiative.[28] Delaware, Maryland, and Virginia have cooperated on issues related to the important poultry industry on the Eastern Shore.

MARYLAND AND GLOBALIZATION

Globalization has been meaningful for Maryland demographically and economically. From 1990 to 2000 the U.S. Census Bureau reported that fully one-third (178,000) of the state's population increase was a result of foreign immigration. Although its relative rankings fell during the second half of the twentieth century, the Port of Baltimore has found specialized markets and in 2007 ranked first in vehicle exports, twelfth in cargo value, and thirteenth in total cargo by volume among the nation's ports.[29]

Primary responsibility for the development of international trade resides with the Maryland Department of Economic Development and the Department of Transportation, although numerous other state agencies are involved. In 1999 the Governor's Subcabinet on International Affairs was created by executive order to coordinate international activities. This subcabinet group, which includes the state departments of economic development, agriculture, transportation, and the environment, concentrates on the state's global efforts. The Office of the Secretary of State also supervises Maryland's nine sister-state programs. Higher education plays a significant role in Maryland's international relations, as more than 13,000 foreign students are enrolled in the state's colleges and universities.

The private and nonprofit sectors of Maryland's economy are active internationally. The Maryland China Business Council, established in 1995, and the Japanese Business Council are two examples of growing commercial associations. Maryland's extensive nonprofit sector, such as the International Red Cross and the worldwide Brethren Relief Center, are major contributors to international humanitarian aid.

SUMMARY

Maryland's federal relations will remain inextricably linked to its close proximity to the nation's capital. The implementation of the programs of the federal government will always be aided and supplied by Maryland residents and businesses. In a rapidly changing global environment, with an emphasis on education and technology, the economic, governmental, and political prospects for Maryland are positive and hopeful. With its unique demographic diversity and predominantly urban characteristics, the state is likely to continue to be a progressive laboratory of democracy in the federal system.

Regardless of political party or ideology, Maryland has become an irresistible place for presidents to use as a backdrop for their bully pulpit and public policy initiatives because of its proximity to the nation's capital. In addition to the daily national news coverage generated by White House activities, a quick presidential visit to a neighboring Maryland locale yields certain coverage in the *Washington Post* and the Washington television market for all those who do business with the federal government or simply visit the nation's capital.

President Clinton and Vice President Gore visited Maryland numerous times to push policy initiatives and commemorate national events. President George W. Bush visited Maryland regularly to make news about social security, national security, homeland security, education, and international trade; in the two-month span from November 27, 2007, through January 28, 2008, the president convened a peace conference at the Naval Academy, visited a church in Mt. Airy, Carroll County, on World AIDS Day, toured a manufacturing plant in Frederick to highlight a proposed economic stimulus package, and visited a job assistance and counseling service for ex-offenders to mark the seventh anniversary of the White House's Faith Based and Community Initiatives.[30] President Obama has continued the practice, with policy addresses on education, the environment, and health care given with a Maryland backdrop and audience.[31]

Presidents from Franklin D. Roosevelt on have used the secluded facilities at historic Camp David in Frederick County for official business as well as a personal retreat.[32] Constructed by the Works Projects Administration during the Depression, this presidential site has hosted international leaders for discussions and negotiations, such as British Prime Minister Winston Churchill and Soviet Premier Nikita Khrushchev during the cold war. President Carter hosted Israeli Prime Minister Menachem Begin and Egyptian President Anwar Sadat to broker the Camp David Accords. President Reagan spent more time at Camp David than any other president (517 days). Presidents George W. Bush and Jimmy Carter each spent more than a year of their terms at this wooded Catoctin Mountain location.

Ironically presidents and their surrogates are more likely to use Maryland as a stage for press conferences after an election than during a presidential election campaign year, when the state's electoral votes are infrequently sources of national campaign competition. As a pragmatic, progressive government, Maryland will continue to welcome this presidential attention, especially when accompanied by program initiatives and the expenditure of federal dollars.

CHAPTER THIRTEEN

Local Governments in Maryland

County governments are large enough to cope, and small enough to care.
Congresswoman Gladys Spellman

In Maryland local government the counties came first and have stayed first. St. Mary's County, the site of initial colonization at the junction of the Potomac River and the Chesapeake Bay, was created in 1637. Ten other counties were organized in the seventeenth century and nine in the eighteenth century. Their names were an extension of the Calvert family's proprietary power for estates (Baltimore County and Baltimore City), a wife (Anne Arundel), a sister (Caroline), a daughter (Talbot), a friend (Dorchester), and the proprietors themselves (Calvert, Cecil, Charles, Frederick, and Harford). Maintaining royal favor, always a Calvert family priority, was reflected by Queen Anne's County and Prince George's County, the latter named for Queen Anne's husband. After the American Revolution the names of newly created Maryland counties shifted to the national hero (Washington), home state personalities of merit and renown (Carroll, Garrett, Howard, and Montgomery), and Native American origins (Allegany and Wicomico; see Map 13-1).

Although Maryland is certainly a relatively sophisticated and cosmopolitan state, counties provide a parochial sense of place. Francis Beirne wrote, "Every Baltimorean carries a book about his city under his belt,"[1] and that sense of local identification and pride typically extends to every county. Ask a Marylander where he or she is from, and the response, more often than not, is the county of residence. This makes sense given the centralized political and governmental importance of the county unit. Unlike

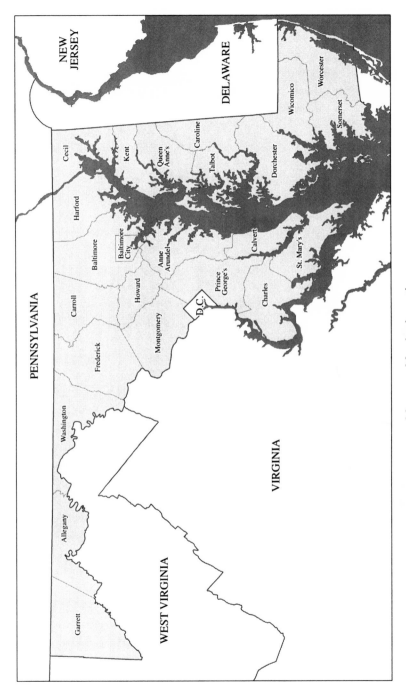

Map 13-1. Maryland counties

its neighbors to the north, Maryland follows the southern model of local governance, in which counties predominate over smaller subdivisions.

Maryland counties perform complex and multiple functions. They serve and act as local governors in making public policy. The majority of Maryland citizens perceive their county as the primary provider of public services such as education, roadways, public safety, libraries, recreation and parks, water supply, waste removal, and zoning.[2] Counties also implement federal and state programs and public policies such as social services, workforce training, environmental protection, and public health.

The diversity and pluralist nature of the state are reflected in its subdivisions. Although the range of county land areas is comparatively narrow, between 215 and 662 square miles, county populations and densities vary widely (see Table 13-1). Several, such as Baltimore, Montgomery, and Prince George's counties, can be considered mini-states. Each contains a massive population, and each tax and spend more per year than several states. In contrast seven rural counties contain fewer than 50,000 people each. Growing minority populations provide wide variations in the racial and ethnic compositions of counties. As a result of growth and migration patterns some Maryland counties have become more predominantly white. As Table 13-1 shows, Maryland's economic affluence is also very unevenly distributed. Mean household income is above or hovers close to six figures in seven counties, but in six rural counties and Baltimore City income is less than half of the two highest ranking counties, Montgomery and Howard.

In addition to the twenty-three counties and Baltimore City (which functions under state law as both a municipality and a county), scattered across the state are 156 incorporated municipalities that vary in population from fewer than twenty to nearly 60,000. Maryland is one of thirty states that have no townships, and there are no independent or multijurisdictional school systems. Public school districts are coterminous with county boundaries and are administered by county boards of education and a board of education for Baltimore City. Some states have opted for a multitude of special districts, single-function units that provide a specialized service. In 2007 Maryland's special districts numbered only seventy-six, the fourth fewest among the states.[3]

Maryland has ten intercounty agencies that employ a regional approach to public services. Two of the most significant operate in the Washington metropolitan area. The Maryland-National Capital Park and Planning Commission, established in 1927, controls planning and zoning in Montgomery County and Prince George's County and maintains parks and recreational

Table 13-1: Profile of Maryland counties and Baltimore City

Subdivision	Population	Density per sq. mile	Type	Median household income
Montgomery	971,777	1,966	charter	$ 93,199
Prince George's	863,420	1,775	charter	70,525
Baltimore	805,029	1,345	charter	63,204
Baltimore City	620,961	7,685	charter	39,115
Anne Arundel	537,656	1,293	charter	82,243
Howard	287,085	1,139	charter	102,175
Harford	244,826	556	charter	76,297
Frederick	233,385	352	commission	80,129
Carroll	167,134	372	commission	79,287
Washington	147,430	322	commission	50,297
Charles	146,551	318	code	87,546
St. Mary's	105,151	291	commission	76,022
Cecil	101,108	290	commission	65,812
Wicomico	98,733	262	charter	50,445
Calvert	88,737	412	commission	91,088
Allegany	75,087	177	code	38,592
Worcester	51,454	109	code	51,825
Queen Anne's	47,798	128	code	81,173
Talbot	37,782	140	charter	62,058
Caroline	33,066	103	code	58,493
Dorchester	32,618	59	charter	45,880
Garrett	30,097	46	commission	44,100
Somerset	26,470	81	commission	40,977
Kent	20,197	72	code	46,449

Sources: U.S. Census Bureau, Census 2010; 2007–2009 American Community Survey.

areas in the state's two most populous jurisdictions. The water supply and sewage systems for those jurisdictions are administered by the Washington Suburban Sanitary Commission, which was created in 1918 by the Maryland General Assembly.

Maryland's 256 local governmental units place it close to the bottom in the nation in absolute numbers, forty-sixth, ahead of only Alaska, Hawaii, Rhode Island, and Nevada.[4] One consequence of this simplified local governance system is the reduction of functional overlap and authority fragmentation. At the county level service and policy responsibility is focused and accountable, with very real political consequences if voters are dissatisfied.

THE DEVELOPMENT OF MARYLAND'S
COUNTY GOVERNMENTS

As in all states, county governments in Maryland are nonsovereign cre-
ations and, as the jurist John Dillon declared, "creatures of the state."[5] All
local powers are derived from the Maryland Constitution and the statutes
passed by the general assembly. Without a delegation of power from these
sources, local government action cannot proceed with legality. In this context three basic forms of local county governance have evolved.

The oldest is the *county commission*, which all Maryland counties employed prior to 1948. During the colonial period county governments were
administered by the local courts. Following the Revolution the general assembly established levy courts, made up of justices of the peace, in each
county to ascertain local governmental expenditures and pay for them with
local property tax assessments. Boards of county commissioners supplanted the levy courts in 1827 and grew out of the expanding needs of the state
legislature to help collect taxes and to build roads and bridges. Commissioners were made locally elected positions by the 1851 constitution. Article VII of the 1867 constitution recognized the county commissioners' role
by continuing their direct election by county voters, but directed that the
composition, pay, powers, and duties of county commissioners be determined by the state legislature.

Consequently a considerable body of statutory law, found primarily in Article 25 of the *Annotated Code of Maryland*, has developed over
the years. The general assembly may enact public general laws that per-
tain to all counties equally, or public local laws that apply a specific policy to a specific county. The reality of this arrangement meant that county commissioner governments concentrated on local public works, while
the legislature, in particular the county delegations in the general assembly,
maintained control of local public policies on a wide range of issues, from
alcohol to taxation. When the state governmental agenda and local government responsibilities were minimal, this made political and institutional
sense. By the beginning of the twentieth century, however, the growth of
statewide concerns and increase in many county populations made legislative local control more time-consuming and more complex. By 1904 over
half of the legislation considered by the general assembly was local bills.
The Maryland State Bar Association, as well as other progressive forces,
urged reform of county government.[6] In 1915 the general assembly passed
and the voters ratified a county home rule constitutional amendment autho-

rizing a county to have a charter drafted and submitted to county voters for approval, providing for enhanced local self-government.[7]

Curiously Maryland counties did not respond to the home rule option for several decades. Montgomery County was the first to adopt its charter, in 1948. Nine other counties slowly followed: Baltimore County (1956), Anne Arundel and Wicomico (1964), Howard (1968), Prince George's (1970), Harford (1972), Talbot (1973), Dorchester (2002), and Cecil (2010). Given county reluctance for home rule, the general assembly remained swamped by local bills for much of the twentieth century. Legislators found themselves preoccupied by "approving matters like restaurant license fees for one county or a dog leash ordinance for another."[8] In the early 1950s about 70 percent of all Annapolis legislation was local in origin. A study commission recommended a mandatory home rule constitutional amendment for all of the then 151 incorporated municipalities in the state, which the general assembly passed and the voters ratified in 1954.[9] But although "municipal home rule virtually eliminated municipal bills," county bills continued to proliferate.[10]

To enable counties to more easily adopt home rule, the general assembly proposed a code home rule procedure in 1965. This provides a streamlined and simplified option designed to overcome local resistance to the charter process. Maryland voters approved the constitutional amendment, Article XI-F, "Home Rule for Code Counties," in 1966. A code county is a combination of charter and commissioner forms. Its adoption means that a county has county commissioners as the governing body but with increased delegated powers from the state. Code counties do not have a charter but possess extensive authority to pass, amend, or repeal local ordinances. Although the original legislative intent probably viewed code home rule as an intermediate stage between commissioner and home rule governance, code county policy power is often liberally construed and approximates home rule to a considerable extent.[11] A county attains code status when the county commissioners, by a two-thirds vote, place on the local ballot a resolution for code home rule and obtain approval from county voters at the next general election. Six Maryland counties have adopted code home rule; Kent was the first in 1970, followed by Allegany (1974), Worcester (1976), Caroline (1984), Queen Anne's (1990), and Charles (2002).

Both the charter and code home rule options represent a more centralized administrative approach and significantly reduce county dependence on representation in the Maryland General Assembly. The political appeal of these measures to modernizing forces was evident. Every county, except Somerset on the lower Eastern Shore, produced reform movements that brought charter or code home rule proposals to county voters. However, local acceptance of home rule often proved an arduous, contentious, and protracted process. Although charters were approved by Anne Arundel, Baltimore, Harford, Talbot, and Wicomico counties on the first try, home rule was initially rejected by Howard and Montgomery counties' voters before a second successful campaign. Voters in Prince George's County rejected creating a charter board three times between 1952 and 1964, before approving a charter drafting board in 1968 and ratifying home rule in 1970. Cecil County approved a charter in 2010, after five unsuccessful efforts. Washington County defeated a charter proposal in the 2008 presidential primary election. One commissioner county is especially resistant to home rule efforts: voters in Carroll County rejected charter or code home rule ballot propositions five times between 1968 and 2006.[12]

Beyond the constitutional procedures and the establishment of any form of county home rule, the state constitution authorizes the general assembly to develop specific home rule powers for counties. These powers are found in the Express Powers Act, which provides for thirty-two powers granted to county government, such as the acquisition and sale of property, zoning and planning, the creation of county agencies, property taxation, borrowing funds, and issuing county bonds.[13]

Charter Counties

The six most populous, high-density counties, all located in the Central Maryland core, have charter home rule government, and four Eastern Shore counties (Cecil, Dorchester, Talbot, and Wicomico) have adopted charter government. Wicomico adopted the county executive–county council system in 2004, and Dorchester and Talbot employ a council-manager structure that extends executive functions and responsibilities to a full-time professional county manager who serves at the pleasure of the county council. Talbot County elects five council representatives at-large. Harford, Montgomery, and Wicomico counties have council members elected at-large and by district. Council members are elected solely from districts in Anne Arundel, Baltimore, Cecil, Howard, and Prince George's counties. All council representatives and county executives serve four-year terms, with elections held in gubernatorial election years.

Montgomery, Prince George's, Anne Arundel, Baltimore, Cecil, Harford, Howard, and Wicomico counties utilize the county executive–county council model of local governance, with a distinct separation of executive and legislative powers. The more populous subdivisions, once largely rural, experienced sustained substantial growth in the wave of suburbanization that followed the Second World War. Home rule charter, more often than not, was the instrument that suburban reformers, composed of "nonpartisan neighborhood improvement associations, good government leagues, service clubs, and groups such as the League of Women Voters," used to topple once dominant and countywide Democratic organizations.[14] For a time during the 1960s and 1970s local Republicans benefited from alliances with these reform groups and won several county executive contests in Anne Arundel, Baltimore, Montgomery, and Prince George's counties. By the 1980s and 1990s Montgomery County and Prince George's County consistently elected Democratic county executives. In addition to Spiro Agnew, elected as Baltimore County executive in 1962, Republicans won one other county executive term in that county, in 1990. Republicans and Democrats have competed fairly evenly in Anne Arundel and Howard counties since they became charter counties. Despite Ehrlich's victory in the 2002 general election, Democrats won every county executive contest except in Harford County. In 2006 Republicans retained the Harford County executive post, and Republican John R. Leopold, a former member of the general assembly, was elected county executive in Anne Arundel County. Democrats won all the other county executive races. Of the seventy-two council positions in the chartered counties, Democrats won 78 percent of the seats. No Republicans serve on the Montgomery and Prince George's county councils or on the fifteen-member Baltimore City Council. After the 2010 general election Democrats hold a 5 to 2 majority in Baltimore County and a 4 to 1 majority in Howard County. Republicans won a 4 to 3 majority in Anne Arundel County, a 5 to 2 majority in Harford County, and a 6 to 1 majority in Wicomico County.

Code Home Rule Counties

Considered the quiet alternative to charter government, code home rule has been adopted by local voters in six Maryland counties. Four are on the Eastern Shore (Kent, Worcester, Caroline, and Queen Anne's) and one each in Southern Maryland (Charles) and Western Maryland (Allegany). Code counties retain the county commissioner office title, and the number of commissioners range from three to seven. The method of selection of county commissioners in code counties varies. The traditional at-large countywide election remains in Allegany, Caroline, Kent, and Worcester counties. In Queen Anne's County four commissioners are elected by district and one at-large countywide. In Charles County five are elected at-large, four of whom are required to reside in certain districts and one designated as running countywide for president of the county commissioners. Code county commissioners are elected for four-year terms. Of the twenty-six commissioners elected in the 2010 general election, nine were Democrats and seventeen were Republicans. Charles and Kent have Democratic majorities; Republicans control Allegany, Caroline, Queen Anne's, and Worcester counties.

Commissioner Counties

Eight counties had the commissioner form of governance in 2010 and are located in every region of the state: in Central Maryland (Carroll County), Western Maryland (Frederick, Garrett, and Washington), Southern Maryland (Calvert and St. Mary's), and the Eastern Shore (Cecil and Somerset). The number of commissioners ranges from three to five. After the 2010 general election Carroll County had five commissioners, leaving Garrett County in far Western Maryland the only county having the historical three-commissioner form of governance. The method of electing commissioners varies among the jurisdictions. In 2010, commissioners ran at-large in Caroline, Frederick, Garrett, and Washington counties. In Carroll and Somerset counties, commissioners ran in five distinct districts. In Calvert and Cecil, commissioners ran at-large but were required to live in specified districts in the county. St. Mary's County elects a president of the county commission at-large and also votes for four commissioners at-large, each of whom are required to live in a defined district. All commissioners, except in Cecil County, serve four-year terms and are elected in the Maryland gubernatorial and General Assembly cycle. In 2000 Cecil County won approval of a state constitutional amendment to authorize its commissioners to run in staggered terms, with two elected in the presidential election cycle and three in the gubernatorial election cycle.[15] Maryland Republicans won all but four of the thirty-six county commissioner seats contested in the 2010 election and control the county commission in all but Somerset County.

Baltimore City

Called "Charm City" by its boosters or just plain "Bawlmer" in the vernacular of its residents, Baltimore City falls into its own unique category. Established initially within Baltimore County in 1729 and incorporated in 1796, the city was separated from Baltimore County under a special provision of the 1851 Maryland Constitution. Baltimore City has a unique status, as detailed in Article XI of the current Maryland Constitution. The city was granted broad powers of self-government in 1898 by the general assembly and, under state law, functions as both a municipality and a county.[16] Its mayor-council structure reflects municipal government, but its constitutional home rule status provides the city with the legal equivalency of a charter county. Unlike the other home rule counties, Baltimore derives its express powers from public local laws enacted by the general assembly and those included in the Baltimore City Charter. The state legislature no longer makes public local law for Baltimore, but if the city wants to modify its existing grant of powers it must obtain legislative approval and then await statewide voter ratification of the appropriate constitutional amendment. The city charter was last partially revised, updated, and approved by the voters in 1994.

Baltimore voters elect three local officials citywide: the mayor, the president of the city council, and the comptroller. In both formal chartered authority and in political practice, the mayor heads an extremely strong and centralized mayoral system that combines extensive executive powers of appointment with fiscal control of city finances through the five-member board of estimates and an executive budget process. Although the president of the city council presides over the board and the comptroller serves as the secretary, the mayor controls the board of estimates by a 3 to 2 margin because the remaining members are the mayor-appointed city solicitor and the director of public works. The board of estimates develops the budget, awards all city contracts, and supervises procurement purchases for the city.

Legislative authority resides in a fifteen-person city council elected from fourteen single-member districts and a citywide elected city council president. The council can only reduce items in the executive budget and generally assumes a reactive stance to mayoral initiatives. If the mayor vetoes a council action, it takes an extraordinary three-fourths council vote to override, an action that rarely occurs. The predominant role of council representatives is to be a advocacy service for Baltimore's 120 neighborhoods.

In Baltimore "neighborhood is next to motherhood."[17] Community associations are exceptionally well established and often well led by local activists. Some even have their own unique flags, and programs, such as residential parking, have a history of percolating up from the grassroots level. Matthew A. Crenson, a professor of political science at Johns Hopkins University, argues that Baltimore community organizations promote informal governance, which resolves innumerable problems within neighborhoods. This reduces demands on City Hall, enhances its leadership, and provides "sufficient breathing space to plan for large scale undertakings."[18]

As a population center and an economic force, Baltimore City served as the focus of Maryland for well over a hundred years. The city contained over half of the entire state population in 1920 and generated almost two-thirds of the state's total economy. But the allure of the suburbs and rising urban pathologies promoted a decline that afflicted Baltimore and virtually every industrialized American city in the twentieth century. Baltimore's population plummeted by almost 30 percent from 1970 to 2000, and its share of the statewide population dropped from 23 to only 14 percent. In 1990 Baltimore City fell behind Montgomery County as the most populous subdivision; by 2000 it was fourth, having been surpassed by Prince George's County and Baltimore County. As the historian George Callcott noted, the population decline meant "the replacement of wealth by poverty, power by powerlessness."[19]

A Baltimore revival was championed during the administration of William Donald Schaefer, a four-term mayor (1971–86) who, thanks to forceful determination and executive management skills, created downtown Baltimore as a tourist destination through an array of public works and joint public-private ventures. The Inner Harbor project replaced rotting wharfs and decaying dockyards with such attractions as the National Aquarium, the Maryland Science Center, and Harborplace, two shop- and restaurant-laden pavilions constructed and administered by the Maryland-based Rouse Corporation. Overcoming grassroots resistance, Schaefer established a "Baltimore Renaissance" that outdrew Disney World in 1981. Yet even in the Schaefer years declining public schools and rising crime rates prompted the continued hemorrhage of citizens.

The Baltimore dynamic established by Schaefer stalled somewhat during the 1990s. Kurt L. Schmoke, Baltimore's first elected African American mayor, served three consecutive terms, from 1987 to 1999. Schmoke, a graduate of Baltimore's elite City College secondary school, Yale University, and Harvard Law School, began his twelve-year tenure accompanied by high hopes and lofty expectations. His earnest and thoughtful style proved somewhat unsuited to the daily pressures of urban problems and politics. Schmoke was frustrated by, and seemed unable to reduce, lawless drug dealing and soaring city homicide rates that ultimately exceeded three hundred per year. The former *Baltimore Sun* reporter David Simon wrote a best-selling compendium of the urban free-fire zones, and city native Barry Levinson brought Simon's *Homicide* to television.[20] Baltimore was perceived as stagnating, acclaimed only for violent crime and other urban pathologies.

When Mayor Schmoke declined to run for a fourth term, a young and forceful city councilman, Martin O'Malley, won the 1999 mayoral election after a contested multicandidate primary election. At thirty-six he became the youngest mayor in the city's history. During his tenure O'Malley endeavored to revive the Baltimore Renaissance. Broadening the Comstat crime-fighting program of New York City by applying it to essential city services, he developed the CitiStat system to enhance agency responsiveness and accountability. Partnerships with the Baltimore corporate community endeavored to cut municipal expenditures, and "a new air of optimism," credited by many to O'Malley, helped him easily win reelection in 2004.[21] O'Malley and Baltimore accumulated national recognition and acclaim from such media outlets as *Esquire*, *Time*, the *New York Times*, and the *Wall Street Journal*.[22]

In the 2006 gubernatorial campaign O'Malley highlighted substantial reductions in crime, significant expansions in drug treatment funding and centers, improved city schools, and $7 billion in new development and construction. His subsequent victory over incumbent Republican governor Ehrlich elevated (by charter mandate) City Council President Shelia Dixon to mayor of Baltimore City on January 17, 2007, the first woman to hold the city's top office. After the 2007 mayoral election Baltimore City became the largest major city in the United States with African American women holding the top three elected offices of mayor, president of the city council, and comptroller. Council President Stephanie Rawlings Blake subsequently became mayor, in February 2010, after Dixon resigned during a trial on ethics violations.[23] She was elected in 2011 to a full term.

Politically Baltimore City is the most Democratic subdivision in Maryland. Democrats outnumber Republicans by 8 to 1, and the de facto election day for city and state legislative offices is the Democratic primary. All city elected officials are Democrats. In the 2004 general election O'Malley won reelection with 88 percent of the vote, President of City Council Shelia Dixon garnered 84 percent, and Comptroller Joan Pratt ran unopposed. The entire fifteen-member city council, last elected in 2007, is Democratic. In five of fourteen city single-member council districts, Green Party candidates outpolled their Republican competitors in the 2004 mayoral general election. Emphasizing the political inclinations of city voters, Barack Obama received nearly 87 percent of the city votes cast for president in the 2008 presidential general election.

LOCAL FISCAL MANAGEMENT:
REVENUE AND SPENDING PATTERNS

In fiscal year 2010 Maryland counties and Baltimore City made an aggregate $26.5 billion in expenditures.[24] Montgomery County ranked first, with

$5.5 billion, followed by neighboring Prince George's ($3.9 billion), Baltimore City ($3.6 billion), and Baltimore County ($3.1 billion). Kent County on the Eastern Shore, the county with the smallest population in the state, spent the least, at $79.4 million. County revenues are generated from a variety of sources, but intergovernmental funds provide almost a third. As a single source, state grants provided over 26 percent of county revenues. In ten subdivisions (Allegany, Baltimore City, Caroline, Cecil, Dorchester, Garrett, St. Mary's, Somerset, Washington, and Wicomico) state aid regularly accounts for over one-third of total revenues. In fiscal year 2010 state and federal intergovernmental aid provided over 50 percent of all revenue in Allegany, Caroline, Dorchester, Somerset, and Wicomico counties, areas where mean household incomes are among the lowest in the state.

Over half of state aid to local jurisdictions in Maryland is allocated according to need-based measures, so affluent counties receive a much smaller percentage of state grants than less wealthy subdivisions. For example, state grants to Montgomery and Howard counties, which have the highest average household incomes, account for between 15.4 and 21.5 percent of their total revenues. Wealthier counties generate a considerably higher percentage of their revenues from their own taxing mechanisms. In the case of Montgomery County, nearly 80 percent of its revenue comes from its own-source taxes, service charges, and proceeds from debts. In contrast Allegany County, with the lowest average household income, generates less than half of its revenue locally.

After state grants, the second largest revenue source for Maryland counties is the traditional property tax, which provides an average of 22 to 25 percent of all local revenues. In Maryland all properties must be appraised once every three years by the state Department of Assessments and Taxation. The local jurisdiction determines its own tax rate, applied per $100 of appraised value. County property tax rates vary in accordance with a variety of factors, including the overall assessable base, annual growth in the assessable base, local charter restrictions on property tax increases, and public service expectations and needs. Urban areas such as Baltimore City typically contain high proportions of property owned by organizations exempt from local taxation such as nonprofits and religious groups; this drives up the property tax rate in cities in comparison to surrounding suburban and outlying rural jurisdictions.

In fiscal year 2009 the property tax rate of Baltimore City, $2.228 per $100 of assessed value, was over twice that of the next highest subdivision, suburban Baltimore County, at $1.10, and almost five times more than the lowest tax rate, Talbot County on the Eastern Shore, with a rate of $0.449 per $100 assessed value.[25] Although Baltimore City had the sixth highest total assessable property base, over $33.4 billion, for fiscal year 2009, its per capita assessable base of $52,917 ranked twenty-third of the twenty-four Maryland subdivisions. In contrast Worcester County, with a population less than 8 percent of Baltimore City's, has an assessable base in excess of $20 billion, putting it first in the state on a per capita assessable property tax base of an extraordinary $403,973.[26] Worcester contains the popular seashore vacation destination of Ocean City and numerous second homes, condominiums, and high-end retirement communities.

Ranking third and producing approximately 16 percent of county revenue is the local income tax. First authorized by the Maryland General Assembly in 1967 to offset rising property tax rates, the local income tax is administratively piggybacked by the state office of the comptroller on payroll withholdings and annual state income tax returns. In addition the counties are authorized to adopt an income tax that can range from 1 to 3.2 percent of Maryland taxable income. Three counties (Howard, Montgomery, and Prince George's) charge the 3.2 percent maximum, while Worcester County again maintains the lowest tax rate, 1.25 percent.

Other local taxes in Maryland include real estate transfer taxes (imposed by eighteen subdivisions), recordation taxes, hotel and motel taxes (levied by twenty subdivisions), admissions and amusement taxes (every subdivision except Caroline County), and mobile home and trailer park taxes (twenty subdivisions). Together these provide about 7–8 percent of all county revenues. Various service charges, fines, debt proceeds, and miscellaneous sources produced an additional average of 21 percent of all county revenues.

Over time the reliance on property tax revenues has diminished as the county income tax receipts have increased. In fiscal year 1984 Maryland counties collected $1,397,922,429 from their respective property taxes, while income tax revenue totaled $732,802,646, or 52 percent of the property tax returns. Twenty years later, in fiscal year 2004, county property tax revenues increased 323 percent to $4,507,420,637, and county income tax receipts jumped 432 percent to $3,159,956,305, or 70 percent of the 2004 property tax revenues. In 2010 property tax revenue was over $7 billion and income tax revenue nearly $3.7 billion.

The state of Maryland exercises a high degree of control over local budgetary procedures. All local governments are required to have a balanced budget, employ uniform accounting procedures, and follow a common fiscal year established by the state. Counties are required to conduct an independent postaudit, and the audit content is specified by state law.

Maryland counties typically spend over 95 percent of their annual collective revenue. The yearly county budgets reflect the characteristics of the county, priorities of the state, and, to a lesser extent, the policy preferences of local officials. The most substantial spending falls into three major categories: education, public works, and public safety. Primary and secondary education appropriations consumed almost half (48 percent) of county budgets in fiscal year 2007, with four counties (Cecil, Somerset, Washington, and Wicomico) devoting over 58 percent of their funding. Baltimore City, the recipient of substantial state and federal aid to education, allocated 35 percent of its budget. County expenditures average about 11 percent for public works, which includes such items as transportation, sewer systems, solid waste collection and disposal, and water supply. Densely populated subdivisions spent more on public safety; Baltimore City was the highest, with nearly 17.5 percent spent on police and fire protection. Rural counties fall considerably below the statewide average of 11 percent, in part because volunteer fire protection units remain standard in those areas. In addition the Maryland State Police (the de facto police in some jurisdictions) as well as local sheriff's departments provide police protection in rural areas.

Overall Maryland counties are in strong financial shape and reflect a fiscally conservative approach within an economically affluent society that has typified state governance for decades. County bonds rank high; Baltimore, Garrett, Howard, and Montgomery counties hold the coveted triple-A designation from all of the major municipal bond rating companies. In addition counties maintain considerable rainy-day funds and unreserved general fund balances that averaged 12.1 percent of general fund revenues in fiscal year 2009.[27]

MARYLAND MUNICIPAL GOVERNMENT

Almost fifty years after the first counties were established the colonial assembly enacted the "town act" in 1683, which authorized county governments to select land sites, establish communities, and provide for their governance. The first incorporated was St. Mary's City, the original state capital. For almost three hundred years the Maryland General Assembly retained governing authority over the state's municipalities. Each had an individual act of incorporation and a charter enacted as a public law by the state legislature. Such charters were quite detailed, spelling out the boundaries, organization, voter qualifications, revenue-raising authority, and functional powers of the specific municipality. In reality, however, each incorporated city or town was extremely dependent on "the good graces of the General Assembly to grant to each of them the individual powers required to address even the most ordinary local issues."[28]

The relationship between the state and municipal governments changed in 1954, when Maryland voters ratified the Municipal Home Rule Amendment (Article XI-E), which extended home rule to previously incorporated municipalities. The amendment provided authority to cities and towns to enact, revise, and amend their own charters. It also shifted the responsibility of municipal incorporation from the state legislature to affected property owners and the respective counties. The general assembly retained control over new forms of municipal taxation, tax limits, and tax debt. Article 23A of the *Annotated Code of Maryland* contains the basic general law applied to municipalities, providing for their creation, annexation, and other express powers. Because of individual charter differences, none of the existing municipalities exercise all of the powers provided by law. Today the procedure of municipal incorporation requires a minimum population of three hundred residents, local initiative, local petitions, and, most important, the approval of the county governing body.

Despite considerable suburban population growth, only five new incorporations, all in Montgomery County, have been chartered since 1954. Excluding Baltimore City, Maryland has 156 municipal corporations scattered across twenty-one of its twenty-three counties. Neither Howard County nor Baltimore County in Central Maryland has a municipal corporation within its boundaries. Prince George's County has the most municipalities, with twenty-seven, and Montgomery County the next highest, with nineteen. Almost 890,000 people, over 15 percent of Maryland's 5.8 million residents, live the 156 municipalities. The 2010 census found the largest was the city of Frederick, with a population of 65,239, and the smallest was Port Tobacco, with only thirteen. In addition to Frederick, three other Maryland cities have population in excess of 50,000 (Rockville and Gaithersburg in Montgomery County and Bowie in Prince George's County). Only six others have populations in excess of 20,000 with the large majority of Maryland municipalities having less than 10,000 residents.

There are a number of local governmental formats that Maryland municipalities employ, but three basic forms predominate: the mayor-council, commission, and council manager. Most prevalent, especially in larger municipalities such as Annapolis, Frederick, Rockville, and Westminster, is the mayor-council system, with separation between executive and legislative authority. This form accounts for 69 percent of municipal governance.

The mayor is typically popularly elected, independent of the council, and charged with some executive responsibilities. The council is separately elected either by district or at-large and is primarily responsible for legislative matters. There are strong and weak mayor forms depending on the municipal charter and veto power.

The commission form is used by about 21 percent of Maryland municipalities. In these the local legislative and executive functions are merged in a single board, although one commissioner may serve as president or chair. Four municipalities have retained the old English title "burgess" to designate this position. The remaining 10 percent rely on the council-manager form, which consists of a directly elected council responsible for policy and executive as well as legislative functions. The council hires a professional manager with authority over the daily administration of the municipality.

Under any formal municipal organization an important trend is the growing reliance of part-time elected officials on full-time municipal professionals. Most elected municipal officers are essentially volunteers, as compensation is minimal and turnover high. Full-time and trained professional managers provide institutional memory and administrative skills. According to the Maryland Municipal League, there are 114 municipal managers as well as sixteen "circuit-rider" administrators who service multiple municipalities.[29]

The election of municipal officials is a matter of considerable local discretion. Both the scheduling of elections and the terms elected officials serve are resolved by each municipality in accordance with its own charter. Most municipal elections are conducted in May and are nonpartisan. Voter turnout is often quite low, typically in the 5 to 15 percent range of registered voters, but can spike significantly on occasions of local issue disputes or challenges to incumbents.

Municipal Revenues and Budgets

Maryland's municipalities collected nearly $1.4 billion in revenues in fiscal year 2010, with local property and income taxes accounting for 44 percent, service charges 30 percent, intergovernmental grants and aid 15 percent, and the remaining funds raised from debt proceeds, fines, and other taxes. According to a 2005 Maryland Municipal League Survey, the most common services provided by at least two-thirds of the 156 municipalities are street lighting, trash collection, street maintenance, and snow removal.[30] Building and housing code enforcement, leaf collection, maintaining a water supply, publishing a town newsletter, planning, police protection, and public works are other services performed by a substantial number of Maryland's municipalities.

MARYLAND COUNTIES AND MUNICIPALITIES
AS INTEREST GROUPS

The critical role and growing contribution of state aid to county fiscal health was not achieved by accident. Maryland counties have long served as forceful advocates for their own local interests. Meetings of various county commissioners to lobby the general assembly for increased school and road funding date back to the early 1930s, and the Maryland County Commissioners Association was organized in 1951. When Baltimore City joined in 1968, MCCA became MACO, the Maryland Association of County Organizations.

MACO has developed into a powerful and influential player that develops its own yearly legislative agenda that governors and the general assembly leadership ignore at their own peril. The annual MACO convention, held in Ocean City during the summer, attracts droves of statewide, legislative, and local elected and appointed officials. Typically the governor will preview an upcoming gubernatorial agenda in a keynote speech and work the local officials to initiate the coalition-building process. County projects such as senior citizen centers, noise abatement walls along busy highways, and even sidewalks funded by state bonds are the political favors that Maryland governors can provide once the general assembly session begins. In turn local officials can help mobilize grassroots support for gubernatorial initiatives and reelection campaigns.

The prime directives of MACO legislative advocacy have been protecting local governmental powers, preserving their autonomy, resisting unwanted state regulation of county policies, and reducing local fiscal dependence on the property tax.[31] Lobbying by MACO played a significant role in the passage of the code home rule option and the county piggyback income tax and the inclusion of local planning and zoning decisions in the Smart Growth acts. Working through an established legislative committee with representatives from all twenty-four jurisdictions, MACO typically adopts positions on fifty to a hundred bills each general assembly session and secures 75 percent of its objectives.[32] The legislation ranges over a wide variety of policy areas, such as school construction, public employee benefits, recycling, land preservation, and public safety.

The counterpart of MACO for Maryland municipalities is the Maryland Municipal League, founded in 1936. With a staff of twelve, the MML serves as an information clearinghouse, provides information technology training, and advocates for the legislative interests of municipalities in the Maryland General Assembly. Recent legislative objectives have included protecting the annexation powers of municipalities, ensuring managed growth, enabling municipalities to establish special public safety taxing districts, and securing funding for programs that provide revitalization, open space, parks, and playgrounds.

Both MACo and MML are well-established players in Annapolis. General assembly committee chairs often seek their positions before proceeding on bills, and the legislature frequently mandates MACo and/or MML representation on task forces and study commissions focused on county or municipality problems. Given the established and effectual lobbying presence of MACo and MML, the policy preferences of Maryland's local governments are routinely considered and more often heeded than defeated.

SUMMARY

Local governments in Maryland reflect the diversity of the state. While all experience the constant demands of public education, public safety, public health, and maintenance of public works infrastructure, different Maryland counties and municipalities often deal with very different problems. For Baltimore City, plagued by endemic drug use, public safety and the expansion of drug treatment facilities are paramount. Allegany County in Western Maryland deals with a declining and aging population in a local economy drained of well-paying jobs. Environmental protection and regulation create policy tensions in the growing Eastern Shore counties and municipalities.

Managing rapid growth is a common concern. Fifteen Maryland counties experienced population increases greater than 10 percent from the 2000 census to the 2010 census, with school overcrowding and traffic gridlock the inevitable results.[33] Yet despite the challenges of the twenty-first century, Maryland counties remain fiscally strong and administratively competent centers of responsive government. Because of the importance of state aid, counties have forged a stable and institutionalized relationship with state government characterized generally by mutual consultation and cooperation. With these assets the primacy of counties in Maryland local governance will persist over the long term.

CHAPTER FOURTEEN

Maryland's Future

Marylanders in a sense developed a culture all their own . . . a sensibility founded on compromise given conflict, on toleration given differences among people and their failings, on the pursuit of happiness given the brevity of life.

Robert Brugger, Maryland historian

From a political perspective twenty-first century Maryland has become a more polarized state, with Democratic and Republican candidates and parties operating in very different, separate spheres of supporters, priorities, and proposed policies. Maryland Democrats confronted a four-year challenge to their dominance with the loss of the governor's office in 2002 but retained effective policy control because of general assembly leadership that successfully defied gubernatorial opposition on major issues.

While the former Republican Party chairman John Kane once boasted of changing Maryland into a "legitimate two-party state," there were no such claims after the 2006 election.[1] Martin O'Malley's 53 to 46 percent defeat of Ehrlich, Ben Cardin's comfortable 54 percent victory for the U.S. Senate over Lieutenant Governor Michael Steele, and the routs of Republican opponents for attorney general and comptroller by Doug Gansler and Peter Franchot all reflected a restoration of historical Democratic dominance. The pattern continued in 2010, when Maryland voters delivered a landslide mandate to Governor O'Malley and the entire statewide Democratic slate despite a national Republican surge.

Certainly reviewing the numbers that count, elective offices held and overall voter registration, Democrats hold a commanding lead in Maryland, and regarding it as a competitive two-party state stretches the political data and even partisan imagination well past the breaking point. There are no statewide Republican officeholders and only two Republican congressmen after the 2010 gubernatorial general election. The Republican Party has only two county executives as its highest state and local officeholders, and both, Anne Arundel County's John R. Leopold and David R. Craig of Harford County, appear to be at the apogee of their political careers. In the "Big Three" bastions of Democratic power, Baltimore City, Montgomery County, and Prince George's County, not a single Republican holds elective office at either the state or local level. Republican voter registration, though it improved from its 1978 low of 23 percent, peaked at 30 percent in 2002 and receded to 27 percent in 2010.

At a 2006 preelection fund-raiser Governor Ehrlich identified his party's stakes: "We have one shot. It comes around every 40 or 50 years. . . . It's not coming around in our lifetimes again."[2] Unfortunately for Ehrlich, he was prescient about 2010, and the immediate Maryland Republican future for statewide offices appears bleak. Robert Ehrlich represented the twenty-first-century totality of his party, and losing the last two gubernatorial elections may close his notable electoral career. Thirty-four years between governorships, Agnew's and Ehrlich's, is an extremely long sojourn in the political wilderness, and another protracted losing streak could loom. Perhaps new issues and personalities will emerge that will prove beneficial to Maryland Republican prospects. There are deep cycles in Maryland state politics that invariably weaken seemingly permanent majorities, but for now the Maryland Republican future in statewide elections rests primarily on this somewhat abstract hope.

The present realities of Marylanders' electoral behavior are displayed in the growing intensity of the differences between the counties and a deepening partisan polarization. Voting patterns amply reflect the growing political divide. In the past five presidential elections (1992–2008) fifteen counties steadfastly supported the Republican candidate and four counties (Baltimore, Howard, Montgomery, and Prince George's) and Baltimore City always voted Democratic.

The strength of Republican or Democratic support within most counties has also intensified. Very few jurisdictions in Maryland, if any, can be considered average. Only four counties (Baltimore, Charles, Howard, and Montgomery) had Obama and McCain numbers that were within ten percentage points of their state totals, while ten jurisdictions (Baltimore City and Allegany, Caroline, Carroll, Cecil, Garrett, Harford, Prince George's, Queen Anne's, and Worcester counties) were more than twenty points away. In contrast nineteen Maryland counties were within ten percentage points of the state average in the presidential elections of 1976 (Carter versus Ford) and 1980 (Reagan versus Carter).

Electoral polarization in gubernatorial elections is also pronounced. In the past five elections (1994–2010) the three Democratic candidates, Parris Glendening, Kathleen Kennedy Townsend, and Martin O'Malley, carried Baltimore City, Montgomery County, and Prince George's County. Glendening won Allegany and Howard counties once, in his successful 1998 re-election. O'Malley also carried Howard County in 2006 and 2010 but lost in Allegany County. He also picked up Charles County in southern Maryland, where in-migration from the Washington suburbs is bolstering Democratic strength, and narrowly won Baltimore County in 2010, Ehrlich's former home base. Republicans Sauerbrey and Ehrlich carried every other county in the state. Table 14-1 displays the popular vote winner by political party in both presidential and gubernatorial elections in Maryland's twenty-four subdivisions from 1988 through 2010.

In 1986 William Donald Schaefer, running for his first term as governor, captured every Maryland subdivision against token opposition, winning with 82 percent of the vote (see chapter 3 for an account of that campaign). Since then eleven counties—six on the Eastern Shore (Caroline, Cecil, Queen Anne's, Talbot, Wicomico, and Worcester), three in Western Maryland (Frederick, Garrett, and Washington), and two suburban jurisdictions in Central Maryland (Anne Arundel and Carroll)—have always gone Republican. In sharp contrast Baltimore City, Montgomery County, and Prince George's County voted consistently for the Democratic candidates by wide majorities. Whereas Baltimore City's share of the total vote has diminished over the past two decades, both Prince George's and Montgomery's have grown substantially. Montgomery County has become far and away number one in both potential and real vote power; in the 2008 election turnout was nearly 80 percent of its 557,910 registered voters, producing a record 443,652 voters. Montgomery's neighbor in the Washington metropolitan area, Prince George's County, ranked third in registered voters for the 2008 general election, with 497,661, and a close second in voter turnout, with 380,925. Together the two counties account for almost one-third of Maryland's registered voters and, in 2006 and 2008, cast more ballots than the combined totals of eighteen of the remaining twenty-two subdivisions. Maryland Democratic strength is concentrated in these urban and older suburban Democratic bastions, while Republican numbers are growing in the outlying counties and several newer and outer suburban metropolitan jurisdictions.

During twelve general elections from 1988 to 2010, seven counties (Al-

Table 14-1: Gubernatorial and presidential election returns by party, 1988–2010

Subdivision	1988	1990	1992	1994	1996	1998	2000	2002	2004	2006	2008	2010
Allegany	R	D	R	R	R	D	R	R	R	R	R	R
Anne Arundel	R	R	R	R	R	R	R	R	R	R	R	R
Baltimore City	D	D	D	D	D	D	D	D	D	D	D	D
Baltimore	R	D	D	R	D	R	D	R	D	R	D	D
Calvert	R	D	R	R	R	R	R	R	R	R	R	R
Caroline	R	R	R	R	R	R	R	R	R	R	R	R
Carroll	R	R	R	R	R	R	R	R	R	R	R	R
Cecil	R	R	R	R	R	R	R	R	R	R	R	R
Charles	R	D	R	R	R	R	D	R	D	D	D	D
Dorchester	R	R	R	R	D	R	R	R	R	R	R	R
Frederick	R	R	R	R	R	R	R	R	R	R	R	R
Garrett	R	R	R	R	R	R	R	R	R	R	R	R
Harford	R	R	R	R	R	R	R	R	R	R	R	R
Howard	R	D	D	R	D	D	D	R	D	D	D	D
Kent	R	R	R	R	D	R	R	R	R	R	D	R
Montgomery	D	D	D	D	D	D	D	D	D	D	D	D
Prince George's	D	D	D	D	D	D	D	D	D	D	D	D
Queen Anne's	R	R	R	R	R	R	R	R	R	R	R	R
St. Mary's	R	D	R	R	D	R	R	R	R	R	R	R
Somerset	R	R	R	R	D	R	D	R	R	R	R	R
Talbot	R	R	R	R	R	R	R	R	R	R	R	R
Washington	R	R	R	R	R	R	R	R	R	R	R	R
Wicomico	R	R	R	R	R	R	R	R	R	R	R	R
Worcester	R	R	R	R	R	R	R	R	R	R	R	R
Maryland	R	D	D	D	D	D	D	R	D	D	D	D

Source: Official election returns of the Maryland State Board of Elections as compiled by John T. Willis.

Note: Unshaded areas indicate subdivisions won by the Democratic candidate. Shaded areas indicate subdivisions won by the Republican candidate.

legany, Calvert, Dorchester, Harford, Kent, St. Mary's, and Somerset) were predominantly Republican; Howard County was the sole predominantly Democrat jurisdiction. Only Baltimore and Charles counties appear to be swing jurisdictions, but with a notable Democratic trend line. During this period Baltimore County recorded seven Democratic and five Republican victories, and Charles chose Republicans six times and Democrats six times, including in the last four.

Polarization also appears in state legislative contests. In state senate races slightly over a third (34 percent) of the legislative districts were uncontested in 2002 and 2006 and 40 percent in 2010. This produces the ultimate polarization: fourteen districts in which the Democratic candidate did not have any Republican opposition and four districts where the Republican candidate did not have any Democratic opposition. Only about a fifth of the forty-seven districts held competitive elections in 2002, 2006, and 2010, when 20 percent or less of the vote separated the partisan candidates.

Partisan polarization is also reflected in voter registration. Democrats are significantly widening their voter registration margin over Republicans in four jurisdictions: Charles, Howard, Montgomery, and Prince George's counties. In other Maryland jurisdictions, Republican registration has made substantial gains over the past twenty years.[3]

The "Two Maryland" concept, introduced in chapter 1, is gaining strength and force in election after election at the state legislative and local levels. Democratic Maryland is multiracial and multiethnic and extends along the I-95 corridor that links the Baltimore and Washington metropolitan areas. These are densely populated areas of 1,500 persons per square mile or more. Some urbanized and high-density suburban precincts in the Maryland Tidewater region, as well as in Western Maryland counties, turn out reliable Democratic majorities. Governor Glendening's Smart Growth initiative, a cluster of policies designed to channel population growth into pre-existing urbanized areas with established infrastructure, served to reinforce Democratic voting tendencies.

Republican Maryland is everywhere else. It's predominantly suburban or rural and overwhelmingly white. Republican Maryland is found in the exurbs newly rising from cornfields and woodlands past. In these areas a sense of community is often provided less by place than by churches, especially rapidly growing evangelical Christian megachurches with congregations numbering in the thousands. These are the cornerstones of Maryland Republican strength.

Electoral polarization in and of itself could be inconsequential if it meant only that Democratic areas vote differently from Republican ones.

However, partisan electoral behavior is rooted in attitudes, values, and beliefs, and these help drive the differences between Maryland Democrats and Republicans. These are not distinctions at the margins; these are often disputes about the very principles of policy. For example, a 2001 *Baltimore Sun* "Maryland Poll" found that majorities along the I-95 corridor supported banning handguns, increasing state aid for Baltimore City's schools, and ending legal discrimination based on sexual orientation. Predominantly Republican areas were far less likely to approve such policies. As Donald F. Norris, a political science professor at the University of Maryland, Baltimore County, noted at the time, "If Maryland supports a liberal agenda, it's because it's a state marked by big pockets of liberal voters."[4] In the case of Washington metropolitan counties, those liberal pockets are very big indeed.

The politicians who represent the "Two Marylands" reflect national trends and national forces. Conservative and moderate Democrats from the Eastern Shore or Western Maryland, once a significant force in the state party, have lost their seats to aggressive Republican challengers. Moderate Republicans in Montgomery County and Prince George's County have lost to more liberal Democrats. The result is a far more partisan and polarized state politics. When Democrats are in control, Maryland policies and programs emerge from a system of compromise and accommodation. Even difficult and controversial issues, such as cutbacks in teachers' pension benefits, mandatory emissions testing for vehicles, and Medicaid coverage for the children of immigrants, legal and illegal alike, were dealt with through executive and legislative consultations and ultimate cooperation. That changed with the 2002 election of Governor Ehrlich. Divided government usually produces partisan conflict, and Maryland proved no exception. Sound-bite rhetoric replaced the conciliatory political language that produces compromised solutions.[5]

The institutional combat between governor and state legislature grew in intensity and scope in every year of Governor Ehrlich's term, polarizing the differences between the Democratic legislative majority and the Republican governor. Ehrlich proposed roughly half the number of legislative initiatives that his Democratic predecessors had, and for the general assembly this provided expanded opportunities to craft statewide policies of progressive intent with pragmatic dimensions. The so-called Walmart bill, which mandated health insurance coverage for employees of any company with 10,000 workers or more (only marketing giant Walmart met that criterion), was a case in point. The intent was to extend health insurance coverage for working uninsured families. While Massachusetts and Vermont opted for far broader programs, the approach of the Maryland General Assembly was more cautious and limited. Similarly state funding for embryonic and adult stem cell research, a measure initiated in the house of delegates, was enacted in 2006. Maryland became only one of five states with such a program, and although its $15 million per year funding was above the annual budgetary allocations of Connecticut, Illinois, and New Jersey, it fell considerably below that of California's $3 billion over a ten-year period. The general assembly also enacted a series of limits on gubernatorial power that may well constrain future chief executives, regardless of party. The governor's broad powers to appoint, dispose of state lands, and promote tourism in television commercials were circumscribed by legislative actions and investigations.

Despite their defeats in 2006 and 2010, Maryland Republicans remain likely to reflect the policy concerns of their national party: pro-business, pro-family, pro–death penalty, antigovernment, antitaxes, anti-abortion, and strongly protective of gun and property rights. The conservative core of the Maryland GOP at the county and legislative-district levels will stay true to its ideological roots. For Maryland Democrats 2002 was a sobering wake-up call that Democrats could no longer emerge victorious statewide by just showing up. Governor O'Malley and his campaign organization represented considerable upgrades from the Democratic efforts four years before. Supplemented by the most extensive and expensive state party operations in Maryland history, O'Malley's campaign agenda emphasized pragmatic but progressive policies on such quality-of-life issues as education, health care, and the environment.

Statewide, Democrats held a registration margin of more than a million voters for the 2010 gubernatorial general election. An equally critical determinant of future Maryland elections centers on the growing portion of voters who decline to specify a party. Unaffiliated and other registered voters now constitute almost 17 percent of the total registered voters in the state, their highest percentage since voter registration was first kept statewide by party in 1914. The number of Marylanders not affiliated with the two major parties has doubled over the past twenty years; between 2000 and 2010 new unaffiliated registered voters provided almost 33 percent of the net overall increase in registered voters statewide. Over 43 percent of these voters reside in Howard, Montgomery, and Prince George's counties, all jurisdictions with significant numbers of federal government employees. Such unaffiliated voters are more likely to support the Democratic activist model of governance, but their allegiance is never certain.

For the immediate future a more polarized and partisan Maryland is likely to persist. The policymaking process will doubtless remain contentious as state Democrats and Republicans score their own respective debating points and play to their core constituencies. The long-term trends of increasing demographic diversity, sheer population growth, and a generalized public preference for activist government keyed to quality-of-life issues project a continued favorable environment for Maryland Democrats. Most statewide and local issues, such as educational concerns, environmental protection, and control of development, play directly to established Democratic strengths. However, the Democratic Party enjoys no absolute monopoly on persuasive leadership in these areas. Statewide contests will certainly be closer if the caliber and quality of Republican challengers increase. The Democratic farm team is far deeper and has the added advantage of coming from the largest jurisdictions in Maryland. The electorate base of Democratic candidates remains the most populous and economically dynamic central core of the state. Republicans must pursue a periphery strategy of the surrounding smaller counties and hope to attract a significant number of Democratic defectors and independent voters. Certainly Ehrlich proved this can be accomplished.

Regardless of individual electoral outcomes, sound leadership that recognizes the challenges that face twenty-first-century Maryland is essential because running state government is about much more than periodic political campaigns. Governing can transcend ideology or partisan disposition, and in Maryland it often does. Even Governor Ehrlich, whose public discourse routinely bashed the "liberal" media and Democrats, rarely strayed from pragmatic policies that were scarcely conservative. His Chesapeake Bay Restoration Act coupled a monthly "flush tax" (the governor preferred terming it a "user fee") on both residential sewer connections and septic tanks to fund upgrades for sixty-six wastewater treatment plants surrounding the Bay. Ehrlich's final budget established record spending levels for Maryland education, and he enlarged considerably the number of gubernatorial pardons and clemency approvals in his single term. Maintaining the pragmatic course while enlarging its progressive content became Governor Martin O'Malley's charge and duty after the 2006 gubernatorial campaign. Governing in the worst economy since the Great Depression has proved demanding, but if incumbent elections are backward mandates and the judgment of the electorate on executive performance, the O'Malley 2010 reelection manifests governing success. After initiating a series of tax increases in his first year, O'Malley compiled a record of innovative approaches, such as the statistics-driven StateStat and BayStat programs, focused economic development grants, the popular four-year tuition freeze at state institutions of higher education, and the opening of slots casinos after

years of delay. Governor O'Malley's second term will prove equally challenging in the task of crafting responsive and effective public policies in a
changed economic and political environment.

By many measures Maryland's assets are significant and enduring, but
the present and the future state of the state are not without substantial problems that future administrations and legislatures will engage, regardless of
party. Ever since World War II Maryland and its local governments have
confronted the benefits and costs of growth. The state's desirability promotes economic growth, population increases, and great diversity, yet these
consequences produce overcrowding, congestion, pollution, and suburban
sprawl. Balancing the positives of growth while controlling, channeling,
and restructuring the negatives is a never-ending struggle. Six major issue
areas will dominate Maryland government at the statewide and local levels
for the decades to come:

Growth and Development: Maryland's multiple advantages—its central location, proximity to Washington, pleasant climate, affluent and educated
workforce, dynamic, diverse, and resilient economy—will continue to attract hordes of new citizens. The state's population is estimated to grow by
more than 1.5 million by the year 2030; if the present trend is any guide,
a substantial proportion of them will be minorities.[6] The multidimensional
pressures of population growth resonate across all governmental sectors,
from local municipalities to Annapolis. While Governor Glendening's
Smart Growth initiatives represented a realistic approach to growth management and planning, these policies and procedures were watered down
and underfunded by the Ehrlich administration, even though the governor
paid lip service to the fundamental principles. Antigrowth candidacies
and campaigns at the local level are increasing in Maryland, especially in
predominantly rural jurisdictions. For example, in 2006 incumbents were
swept out of office in Crisfield, a small municipality on the lower Eastern
Shore, where development issues were prominent in the campaign. More
than 50 percent of the voters participated, an extraordinary turnout for the
June election.[7] Growth issues pose a real and present danger to Maryland
Republicans, whose traditional defense of absolute property rights and
open hostility to strict environmental regulations can easily put them on the
wrong side of growth and development conflicts.

Chesapeake Bay: With waterfront and water-view property values rapidly
escalating, development pressures and sheer population growth along the
Bay and its many tributaries has soared. This in turn has stalled progress in

the enduring struggle to "save the Bay." The premier guardian of Bay vitality, the Chesapeake Bay Foundation (140,000 members), has developed a composite index, a report card of sorts, of thirteen measures of such areas as pollution, habitat, and fisheries. The foundation publishes this index yearly in its "State of the Bay" report. Scores on the index range from one hundred ("pristine") to zero ("dead"). Since 2002 the index has hovered in the upper twenties ("dangerously out of balance"). Particularly troubling are increased quantities of nitrogen and phosphorus pollution that nourishes massive summer algal blooms, reducing water clarity and quality. By late summer the algae dies off and decomposes, the dissolved oxygen content of Bay waters plummets, and the result is a no-fish area, a dead zone that in August 2005 stretched from above the Bay Bridge to almost the mouth of the York River in Virginia. Fully 40 percent of the Chesapeake had substandard oxygen levels, a portent, if concerted and sustained action fails, of a permanently depleted and diminished Bay. Blame for the Chesapeake's deterioration is best summed up by Pogo, Walt Kelly's immortal cartoon character: "We have met the enemy and he is us." The Chesapeake Bay Foundation is more focused in its indictment: "Elected officials have failed to provide the leadership and resources for restoration that is broad enough to make a systemic difference."[8] More must be done to save the Bay.

Traffic and Congestion: Maryland resembles a staging area for the interstate highway system, as such superhighways as I-70, I-83, I-95, I-97, and I-270 crisscross the state. Maryland drivers rank fifth nationally in percentage of travel on interstates, with almost a third of their mileage driven on these superhighways.[9] Both the Washington and Baltimore metropolitan areas are serviced by extensive public transportation systems. The Washington Metro extends its five heavy rail lines, totaling 106 miles, through the suburban communities of Maryland and Virginia. With eighty-six stations, the Washington Metro carries a daily ridership of 535,000, second only to New York City in volume. The Baltimore Metro is far less extensive; its 15.5-mile heavy rail line extends from northwestern Baltimore County to downtown Baltimore, with a short spur to the Johns Hopkins Hospital complex in east Baltimore. The Metro is supplemented by a thirty-mile light rail system that services north-central Baltimore County, Baltimore City, northern Anne Arundel County, and the Baltimore-Washington International Thurgood Marshall Airport. Although Maryland ranks third among the states in the percentage of use of public transportation by workers, fewer than one in ten rely on mass transit.[10] Maryland workers, like the vast majority of Americans, depend on their cars for daily transport. Despite the roadways and mass transit systems, rush hour, especially on the Washington (I-495) and Baltimore (I-695) beltways, has become a misnomer; it's now rush gridlock. According to the Texas Transportation Institute, the Washington metropolitan area ranks first in traffic congestion and Baltimore fifth.[11] Crafting effective transportation policies that ease the traffic and congestion burdens of Maryland's metropolitan areas has become one of the most important governmental imperatives of the twenty-first century.

Crime and Violence: Like America as a whole, Maryland has had its cycles of increasing and decreasing crime rates.[12] Social and economic disparities that often are the root of criminal activity exist in Maryland, notwithstanding the state's high rankings in per capita income and wealth. Violent crime associated with densely populated urban areas affects Maryland insofar as it has an old central core metropolitan city, Baltimore, and the state borders the most economically disadvantaged areas of Washington DC. Most disturbingly Baltimore has been persistently plagued by homicide rates fueled by the raging scourge of drug abuse and territorial drug wars. In the 1970s and 1980s the state embarked on massive prison construction programs that tripled the capacity of the penal institutions. The increased number of criminal laws and a continual struggle to deal with the consequences of drug abuse keeps the criminal justice system busy, the jails full, and crime rates relatively high. For fiscal years 2008 and 2009 an average of 197,675 criminal cases a year were filed in the district courts in Maryland and an average of 83,138 were filed in the circuit courts.[13] The federal 2004 Bureau of Justice Statistics report ranked the state twentieth in overall incarceration rate. Contributing to the saliency of crime as a public policy issue is the influence of television and other media (the "If it bleeds, it leads" syndrome), which drives a perception of crime that often runs counter to reported crime rate statistics.[14] Crime, the fear of it and its harsh realities, will continue to plague many Maryland urban communities, and public officials must continue to grapple with this seemingly entrenched pathology. The cost of public safety and corrections, in which Maryland ranks proportionally high among the states, will require balancing with other priorities.

Health Care: Expenditures for health care now rank as the largest percentage of the Maryland state budget, over $8 billion in fiscal year 2010. Maryland's pragmatic progressivism is reflected in its acceptance and expansion of federal programs. Medicaid coverage has been extended to persons with income up to 250 percent of the minimum poverty levels and covers more that 830,000 state residents. When Congress prohibited federal Medicaid expenditures for immigrants, Maryland continued coverage with state funds under Governor Glendening. When some funds were cut by Governor Ehrlich, the Maryland General Assembly forced a partial restoration. The state legislature has demonstrated a willingness to take on difficult health care issues, including successful opposition to the request of Blue Cross/Blue Shield to change from a nonprofit to a private for-profit entity and support for the extension of medical benefits to pregnant women, children, and seniors. Strong public expectations for health care combined with the fiscal consequences of meeting public demands will keep health care at the forefront of public policy concerns in Maryland for the short- and long-term future.

Education: Public and group pressure for improved educational curriculum, facilities, and opportunity, buttressed by a state constitutional mandate for "a thorough and efficient" system of public education, is unlikely to be lessened in Maryland's future. Record increases in the level of state funding of public education over the past ten years have not lessened the demand for more financial resources from local boards of education, county governments, parent-teacher associations, education advocacy groups, teachers' and employee unions, and voters. With fiscal responsibility separated from administrative responsibility under Maryland's system of elementary and secondary education, management tensions will persist. The rising costs of higher education will ensure that the issues of access, affordability, and quality remain on the minds of Marylanders as the state seeks to meet the job requirements of expanding high technology, biotechnology, health care, and government service industries as well as the expectations of its citizens.

SUMMARY

Maryland's public policy agenda for the twenty-first century is certainly full. Given the state's history and political culture, as well as anticipated growth patterns, this is to be expected. The post–World War II American dream put deep roots into the Maryland terrain, with suburban expansions that have spread far beyond metropolitan confines. The demographic diversity of Maryland, long established, has meant that many of these suburbs reflect a pluralistic tapestry unknown in more homogeneous states. The Central Maryland I-95 corridor, the densely populated urban and suburban core of the state, and the vote-rich base of Democratic dominance typify this growing demographic diversity. The two metropolitan areas, Baltimore in the north and Washington in the southwest, are growing ever closer, creating greater economic, political, and social interdependency. Traditional parochial animosities between the Baltimore and Washington metropolitan areas are clearly on the decline. Over the past six decades Maryland has managed diverse growth with skill and stability that is a tribute to the wisdom of its past and present political leadership. Even greater tasks lie ahead in the twenty-first century.

The issues identified in this book will collectively perplex, frustrate, and even inspire future generations of Maryland public policymakers, Democrats and Republicans alike. The Free State has faced challenges before and resolved them with a unique blend of idealism tempered by pragmatism and a tolerant compassion blended with fiscal prudence. Maryland will not only endure but will prosper in the decades to come and provide both the region and the nation with a positive model for productively progressive policies. Maryland's pragmatic sensibility can serve as both a guide and a rule for the future of politics and government within the nation's state and local governments.

CHAPTER FIFTEEN

Further Reference for Maryland Study

The study of Maryland politics and government is enriched by the existence of a substantial supply of original source documents, a wealth of official government publications and reports, informed secondary works, and a bountiful collection of newspapers, journals, and periodicals. The selected sources for study and reference were chosen because of their value to understanding Maryland's politics and government and do not represent an attempt to catalogue all of the significant works describing the rich heritage of Maryland.

ORIGINAL SOURCE DOCUMENTS

Significant original source documents have been collected and maintained by the Maryland State Archives, the Maryland Historical Society in Baltimore, the Enoch Pratt Free Library Main Branch in Baltimore City, the McKeldin Library at the University of Maryland in College Park, and the Milton Eisenhower Library of Johns Hopkins University, located on its central Homewood Campus in Baltimore City. Local historical societies and county and municipal offices have original source documents available for review, research, and study.

The Maryland State Archives, an independent state agency, is a treasure trove of government records, genealogy resources, newspapers, and other important Maryland historical documents. It is the official repository for numerous state, county, and municipal government records. The holdings of the state archives date to 1634 and are preserved in an exemplary, climate-controlled facility with over 330,000 cubic feet of storage space.

The Maryland Historical Society, founded in 1844 under a charter from the state legislature, has more than 6.2 million books, manuscripts, prints, photographs, genealogy indexes, works of art, and cultural artifacts in its collections, covering four centuries for potential research. The Enoch Pratt Free Library, the designated State Library Resource Center for Maryland, opened its doors in 1886. Virtually every book on Maryland's history, government, and politics can be found there, along with official national, state, and local government publications. Its Maryland Room contains a researcher's delight of vertical files, maps, and unique publications.

CONTEMPORARY GOVERNMENT RECORDS AND REPORTS

The Maryland Manual: A Guide to Maryland Government, published biennially by the Maryland State Archives, is a compendium of Maryland governmental matters. The *Maryland Manual* was first published in 1895 and annually thereafter until 1940, when biennial publication began. The three branches of government, local government, boards, and commissions are described in useful detail, including biographies of executive, legislative, and judicial public officials. The information is also available through *Maryland Manual On-line*, located on the website of the Maryland State Archives.

The annual report and the annual statistical report of the Maryland judiciary provide straightforward information about the composition and workload of the state judicial branch of government. The State Law Library, created in 1826, is located in the Court of Appeals building in Annapolis and maintains a collection of more than 400,000 books and other resources to serve the research needs of the judiciary as well as the executive and legislative branches of government and the general public.

Official information on the actual year-end revenue and expenditures of state government may be found in the annual reports of the comptroller of Maryland and the state treasurer. The *Joint Chairmen's Report*, prepared by the Department of Legislative Services shortly before the adjournment of the regular annual session of the Maryland General Assembly, sets forth the legislative actions on the annually approved budget, including reductions, contingencies, restrictions, and budget bill language. The *Fiscal Digest*, prepared by the Maryland Department of Budget and Management, is considered the official record of approved expenditures and revenues for each fiscal year. The department also prepares the annual capital budget for the state and publishes the rolling five-year capital improvement program.

The annual reports published by cabinet departments and other state agencies, as well as by local government entities, provide a plethora of information about the annual operation of state and local government. The Department of Legislative Services of the Maryland General Assembly has produced the *Legislative Handbook Series* every four years since 1970. This is a multivolume series that sets forth in a useful manner the essentials of state and local government, including organizational structure, functions, budgets, programs, and services. The department also produces excellent reports on special topics with selected recent reports available on its website.

SECONDARY SOURCES

Of all the overviews of Maryland history from its inception to contemporary times, Robert J. Brugger's *Maryland: A Middle Temperament* stands as the master work. Commissioned by the Maryland Historical Society to mark the 350th anniversary of the state's founding, the book is thoroughly researched and eminently readable. There is no better guide to the sweep of Maryland history and the public character of the state. The lengthy volume compiled for the national bicentennial, *Maryland: A History 1632–1974*, edited by Richard Walsh and William Lloyd Fox, contains chapters on the major eras in Maryland's governmental and political evolution produced by leading state scholars. George H. Callcott's *Maryland and America: 1940 to 1980* is also very valuable for its detailed analysis of the demographic and economic dynamics that drove state politics and public policies after World War II.

There are scores of publications that examine various historical eras and aspects of Maryland politics and government. An abbreviated list of informative books on Maryland history and historical periods and selected biographies for further study is presented below.

Baker, Jean H. *Ambivalent Americans: The Know-Nothing Party in Maryland*. Baltimore: Johns Hopkins University Press, 1977.
———. *The Politics of Continuity: Maryland Political Parties from 1858 to 1870*. Baltimore: Johns Hopkins University Press, 1973.
Bode, Carl. *Maryland: A Bicentennial History*. New York: Norton, 1978.
Brugger, Robert J. *Maryland: A Middle Temperament*. Baltimore: Johns Hopkins University Press in association with the Maryland Historical Society, 1988.
Callcott, George H. *Maryland and America: 1940 to 1980*. Baltimore: Johns Hopkins University Press, 1985.

Callcott, Margaret Law. *The Negro in Maryland Politics 1870–1912*. Baltimore: Johns Hopkins University Press, 1969.

Crooks, James B. *Politics and Progress: The Rise of Urban Progressivism in Baltimore 1895 to 1911*. Baton Rouge: Louisiana State University Press, 1968.

Dozer, Donald Marquand. *Portrait of the Free State: A History of Maryland*. Cambridge MD: Tidewater, 1976.

Everstine, Carl N. *The General Assembly of Maryland*. 3 vols. Charlottesville VA: Michie, 1980–84.

Evitts, William J. *A Matter of Allegiances: Maryland from 1850 to 1861*. Baltimore: Johns Hopkins University Press, 1974.

Helmes, Winifred G., ed. *Notable Maryland Women*. Cambridge MD: Tidewater, 1977.

Hughes, Harry R., with John W. Frece. *My Unexpected Journey: The Autobiography of Governor Harry Roe Hughes*. Charleston SC: History Press, 2006.

Jacobs, Bradford. *Thimbleriggers: The Law v. Governor Marvin Mandel*. Baltimore: Johns Hopkins University Press, 1984.

Kirwin, Harry W. *The Inevitable Success: Herbert R. O'Conor* Westminster MD: Newman Press, 1962.

Lambert, John R., Jr. *Arthur Pue Gorman*. Baton Rouge: Louisiana State University Press, 1953.

Land, Aubrey C., Lois Green Carr, and Edward C. Papenfuse, eds. *Law, Society, and Politics in Early Maryland*. Baltimore: Johns Hopkins University Press, 1977.

Parks, A. Franklin, and John B. Wiseman, eds. *Maryland: Unity in Diversity*. Dubuque IA: Kendall/Hunt, 1990.

Phillips, Christopher. *Freedom's Port: The African American Community of Baltimore, 1790–1860*. Chicago: University of Illinois Press, 1997.

Radoff, Morris L., ed. *The Old Line State: A History of Maryland*. 3 vols. Annapolis: Hall of Records Commission, State of Maryland, 1971.

Smith, Fraser C. *William Donald Schaefer: A Political Biography*. Baltimore: Johns Hopkins University Press, 1999.

Walsh, Richard, and William Lloyd Fox, eds. *Maryland: A History 1632–1974*. Baltimore: Maryland Historical Society, 1974.

White, Frank F., Jr. *The Governors of Maryland, 1777–1970*. Annapolis: The Hall of Records Commission, State of Maryland, 1970.

Willis, John T. *Presidential Elections in Maryland*. Mt. Airy MD: Lomond Publications, 1984.

MARYLAND PUBLIC OPINION

The annual public opinion survey conducted by the Schaefer Center for Public Policy at the University of Baltimore is an invaluable source for the study of contemporary Maryland opinion and attitudes on a wide variety of governmental and political topics. See *Maryland Policy Choices*, 1992–98 and 2002–9. Especially in gubernatorial and presidential election years, the *Baltimore Sun* and the *Washington Post* regularly commission and publish political public opinion surveys to inform their journalism and their readers.

NEWSPAPERS, JOURNALS, AND MAGAZINES

The free press has played an important role in Maryland politics and government throughout its history. Newspapers and journals are often the sole or most accessible source of election information contemporaneous with the period, personality, or event being researched. It should be noted that these publications were frequently very partisan, and material should be cross-checked. The Maryland State Archives houses a substantial collection of newspapers, as does the Enoch Pratt Library.

Information about early Maryland newspapers and journals is presented in Clarence S. Brigham, *History and Bibliography of American Newspapers, 1690–1820*, 2 vols. (Worcester MA: American Antiquarian Society, 1947), 1:218–70, and Gregory Winifred, ed., *America Newspapers 1821–1936: A Union List of Files Available in the United States and Canada* (New York: H. W. Wilson, 1937), 257–68. J. Preston Dickson, *Newspapers of Maryland's Eastern Shore* (Centreville MD: Tidewater, 1986), contains a history of that region's free press.

Published since May 17, 1837, the *Baltimore Sun* is a significant source of information. A book marking the paper's 100th anniversary describes its role: Gerald W. Johnson, Frank R. Kent, H. L. Mencken, and Hamilton Owens, *The Sunpapers of Baltimore 1837–1937* (New York: Knopf, 1937). In recent years the *Washington Post* has exceeded the *Baltimore Sun* in daily subscribers residing in Maryland and should now be considered among the state's most influential media. Also important to government and politics are the twelve other daily newspapers published throughout the state which have influence in their respective areas.

The *Maryland Historical Magazine*, published by the Maryland Historical Society since 1906, contains a veritable warehouse of information. The *Maryland Historical Magazine* has regularly published a compilation of articles, books, and doctoral dissertations since 1975 that is useful as a research tool. See, for example, "Maryland History Bibliography, 2006: A Selected List," *Maryland Historical Magazine* 102, no. 2 (2007).

The Internet has made official government publications and information significantly more widely available and accessible to scholars, researchers, and the general public. Through the official government portal of the State of Maryland a seemingly limitless amount of information about state government can be accessed at www.maryland.gov. The direct link to the Maryland General Assembly is http://mlis.state.md.us/, to the Maryland Office of Governor is www.gov.state.md.us/, and to the Maryland Judiciary is www.courts.state.md.us/. The website of the Maryland State Board of Elections contains information about voter registration, election results, and campaign finance requirements and reports and may be accessed at www.elections.state.md.us/. The website of the Maryland State Data Center at the Department of Planning, www.mdp.state.md.us/msdc/, contains numerous reports, tables, and maps regarding state demographics and land use.

All of Maryland's counties and Baltimore City have independent websites that contain a varying quantity and quality of information and that may be accessed independently or through links on the state website.

The major centers for research on Maryland politics and government also maintain websites. Especially noteworthy are the Maryland State Archives, where original copies of numerous founding documents can be viewed at www.msa.md.gov, the Enoch Pratt Free Library at www.prattlibrary.org, and the Maryland Historical Society at www.mdhs.org.

Notes

1. THE MARYLAND IDENTITY

H. L. Mencken, "The Home of the Crab," in *The Impossible H. L. Mencken: A Selection of His Best Newspaper Stories*, ed. Marion Elizabeth Rodgers (New York: Anchor Books, 1991), 138.

1. *Scott v. Sandford*, 60 U.S. 393 (1856). See Jesse H. Choper et al., *Constitutional Law: Cases, Comments, Questions* (St. Paul MN: West Group, 2001), 1156.

2. Jean H. Baker, *The Politics of Continuity: Maryland Political Parties from 1858 to 1870* (Baltimore: Johns Hopkins University Press, 1973), 7.

3. U.S. Census Bureau, *Current Population Survey, 2006 to 2008 Annual Social and Economic Supplements* (Washington DC: Government Printing Office, 2008); U.S. Census Bureau, *American Fact Finder, Census 2000 Summary File 1* (Washington DC: Government Printing Office, 2005), table GCT-PH 1.

4. Michael Barone et al., *The Almanac of American Politics 1992* (Washington DC: National Journal Group, 1991), 538.

5. Quoted in John T. Willis, *Presidential Elections in Maryland* (Mt. Airy MD: Lomond, 1984), 137.

6. Bradford Jacobs, *Thimbleriggers: The Law v. Governor Marvin Mandel* (Baltimore: Johns Hopkins University Press, 1984), xix.

7. Ryan Polk, "The Origin of 'the Old Line State'" (Annapolis: Maryland State Archives, 2005). This article, tracing the origin and use of this nickname, may be viewed on the state archives website, www.aomol.net/html/oldline.html.

8. Dorothy M. Brown, "Maryland between the Wars," in *Maryland: A History 1632–1974*, ed. Richard Walsh and William Lloyd Fox (Baltimore: Maryland Historical Society, 1974), 712.

9. Christopher Phillips, *Freedom's Port: The African American Community of Baltimore, 1790–1860* (Chicago: University of Illinois Press, 1997), 8.

10. Robert J. Brugger, *Maryland: A Middle Temperament* (Baltimore: Johns Hopkins University Press, Maryland Historical Society, 1988), 781.

11. John R. Wennersten, "The Almighty Oyster: A Saga of Old Somerset and the Eastern Shore, 1850–1920," in *Maryland: Unity in Diversity*, ed. A. Franklin Parks and John B. Wiseman (Dubuque IA: Kendall/Hunt, 1990), 147–53. Long-handled tongs or "nippers" were used to harvest shallow-water oyster beds. Iron dredges were employed for harvesting oysters in deeper water.

12. Baker, *Politics of Continuity*, 8.

13. Brugger, *Maryland*, 564.

14. Quoted in Carl Bode, *Maryland: A Bicentennial History* (New York: Norton, 1978), 90.

15. Bode, *Maryland*, 90–91.

16. Baker, *Politics of Continuity*, 8.

17. Bode, *Maryland*, 91.

18. Brugger, *Maryland*, 333.

19. U.S. Census Bureau, *American Fact Finder* (Washington DC: Government Printing Office, 2005), tables GCT-P11 and GCT-P13.

20. Maryland Port Administration, "Port Report," *The Port of Baltimore*, January/February 2008, 20–27; Maryland Port Administration, "Port Report," *The Port of Baltimore*, July/August 2008, 9.

21. Franklin L. Burdette, "Modern Maryland Politics and Social Change," in *Maryland: A History 1632–1974*, ed. Richard Walsh and William Lloyd Fox (Baltimore: Maryland Historical Society, 1974), 833.

22. George H. Callcott, *Maryland and America, 1940 to 1980* (Baltimore: Johns Hopkins University Press, 1985), 59.

23. Larry Carson, "Howard Officials Tout Health Plan," *Baltimore Sun*, October 16, 2007; Susan DeFord and Mary Otto, "Howard Unveiling Its Health Program," *Washington Post*, October 16, 2007.

24. Bode, *Maryland*, 196.

25. G. H. Callcott, *Maryland and America*, 27.

26. Jacobs, *Thimbleriggers*, 69.

27. In 2008 only seven states earned the triple-A rating; the others were Delaware, Georgia, Missouri, North Carolina, Utah, and Virginia. Joint Legislative Audit and Review Commission, "Virginia Compared to Other States, Bond Ratings," Virginia General Assembly, January 2008.

28. U.S. Bureau of the Census, *Census 2000 PHC-T-6, Population by Race* (Washington DC: Government Printing Office, 2001), table 2.

29. American Jewish Committee, *American Jewish Year Book* (New York: American Jewish Committee, 2006), 159–60, table 1.

30. Maryland Department of Labor, Licensing and Regulation, Office of Work-

force Information and Performance, *Employment and Payrolls: Second Quarter 2008*, Baltimore, December 2008, 6–8.

31. Brugger, *Maryland*, x; Donald Marquand Dozer, *Portrait of the Free State: A History of Maryland* (Cambridge MD: Tidewater, 1976), 415.

2. A MARYLAND POLITICAL HISTORY

Philip L. Barbour, ed., *The Complete Works of Captain John Smith* (Chapel Hill: University of North Carolina Press, 1986), 1:144.

1. Quoted in Brugger, *Maryland*, 7.
2. Matthew Page Andrews, *History of Maryland: Province and State* (Garden City NY: Doubleday, Doran, 1929), 13.
3. William T. Russell, *Maryland: The Land of Sanctuary* (Baltimore: J. H. Furst, 1907), 29.
4. Audrey C. Land, "Provincial Maryland," in *Maryland: A History 163 2–1974*, ed. Richard Walsh and William Lloyd Fox (Baltimore: Maryland Historical Society, 1974), 10–11.
5. David Curtis Skaggs, *Roots of Maryland Democracy: 1753–1776* (Westport CT: Greenwood Press, 1973), 13.
6. George H. Callcott, "Heritage and Identity," in *Maryland: Unity in Diversity*, ed. A. Franklin Parks and John B. Wiseman (Dubuque IA: Kendall/Hunt, 1990), 17.
7. Brugger, *Maryland*, 23.
8. Brugger, *Maryland*, 60.
9. Land, "Provincial Maryland," 32.
10. Land, "Provincial Maryland," 41.
11. Richard Walsh, "The Era of the Revolution," in *Maryland: A History 1632–1974*, ed. Richard Walsh and William Lloyd Fox (Baltimore: Maryland Historical Society, 1974), 87.
12. Quoted in Aubrey C. Land, ed., "Sharpe's Confidential Report on Maryland, 1765," *Maryland Historical Magazine* 44 (June 1949): 126–27.
13. Barbara W. Tuchman, *The March of Folly* (New York: Knopf, 1984).
14. For accounts of the burning of the *Peggy Stewart*, see Skaggs, *Roots of Maryland Democracy*, 143–45; Morris L. Radoff, ed., *Old Line State: A History of Maryland* (Annapolis: Hall of Records Commission, State of Maryland, 1971), 37, 186. In *The Colonial Merchants and the American Revolution, 1773–1776* (New York: Facsimile Library, 1939), 392, the historian Arthur Schlesinger noted of this incident that "Annapolis had out-Bostoned Boston."
15. Elmer E. Clark, *The Journals and Letters of Francis Asbury* (Nashville: Abingdon Press, 1958), 1,355.
16. Brugger, *Maryland*, 119.

17. Quoted in Cary Howard, "John Eager Howard: Patriot and Public Servant," *Maryland Historical Magazine* 62 (1967): 304.

18. George H. Callcott, "The Quality of Life in Maryland over Five Centuries," *Maryland Historical Magazine* 96 (fall 2001): 283.

19. Kenneth Carroll, "Religious Influences on the Manumission of Slaves," *Maryland Historical Magazine* 56 (June 1961): 176–97.

20. "Sotweed" is an eighteenth-century term for tobacco. "The Sot-Weed Factor" was a lengthy poem by Ebenezer Cook, who satirized the colonial dependency on the tobacco trade. See E. C. Gent, *Sotweed Redivivus or The Planter's Looking Glass* (Annapolis MD 1730).

21. Tocqueville predicted the demise of slavery in Maryland because of the decline of tobacco farming. Alexis De Tocqueville, *Democracy in America*, ed. J. P. Mayer (New York: Harper Perennial, 1980), 348.

22. Phillips, *Freedom's Port*, 36–37.

23. James S. Van Ness, "Economic Development, Social and Cultural Changes: 1800–1850," in *Maryland: A History 1632–1974*, ed. Richard Walsh and William Lloyd Fox (Baltimore: Maryland Historical Society, 1974), 160.

24. Brugger, *Maryland*, 178.

25. Scott S. Sheads and Anna Von Lunz, "Defenders' Day, 1818–1998: A Brief History," *Maryland Historical Magazine* 93 (fall 1998): 301–15. See also Baltimore-born Walter Lord's account of the pivotal engagement: *The Dawn's Early Light* (New York: Norton, 1972).

26. Phillips, *Freedom's Port*, 13.

27. Joseph E. Morse and R. Duff Green, eds., *Thomas B. Searight's, The Old Pike: An illustrated narrative of the National Road* (Orange VA: Green Tree Press, 1971).

28. Dozer, *Portrait of the Free State*, 396.

29. Brugger, *Maryland*, 333.

30. Dozer, *Portrait of the Free State*, 387.

31. W. Wayne Smith, "Politics and Democracy in Maryland, 1800–1854," in *Maryland: A History 1632–1974*, ed. Richard Walsh and William Lloyd Fox (Baltimore: Maryland Historical Society, 1974), 282–83.

32. Brugger, *Maryland*, 227.

33. Quoted in W. W. Smith, "Politics and Democracy," 282.

34. Ibid.

35. Tocqueville, *Democracy in America*, 242–43.

36. Barbara G. Salmore and Stephen A. Salmore, *Candidates, Parties, and Campaigns: Electoral Politics in America* (Washington DC: Congressional Quarterly Press, 1989), 24.

37. Quoted in Brugger, *Maryland*, 228.

38. Mason Parsons quoted in W. W. Smith, "Politics and Democracy," 287.

39. Brugger, *Maryland*, 228.

40. Willis, *Presidential Elections in Maryland*, 247.

41. Quoted in Dozer, *Portrait of the Free State*, 356.

42. W. W. Smith, "Politics and Democracy," 281.

43. W. W. Smith, "Politics and Democracy," 275.

44. Baker, *Politics of Continuity*, 11.

45. Phillips, *Freedom's Port*, 195.

46. Van Ness, "Economic Development," 213.

47. Although Baltimore City was the center of Know Nothing strength in Maryland, the party had many supporters in rural areas as well. In Western Maryland the *Hagerstown Herald and Torch* editorialized this sentiment in support of the party. See W. W. Smith, "Politics and Democracy," 305. See also Jean H. Baker. *Ambivalent Americans: The Know-Nothing Party in Maryland* (Baltimore: Johns Hopkins University Press, 1977).

48. Bode, *Maryland*, 95.

49. Bode, *Maryland*, 96.

50. Brugger, *Maryland*, 260.

51. W. W. Smith, "Politics and Democracy," 305.

52. J. Thomas Scharf, *History of Baltimore City and County* (Philadelphia: Louis H. Everts, 1881), 787.

53. Biographers and historians have speculated that Edgar Allan Poe was "cooped" in 1849 and died from the experience. Poe is buried in Westminster Burying Grounds, located in downtown Baltimore. See for example, Bode, *Maryland*, 99–100. The campaign tactics of the American Know Nothing Party in Maryland are detailed in Baker, *Ambivalent Americans*, 121–25, 129–34.

54. Richard R. Duncan, "The Era of the Civil War," in *Maryland: A History 1632–1974*, ed. Richard Walsh and William Lloyd Fox (Baltimore: Maryland Historical Society, 1974), 326.

55. Baker, *Politics of Continuity*, 33.

56. Baker, *Politics of Continuity*, 4.

57. Duncan, "Civil War," 330.

58. Baker, *Politics of Continuity*, 28.

59. Phillips, *Freedom's Port*, 145.

60. Phillips, *Freedom's Port*, 234, 239.

61. Dozer, *Portrait of the Free State*, 430–31.

62. Phillips, *Freedom's Port*, 200–203.

63. Phillips, *Freedom's Port*, 84, 236.

64. Van Ness, "Economic Development," 232.

65. Brugger, *Maryland*, 246.

66. Phillips, *Freedom's Port*, 27.
67. Brugger, *Maryland*, 245.
68. Susan Cooke Soderberg, *Lest We Forget: A Guide to Civil War Monuments in Maryland* (Shippensburg PA: White Mane, 1995), 95.
69. Duncan, "Civil War," 341.
70. Adopted as the state song in 1939, "Maryland, My Maryland," written by James Ryder Randall, is sung to the tune of the Christmas carol "O, Tannenbaum." Md. Laws 969, chap. 451 (1939), codified as "State Government Article," *Annotated Code of Maryland*, sec. 13–307. The Maryland historian Donald Dozer notes that the first, fifth, and ninth stanzas are usually cut because of their warlike and blatantly biased rhetoric. Dozer, *Portrait of the Free State*, 463.
71. Some, like Lawrence Denton, argue that only the Union Army prevented Maryland from seceding. He claims that "if free to choose, Maryland would have opted to join the Southern Confederacy." Lawrence M. Denton, *A Southern Star for Maryland: Maryland and the Secession Crisis* (Baltimore: Publishing Concepts, 1995), 127. Donald Dozer concurs, maintaining that public opinion was "deposed to favor secession." Dozer, *Portrait of the Free State*, 462. The historian Jean Baker debunks such arguments, quoting William Schley, a prominent contemporary Baltimore attorney, who wrote, "There has never been a moment when Maryland could have been forced into secession." Baker, *Politics of Continuity*, 54. Another study of the period concluded, "Maryland was Unionist in sentiment, it is clear, though its choice was made manifest by its acquiescence to federal force rather than entirely by its own actions." William J. Evitts, *A Matter of Allegiances: Maryland from 1850–1861* (Baltimore: Johns Hopkins University Press, 1974), 191. Reflecting a typical Maryland attitude is the judgment of Carl Bode, who reviewed the controversy and concluded, "Nobody knew then, and nobody knows now whether the main sympathies lay with the North or the South." Bode, *Maryland*, 127.
72. Van Ness, "Economic Development," 235.
73. Baker, *Politics of Continuity*, 78.
74. Brugger, *Maryland*, 277.
75. Duncan, "Civil War," 338.
76. Brugger, *Maryland*, 274.
77. Brugger, *Maryland*, 279.
78. Quoted in George William Brown, *Baltimore and the Nineteenth of April, 1861* (Baltimore: Johns Hopkins University, 1887; reprint, Baltimore: Maclay, 1982), 90. For a further discussion of Taney's decision in *Ex parte Merryman*, 17 Fed. Cases 9,487, Circuit Court, District of Maryland, 1861, see Baker, *Politics of Continuity*, 58–62.
79. Dozer, *Portrait of the Free State*, 451.

80. Duncan, "Civil War," 353.
81. Willis, *Presidential Elections in Maryland*, 50.
82. Baker, *Politics of Continuity*, 62.
83. Baker, *Politics of Continuity*, 180.
84. Willis, *Presidential Elections in Maryland*, 51.
85. Frank Kent, *The Story of Maryland Politics* (Garden City NJ: Doubleday Page, 1923; reprint, Hatboro PA: Tradition Press, 1968), 33.
86. Bode, *Maryland*, 138.
87. Baker, *Politics of Continuity*, 202.
88. Jacobs, *Thimbleriggers*, 26.
89. Quoted in Bode, *Maryland*, 137.
90. Bode, *Maryland*, 136.
91. Brugger, *Maryland*, 393.
92. Bode, *Maryland*, 137.
93. Jacobs, *Thimbleriggers*, 25.
94. Quoted in Jacobs, *Thimbleriggers*, 26.
95. James B. Crooks, "Maryland Progressivism," in *Maryland: A History 1632–1974*, ed. Richard Walsh and William Lloyd Fox (Baltimore: Maryland Historical Society, 1974), 604.
96. Quoted in Brugger, *Maryland*, 405.
97. Leigh Bonsal quoted in Crooks, "Maryland Progressivism," 613.
98. Brugger, *Maryland*, 422.
99. For a well-researched and informative description of these disenfranchisement efforts, see M. Callcott, *The Negro in Maryland Politics, 1870–1912* (Baltimore: Johns Hopkins University Press, 1969), 101–38. See also James B. Crooks, *Politics and Progress: The Rise of Urban Progressivism in Baltimore, 1895–1911* (Baton Rouge: Louisiana State University Press, 1968), 55–72.
100. Calcott, *Negro in Maryland Politics*, 126.
101. Crooks, "Maryland Progressivism," 662.
102. Crooks, "Maryland Progressivism," 669.
103. Dozer, *Portrait of the Free State*, 527: Crooks, "Maryland Progressivism," 662.
104. Brugger, *Maryland*, 450–51.
105. Eleanor Bruchey, "The Industrialization of Maryland 1860–1914," in *Maryland: A History 1632–1974*, ed. Richard Walsh and William Lloyd Fox (Baltimore: Maryland Historical Society, 1974), 398.
106. D. M. Brown, "Maryland between the Wars," 672.
107. Mencken, *Impossible H. L. Mencken*, 293.
108. Brugger, *Maryland*, 454–58.
109. Brugger, *Maryland*, 457.
110. Sherrilyn A. Ifill, *On the Court-House Lawn: Confronting the Legacy of*

Lynching in the Twenty-first Century (Boston: Beacon Press, 2007), 39, 80, 91, 101–3.

111. Frank Kent quoted in Brugger, *Maryland*, 497.

112. Jacobs, *Thimbleriggers*, 39–40; D. M. Brown, "Maryland between the Wars," 675.

113. Brugger, *Maryland*, 453.

114. Quoted in Bode, *Maryland*, 177.

115. Albert C. Ritchie quoted in D. M. Brown, "Maryland between the Wars," 740.

116. Brugger, *Maryland*, 509; Jacobs, *Thimbleriggers*, 36.

117. G. H. Callcott, *Maryland and America*, 53.

118. D. M. Brown, "Maryland between the Wars," 746–47.

119. D. M. Brown, "Maryland between the Wars," 752.

120. Brugger, *Maryland*, 514. See also Linda M. Burrell, ed., *Maryland's 157: The Incorporated Cities and Towns* (Annapolis: Maryland Municipal League, 2000), 156.

121. G. H. Callcott, *Maryland and America*, 28.

122. Dozer, *Portrait of the Free State*, 569.

123. Brugger, *Maryland*, 541.

124. Brugger, *Maryland*, 532.

125. G. H. Callcott, *Maryland and America*, 103.

126. G. H. Callcott, *Maryland and America*, 61.

127. Brugger, *Maryland*, 569.

128. G. H. Callcott, *Maryland and America*, 105.

129. G. H. Callcott, *Maryland and America*, 103.

130. Jacobs, *Thimbleriggers*, 52.

131. Burdette, "Modern Maryland Politics."

132. G. H. Callcott, *Maryland and America*, 107.

3. CONTEMPORARY POLITICAL PATTERNS

Louis Goldstein quoted in C. Fraser Smith, "Is Campaign Tone a Tonic or a Turnoff?" *Baltimore Sun*, October 5, 2002.

1. Kent, *The Story of Maryland Politics*, 210.

2. Quoted in Dozer, *Portrait of the Free State*, 538.

3. Jacobs, *Thimbleriggers*, 55.

4. Quoted in G. H. Callcott, *Maryland and America*, 140.

5. G. H. Callcott, *Maryland and America*, 215.

6. Jerrold G. Rusk, *A Statistical History of the American Electorate* (Washington DC: CQ Press, 2001), 52, 75; Curtis Gans, "Anger Fear and Youth Propel Turnout to Highest Level Since 1960," news release, Committee for the Study of the American Electorate, December 18, 2008, 6, 14.

7. Alliance for Better Campaigns, *Gouging Democracy: How the Television Industry Profiteered on Campaign 2000*, Washington DC, 2001, 16.

8. U.S. Census Bureau, *Consolidated Federal Funds Report for Year 2009* (Washington DC: Government Printing Office, 2010), tables 1 and 14; National Science Foundation, Division of Science Resources Statistics, "Science and Engineering State Profiles: 2003–05," www.nsf.gov/statistics/nsf07322/ (accessed July 30, 2008).

9. For job performance ratings throughout Governor Schaefer's tenure, see Mason-Dixon Political/Media Research, Inc., "Maryland Poll," displayed in *Baltimore Sun*, January 11, 1995, and *Washington Post*, January 17, 1995.

10. Thad Beyle, "Pete Wilson for President?," *State Government News*, January 1995, 26.

11. Thomas W. Waldron and Michael James, "Ruling Is Likely Today in Sauerbrey Challenge," *Baltimore Sun*, January 13, 1995.

12. Marcia Myers, "Election Theft Ruled Out," *Baltimore Sun*, August 24, 1995.

13. See, for example, Rick Lowry, "Early and Often-absentee Voting Fraud," *National Review*, June 17, 1996; "Vote Fraud: A National Disgrace," *Reader's Digest*, June 1995.

14. C. Fraser Smith, "Race for 1998 Starts," *Baltimore Sun*, October 13, 1996.

15. Scott Wilson, "Negative Ads Fill the Air in Maryland," *Washington Post*, October 27, 1998.

16. In Michael Barone et al.'s *The Almanac of American Politics 2002*, (Washington DC: National Journal, 2001), 707, Charlie Cook's call for the Maryland gubernatorial race with Townsend as the presumptive heir was rated "safe."

17. David Nitkin and Sarah Koenig, "Townsend's Candidacy Still Shines," *Baltimore Sun*, January 11, 2002.

18. Thad Beyle, "Governors: Elections, Campaign Costs and Powers," in Council of State Governments, *The Book of the States* (Lexington KY: Council of State Governments, 2008), 167.

19. Mark Cheshire, "On the Record with Kathleen Kennedy Townsend," *Daily Record*, May 18, 2002.

20. Richard Dresser, "Ehrlich Fires Up Attack Rhetoric," *Baltimore Sun*, September 25, 2001.

21. Sarah Koenig and David Nitkin, "Shelling Out for Clambake or Crabfeast," *Baltimore Sun*, July 21, 2002.

22. Quoted in "GOP Chiefs Urge End to Infighting," *Washington Times*, December 10, 2001.

23. C. Fraser Smith, "At Heart of Campaign Is Chance for Change," *Baltimore Sun*, October 27, 2002.

24. Tim Craig, "Schaefer Camp Divided on Governor," *Baltimore Sun*, October 31, 2002.

25. Michael Dresser, "Ehrlich Donors Largely in State," *Baltimore Sun*, October 26, 2002.

26. Michael Dresser, "Townsend Camp Nearly Doubles GOP on Salaries," *Baltimore Sun*, November, 28, 2002.

27. Tim Craig, "Ehrlich Takes Offensive in Ad on Crime," *Baltimore Sun*, October 25, 2002.

28. Howard Libit, "Ehrlich Edges Past Townsend in New Poll," *Baltimore Sun*, October 30, 2002.

29. Thomas F. Schaller, "Governor Leaves a Big Repair Job," *Baltimore Sun*, November 22, 2002.

30. Edward Ericson Jr., "If Gov. Robert Ehrlich Isn't Who the Sun Says He Is, Then Who Is He?," *City Paper (Baltimore)*, October 25, 2006.

31. Andrew A. Green and David Nitkin, "An Early Edge for Ehrlich's Rivals," *Baltimore Sun*, November 6, 2005.

32. Eric Siegel, "Baltimore, Feel Free to Celebrate Your Election Victory," *Baltimore Sun*, November 16, 2006.

33. Andrew Green and Doug Donovan, "Voters Get Their Turn," *Baltimore Sun*, November 7, 2006.

34. Robert Barnes and Matthew Mosk, "Poll Puts Maryland Democrats in the Lead," *Washington Post*, October 29, 2006; Siegel, "Celebrate Your Election Victory."

35. All copy of Ehrlich's and O'Malley's political commercials are from "Campaign Ad Watch," a presentation and review of television advertising run by the gubernatorial candidates presented in the *Baltimore Sun* during the 2006 campaign from July through the November general election. See, for example, John Fritze, "O'Malley Rebuts Ehrlich Ad: Campaign Ad Watch," *Baltimore Sun*, October 24, 2006; Doug Donovan, "Mayor Focuses on Record: Campaign Ad Watch," *Baltimore Sun*, August 24, 2006; Andrew A. Green, "Ehrlich Focuses on Schools: Campaign Ad Watch," *Baltimore Sun*, August 31, 2006.

36. Matthew Mosk, "With Choice of Gubernatorial Partner, Ehrlich Woos Female Voters," *Washington Post*, June 30, 2006.

37. Ericson, "If Gov. Ehrlich," 25.

38. Green and Donovan, "Voters Get Their Turn."

39. Andrew Green and Doug Donovan, "Two Rivals Clash with Two Styles," *Baltimore Sun*, October 15, 2006.

40. "O'Malley for Governor," editorial endorsement, *Baltimore Sun*, October 29, 2006.

41. Josh Mitchell, "O'Malley Got Boost from Balto. Co. Executive," *Baltimore Sun*, November 11, 2006.

42. John Fritze, "O'Malley Outspent Ehrlich on TV ads," *Baltimore Sun*, November 30, 2006.

43. Ovetta Wiggins and Avis Thomas-Lester, "Misleading GOP Handouts Called a Political Low Point," *Washington Post*, November 8, 2006.

44. Timothy B. Wheeler, "A Win Built in the 'Burbs," *Baltimore Sun*, November 9, 2006.

45. Poll results are from the exit polls conducted by Edison Media Research, as presented in "America Votes 2006," a website maintained by CNN.com at *www.cnn.com/ELECTION/2006/ (accessed February 12, 2007 and June 26, 2008)*.

46. Quoted in Len Lazarick, "How Ehrlich Lost: In the Margins," *Baltimore Examiner*, November 11, 2006.

47. Barnes and Mosk, "Democrats in the Lead."

48. The television commercials for the Democratic ticket during the 2010 gubernatorial election may be viewed on the O'Malley-Brown website, www.martinomalley.com (accessed February 25, 2011).

49. John Wagner, Aaron C. Davis, and Jon Cohen, "Ehrlich's GOP Traction Slipping," *Washington Post*, October 25, 2010; John Wagner and Aaron C. Davis, "Murky Message, Less Money Hurt Ehrlich's Odds," *Washington Post*, November 4, 2010.

50. Annie Linskey, "Sarah Palin Steps into Md. Politics with Endorsement," *Baltimore Sun*, August 4, 2010; John Wagner, "Palin Backs Murphy in GOP Governor's Race, Surprising Mostly Everyone," *Washington Post*, August 5, 2010.

51. Aaron C. Davis and John Wagner, "Where O'Malley Goes, Obama Accolades Flow," *Washington Post*, October 7, 2010; Julie Bykowicz and Annie Linskey, "Obama Hails O'Malley," *Baltimore Sun*, October 8, 2010.

52. Julie Bykowicz and Annie Linskey, "O'Malley Widens Lead over Ehrlich," *Baltimore Sun*, October 23, 2010. The television commercials for Republican candidate Robert Ehrlich may be viewed at www.candidateblogs.baltimoresun.com/bob-ehrlich/ (accessed February 25, 2011).

4. MARYLAND PUBLIC OPINION

G. H. Callcott, "Heritage and Identity," 20.

1. Ronald C. Lippincott and Larry W. Thomas, "Maryland: The Struggle for Power in the Midst of Change, Complexity, and Institutional Constraints," in *Interest Group Politics in the Northeastern States*, ed. Ronald J. Hrebenar and Clive S. Thomas (University Park: Pennsylvania State University Press, 1993), 133.

2. Bernard C. Hennessy, *Public Opinion* (Belmont CA: Wadsworth, 1965), 105.

3. U.S. Bureau of the Census, *Census 2000, Summary File 3, Maryland, Ancestry Profile 1* (Washington DC: Bureau of the Census, 2002).

4. Brugger's epilogue to his masterful history describes the Maryland sensibility, both "democratic and diverse," as something uniquely American. Brugger, *Maryland*, 673–76. See also G. H. Callcott, "Heritage and Identity," 15–23.

5. Don Haynes et al., *Maryland Policy Choices, 1992–1998, 2002–2009* (Baltimore: Schaefer Center for Public Policy, University of Baltimore, 1992–2009).

6. Ronald W. Reagan, First Inaugural Address, January 20, 1981, in *The Inaugural Addresses of the Presidents*, ed. John Gabriel Hunt (New York: Gramercy Books, 2003), 473.

7. Lloyd A. Free and Hadley Cantril, *The Political Beliefs of Americans* (Long Island City NY: Simon and Schuster, 1968), 36.

8. U.S. Department of Justice, Bureau of Justice Statistics, "State Crime Estimates, 1960–2005," www.ojp.usdoj.gov/bjs.

9. Brugger, *Maryland*, 464–65.

10. Mencken, *Impossible H. L. Mencken* 452.

11. Tom Horton, *Bay Country* (Baltimore: Johns Hopkins University Press, 1987), 212.

12. See CNN exit polls conducted by Edison Media Research, as presented in "Election Center 2008," www.cnn.com/ELECTION/2008/results/polls/#MDPoop1 *(accessed on December 17, 2008). See also* Gerald C. Wright Jr., Robert S. Erikson, and John P. McIver, "Measuring State Partisanship and Ideology with Survey Data," *Journal of Politics* 47, no. 2 (1985): 469–89; David Nitkin and JoAnna Daemmrich, "Maryland Voters Strongly behind Kerry, Poll Shows," *Baltimore Sun*, October 28, 2004.

13. Maryland Constitution, Art. XVI, sec. 2.

14. An Act concerning Handguns, Md. Laws 3489, chap. 533 (1988).

15. Karyn Strickler, interview by authors.

16. An Act concerning Abortion, Md. Laws 5, chap. 1 (1991).

5. POLITICAL PARTIES, INTEREST GROUPS, AND CORRUPTION

Paul Winchester, *Men of Maryland Since the Civil War* (Baltimore: Maryland County Press Syndicate, 1923), 20.

1. Willis, *Presidential Elections in Maryland*, 29–30.

2. G. H. Callcott, *Maryland and America*, 133–36. McKeldin was the only Republican governor south of the Mason-Dixon Line during the 1950s. He was accorded the honor of nominating Dwight D. Eisenhower for president at the Republican National Convention in 1952. Senator Mathias was often cited as one of the most liberal Republicans during his congressional service. Senators Sarbanes and Mikulski began their congressional careers upsetting more establishment Democratic opponents in party primary elections.

3. Samuel Eldersveld and Hanes Walton, *Political Parties in American Society*, 2nd ed. (Boston: Bedford/St. Martin's Press, 2000), 125–26.

4. "Elections Article," *Annotated Code of Maryland*, secs. 4-201–203.

5. David Nitkin, "State GOP's two-party bash," *Baltimore Sun*, October 7, 2003.

6. Antero Pietila, "Clubhouses Empty, Political Clout Gone," *Baltimore Sun*, December 14, 2003.

7. Survey data collected by the authors.

8. Brugger, *Maryland*, 134.

9. Van Ness, "Economic Development," 195–96.

10. Brugger, *Maryland*, 322–28.

11. Van Ness, "Economic Development," 199; Bruchey, "Industrialization of Maryland," 455.

12. Brugger, *Maryland*, 580.

13. G. H. Callcott, *Maryland and America*, 181.

14. David Nitkin, "Ehrlich Scolds Businesses for Lack of Lobbying," *Baltimore Sun*, April 23, 2004.

15. Lippincott and Thomas, "Struggle for Power," 138.

16. Lippincott and Thomas, "Struggle for Power," 145.

17. National Center for Public Integrity, "State Lobbying Totals, 2004–2006. Hired Guns: A Comprehensive Look at Lobbying in the 50 States" (Washington DC: National Center for Public Integrity, 2007).

18. State of Maryland, State Ethics Commission, *Twenty-ninth Annual Report*, Annapolis, 2008, appendix D.

19. Lippincott and Thomas, "Struggle for Power," 150.

20. State Ethics Commission, *Twenty-ninth Annual Report*, 8.

21. Quoted in Keith F. Girard, "The Connection Machine," *Warfield's* 4 (May 1989): 85.

22. See L. Harmon Zeigler, "Interest Groups in the States," in *Politics in the American States*, ed. Virginia Gray, Herbert Jacob, and Kenneth Vines (Boston: Little, Brown, 1983), 102; Michael Engel, *State and Local Politics* (New York: St. Martin's Press, 1985), 241.

23. Lippincott and Thomas, "Struggle for Power," 143–46.

24. Lippincott and Thomas, "Struggle for Power," 160.

25. Quoted in Common Cause of Maryland, *Payout 2004* (Washington DC: Common Cause of Maryland, 2005), 39.

26. Lippincott and Thomas, "Struggle for Power," 146–49.

27. M. James Kaufman, "Are All Lobbyists Equal?," unpublished manuscript, July 2002.

28. Alan Rosenthal, *The Third House: Lobbyists and Lobbying in the States* (Washington DC: Congressional Quarterly Press, 1993), 56.

29. Catherine Pierre, "Grassroots Guru," *Johns Hopkins Magazine* 56 (September 2004): 39–44; Michael Pertschuk, *The DeMarco Factor* (Nashville TN: Vanderbilt University Press, 2010).

30. Clive S. Thomas and Ronald J. Hrebenar, "Interest Groups in the States," in

Politics in the American States: A Comparative Analysis, ed. Virginia Gray and Russell Hanson (Washington DC: Congressional Quarterly Press, 1999), 137.

31. Lippincott and Thomas, "Struggle for Power," 157–58.

32. Kaufman, "Are All Lobbyists Equal?," analysis by authors.

33. Betty Zisk, *Local Interest Politics: A Two-Way Street* (Indianapolis IN: Bobbs-Merrill, 1973), 1.

34. Rosenthal, *The Third House*, 208.

35. David Nitkin and Michael Dresser, "Gambling Lobby Led Spending during Session," *Baltimore Sun*, June 3, 2004.

36. Lippincott and Thomas, "Struggle for Power," 163.

37. Jacobs, *Thimbleriggers*, 42.

38. Jacobs, *Thimbleriggers*, 42–43.

39. John Petrie, "Collection of H. L. Mencken's Quotes," University of Georgia, http://jpetrie.myweb.uga.edu/mencken.html *(accessed August 1, 2009).*

40. G. H. Callcott, *Maryland and America*, 296–97.

41. G. H. Callcott, *Maryland and America*, 65.

42. G. H. Callcott, *Maryland and America*, 298.

43. Kaufman, "Are All Lobbyists Equal?," 6.

44. Brugger, *Maryland*, 653.

45. Brugger, *Maryland*, 648.

46. Justin P. Coffey, "Spiro T. Agnew and Middle Ground Politics," *Maryland Historical Magazine* 98 (winter 2003): 441–55.

47. Burdette, "Modern Maryland Politics," 795–96.

48. Jacobs, *Thimbleriggers*, 101.

49. Jacobs, *Thimbleriggers*, 83.

50. Jacobs, *Thimbleriggers*, 207.

51. *U.S. v. Mandel*, 672 F. Supp. 864 (D.Md. 1987), 862 F.2d 1067, cert. den. 491 U.S. 906 (1989), relying on *McNally v. U.S.*, 483 U.S. 350 (1987).

52. Timothy Phelps and Donald Kimmelman, "Hughes Pledges Break with Past in His Inaugural," *Baltimore Sun*, January 18, 1979.

53. Md. Laws 13, chap. 5 (1972), codified in "State Government Article," *Annotated Code of Maryland*, sec. 2-701, et seq.

54. Ryan Davis, "Maryland Is Bullish on Ethics Panels," *Baltimore Sun*, August 1, 2003.

55. Matthew Dolan, "Guilty Plea Seals Bromwell Descent; Former MD. Senator Took Bribes; Helped Firm Gain Contracts," *Baltimore Sun*, July 25, 2007; Philip Rucker, "Former Senator Pleads Guilty to Racketeering," *Washington Post*, July 25, 2007.

56. "Paul Schwartzman and Ovetta Wiggins, From Political Outsider to Gilded Insider," *Washington Post*, June 6, 2011; Ruben Castaneda and Miranda S. Spiv-

ack, "Johnson Admits Accepting Bribes," *Washington Post*, May 18, 2011; and Ian Urbina, "Mayor Agrees to Step Down in Baltimore in Theft Case," *New York Times*, January 7, 2010.

57. Karl Vick, "Md. Lobbyist Avoids Prison in Fraud Case," *Washington Post*, April 22, 1995; Blair Lee IV, "Bruce Bereano's Best Little Whorehouse in Maryland," *Montgomery Journal*, April 25, 1995.

58. *U.S. v. Bereano*, 161 F.3d 3 (4th Cir. 1998) (table decision), cert den. 526 U.S. 1130 (1999); Ruben Castaneda, "Md. Lobbyist Resentenced to Halfway House; Bereano Also Gets Home Detention," *Washington Post*, December 5, 1998.

59. *Attorney Grievance Commission v. Bereano*, 357 Md. 321 (2000); Daniel LeDuc, "Lining Up for Lobbyist: Political Heavyweights Pleading Bereano's Case in Md. Disbarment Hearing," *Washington Post*, September 22, 1999.

60. Thomas W. Waldron, "Evans Gets 2½ Years for Fraud: Judge, Defendant Agree on Need for Reform in Annapolis," *Baltimore Sun*, September 30, 2000; "'Culture of Corruption' in General Assembly Lobbyist Jailed," editorial, *Baltimore Sun*, October 3, 2000.

61. Md. Laws 1571, 1607, chaps. 129,130 (1999); Md Laws 3394, chap. 631 (2001). For an explanation of these restrictions, see State of Maryland, State Ethics Commission, *Twenty-third Annual Report*, Annapolis, 2001, 7–10. For an example of critical media coverage, see Thomas W. Waldron, "Ways of Lobbyists Exposed—Again," *Baltimore Sun*, July 16, 2000.

62. *State Ethics Commission v. Evans*, 382 Md. 370 (2004); Michael Dresser, "Lobbyist Convicted of Fraud Allowed to Continue Career," *Baltimore Sun*, July 31, 2004.

63. *Bereano v. State Ethics Commission*, 403 Md. 716 (2008). See Michael Dresser, "Pact May Be Ethics Breach," *Baltimore Sun*, June 13, 2002; Michael Dresser, "Bereano's Contract Dismays Lawmakers," *Baltimore Sun*, June 14, 2002.

64. Jeff Barker and Michael Dresser, "Lobbyists Not Hobbled by Reforms," *Baltimore Sun*, June 2, 2001.

65. Lori Montgomery, "Md. Sunshine Law at Issue," *Washington Post*, November 8, 2003; "A Poor Choice," editorial, *Baltimore Sun*, February 24, 2003; David Nitkin, "Ehrlich Names Mandel to Md. Board of Regents," *Baltimore Sun*, February 21, 2003.

66. Stephanie Desmon, Tim Craig, and Ivan Penn, "Mitchell IV Forced to Quit $92,000-a-year Md. Housing Job," *Baltimore Sun*, February 25, 2003; "Fire Mitchell," editorial, *Baltimore Sun*, February 16, 2003.

6. THE MARYLAND CONSTITUTION

John P. Wheeler Jr. and Melissa Kinsey, *Magnificent Failure: The Maryland Constitutional Convention of 1967–1968*, State Constitutional Convention Studies, 3 (New York: National Municipal League, 1970), iv.

1. Daniel J. Elazar, "The Principles and Traditions Underlying State Constitutions," *Publius* 12 (winter 1982): 11–25.

2. The numbering of articles in the declaration of rights extends to forty-seven (47), but Article 38, requiring state approval of property transfers to religious entities, was repealed and is listed as vacant. Acts of 1947, chap. 623 (ratified November 2, 1948).

3. The numbering of articles in the Constitution of Maryland extends to XXIX, but Article X is designated as vacant. It provided for a superintendent of labor and agriculture to be elected only for a single term of four years unless extended by the general assembly, which was not done.

4. Acts of 2007 special session, chap. 5 (ratified November 4, 2008).

5. Aubrey C. Land, *Colonial Maryland: A History* (Millwood NY: Kraus International Publishers, 1981); Skaggs, *Roots of Maryland Democracy*.

6. For a complete text of the original Maryland Declaration of Independence, see *Proceedings of the Convention of the Province of Maryland Held in the City of Annapolis in 1774, 1775, and 1776* (Jonas Green, 1836). The origin of the Maryland Declaration of Rights is discussed in Dan Friedman, "The History, Development, and Interpretation of the Maryland Declaration of Rights," 71 *Temple Law Review* 637 (1998). See also John C. Rainbolt, "A Note on the Declaration of Rights and the Constitution of 1776," *Maryland Historical Magazine* 66 (winter 1971): 420.

7. *Proceedings of the Convention*, 220.

8. For a description of the convention debates, see Andrews, *History of Maryland*, 327–32; Edward C. Papenfuse and Gregory A. Stiverson, eds., *The Decisive Blow Is Struck: A Facsimile Edition of the Proceedings of the Constitutional Convention Proceedings 1776 and the First Maryland Constitution* (Annapolis MD: Hall of Records Commission, Department of General Services, 1977), 1–7.

9. The drafting committee appointed by the constitutional convention were George Plater, chair of the convention, Charles Carroll (barrister), Charles Carroll of Carrollton, Samuel Chase, Robert Goldsborough, William Paca, and Matthew Tilghman. Thomas Johnson, Maryland's first state governor, later joined the committee.

10. 1776 Maryland Constitution, sec. 15.

11. James Madison, *The Federalist Papers, No. 63* (New York: Bantam Books, 1982), 323–24.

12. 1776 Maryland Constitution, sec. 59.

13. James H. F. Brewer, "The Democratization of Maryland, 1800–1837," in *Old Line State: A History of Maryland*, ed. Morris L. Radoff (Annapolis: Hall of Records Commission, State of Maryland, 1971), 49–66; Bernard C. Steiner, *Citizenship and Suffrage in Maryland* (Baltimore: Cushing, 1895), 29–30;

Thorton Anderson, "18th Century Suffrage: The Case of Maryland," *Maryland Historical Magazine* 76 (summer 1981): 141–58.

14. Chap. 20, Laws of Maryland, 1802; chap. 33, Laws of Maryland, 1810.

15. For a discussion of the efforts of the Whig state senate electors, see Andrews, *History of Maryland*, 462–64; Carl N. Everstine, *The General Assembly of Maryland: 1776–1850* (Charlottesville VA: Michie, 1982), 453–97; W. W. Smith, "Politics and Democracy," 273–79.

16. State of Maryland, Constitutional Convention Commission, *Report to the Governor of Maryland, the General Assembly of Maryland and the People of Maryland*, Annapolis, 1967, 40–41.

17. *Maryland Committee for Fair Representation v. Tawes*, 377 U.S. 656 (1964).

18. George L. Radcliffe, *Governor Thomas Holiday Hicks and the Civil War* (1907; reprint, Baltimore: Johns Hopkins University Press, 1965).

19. Willis, *Presidential Elections in Maryland*, 65–66.

20. Baker, *The Politics of Continuity*, 195.

21. There have been two proposed amendments that passed the general assembly but were not placed on the ballot for consideration by the voters: Md. Laws 1123, chap. 547 (1916), which provided for changing the term of county sheriffs from two years to four years; and Md. Laws 979, chap. 348 (1929), which provided for an increase in the compensation of members of the general assembly. The term of the county sheriff was subsequently increased to four years by a constitutional amendment ratified in 1946 (Acts of 1945, chap. 786). After defeats of proposed constitutional amendments in 1934 and 1939 an increase in compensation for the members of the general assembly was approved by voters in 1942 (Acts of 1941, chap. 695).

22. Although passed by Maryland voters in 1915, it was not until 1948 that Montgomery County became the first county to take advantage of the opportunity to establish a charter and gain home rule over local matters.

23. An amendment to establish an independent compensation commission for the Maryland General Assembly was ratified by the voters in 1970 (Acts of 1970, chap. 543 amending section 15, article III), and a salary commission for the governor and lieutenant governor was ratified in 1976 (Acts of 1976, chap. 543, amending section 21, article II).

24. Maryland Constitution, art. XIV, sec. 2.

25. *Board of Supervisors of Elections for Anne Arundel County v. Attorney General of Maryland*, 248 Md. 417 (1967).

26. The constitutional convention commission produced a substantial body of work that was deposited in the Enoch Pratt Free Library in Baltimore, the University of Maryland library, the Maryland State Library in Annapolis, and the Johns Hopkins University library. *The Report of the Constitutional Convention Commission* was published by the State of Maryland in a bound volume printed by

King Brothers of Baltimore, dated August 25, 1967. A larger, separate volume of *Constitutional Revision Study Documents* was published on June 15, 1968.

27. "Arrogance in Maryland," editorial, *Washington Post*, October 13, 1967.
28. Dan Friedman, "Magnificent Failure Revisited: Modern Maryland Constitutional Law from 1967 to 1998," 58 *Maryland Law Review* 528 (1999); Dan Friedman, *The Maryland State Constitution: A Reference Guide* (Westport CT: Praeger, 2006), 9–10.

7. THE MARYLAND GENERAL ASSEMBLY

1. Alan Rosenthal, *Heavy Lifting: The Job of the American Legislature* (Washington DC: CQ Press, 2004), 2.
2. Carl N. Everstine, *The General Assembly of Maryland: 1634–1776* (Charlottesville VA: Mitchie, 1980), 39.
3. Everstine, *General Assembly 1634–1776*, 48.
4. Madison, *Federalist Papers No. 63*.
5. Burdette, "Modern Maryland Politics," 852.
6. G. H. Callcott, *Maryland and America*, 227.
7. Rosenthal, *Heavy Lifting*, 172.
8. Brugger, *Maryland*, 630.
9. G. H. Callcott, *Maryland and America*, 227.
10. William S. James, "Recollections of William S. James" (unpublished), quoted in Department of Legislative Services, *Under the Dome: The Maryland General Assembly in the 20th Century* (Annapolis MD: Department of Legislative Services, 2001), 4.
11. Quoted in "Recollections of William S. James," 8.
12. G. H. Callcott, *Maryland and America*, 227.
13. See George Stockton Wills II, "The Reorganization of the Maryland General Assembly, 1966–1968: A Study of the Politics of Reform" (PhD diss., Johns Hopkins University, 1969); Alan Rosenthal, *Strengthening the Maryland Legislature: An Eagleton Study and Report* (New Brunswick NJ: Rutgers University Press, 1968).
14. Rosenthal, *Strengthening the Maryland Legislature*, 170–71.
15. Council of State Governments, *Book of States: 2008*, 97–99.
16. Council of State Governments, *Book of States: 2008*, 100–104.
17. National Conference of State Legislatures, www.ncsl.org/ncsldb/elect98/partcomp.cfm?yearsel=2004 (accessed January 22, 2006).
18. National Conference of State Legislatures, www.ncsl.org/programs/legismgt/about/legislator_overview.htm (accessed August 1, 2005).
19. *In re Legislative Districting of the State*, 370 Md. 312 (2002); *In re Legislative Districting*, 331 Md. 574, 614 (1993).

20. David Nitkin and Michael Dresser, "Court Revises Political Map: City Loses Seats, Influence; Baltimore County Gains," *Baltimore Sun*, June 22, 2002.

21. Center for American Women and Politics, National Conference of State Legislatures, www.ncsl.ors/wln/womenInOffice2006.htm and www.ncsl.org/programs/legismgt/about.afrAmermain.htm.

22. Alan Rosenthal, *Legislative Life: People, Process, and Performance in the States* (New York: Harper and Row, 1981), 126.

23. Rosenthal, *Heavy Lifting*, 19.

24. Department of Legislative Services, Maryland General Assembly, "2006 Membership Profile," Annapolis, 2006.

25. Samuel I. (Sandy) Rosenberg, unpublished legislative diary, January 22, 2003. Delegate Rosenberg currently represents the Forty-first Legislative District in Baltimore City. He has been a member of the Maryland House of Delegates since 1983.

26. Rosenthal, *Heavy Lifting*, 22.

27. Rosenthal, *Heavy Lifting*, 80.

28. The ten "inner circle" members include the house of delegates party leaders, the president pro tem, and committee chairs. The "outer circle" members include committee vice chairs and selected delegation leaders and veteran delegates.

29. Alan Rosenthal, *Governors and Legislators: Contending Powers* (Washington DC: CQ Press, 1990), 43.

30. Rosenberg diary, February 11, 2003.

31. State Senator George W. Della Jr., personal interview. Senator Della represented the Forty-sixth Legislative District, located in Baltimore City. He had been a member of the Maryland General State Senate since 1983 and previously served on the Baltimore City Council from 1976 to 1983.

32. "State Finance and Procurement Article," *Annotated Code of Maryland*, secs. 8-104–8-116.

33. *Bayne v. Secretary of State*, 283 Md. 560 (1978).

34. Rosenberg diary, January 13, 2005.

35. Rosenthal, *Heavy Lifting*, 180.

36. Andrew Green, "Legislators Override 6 More Vetoes, Bringing Total to 13," *Baltimore Sun*, January 20, 2006.

37. Michael Olesker, "Ehrlich Took Slots Plan and Fumbled It for a Loss," *Baltimore Sun*, April 8, 2003.

38. Michael Dresser and Greg Garland, "Slots Effort Seen Losing Ground in Assembly," *Baltimore Sun*, March 7, 2003.

39. Stephanie Desmon, Tim Craig, and Ivan Penn, "Mitchell IV Forced to Quit $92,000-a-year Md. Housing Job," *Baltimore Sun*, February 25, 2003.

40. David Nitkin, "Beaches, Woods, Parks Up for Sale," *Baltimore Sun*, November 18, 2004.

41. John Wagner and Matthew Mosk, "Democrats Approve Agenda in Final Push," *Washington Post*, April 12, 2005. See *Schisler v. State of Maryland*, 394 Md. 519 (2006)(challenge to legislative reconstituting Public Service Commission); *Lamone v. Capozzi*, 396 Md. 53 (2006)(challenge to early voting procedures passed by legislature).

42. C. Fraser Smith, "Muddling Through in This New Age of Partisanship," *Baltimore Sun*, December 21, 2003.

43. Howard Libit and Greg Garland, "Democrats Cry Foul over GOP Tactic," *Baltimore Sun*, March 16, 2004.

44. *Smigiel v. Franchot*, 410 Md 302 (2009).

45. Quoted in Matthew Mosk, "Ehrlich Warns Democrats on Questioning Integrity," *Washington Post*, July 24, 2005.

8. THE MARYLAND GOVERNOR AND THE EXECUTIVE BRANCH

Charles James Rohr, *The Governor of Maryland: A Constitutional Study* (Baltimore: Johns Hopkins University Press, 1932), 164.

1. See Thad Beyle, "The Governors," in *Politics in the American States: A Comparative Analysis*, 8th ed., ed. Virginia Gray and Russell Hansen (Washington DC: CQ Press, 2003); Robert Jay Dilger, "A Comparative Analysis of Gubernatorial Enabling Resources," *State and Local Government Review* 27, no. 2 (1995): 118–26.

2. Maryland Constitution, art. II, sec. 5.

3. Maryland Constitution, art. II, sec. 1 and sec. 10A.

4. For background on the economic, social, and political environment in Maryland before and after statehood, see Walsh, "The Era of Revolution," 55–80; Skaggs, *Roots of Maryland Democracy*; Ronald Hoffman, *A Spirit of Dissension: Economics, Politics and the Revolution of Maryland*, Maryland Bicentennial Studies (Baltimore: Johns Hopkins University Press, 1974); Philip A. Crowl, *Maryland during and after the Revolution* (Baltimore: Johns Hopkins University Press, 1943); Charles A. Barker, "The Revolutionary Impulse in Maryland," *Maryland Historical Magazine* 100 (summer 2005): 261–71.

5. 1776 Maryland Constitution, sec. 26.

6. 1776 Maryland Constitution, secs. 20–23; Acts of 1836, chap. 197, ratified and confirmed on February 13, 1838; Acts of 1838, chap. 84. For accounts of the political machinations leading to the popularly elected governor, see Bernard C. Steiner, "The Electoral College for the Senate of Maryland and the Nineteen Van Buren Electors," in *American Historical Association Annual Report for 1895* (Washington DC: Government Printing Office, 1896), 150–51; A. Clarke Hagensick, "Revolution or Reform in 1836: Maryland Preface to the Dorr Rebellion," *Maryland Historical Magazine* 57 (December 1962): 346–66.

7. For a journalistic account of the state party politics from the Civil War through the Age of Reform, see Kent, *Story of Maryland Politics*.

8. For a description of the work of the Goodnow Commission with relevant period citations, see Rohr, *Governor of Maryland*, 148–54.

9. Emerson C. Harrington, Comptroller's Office, *Annual Report of the Comptroller of Maryland to the General Assembly for the Fiscal Year Ended September 30, 1913*, Baltimore, 1913, v–xv.

10. Acts of 1916, chap. 159 (ratified November 7, 1916).

11. For an account of Ritchie's efforts to reorganize the executive branch of Maryland state government, see Rohr, *Governor of Maryland*, 124–34.

12. Letter of transmittal from John N. Curlett, chairman, to Governor J. Millard Tawes, accompanying *The Report of the Commission for the Modernization of the Executive Branch of the Maryland Government*, Baltimore, January 10, 1967.

13. *Report of the Constitutional Convention Commission* (Baltimore: King Brothers, August 25, 1967), 147–74; Constitutional Convention Commission of Maryland, *Constitutional Revision Study Documents* (Baltimore: King Brothers, 1968), 151–86.

14. Acts of 1947, chap. 109 (ratified November 2, 1948).

15. Acts of 1959, chap. 604 (ratified November 8, 1960).

16. Acts of 1995, chap. 114 (ratified November 5, 1996).

17. *Report of the Governor's Salary Commission*, Annapolis, January 2006, 2, 40. See also Council of State Governments, *Survey of State Government Finances*, February 2007.

18. "State Financial and Procurement Article," *Annotated Code of Maryland*, sec. 7-213 (Michie, 2006).

19. Maryland Constitution, art. III, sec. 4.

20. Acts of 1970, chap. 532 (ratified November 3, 1970).

21. Harry Roe Hughes with John W. Frece, *My Unexpected Journey: The Autobiography of Harry Roe Hughes* (Charleston SC: History Press, 2006), 129–30, 138–39.

22. 1851 Maryland Constitution, art. VI, sec. 2.

23. For a summary of the accomplishments of Comptroller Louis L. Goldstein, see Office of Comptroller, *Annual Report of the Comptroller for Fiscal Year 1998*, Annapolis, 1998.

24. *Abrams v. Lamone*, 394 Md. 305 (2006).

25. Maryland Constitution, art. II, secs. 22–23.

26. For a description of the prior experience of the nation's governors, see Larry Sabato, *Goodbye to Good-Time Charlie*, 2nd ed. (Washington DC: CQ Press, 1983), 33–40; Rosenthal, *Governors and Legislatures*, 20–21; Beyle, "Governors: Elections," 145–49.

27. At the special session of the Maryland General Assembly held on January 7, 1969, the votes to succeed Spiro Agnew as governor were cast as follows: 123 for Marvin Mandel; twenty-six for Rogers C. B. Morton, then a Republican congressman representing the First Congressional District; fifteen for Francis X. Gallagher, then a member of the house of delegates from Baltimore City; and thirteen for William S. James, then president of the state senate. Maryland General Assembly, *Journal of Proceedings of the House of Delegates*, special sess., January 7, 1969, 87. This vote reflected not only the partisan division between Democrats and Republicans but also an ideological divide among Democrats that has continued for over forty years.

28. Rosenthal, *Governors and Legislatures*, 68; Edward J. Miller, "Gubernatorial Support in a State Legislature: The Case of Maryland," paper delivered at the annual meeting of the American Political Science Association, San Francisco, September 2–5, 1975, 19.

29. See Governor's Commission on the Modernization of the Executive Branch of State Government, *Modernizing the Executive Branch*, Annapolis, 1967; Constitutional Convention Commission of Maryland, *Report of the Constitutional Convention Commission* (1967); Constitutional Convention Commission of Maryland, *Constitutional Revision Study Documents*, (1968), 151–86; Commission on Executive Reorganization, *Executive Reorganization: A Comprehensive Plan for Maryland* (1969).

30. G. H. Callcott, *Maryland and America*, 289. Notwithstanding personal travails resulting from his federal indictment in November 1975, Mandel relished being a part of rallying his supporters to hand Jimmy Carter a popular electoral defeat in the Maryland primary held on May 18, 1976, by supporting the late candidacy of Jerry Brown.

31. Bentley Orrick, "Mandel Gets Re-election Head Start: Affair at Civic Center Raises Record $1 Million, Cornering Money Market for Mandel Re-election," *Baltimore Sun*, May 23, 1973; Richard M. Cohen, "Mandel Near $1 Million for Campaign: 8,000 at Baltimore Party Contribute $750,000," *Washington Post*, May 23, 1973.

32. For an account of this part of the Mandel era, see G. H. Callcott, *Maryland and America*, 289–93.

33. G. H. Callcott, *Maryland and America*, 293–96. See also Richard M. Cohen and Jules Witcover, *A Heartbeat Away: Of Vice President Spiro T. Agnew* (New York: Viking, 1974), 7, 61.

34. The legal history and trial evidence are reviewed in "United States v. Mandel: The Mail Fraud and En Banc Procedural Issues," 40 *Maryland Law Review* 550 (1981). See also *U.S. v. Mandel*, 602 F.2d 653 (4th Cir. 1979) (en banc) cert. denied 445 U.S. 696 (1980); Jacobs, *Thimbleriggers*.

35. G. H. Callcott, *Maryland and America*, 296.
36. A brief account of this protest may be found in Alan M. Wilner, *The Maryland Board of Public Works: A History* (Annapolis MD: Hall of Records Commission 1984), 113–15. See also Hughes, *My Unexpected Journey*, 111–17.
37. See the official biography of Harry Hughes in *Maryland Manual: 1985–1986* (Annapolis: Maryland State Archives, 1985), 19.
38. The landmark environmental legislation of the Hughes administration was titled the Chesapeake Bay Critical Area Protection Program and is codified in "Natural Resources Article," *Annotated Code of Maryland*, secs. 8-1801–1817.
39. Wilbur D. Preston Jr., *Report of the Special Counsel on the Savings and Loan Crises*, presented to the Maryland General Assembly, State of Maryland, January 8, 1986; John W. Frece, "Banking Crisis Perils Political Reputations," *Baltimore Sun*, May 19, 1985.
40. "Governor William Donald Schaefer," *Baltimore Magazine*, May 17, 1987, 25.
41. C. Fraser Smith, *William Donald Schaefer: A Political Biography* (Baltimore: Johns Hopkins University Press, 1999).
42. See the official biography of William Donald Schaefer in *Maryland Manual: 1994–1995* (Annapolis MD: State Archives, 1994), 27–28.
43. Fern Shen, "Schaefer Assailed for Shore Remark," *Washington Post*, February 5, 1991; "Schaefer Comment Annoys Lawmakers," *Washington Post*, February 3, 1991; C. F. Smith, *A Political Biography*, 310–22.
44. Peter Jensen, "Schaefer Buries Hatchet with Shore Legislators", *Baltimore Sun*, February 4, 1991; John Roll, "A Contrite Schaefer Apologizes to the Eastern Shore," *Baltimore Sun*, February 12, 1991.
45. Howard Schneider and Fern Shen, "Acid in Schaefer's Pen Makes Some Fear What's in His Head," *Washington Post*, February 10, 1991; Roger Simon, "Schaefer's 'Not Nuts,' but Finds Much in Maryland to Fault," *Baltimore Sun*, March 25, 1991; Thomas W. Waldron, "Schaefer Sends Critic a Bizarre Greeting," *Baltimore Evening Sun*, December 20, 1991.
46. For job performance ratings throughout Governor Schaefer's tenure, see "Maryland Poll," by Mason-Dixon Political/Media Research, Inc., as displayed in the *Baltimore Sun*, January 11, 1995, and in the *Washington Post*, January 17, 1995.
47. John W. Frece, "Schaefer Spurns Democrats, Backs Bush," *Baltimore Sun*, October 30, 1992; Richard Tapscott, "Gov. Schaefer Throws Support to Bush: Md. Democrats Call Cross-Party Endorsement 'Regrettable,' 'Sad,'" *Washington Post*, October 31, 1992; John W. Frece, "Schaefer Spared Party's Scolding," *Baltimore Sun*, November 8, 1992; Richard Tapscott, "Uncensored Schaefer Is Uncensured: Top Democrat Survives His Backing of Bush," *Washington Post*, November 8, 1992.

48. William Thompson, "The Schaefer Style: Tantrums Seen Used as Management Tool," *Baltimore Sun*, July 20, 1990; Peter Carlson, "King Crab: Why Is William Donald Schaefer So Cranky?," *Washington Post Magazine*, January 10, 1993.

49. Melody Simmons and Nicholas Sohr, "Baltimore Says Goodbye to William Donald Schaefer," *Daily Record*, April 25, 2011; Michael Dresser, "William Donald Schaefer, Governor and Mayor, Dies," *Baltimore Sun*, April 19, 2011; Adam Bernstein, "William Donald Schaefer Dies at 89: Maryland Governor, Baltimore Mayor Had Trademark Style," *Washington Post*, April 18, 2011; and C. Fraser Smith and Melody Simmons, "William Donald Schaefer: 1921–2011," *Daily Record*, April 18, 2011.

50. Edward Gunts, "Schaefer Leaves His Mark—and Name," *Baltimore Sun*, July 23, 1994.

51. *Sauerbrey v. State Administrative Board of Election Laws*, Circuit Court for Anne Arundel County, January 13, 1995; Thomas W. Waldron and Michael James, "Judge Rejects Vote Challenge by Sauerbrey," *Baltimore Sun*, January 14, 1995; David Montgomery, "Sauerbrey's Bid to Overturn Md. Vote Rejected by Judge," *Washington Post*, January 14, 1995.

52. John W. Frece, "Schaefer's Parting Shot: A Symbolic Budget; Glendening's Leaner Plan to Prevail," *Baltimore Sun*, December 15, 1994; Fern Shen, "Bowing Out Unbowed: In Final Days, Schaefer's Busy Shepherding Projects, Spending Surplus," *Washington Post*, January 13, 1995.

53. See Frank Langfitt and Thomas W. Waldron, "Glendening Aides Get Special Pension," *Baltimore Sun*, January 28, 1995; "Glendening Forgoes Early P.G. Pension," *Washington Post*, January 31, 1995; John W. Frece, "Glendening Revelations Raise Credibility Questions," *Baltimore Sun*, February 26, 1995.

54. Ann O'M. Bowman and Richard C. Kearney, *State and Local Government*, 6th ed. (Boston: Houghton Mifflin, 2005), 328–29.

55. Maryland Gun Violence Act of 1996, Md. Laws 3139, chap. 561 (1996); Responsible Gun Safety Act of 2000, Md. Laws 6, chap. 2 (2000).

56. Jon Jeter, "Md. Shields Jobs from Welfare Law," *Washington Post*, May 4, 1997.

57. AntiDiscrimination Act of 2001, Md. Laws 2112, chap. 340 (2001).

58. Josh Kurtz, "The Capital Report," *Montgomery Gazette*, July 11, 1997; "Changing Political Persona," editorial, *Baltimore Sun*, October 8, 2000.

59. Office of Governor, "Governor Ehrlich Outlines FY '05 Legislative Initiatives," news release, January 22, 2004.

60. "Pound Foolish," editorial, *Baltimore Sun*, August 29, 2005; "Surpluses and Luck," editorial, *Washington Post*, July 24, 2005; "What Surplus?," editorial, *Washington Post*, July 20, 2005.

61. "State Budget Baloney," editorial, *Baltimore Sun*, November 3, 2006; Maryland Department of Legislative Services, *Issue Papers: 2008 Legislative Session*, Annapolis, December 2007, 5.

62. *Ehrlich v. Perez*, 394 Md. 691 (2006).

63. Andrew A. Green, "Potential Land Sale by State Criticized," *Baltimore Sun*, October 1, 2004; Matthew Mosk, "Md. Builder Backs Off St. Mary's Land Deal," *Washington Post*, November 9, 2004.

64. David Nitken, "Ehrlich Calls Multiculturalism 'Bunk,' 'Damaging to Society,'" *Baltimore Sun*, May 9, 2004.

65. Lena H. Sun and Matthew Mosk, "Ehrlich's Hirings, Firings Reached Deep in Ranks," *Washington Post*, June 19, 2005. See also Matthew Mosk, "Ehrlich Staffer Endorsed Firing," *Washington Post*, September 23, 2005; Larry Carson, "Ex–State Worker Sues Ehrlich Administration," *Baltimore Sun*, January 20, 2006.

66. Special Interim Committee on State Employee Rights and Responsibilities, *Report to Maryland General Assembly*, Annapolis, 2006. The recommendations of this committee resulted in the passage of the State Employees' Rights and Protection Act of 2007, Md. Laws 3799, chap. 592 (2007).

67. Daniel LeDuc, "Leaders of Md. GOP Preach Unity," *Washington Post*, December 9, 2001.

68. Robert L. Ehrlich Jr., "What We've Achieved in Maryland," *Washington Post*, April 27, 2005; Earl Kelly, "Ehrlich's To-do List Is Long at Midterm," *The Capital*, December 12, 2004; Robert L. Ehrlich Jr., "A Loser for Maryland: Busch's Push for Higher Taxes," *Washington Times*, April 5, 2004.

69. Letters from the executive, Governor Robert L. Ehrlich Jr., to the president of the senate and speaker of house, May 26, 2006.

70. Acts of 2005, chap. 617 (ratified November 7, 2006).

71. Stephen Kiehl, "Two Sun Journalists Target of Ban," *Baltimore Sun*, November 20, 2004; "Shooting Messengers," editorial, *Baltimore Sun*, November 23, 2004. The *Baltimore Sun*'s lawsuit seeking to overturn Governor Ehrlich's action was unsuccessful. See *The Baltimore Sun Co. v. Ehrlich*, 437 F.2d 410 (C.A. 4th, 2006).

72. Justin Fenton, "Tone Changes in Annapolis," *Baltimore Sun*, February 1, 2007.

73. E. J. Dionne, "A Governor Unafraid of Government," *Washington Post*, November 23, 2007.

74. Jonathan Walter, "Public Officials of the Year: Driven by Data," *Governing*, November 2009, 32.

75. Quoted in John Wagner, "O'Malley Victories Come at a Price," *Washington Post*, April 9, 2008.

76. Associated Press, "Observers: O'Malley Opposition to Death Penalty a Smart Move," *Carroll County Times*, March 13, 2007.

77. Maryland League of Conservation Voters, "Gubernatorial Mid-Term Report Card: Governor O'Malley Earns A–for Environmental Record," news release, July 22, 2008.

78. *Education Week's Quality Counts, 2010 Report* (Washington DC: National Center for Education Information, 2010).

79. Aaron C. Davis, "NEA Names O'Malley Education Governor of the Year," *Washington Post*, June 30, 2010.

9. THE MARYLAND JUDICIARY

This quotation comes from a speech titled "The Sword and the Robe" *that* Justice Marshall made to the second circuit judicial conference on May 8, 1981.

1. *Bell v. State*, 227 Md. 302, (1962); *rev'd.* 378 U.S. 226 (1964).

2. Michael Abramowitz and Saundra Torry, "For First Time, a Black Judge Heads Maryland High Court," *Washington Post*, October 24, 1996. For a profile of Chief Judge Bell, see Wil S. Hylton, "Burden of Proof," *Baltimore Magazine*, March 1997, 47.

3. U.S. Supreme Court justices from Maryland have been Thomas Johnson (1791–93), Samuel Chase (1796–1811), Gabriel Duvall (1811–35), Roger Brooke Taney (1836–64), and Thurgood G. Marshall (1967–91). Attorneys general have been William Pinkney (1812–14), William Wirt (1831–33), Roger Brooke Taney (1831–33), John Nelson (1843–45), Reverdy Johnson (1849–50), and Charles J. Bonaparte (1906–9). Solicitors general have been Philip B. Perlman (1947–52), Simon E. Sobeloff (1954–56), and Thurgood G. Marshall (1965–67).

4. For an overview of the early Maryland courts, see Carroll T. Bond, *Proceedings of the Maryland Court of Appeals: 1695–1729* (Washington DC: American Historical Society, 1933; reprint, Millwood NY: Kraus, 1975); Elbert M. Byrd Jr., *The Judicial Process in Maryland* (College Park: Bureau of Governmental Research, University of Maryland, 1961), 1–17.

5. 1776 Maryland Constitution, sec. 56.

6. Acts of 1804, chap. 55, ratified in the succeeding general assembly session on January 25, 1806, as Acts of 1805, chap. 65.

7. See Acts of 1963, chap. 744 (ratified November 3, 1964), pertaining to Montgomery County; Acts of 1972, chap. 374 (ratified November 7, 1972), pertaining to Harford County. In these two counties the duties of the orphans' court are handled by their respective circuit courts.

8. See Harry W. Kirwan, *The Inevitable Success: A Biography of Herbert R. O'Conor* (Westminster MD: Newman Press, 1962), 369–81. See also Morris A. Soper, "Reorganization of the Court of Appeals," 8 *Maryland Law Review* 91–119 (1944).

9. Acts of 1965, chap. 773 (ratified November 8, 1966); Acts of 1974, chap. 886 (ratified November 5, 1974). The powers, duties, and responsibilities of the

commission on judicial disabilities are set forth in the "Courts and Judicial Proceedings Article," *Annotated Code of Maryland*, secs. 13-401–403.

10. Acts of 1976, chap. 542 (ratified November 2, 1976).

11. Acts of 1980, chap. 523 (ratified November 4, 1980).

12. For example, compare Governor Glendening's Executive Order 01.01.1999.08 with Governor Ehrlich's Executive Order 01.01.2003.09 and Governor O'Malley's Executive Order 01.01.2007.08. See also Editorial Advisory Board, "Protecting the Public's Faith in Judicial Selection," *Daily Record*, June 13, 2008.

13. Administrative Office of the Courts, *Maryland Judiciary: Annual Statistical Abstract, Fiscal Year 2010*, Annapolis, 2011, table DC-2.

14. Administrative Office of the Courts, *Maryland Judiciary*, table CC-1.2.

15. Maryland Constitution, art. IV, sec. 14A.

16. The jurisdiction of the court of special appeals is codified in "Courts and Judicial Proceedings Article," *Annotated Code of Maryland*, sec. 12-308.

17. Informative works on the history and work of the Maryland Court of Appeals are Carroll T. Bond, *The Court of Appeals of Maryland: A History* (Baltimore: Barton-Gillet, 1928); William L. Reynolds II, "The Court of Appeals of Maryland: Roles, Work and Performance," 37 *Maryland Law Review* 1 (1977); Dennis M. Sweeney, "The Murphy Years: A View from the Trial Court," 56 *Maryland Law Review* 636 (1997); Alan M. Wilner, "A Humble Giant," 56 *Maryland Law Review* 631 (1997). The *Maryland Law Review* has regularly published a review of the decisions of the court of appeals since 1975.

18. Acts of 1960, chap. 11 (ratified November 18, 1960) increased the number of judges on the court of appeals from five to seven, increased the number of appellate circuits from five to six, modified the placement of counties within judicial appellate circuits, and granted Baltimore City two judges in the new sixth appellate circuit.

19. Acts of 1975, chap. 551 (ratified November 2, 1976).

20. Maryland Constitution, art. III, sec. 5.

21. The jurisdiction of the court of appeals is codified in "Courts and Judicial Proceedings Article," *Annotated Code of Maryland*, sec. 12-307. See also William L. Reynolds, "The Court of Appeals of Maryland: Roles, Work and Performance," 37 *Maryland Law Review* 1 (1977).

22. In the nineteenth century the orphans' courts played an instrumental role in sustaining various forms of indentured labor during the long transition from a slave economy. Even after the abolition of slavery the powers of the court were dubiously and shamefully used to keep black Marylanders in various forms of servitude. See T. Stephen Whitson, "Manumission and Apprenticeship in Maryland, 1770–1870," *Maryland Historical Magazine* 101 (2006): 55–71.

23. The composition and duties of the Maryland Tax Court are detailed in "Tax General Article," *Annotated Code of Maryland*, secs. 3-101–113.

24. The jurisdiction and authority of the Board of Contract Appeals is set forth in "State Government Article," *Annotated Code of Maryland*, secs. 15-205–212.

25. The Office of Administrative Hearings is codified in "State Government Article," *Annotated Code of Maryland*, secs. 9-1601–1610.

26. Administrative Office, "Maryland Judiciary at a Glance," *Statistical Digest, Fiscal Year 2008*.

27. Acts of 1980, chap. 717 (ratified November 4, 1980). The judicial compensation commission is codified in the "Courts and Judicial Proceedings Article," *Annotated Code of Maryland*, sec. 1-708, et seq. Under the state law, members of the judiciary receive the same percentage cost-of-living increase granted to all state employees but need specific legislative approval for general salary increases. Section 1-(703(b), "Courts and Judicial Proceedings Article," *Annotated Code of Maryland*.

28. Maryland Constitution, art. IV, sec. 4.

29. Maryland Constitution, art. III, sec. 26.

30. Maryland Constitution, art. IV, secs. 4A and 4B.

31. Acts of 1996, chap. 113 (ratified November 5, 1996).

32. Acts of 1975, chap. 551 (ratified November 2, 1976).

33. "Sitting Judges Face Challengers in Five Circuits in September Primary," *Bar Bulletin* (Maryland State Bar Association Newsletter), August 15, 2006. See also the Maryland Judicial Campaign Conduct Committee, Inc. website, www.mdjcc.org/home.html (accessed July 1, 2008).

34. Commission on the Future of Maryland Courts, *Final Report Presented to the Governor and the General Assembly of Maryland*, Annapolis, 1996, 56–60; Administrative Office of the Courts, Commission to Study the Judicial Branch of Government, *Report of the Commission*, Annapolis, 1982, 81–87; Commission on Judicial Reform, *Final Report to the Governor and General Assembly of Maryland*, Baltimore, 1974, 26–31.

35. *Whittington v. Polk*, 1 Harris and Johnson 150, 155–57 (1802). See also *Crane v. Meginnis*, 1 Gill and Johnson 463 (1829); *University of Maryland v. Williams*, 9 Gill and Johnson 365 (1838); *Thomas v. Owens*, 4 Md. 189 (1853); *Dowling v. Smith*, 9 Md. 242 (1856); *Cantwell v. Owens*, 14 Md. 215 (1859); and *Humphreys v. Walls*, 169 Md. 292 (1935).

36. *Magruder v. Swann*, 25 Md. 173 (1866).

37. *In re Legislative Districting of the State*, 370 Md. 312 (2002). See also Brooke Erin Moore, "Opening the Door to Single Government: The 2002 Redistricting Decision Gives the Courts Too Much Power in an Historically Political Arena," 33 *University of Baltimore Law Review* 123 (2003).

38. *Office of Governor v. Washington Post Company*, 360 Md. 520 (2000).

39. *Lewis v. Department of Natural Resources*, 377 Md. 382 (2003); *MedStar Health v. Maryland Health Care Commission*, 376 Md. 1 (2003).

40. *Green Party v. Board of Elections*, 377 Md. 127 (2003).

41. *State v. Brookins*, 380 Md. 345 (2004).

42. *Lamone v. Capozzi*, 396 Md. 53 (2006); *Abrams v. Lamone*, 394 Md. 305 (2006).

43. *Schisler v. State of Maryland*, 394 Md. 519 (2006).

44. *Ehrlich v. Perez*, 394 Md. 691 (2006).

10. THE POLITICS OF TAXATION AND SPENDING

Maryland's legendary and colorful comptroller, Louis L. Goldstein, regularly recited this dictum in his numerous speeches throughout the state, second only to his trademark close, "God bless y'all real good." A flavor of Comptroller Goldstein's unique, endearing, and positive approach to politics and government may be gleaned from Frank Ahrens, "Still Running Like a Charm," *Washington Post*, July 21, 1997; John W. Frece, "Ambassador of Maryland," *Baltimore Sun*, February 9, 1984.

1. Standard & Poor's, "Maryland Credit Profile," *Public Finance*, July 14, 2010.

2. Moody's Investor Service, *Municipal Credit Research Report*, July 14, 2010.

3. National Association of State Budget Officers, *The Fiscal Survey of States*, Washington DC, 2000–2010, table A-1.

4. Maryland Constitution, art. III, sec. 52(3). During the initial year of a governor's term of office the budget does not have to be submitted until ten days after the convening of the legislature. The general assembly may also extend the time for submission of the budget.

5. Maryland Constitution, art. III, sec. 52(8).

6. Acts of 1978, chap. 971 (ratified November 7, 1978).

7. *Bayne v. Secretary of State*, 283 Md. 560, 574 (1978).

8. Department of Legislative Services, Maryland General Assembly, *Joint Chairmen's Report*, Annapolis, April 2005, xxvii–lxx.

9. "State Finance and Procurement Article," *Annotated Code of Maryland*, sec. 8-101–114.

10. An Act concerning Spending Affordability, Md. Laws 3472, chap. 585 (1982).

11. Maryland General Assembly, Spending Affordability Committee, *2010 Interim Report*, Annapolis, December 2010, 2.

12. An Act concerning Bonds of State Units and Public Instrumentalities, Md. Laws 1072, chap. 246 (1987); An Act concerning Department of Transportation-County Revenue Bonds, Md. Laws 2699, chap. 539 (1993); An Act concerning Department of Transportation-Special Bonds and Borrowings, Md. Laws 3758, chap. 470 (2002).

13. Office of the Treasurer of Maryland, *2004 Annual Report*, Annapolis, 2002, 11.
14. An excellent reference for understanding this unique governmental institution is Wilner, *Board of Public Works*.
15. "State Finance and Procurement Article," *Annotated Code of Maryland*, sec. 8-134.
16. "State Finance and Procurement Article," sec. 7-213.
17. The Federation of Tax Administrators, "State Individual Income Taxes," Washington DC, www.taxadmin.org/fta/rate/ind_inc.html (accessed May 9, 2007 and August 31, 2010).
18. Department of Legislative Services, Office of Policy Analysis, *Maryland's Revenue Structure*, vol. 3, *Legislative Handbook Series*, Annapolis, 2006, 39–50.
19. An Act concerning Office of Comptroller-Tax Compliance, Holding Companies, Md. Laws 2632, chap. 556 (2004).
20. Maryland Higher Education Commission, *2007 Data Book: Creating a State of Achievement*, Annapolis, 2007, 29.
21. An Act Concerning Transportation Trust Fund—Transportation Financing—Increased Revenues, Md. Laws 41, chap. 9 (2004); Budget Reconciliation and Financing Act of 2004, Md. Laws 1891, 1921–22, chap. 430 (2004).
22. An Act to Add New Section 264B to Article 27 of Annotated Code of Maryland, Md. Laws 1345, chap. 617 (1963).
23. Michael A. Abramowitz, "Md. Governor Rules Out Slot Machines," *Washington Post*, August 13, 1996; Parris N. Glendening, "No Casinos, No Slot Machines," *Washington Post*, August 18, 1996.
24. Maryland Constitution, art. III, sec. 34.
25. "State Finance and Procurement Article," *Annotated Code of Maryland*, sec. 8-134,
26. Maryland's unique tax assessment structure is codified in "Tax-Property Article," *Annotated Code of Maryland*, secs. 2-101–221.
27. Maryland General Assembly, Capital Debt Affordability Committee, *Report on Recommended Debt Authorization for Fiscal Year 2010*, Annapolis, 2010, 18, 77.
28. Maryland Budget and Tax Policy Institute, *Chartbook on Taxes in Maryland*, 3rd ed., Silver Spring, MD, January 2002, iii.
29. Department of Legislative Services, Office of Policy Analysis, *Revenue and Expenditure Comparison for Maryland and Selected States*, Annapolis, August 22, 2002, 3,4,7.
30. Maryland State Department of Education, *The Fact Book, 2009–2010: A Statistical Handbook*, Baltimore, 2010, 5–7.
31. 1864 Maryland Constitution, art. XIII.
32. *Board of Education of Prince George's County v. Waeldner*, 298 Md. 354 (1984).
33. *Hornbeck v. Somerset County*, 295 Md. 597, 693 (1983).

34. An Act concerning New Baltimore City Board of School Commissioners, Md. Laws 1529, chap. 105 (1997).
35. An Act concerning Commission on Education Finance, Equity, and Excellence, Md. Laws 3413, chap. 601 (1999).
36. Bridge to Excellence in Public Schools Act, Md. Laws 2158, chap. 288 (2002).
37. Bridge to Excellence in Public Schools Act—Trigger Provision-Repeal, Md. Laws 28, chap. 6 (2004). Message from the executive, Governor Robert L. Ehrlich Jr., to the speaker of the house, March 4, 2004, may be found in Maryland House of Delegates, *Journal of Proceedings*, 2004 regular session, March 8, 2004, 1262–63.
38. An act to provide for the State assumption, under certain conditions, of the costs of public school construction . . . , Md. Laws 1301, chap. 646 (1971).
39. See, for example, Sarah Breitenbach, "Officials Bemoan Scant School Construction Funds," *Frederick News-Post*, May 27, 2008; Mary Gail Hare, "County School Plans in Works; Construction Projects Worth $140 Million Set to Start without Promise of State Funds," *Baltimore Sun*, March 18, 2007.
40. Maryland General Assembly, Task Force to Study Public Schools Facilities, *Final Report*, Annapolis, February 2004, iii.
41. See, for example, National Education Goals Panel, *Education Week's Quality Counts, 2001 Report* (Washington DC: National Center for Education Information, 2001); *Education Week's Quality Counts, 2009 Report*, ranking Maryland first among the fifty states.
42. An Act concerning concerning Administration Action Plan for Higher Education 1988, Md. Laws 2370, chap. 246 (1988).
43. "Education Article," *Annotated Code of Maryland*, title 11.
44. An Act concerning the University of Maryland Medical System, Md. Laws 1641, chap. 288, (1984).
45. *Roemer v. Board of Public Works of Maryland*, 426 U.S. 736 (1976). See An Act to Add Aid to Non-Public Institutions of Higher Education, Md. Laws 1309, chap. 626 (1971). These provisions are codified in "Education Article," *Annotated Code of Maryland*, secs. 17-101–106.
46. Higher Education Commission, *2007 Data Book*, 26.
47. Department of Legislative Services, Special Committee on Higher Education Affordability and Access, *Final Report to the Maryland General Assembly*, Annapolis, February 2004, 8, 11.
48. *Final Report to the Maryland General Assembly*, 13.
49. Tax Reform Act of 2007, Md. Laws 48, 79–81, chap. 3 (special session 2007).
50. Children and Family's First Health Care Act of 1998, Md. Laws 1065, chap. 110 (1998); Maryland Health Programs Expansion Act of 2000, Md. Laws 170, chap. 16 (2000).

51. Center on Budget and Policy Priorities, Kaiser Commission on Medicaid and the Uninsured, "Income Eligibility for Children's Regular Medicaid and Medicaid-funded SCHIP's Medicaid Expansions" and "Income Eligibility Levels for Pregnant Women," www.statehealthfacts.org/comparetable (accessed June 18, 2008).

52. The Targeted Local Health Department Program was created in 1997 and was funded at over $57 million in fiscal year 2007.

53. Maryland Pharmacy Assistance Program, Md. Laws 1209, chap. 99 (1993).

54. Office of Policy Analysis, *Government Services*, vol. 2, *Legislative Handbook Series* (Annapolis MD: Department of Legislative Services, 2006), 183.

55. "Human Services Article," *Annotated Code of Maryland*, sec. 3-301.

56. See Irene Lurie, "State Welfare Policy," in *The State of the States*, ed. Carl E. Van Horn (Washington DC: CQ Press, 2006), 169–70, 182.

57. Maryland Department of Public Safety and Correctional Services, Division of Correction, *Annual Report-2009*, Towson, 2009, 51.

58. The legislative history of state assistance for local prison construction facilities is reported as a note to Md. Laws. 445, chap. 54 (1999) at 847–49. The provisions have been codified as "Correctional Services Article," *Annotated Code of Maryland*, sec. 11-104.

59. See and compare Department of Legislative Services, Maryland General Assembly, *Joint Chairmen's Report*, Annapolis, fiscal years 2002 through 2010.

11. "PLEASANT LIVING" POLICIES AND POLITICS

William A. Brooks, *The Oyster* (Baltimore: Johns Hopkins Press, 1891; reprint, Johns Hopkins University Press, 1996), 3. Citations are to the 1996 paperback edition.

Horton, *Bay Country*, 215.

1. H. L. Mencken, *Happy Days* (New York: Knopf, 1940), 55.

2. For a naturalist's perspective, see Gilbert C. Klingel, *The Bay* (Baltimore: Johns Hopkins University Press, 1934; reprint, New York: Dodd Mead, 1951); William W. Warner, *Beautiful Swimmers: Watermen, Crabs and the Chesapeake Bay* (New York: Little, Brown, 1976).

3. Maryland Department of Transportation, "Marylanders Show Their Support for the Chesapeake Bay This Summer Driving Season: One out of Ten Marylanders Have Purchased a Treasure the Chesapeake License Plate," news release, June 12, 2006.

4. The 1903 and 1907 platforms of the Maryland Democratic Party and Maryland Republican Party may be found in *The Sun Almanac for 1904* (Baltimore: A. S. Abell, 1904), 37–39, and *The Sun Almanac for 1908* (Baltimore: A. S. Abell, 1908), 158–59, 162–63.

5. Brooks, *The Oyster*, xii–xvi, 1–2, 211.

6. See Arthur W. Sherwood, *Understanding the Chesapeake* (Queenstown MD: Tidewater Publishers, 1973); Tom Horton and Wm. M. Eichbaum, *Turning the Tide: Saving the Chesapeake Bay* (Washington DC: Island Press 1991); Howard R. Ernst, *Chesapeake Bay Blues: Science, Politics, and the Struggle to Save the Bay* (Lanham MD: Rowman and Littlefield, 2003); Tom Horton, "Hanging in the Balance: Chesapeake Bay," *National Geographic*, June 1993, 2–35.

7. See Brian Wingfield and Miriam Marcus, "America's Greenest States," *Forbes*, October 17, 2007; Pamela Wood, "Md. Clean Energy Efforts Praised," *Carroll County Times*, November 17, 2007; Chris Kromm, Keith Ernst, and Jaffer Barrett, "Green Rankings for the States," in *Gold and Green 2000* (Durham NC: Institute for Southern Studies, November 2000).

8. "Natural Resources Article," *Annotated Code of Maryland*, secs. 3-201 to 3-211, 5-901 to 9-911.

9. "Natural Resources Article," secs. 8-1801 to 8-1817.

10. Keith Schneider, "Ending Sprawl Isn't about Stopping All Development," *Detroit Free Press*, February 22, 1998.

11. Neal R. Peirce, "Maryland's Smart Growth Law: A National Model?," *Nation's Cities Weekly*, April 28, 1997, 5.

12. Healthy Air Act, Md. Laws 129,692, chaps. 23,301 (2006), codified as "Environment Article," *Annotated Code of Maryland*, secs. 2-1001 to 2-1005.

13. Maryland Energy Efficiency Standards Act, Md. Laws 3,18, chaps. 2,5 (2004).

14. Electricity Regulation—Renewable Energy Portfolio Standard and Credit Trading-Maryland Renewable Energy Fund, Md. Laws 2258,2278, chaps. 487,488 (2004).

15. Maryland Clean Cars Act of 2007, Md. Laws 1017, chap. 111 (2007); Environment Phosphorus Dishwashing Detergent, Md. Laws 1450, chap. 187 (2007); Stormwater Management Act of 2007, Md. Laws 1148, chap. 121 (2007); Renewable Energy Portfolio Standard—Solar Energy, Md. Laws 1092, chap. 119 (2007).

16. Chesapeake and Atlantic Coastal Bays Critical Area Protection Program—Administrative and Enforcement Provisions, Md. Laws 1092, chap. 119 (2008); EMPOWER Maryland Energy Efficiency Act of 2008, Md. Laws 892, chap. 131 (2008); Renewable Portfolio Standard Percentage Requirements—Acceleration, Md. Laws 833,839, chaps. 125,126 (2008); High Performance Buildings Act, Md. Laws 825, chap. 124 (2008).

17. The Bay Restoration Fund, Md. Laws 1571, chap. 428 (2004). House Bill 491 was introduced by request of the Ehrlich administration's Department of Planning in the 2004 regular session of the Maryland General Assembly. Maryland House of Delegates, *Journal of Proceedings*, 2004 regular session, February 2, 2004, 362.

18. "Smart Growth and Neighborhood Conservation Policy," Md. Exec. Order no. 01.01.1998.04 (1998); Office of Smart Growth, Md. Laws 3040, chap. 566 (2001) codified as "State Government Article," *Annotated Code of Maryland*, secs. 9-1401–1406.

19. Smart, Green, and Growing: The Sustainable Growth Commission, Md. Laws 3392,3402, chaps. 488, 489 (2010).

20. Smart, Green, and Growing—The Sustainable Communities Act of 2010, Md. Laws 3326. chap. 487 (2010).

21. "Smart Growth @ 10: A Critical Examination of Maryland's Landmark Land Use Program," a conference held at the University of Maryland, College Park, October 3–5, 2007. Papers from the conference are accessible on the Center for Smart Growth website, www.smartgrowth.umd.edu/. See also John W. Frece, "Twenty Lessons From Maryland's Smart Growth Initiative," *Vermont Journal of Environmental Law* 6 (2004–5): 106.

22. Janet S. Owens, "BWI Corridor Is Anne Arundel's Gold Coast," *Business Monthly*, May 2003, 5.

23. James Lighthizer, "Transportation: A Key Element in Sustainable Communities," in *Land Use in America: The Report of the Sustainable Use of Land Project*, ed. Henry L. Diamond and Patrick F. Noonan (Washington DC: Island Press, 1996), 173.

24. Ike Wilson, "County Approves 3,051 Acres for Farmland Preservation," *Frederick News Post*, February 4, 2010, 1.

25. Carroll County Planning and Zoning Commission, *2007 Planning Annual Report*, Westminster MD, January 2007, 29–31.

26. Frederick County, sec. 1-13–55 (Am. Legal Publishing, 2007).

27. *Washington County Code*, sec. 1-1101 (2007); Ordinance No. ORD-09-01, "Ordinance for the Establishment of Agricultural Preservation Districts" (adopted January 13, 2009).

28. See Baltimore County Council, *Baltimore County Master Plan 2010*, February 22, 2000, 1–11.

29. Susan DeFord, "Offer More for Land, Robey Says; He Wants to Rekindle Preservation Effort," *Washington Post*, March 2, 2006.

30. Howard County Commission on the Environment and Sustainability, *Final Report*, Columbia MD, August 28, 2007; Susan DeFord, "Howard Chief Pushes Green Development; Stricter Standards Sought for Energy Use, Design," *Washington Post*, June 13, 2007; Susan DeFord, "Ulman Lays Out His Early Initiatives," *Washington Post*, February 22, 2007.

31. Complementary state programs include brownfields voluntary cleanup, community legacy, job creation tax credits, historic structure tax credits, and neighborhood and business revitalization.

32. See, for example, Rona Kobell and Chris Guy, "Primed for Growth: Developers Want to Build Thousands of Homes on the Shore. But Is the Area Ready?," *Baltimore Sun*, July 2, 2006; Laura McCandlish, "Growth Takes Big Hit in Vote: Projects Rejection in Mount Airy Seen as an Indicator for the General Election," *Baltimore Sun*, May 3, 2006; Eugene L. Meyer, "On the Bay, a Developing Battle; Annexation Proposal Splits Quiet, Quaint St. Michaels," *Washington Post*, April 22, 1997.

33. Sierra Club, *Solving Sprawl: 1999 Sierra Club Sprawl Report* (Washington DC: Sierra Club Foundation, 1999).

34. Maryland Agricultural Land Preservation Foundation, *Annual Report for Fiscal Year 2002*, Annapolis, August 1, 2003, 37.

35. Associated Press, "Maryland Lawmakers OK New Blue Crab Limits," *Daily Record (Baltimore)*, May 22, 2008; David A. Fahrenthold, "Alarm over Blue Crab Decline," *Washington Post*, April 16, 2008; Rona Kobell, "Step Up Efforts to Save Oysters, Governor Says," *Baltimore Sun*, April 26, 2007.

36. Candus Thomson, "Md. Told to Halve Rockfish Catch; Regulators Impose 30,000 Fish Quota," *Baltimore Sun*, January 30, 2007.

37. Tom Horton, "Reality Differs a Bit from People's Words, Actions on Growth," *Baltimore Sun*, November 15, 2005; "Agency Failed to Do Its Job: Cambridge Development Plan Ok'd for Wrong Reasons," editorial, *Salisbury Daily Times*, October 27, 2005.

38. Maryland Constitution, Art. XII, sec. 3(B); Acts of 2005, chap. 617 (ratified November 7, 2006).

39. Schaefer Center for Public Policy, *Maryland Policy Choices: 2006* (Baltimore: University of Baltimore, January 2006), 33.

40. Andrew A. Green, "Ehrlich Offers 'Green' Funding," *Baltimore Sun*, January 17, 2006.

41. The phrase "Land of Pleasant Living" was popularized by Arthur Deute, who bought the Baltimore-based National Brewing Company in 1935. Inspired by Capt. John Smith's early 1600s observations of the Chesapeake Bay, Deute utilized the phrase in the marketing of his popular, locally brewed beer. Caroline County adopted the phrase as part of its county seal and flag in 1984, during the state's 350th anniversary celebration. The phrase is frequently used in government and commercial brochures, documents, and reports as well as being a catchphrase in public speeches.

12. MARYLAND IN THE FEDERAL SYSTEM

1. An Act for establishing the temporary and permanent seat of the Government of the United States, Stats at Large of USA, vol. 1, chap. XXVII, 214 (1861).

2. Constance McLaughlin Green, *Washington: A History of the Capital, 1800–1850* (Princeton NJ: Princeton University Press, 1962), 7–14; John C. Miller, *Alexander Hamilton and the Growth of the New Nation* (New York: Harper and Row, 1959), 238–54; Norman K. Risjord, *Chesapeake Politics: 1781–1800* (New York: Columbia University Press, 1978), 363–93.

3. Willis, *Presidential Elections in Maryland*, 4–19.

4. For insight into the Maryland perspective on the federal view of the state at the beginning of the Civil War, see Radcliffe, *Governor Hicks and Civil War*.

5. Representing the state's First Congressional District from 1991 to 2009, Congressman Wayne Gilchrest from Kent County on the Eastern Shore consistently ranked as one of the most environment-friendly Republicans. Congresswoman Connie Morella from Montgomery County, who represented the Eighth Congressional District for sixteen years (1987–2003), regularly drew support from public employee unions and women's groups that traditionally supported Democrats. See summary of interest group rankings presented in Michael Barone and Grant Ujifusa, *The Almanac of American Politics 2000* (Washington DC: National Journal Group, 1999), 744–46, 761–63.

6. "State Government Article," *Annotated Code of Maryland*, sec. 2-901–906.

7. John W. Frece, "Schaefer Spurns Democrats, Backs Bush," *Baltimore Sun*, October 30, 1992; Richard Tapscott, "Gov. Schaefer Throws Support to Bush: Md. Democrats Call Cross-Party Endorsement 'Regrettable,' 'Sad,'" *Washington Post*, October 31, 1992.

8. Thomas W. Waldron and Michael Dresser, "Clinton Puts Spotlight on Md. Gun Law; President Attends as Glendening Signs Landmark Legislation," *Baltimore Sun*, April 12, 2000; Daniel LeDuc, "With President on Hand, Gun Locks Become Law; Glendening Signs Measure Requiring Childproof Devices," *Washington Post*, April, 12, 2000.

9. U.S. Census Bureau, *Consolidated Federal Funds Report for Fiscal Year 2009* (Washington DC: Government Printing Office, 2010), tables 1 and 14.

10. U.S. Department of Commerce, Bureau of Economic Analysis, *Regional Economic Accounts* (Washington DC: Government Printing Office, 2006), table SA27N.

11. U.S. Census Bureau, *2006 American Community Survey* (Washington DC: Government Printing Office, 2007), table R2101; U.S. Department of Veterans Affairs, "Veteran Population Model 2007," Washington DC, 2008), table 1-2L.

12. Maryland Department of Business and Economic Development and Office of Military and Federal Affairs, *2005 BRAC State of Maryland Impact Analysis: 2006–2020*, Baltimore, 2007.

13. An Act concerning Base Realignment and Closure Subcabinet, Md. Laws 676, chap. 6 (2007), codified in "State Government Article," *Annotated Code of Maryland*, sec. 9-802.

14. U.S. Census Bureau, *Consolidated Federal Funds Report for Fiscal Year 2009* (Washington DC: Government Printing Office, 2010), tables 1 and 14.

15. U.S. Census Bureau, *Consolidated Federal Funds Report for Fiscal Year 2009.* Compare table 1, p. 1 with table 15, p. 48.

16. See, for example, Dan Thang Dang and Jamie Smith Hopkins, "Security State: Maryland Businesses Fight Terror," *Baltimore Sun*, November 2, 2003; "As Defense Spending Jumps, Md. Companies Get More than Their Share," *Daily Record*, May 6, 2003; Renae Merle, "Defense Earnings Continue to Soar," *Washington Post*, July 30, 2007; Danielle Ulman, "$15 Billion in Defense Contracts Ranks Maryland No. 5 in Nation," *Daily Record*, October 9, 2007.

17. Maryland Department of Planning, Planning Data Services, *Federal Expenditures Increase in Maryland Largest Ever: Procurement Leads the Way*, Baltimore, 2005.

18. Dana Hedgpeth, "Base Shuffle Might Benefit Region," *Washington Post*, August 29, 2005.

19. U.S. Department of Health and Human Services, "Award Trends, Ranking for All Institutions," http://grants1.nih.gov/grants/award/trends/All_Institutions_Rank .htm (accessed February 13, 2010).

20. William Ecenbarger, *Walkin' the Line: A Journey from Past to Present along the Mason-Dixon* (New York: Evans, 2000), 15–17; George Shaun and Virginia Shaun, *The Story of the Delaware-Pennsylvania-Maryland Boundaries* (Annapolis MD: Greenberg, 1963); David S. Thaler, "Mason and Dixon and the Defining of America," *MDHS News*, winter 2009, 16–19; Edward B. Matthews, "History of the Boundary Dispute between the Baltimores and the Penns Resulting in the Original Mason and Dixon Line," *Maryland Geological Survey, Reports*, 7 (1908): 105–203.

21. *Maryland v. West Virginia*, 217 U.S. 1 (1910).

22. See Matthew Page Andrews, *The Founding of Maryland* (New York: D. Appleton Century, 1933), 94–112; Bernard C. Steiner, *Maryland under the Commonwealth: A Chronicle of the Years 1649–1658* (Baltimore: Johns Hopkins Press, 1911).

23. *Stats at Large of USA*, vol. 1, chap. XVII, 214 (1861).

24. *Virginia v. Maryland*, 540 U.S. 56 (2003).

25. Meredith Cohn, "Fewer Cruises to Call in 2008: 'Grandeur' Will Shift to New Va. Terminal," *Baltimore Sun*, April 10, 2007.

26. *Comptroller of the Treasury v. Syl, Inc.*, 375 Md. 59 (2003); Tax Compliance-Holding Companies, Md. Laws 2632, chap. 556 (2004); Tax Compliance-Settlement Period, Md. Laws 2641, chap. 557 (2004).

27. Sales and Use Tax-Tax-Free Week, Md. Laws 3039, 3040, chaps. 576 and 577 (2000); Sales and Use Tax-Tax-Free Period, Md Laws 1139, chap. 191 (2005);

Transportation and State Investment Act, Md Laws 266, 278, chap. 6 (special session 2007). See "Tax—General Article," *Annotated Code of Maryland*, sec. 11-228.

28. Ellen McCarthy, "Young Biotechs, Hungry and Anxious," *Washington Post*, June 2, 2005.

29. Laura McCandlish, "Port Exports Set Record," *Baltimore Sun*, April 23, 2008.

30. See David Woods and David Nitkin, "All Eyes on Annapolis: President Stresses the Common Goal," *Baltimore Sun*, November 27, 2007; Erica Kritt, "Bush Visits Mt. Airy," *Carroll County Times*, December 1, 2007; David Nitken, Matthew Hay Brown, and Jamie Smith Hopkins, "Fast Economic Fix Urged," *Baltimore Sun*, January 19, 2008; David Nitkin, "Bush to Visit City Re-entry Program," *Baltimore Sun*, January 29, 2008.

31. See, for example, "John Fritze, Obama Urges Fleets of Clean Cars," *Baltimore Sun*, April 2, 2011; Liz Bowie, "Obama to Visit Parkville School Monday," *Baltimore Sun*, February 12, 2011; Associated Press, "Obama Speaks on Health Bill in Md.," *Carroll County Times*, June 9, 2010; Paul West, "Obama at UM," *Baltimore Sun*, September 18, 2009.

32. The history and presidential use of Camp David is presented in Kenneth T. Walsh, *From Mt. Vernon to Crawford: A History of Presidents and Their Retreats* (New York: Hyperion, 2005), chap. 19, 272–311.

13. LOCAL GOVERNMENTS IN MARYLAND

Gladys Noon Spellman, quoted in Ellen B. Clarke, ed., *A History of the Maryland Association of Counties: 1951–2002* (Annapolis: Maryland Association of Counties, 2003), 45. Spellman was a Prince George's County Council member from 1971 to 1974, became the first woman president of the National Association of Counties in 1972, and in 1975 was elected to the U.S. House of Representatives, where she served until complications from cardiac arrest led to her seat being declared vacant in 1981.

1. Francis F. Beirne, *The Amiable Baltimoreans* (Baltimore: Johns Hopkins University Press, 1951), 11. In his history of the Maryland General Assembly, Carl N. Everstine, the director of legislative reference from 1952 to 1978, noted in his comprehensive legislative history the "strong county loyalties which have always distinguished the State of Maryland" in the proceedings of constitutional conventions. Everstine, *General Assembly 1776–1850*, 585.

2. Vincent L. Marando and Robert D. Thomas, *The Forgotten Governments: County Commissioners as Policy Makers* (Gainesville: University Presses of Florida, 1977), 23.

3. U.S. Census Bureau, *2007 Census of Governments* (Washington DC: Government Printing Office, 2008), table 3.

4. U.S. Census Bureau, *2007 Census of Governments*, table 3.

5. John F. Dillon, *Commentaries on the Law of Municipal Corporations* (Boston: Little, Brown, 1911), 64–65.

6. Victor K. Tervala, *Home Rule Options in Maryland* (College Park MD: Institute for Governmental Service, 2001), 14–15.

7. Acts of 1914, chap. 416 (ratified November 2, 1915).

8. G. H. Callcott, *Maryland and America*, 230.

9. Acts of 1954, chap. 53 (ratified November 2, 1954).

10. Tervala, *Home Rule Options*, 19.

11. Department of Legislative Services, Office of Policy Analysis, *Legislative Handbook Series*, vol. 6, *Maryland Local Government*, Annapolis, 2006, 40; Tervala, *Home Rule*, 40–41.

12. See Tervala, *Home Rule*, 98-106, for a list of the election results for county referendums on home rule charters and code home rule from 1948 through 1998.

13. The powers granted to the various counties by the general assembly may be found in the *Annotated Code of Maryland*, article 25 for commissioner counties, article 25A for charter counties, and article 25B for code counties.

14. G. H. Callcott, *Maryland and America*, 24.

15. Acts of 1999, chap. 119 (ratified November 7, 2000).

16. *Annotated Code of Maryland*, art. 1, sec. 14(a) states, "The word county shall be construed to include the City of Baltimore unless such construction would be unreasonable."

17. Matthew A. Crenson, *Neighborhood Politics* (Cambridge MA: Harvard University Press, 1983), 292.

18. Crenson, *Neighborhood Politics*, 296–97.

19. G. H. Callcott, *Maryland and America*, 84.

20. David Simon, *Homicide: A Year on the Killing Streets* (New York: Ivy Books, 1991). Simon followed up *Homicide* with *The Corner*, written with Edward Burns, a twenty-year Baltimore City Police veteran. *The Corner* explores the drug culture and its toll on the residents of West Baltimore. David Simon and Edward Burns, *The Corner: A Year in the Life of an Inner City Neighborhood* (New York: Broadway Books, 1997).

21. Christopher Swope, "Restless for Results," *Governing, the Magazine of States and Localities*, April 2001, 20–23.

22. Office of Mayor, Baltimore City, www.ci.baltimore.*md.us/mayor/biography .html* (accessed November 27, 2005).

23. Julie Bykowicz, "Dixon Resigns," *Baltimore Sun*, January 7, 2010; Brendan Kearney, "Plea Deal Ends Corruption Cases, Keeps Record Clear," *Daily Record*, January 6, 2010.

24. Unless noted otherwise, all fiscal data for Maryland counties are drawn from

Department of Legislative Services, *Local Government Finances in Maryland: Fiscal Year Ending June 30, 2010*, Annapolis, 2010, 315–47.

25. Maryland Association of Counties, *Fiscal Year 2009 Report of County Budgets, Tax Rates and Selected Statistics*, Annapolis, 2009, 26.
26. Maryland Association of Counties, *Fiscal Year 2009 Report*, 27.
27. Department of Legislative Services, *Overview of Maryland Local Governments: Finances and Demographic Information*, Annapolis, January 2010, 98.
28. Burrell, *Maryland's 157*, 6.
29. Department of Legislative Services, Office of Policy Analysis, *Legislative Handbook Series*, vol. 6, *Maryland Local Government*, Annapolis, 54.
30. Survey conducted by the Maryland Municipal League, cited in Department of Legislative Services, Office of Policy Analysis, *Legislative Handbook Series*, vol. 2, *Government Services in Maryland*, Annapolis, 2006, 7.
31. Clarke, *Association of Counties*, 39.
32. Clarke, *Association of Counties*, 42.
33. Maryland Department of Planning, State Data Services, "Population for Maryland Jurisdictions: 2010 and 2000," Baltimore, February 2011.

14. MARYLAND'S FUTURE

Brugger, *Maryland*, x.
1. Quoted in Laura Cadiz, "GOP Begins to Focus on 2006," *Baltimore Sun*, November 14, 2004.
2. Quoted in Andrew A. Green, "Confident GOP Raises $750,000 at Dinner," *Baltimore Sun*, September 27, 2006.
3. Richard Norling, "Political Status of Maryland Democrats: Research Needed to Craft a Message to Reverse Party Decline," Norling Research Corporation, December 23, 2004.
4. Howard Libit, "Poll Reveals Contrasts," *Baltimore Sun*, January 14, 2001.
5. For example, see C. Fraser Smith, "Name-calling Won't Win the Budget War," *Baltimore Sun*, March 2, 2003. Michael F. Busch quoted in Michael Olesker, "Ehrlich Took Slots Plan and Fumbled It for a Loss," *Baltimore Sun*, April 8, 2003.
6. The projected state population for 2030 is 6.7 million people. Maryland Department of Planning, Planning Data Services, *Historical and Projected Total Population for Maryland's Jurisdictions*, Baltimore, October 2007. See also Kelly Brewington, "Minorities Fuel Md. Growth," *Baltimore Sun*, August 11, 2005.
7. Chris Guy, "Small Town Backs Sweep," *Baltimore Sun*, June 22, 2006.
8. Chesapeake Bay Foundation, *2005 State of the Bay Report*, Annapolis MD, 2005, 2.

9. Texas Transportation Institute, *2009 Urban Mobility Report*, 32, mobility.tamu.edu/ums/congestion-data/national-congestion-tables.stm (accessed March 3, 2011).

10. Census Bureau, *2006 American Community Survey*, table R0804; http://factfinder.census.gov/ (accessed on July 28, 2008).

11. Texas Transportation Institute, *2009 Urban Mobility Report*.

12. U.S. Department of Justice, Bureau of Justice Statistics, "State Crime Estimates, 1960–2005," www.ojp.usdoj.gov/bjs (accessed April 25, 2010).

13. Administrative Office Courts, *Statistical Digest, 2008–2009*, tables CC-1.2, DC-2.

14. Lisa Frazier, "Report Links Baltimore Crime Fears, TV News," *Washington Post*, June 26, 1998, citing Project on Media Ownership; Dorothy S. Boulware, "Media Disproportionately Connect Youth with Crime and Violence," *Baltimore Afro-American*, April 14–20, 2001, 1.

Index

All topics refer to the state of Maryland, unless otherwise noted.
Page numbers in *italics* indicate *tables* and *maps*.

tended 2010, 84–88; Democratic dominance restored 2006, 78–84; Ehrlich vs. Townsend 2002, 71–77; Glendening vs. Sauerbrey 1998, 69–71; overview, 50–54; Republican near miss 1994, 65–69; voter registration, 54–55, 55; voter turnout patterns, 55–56; voting patterns for county officials, 61, 62; voting patterns for gubernatorial and statewide offices, 58–60, 59; voting patterns for state legislature, 60–61; voting patterns in congressional elections, 56–58; voting patterns in presidential elections, 56

Maryland Cooperative Extension Service, 259

Maryland County Commissioners Association (MCCA), 299

Maryland Court of Appeals, 129, 222

Maryland Declaration of Rights, 1776, 23

Maryland Declaration of Rights and Constitution. *See* Constitution of Maryland

Maryland Energy Efficiency Standards Act of 2004, 257

Maryland Environmental Service, 236, 258

Maryland Environmental Trust, 255

Marylanders Against Handgun Abuse, 114

Maryland Fisheries Services, 258

Maryland for Choice, 107

Maryland General Assembly, 152–75; budgetary power of, 169, 229–30; characteristics of membership, 160–63; committees, 166–69; governor's council, 138, 154, 177, 187, 208; gubernatorial relations, 169–72, 172; history of, 153–56; house of delegates, 153–56, 158, 160, 163–65, 167–68; hybrid nature of, 163–64, 164; leadership, 164–66, 339n28; and modern MD legislature, 157–58; overview, 152–53; partisan polarization, 172–74; representation and redistricting, 158–60, 161; vacancies in, 111

Maryland Gun Violence Prevention Act of 1996, 122

Maryland Health Care Cost Commission, 223

Maryland Higher Education Commission (MHEC), 179, 244

Maryland Insurance Administration, 180

Maryland Jewish Alliance, 114

Maryland Jockey Club, 114, 118

Maryland Judicial Campaign Committee, 222

Maryland League of Conservation Voters, 63, 114

Maryland Monument at Antietam, 35

Maryland Municipal League (MML), 116, 299–300

Maryland National Abortion Rights Action League PAC, 106

Maryland-National Capital Park and Planning Commission, 284

Maryland National Guard, 184

Maryland Policy Choices, 90, 95, 97, 100–104, 266, 318

Maryland politics: two-party state status, 16–17; understanding, 13–16

Maryland Port Administration, 261

Maryland Public Interest Research Group, 63, 114

Maryland Racing Commission, 48, 99

Maryland Stadium Authority, 235

Maryland State Bar Association, 286

Maryland State Board of Elections, 172

Maryland State Education Association, 114, 123

Maryland State Lottery, 235

Maryland State Medical Society, 114, 118

Maryland State Police, 90, 251

Maryland State Teachers Association, 63, 114

Maryland Sustainable Growth Commission, 258

Maryland Tax Court, 217

Maryland Taxpayers Association, 115

Maryland Transportation Authority, 236, 262

Maryland Trial Lawyers' Association, 114, 124

Maryland Woman's Suffrage Association, 42–43

Mason-Dixon Line, 21, 30, 46, 114, 276

mass-based political parties, 27–31

mass transit, Baltimore, 250

Mass Transit Administration (MTA), 260–61

Mathias, Charles Mac, 51–52, 109, 195, 266, 270

In the Politics and Governments of the American States series

Alabama Government and Politics
By James D. Thomas and William H. Stewart

Alaska Politics and Government
By Gerald A. McBeath and Thomas A. Morehouse

Arizona Politics and Government: The Quest for Autonomy,
Democracy, and Development
By David R. Berman

Arkansas Politics and Government, second edition
By Diane D. Blair and Jay Barth

Colorado Politics and Government: Governing the Centennial State
By Thomas E. Cronin and Robert D. Loevy

Delaware Politics and Government
By William W. Boyer and Edward C. Ratledge

Hawai'i Politics and Government: An American State in a Pacific World
By Richard C. Pratt with Zachary Smith

Illinois Politics and Government: The Expanding Metropolitan Frontier
By Samuel K. Gove and James D. Nowlan

Kansas Politics and Government: The Clash of Political Cultures
By H. Edward Flentje and Joseph A. Aistrup

Kentucky Politics and Government: Do We Stand United?
By Penny M. Miller

Maine Politics and Government, second edition
By Kenneth T. Palmer, G. Thomas Taylor,
Marcus A. LiBrizzi, and Jean E. Lavigne

Maryland Politics and Government: Democratic Dominance
By Herbert C. Smith and John T. Willis

Michigan Politics and Government: Facing Change in a Complex State
By William P. Browne and Kenneth VerBurg

Minnesota Politics and Government
By Daniel J. Elazar, Virginia Gray, and Wyman Spano

Mississippi Government and Politics: Modernizers versus Traditionalists
By Dale Krane and Stephen D. Shaffer

Nebraska Government and Politics
Edited by Robert D. Miewald

Nevada Politics and Government: Conservatism in an Open Society
By Don W. Driggs and Leonard E. Goodall

New Jersey Politics and Government:
Suburban Politics Comes of Age, second edition
By Barbara G. Salmore and Stephen A. Salmore

New York Politics and Government: Competition and Compassion
By Sarah F. Liebschutz, with Robert W. Bailey, Jeffrey M. Stonecash,
Jane Shapiro Zacek, and Joseph F. Zimmerman

North Carolina Government and Politics
By Jack D. Fleer

Oklahoma Politics and Policies: Governing the Sooner State
By David R. Morgan, Robert E. England, and George G. Humphreys

Oregon Politics and Government: Progressives versus Conservative Populists
By Richard A. Clucas, Mark Henkels, and Brent S. Steel

Rhode Island Politics and Government
By Maureen Moakley and Elmer Cornwell

South Carolina Politics and Government
By Cole Blease Graham Jr. and William V. Moore

West Virginia Politics and Government
By Richard A. Brisbin Jr., Robert Jay Dilger, Allan S. Hammock,
and Christopher Z. Mooney

West Virginia Politics and Government, second edition
By Richard A. Brisbin Jr., Robert Jay Dilger, Allan S. Hammock,
and L. Christopher Plein

Wisconsin Politics and Government: America's Laboratory of Democracy
By James K. Conant

To order or obtain more information on these or other
University of Nebraska Press titles, visit www.nebraskapress.unl.edu.

CPSIA information can be obtained at www.ICGtesting.com
Printed in the USA
BVOW041341051111

275242BV00007B/3/P